# Clear The Confederate Way!

## The Irish in the Army of Northern Virginia

Kelly J. O'Grady

Civil War Author

*Kelly J. O'Grady*

Savas Publishing Company

*Clear the Confederate Way!*
*The Irish in the Army of Northern Virginia*
by Kelly J. O'Grady

© 2000 Kelly O'Grady

Includes bibliographic references and index

Printing Number
10 9 8 7 6 5 4 3 2
First Edition

ISBN 1-882810-42-2
LCCCN 99-63648

Savas Publishing Company
202 First Street SE, Suite 103A
Mason City, IA 50401

(515) 421-7135 (editorial offices)
(800) 732-3669 (distribution)

This book is printed on 50-lb. acid-free paper. It meets or exceeds the guidelines for permanence and durability of the Committee on Production Guidelines for Book Longevity of the Council on Library Resources

To my mother and father

Jane Atkinson O'Grady
Edward L. O'Grady, 1923-1996

and to Six Generations of O'Gradys in the South

Vulneratus Non Victus

Private Andrew Blakely, a native of Belfast, Ireland, enlisted in the Washington Artillery in New Orleans in 1861. He was only nineteen when he was wounded and captured at Second Manassas. Blakely later worked in the Confederate Treasury Department.

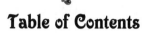

# Table of Contents

# Table of Contents (continued)

# - List of Maps -

# Foreword

The famed Irish Brigade of the Army of the Potomac hewed out an admirable record at Sharpsburg, Fredericksburg, and elsewhere. In recent years, however, the brigade's renown has outstripped the merits of the case—not necessarily in an absolute sense, but certainly relative to similar formations in the same army. The devoted but vain assault toward Marye's Heights at Fredericksburg has become the Irish Brigade's defining, even legendary, moment. Without detracting from what the one brigade did, it is worth noting that no fewer than eight other Northern brigades at Fredericksburg counted losses at the same level as the Irishmen, and Caldwell's Brigade suffered twice as many casualties (including *more* than twice as many killed). Yet only the most devoted of Civil War cognoscenti know of Caldwell's Brigade, and if anyone regularly hymns that worthy unit, they do so without the tiniest glimmer of the popular attention routinely bestowed upon the Irishmen.

Perhaps some of the prominence of the Irish Brigade commanded by General Thomas Francis Meagher is a product of the relentless, frenzied, American preoccupation with matters of race. That obsession cannot account, though, for a parallel phenomenon: a similarly inappropriate chasm separates the reputation of those Federal Irish soldiers from their hard-fighting—but largely ignored—countrymen in Confederate ranks.

Kelly O'Grady's book sets out methodically to supply an antidote for some of those popular misperceptions, and succeeds in the effort with a distinctive flair. Before the reader reaches the index, he will find ample reason to judge O'Grady a success in his avowed effort "to bring some balance to the discussion of Irish participation in the war."

Although his focus is on Irishmen in service to the South, O'Grady devotes a fascinating section of his work to the aftermath of Fredericksburg in the North. The argument convincingly draws related conclusions: that the Irish Brigade's suffering at Fredericksburg understandably was viewed in many quarters as dolorous rather than grand; that men within and without the brigade clearly recognized the arrant bungling of Meagher and other leaders; and that support among Irish people for the Northern war effort waned as a result.

Across the lines, Irishmen were the largest immigrant group in the Confederate military population. Southern Irish soldiers and civilians were notably more ardent in support of their country's cause than were their brethren in the North. That enthusiasm, O'Grady argues, resulted from relatively better treatment afforded the Irish in the South than in the intolerant North. The pro-Confederate stance of many influential Irish Catholic clergy also contributed to Irish-Confederate commitment.

Anyone who has read much about the American Civil War has run across instances of raillery and rivalry across the lines between Irish soldiery serving opposite one another. O'Grady accumulates enough of that anecdotal material to establish the very wide prevalence of Irish comity between foemen. Men of common ancestry, though wearing blue or gray or butternut, clearly enjoyed a sort of ethnic sodality that overlooked the temporary separation by political expedients.

Casual readers probably will not appreciate the appendices as much as the main narrative, but the back matter contains highly useful reference material. Especially valuable are sections devoted to biographical sketches of more than one hundred Irish officers, and short histories of several dozen Irish companies.

Civil War books continue to appear with tidal regularity and in tidal-wave proportions. Most talk about the same subjects over and over again. That is an inevitable and not necessarily undesirable consequence of the intense interest in events of high drama and portent. Most of the flood of books use the same tired material (over and over again), however, and that is inexcusable. Six books attacking Lee's record have appeared recently, for instance, each of them parroting a tendentiously flawed original and none of them employing so much as an iota of new information. O'Grady, by contrast, has taken a fresh look at a subject that is far from exhausted. He throws new light on an interesting aspect of Civil War history, and he dug deeply in a wide array of primary sources in preparing his thesis. The result is a stimulating good book.

Robert K. Krick
Fredericksburg, Virginia

# Preface

She's the most distressful country that ever yet was seen, For they're
hanging men and women there for the Wearin' o' the Green.

— *The Wearing of the Green*, 18th century Irish political lament, Anonymous

We are a band of brothers
and native to the soil,
Fighting for our liberty,
With treasure, blood and toil.

—The Bonnie Blue Flag, Harry McCarthy

In the study of the American Civil War, readers glimpse but fleeting
allusions to Irishmen in Confederate service. At the same time the
Union Irish Brigade has been lauded and lionized in press, poetry,
paint and prose for more than one hundred thirty-five years. This book
seeks to bring some balance to the discussion of Irish participation in the
war. *Clear the Confederate Way!* began as a simple attempt to identify
the Irish troops and leaders of the Confederacy; it developed into a
multifaceted work that resurrects what was a strong pro-Confederate
Irish presence in the wartime South.

Scholars of the war will agree that Irish Confederates often appear in
our investigative frame, but never have been the center of our focus.
Who were these often mentioned, seemingly ubiquitous, but rarely
featured Irishmen of the Confederacy? The answer to this ostensibly
simple question has resulted in this book—the first comprehensive
attempt to catalogue the Irish troops in the Army of Northern Virginia. It
is an objective (though not wholly dispassionate) work describing what
was a significant and substantial Irish contribution to the Confederacy.

# CLEAR THE CONFEDERATE WAY!

As primarily a military history, *Clear The Confederate Way!* focuses on the battlefield exploits of the Irishmen of the South. But by emphasizing a strong biographical component, the book offers more than one-dimensional military narratives. Irish brains and brawn played a significant part in the overall Confederate war effort, but the Irish presence in the South was even larger than its participation in the war. Therefore, this book explores some larger themes.

In the war period, the Irish were the largest immigrant group in the American South and the largest immigrant group in Confederate armies. Their numbers were so great—and their stories so compelling—that by necessity this book is limited only to a study of the Irish in the premier Confederate army, Gen. Robert E. Lee's Army of Northern Virginia. What was often wholehearted support for the Confederacy by the Irish in the South contrasts with Northern Irish reticence for the Union cause. Although in raw numbers many more Irishmen took up the Union banner, historian James M. McPherson noted in his Pulitzer prize-winning book *Battle Cry of Freedom* that the Irish were the most underrepresented immigrant group in Northern armies. In short, Southern Irishmen may have been better Confederates than Northern Irishmen were Federals. The Irish Confederate contribution in uniform comes to life in this book in representative examples of Irishmen in battle. Confederate Irish soldiers participated in every major battle in the Eastern Theater, and Irish Confederate battle experiences present us with some awe-inspiring scenes.

Southern Irish troops were the first in the war to invoke the Gaelic battle cry "Faugh A Ballagh!" translated "Clear the way!" Colonel Patrick T. Moore of the 1st Virginia Infantry and that regiment's Montgomery Guard used the Irish cheer at Manassas in 1861. Another Irish Confederate tableau occurred in camp one night during the 1862 Shenandoah Valley Campaign. Major General Richard Taylor tells us that the raucous Irish troops under his command at Port Republic were impatient to prove themselves against the Irish Yankee general James Shields. These Southern Irishmen boldly predicted victory as they caroused in camp that night. Richard Taylor and his Irishmen would whip Shields the following day. Taylor's description of the scene around Confederate campfires the night before the battle prefigured the words of today's Irish national anthem, "Soldier's Song," which was not written until 1907:

> As 'round our blazing fires we throng, the starry heavens o'er us.
> Impatient for the coming fight, and as we wait the morning light.
> Here in the silence of the night, we'll chant a soldier's song.

Was the scene in the Irish national anthem inspired by this rousing chorus of Irish Confederates?

A third example of Irish Confederates in battle will touch the hearts of all who read it. Irishman John P. Keely, a captain with the 19th Georgia, rescued a wounded Union Irishman from a fire during the Chancellorsville battle. "I paused," explained Keely, "not because he was an enemy, nor did I assist him because he was an Irishman—I knew only that he was helpless, and in imminent danger, and that I could assist him—and I did." This sublimely emotional Irish battle experience involving both Union and Confederate Irishmen could inspire a new Irish monument or commemorative battle painting. Indeed these three exciting examples of Irish Confederates in the war only hint at untapped inspirational events that could be used by artists who heretofore have portrayed only Union Irish troops in the Civil War. The Irish troop units and leaders of the Army of Northern Virginia—the nuts and bolts of this work—are catalogued in Appendices I and II. This information provides a mere beginning for the study of these unsung Irish heroes.

On the political front, wartime Irish opinion in the South and in Ireland, contrary to conventional belief today, was largely pro-Confederate. This fact has been lost in what American historian Joseph M. Hernon Jr. convincingly argues was a revisionist, postwar attempt to gloss over Irish sympathies for the losing side. Many Irishmen then, as today, sympathized with rebellion. In a troubled anti-immigrant period, the 19th century Democratic Party (the party of the South) offered political, economic, and social refuge for Irish—and particularly Catholic immigrants. Evidence of this Democratic Party alliance of "Romanism and rebellion" was later immortalized by derogatory Republican slogans in the 1885 Presidential campaign. The Irish community in America formed this political pact in reaction to its intolerant and even violent experience at the hands of some Northerners, whose nativism and Puritanism were traditional enemies of the Irish people. Many leaders of the 19th century Irish nationalist movement also advocated an Irish allegiance with the South. Most Irish nationalists saw the South's attempt to secede from the American Union as a parallel struggle with Ireland's aim to break away from Britain. One might even go so far as to say that some nationalist revolutionaries viewed the South as a surrogate Ireland and saw Southern secession as an experiment in how an agricultural society might gain its independence from a powerful industrial nation. These issues are more fully developed in Chapter One, "The Politics of Southern Allegiance: Why the Irish Supported the Confederacy." The Roman Catholic Church provided yet another influential group of pro-South Irish leaders in America. The bishops and clergy of the Catholic dioceses in the South were staunch Confederates and exercised tremendous influence over their Irish Catholic flocks. Chapter One's "The Rebel Church: Irish Priests in Confederate Service," explores this overlooked facet of Southern allegiance.

If Hernon's thesis is sound, and strong Irish support for the Confederacy can be proved, how did we get to this amnesic point? Why is Irish allegiance in the war indubitably linked to the Union cause? Why does the Union Irish Brigade stand today as the consummate symbol of Irish participation in the war? The answers to these questions were erected on a single foundation: political expedience.

The Irish Brigade became the main instrument of postwar Northern and Irish revisionists who needed to provide cover for impolitic Irish sympathies in the war. Union patriotism among many Northern Irish was lackluster. Erin's "prodigal sons" in the South were painfully obvious and often well-placed in the Irish community. During the war, Irish nationalist circles in America and Ireland were conspicuous in their pro-Confederate sympathies. In the postwar period, a relentless public relations campaign assured that the Irish Brigade, and not its Confederate counterparts, became the symbol of Irish allegiance in the war. The example of loyal Union service by the Irish Brigade was highly publicized and expertly touted as the only Irish example of war participation. There is evidence of postwar Southern Irish complicity with what was a cynical, political rehabilitation scheme. Irish Confederates left little in the written record about their Southern loyalty,

# Preface

even when they were well positioned to do so. For example, former Confederate officer John D. Keiley Jr., editor of the Irish nationalist *Freeman's Journal* newspaper after the war, did not write of his Confederate past. Thus the paucity of Southern Irish accounts, coupled with the complicity of Northern Irish revisionists, may well account for today's almost complete memory loss of Irish support for the Confederacy. This political censorship also may explain why the true and tragic nature of the Irish Brigade's war service has been lost. The soldiers of that brigade were indeed gallant and brave, but the unit's wanton abuse by incompetent leadership rendered its service less glorious than was presented by the revisionists. Chapter Three's "A Second Look at the Irish Brigade at Fredericksburg," and an analysis of the Civil War career of Irish Brigade commander Thomas F. Meagher, help set the revisionist record straight.

"The Legacy of Fredericksburg: Irish Opinion Turns Against the War," also contained in the book's third chapter, offers another larger theme: that the destruction of the Irish Brigade at Fredericksburg, more than any other single battlefield event, turned Irish opinion in the North and in Ireland almost completely against the Union and the war. This is significant because the Battle of Fredericksburg is remembered today as the brigade's most heroic moment. Wartime opinion-makers, though, saw the Irish storming of Marye's Heights through sad and tragic eyes. The Battle of Fredericksburg, at least in the Irish experience, was the turning point of the war.

"Southern Irish Soldiers and the Mercenary Myth," also found in Chapter Three, disarms long-standing claims by some Southern historians that the Northern armies were filled with Hessian-like hirelings. In fact, Lee's Confederate army at its zenith may have had a higher proportion of foreigners in its ranks than its Northern counterpart. A statistical analysis demonstrates that by percentage, Southern Irishmen served in the Confederate army at the same rate that Northern Irishmen served as Union soldiers. In any event, there were no mercenaries, in the classic sense of the word, in either army, although a few independent soldiers of fortune could be found in both. The foreign presence in the armies did not represent an organized mercenary force. Most of these men were simply new immigrants and future American citizens who took army service as the best available work in their new country. Most of them were Irishmen.

The first chapter in *Clear the Confederate Way!*, entitled "From the Old Sod to the Old First: Irish Immigrants in the American South," explores another common misconception. Southerners often touted the lost cause as the struggle of a purely Anglo-Saxon culture. The South, however, was much more cosmopolitan and multiethnic than is generally recognized. The opening lines to the secessionist anthem "The Bonnie Blue Flag" reinforce the Southern belief in a native born brotherhood:

> We are a band of brothers
> And native to the soil,
> Fighting for our liberty,
> With treasure, blood and toil.

What most do not realize is that an Irishman, Harry McCarthy, wrote those lyrics to match the tune of an old Irish song called "The Jaunting Car." This Rebel hymn was in fact an Irish tune with words by an Irish minstrel. McCarthy was an Irishman with secessionist sympathies. George Hubbard, writing in the 1928 *Confederate Veteran*, noted that McCarthy, a comedian and vocalist billed as the "Irish Nightingale" and the "Arkansas Comedian," sympathized with the South in the war. McCarthy, Hubbard wrote, was a prisoner of war at Johnson's Island, Ohio, when he and Missouri "Swamp Rat" Gen. M. Jeff Thompson wrote another popular Southern song, "Georgia Militia Grabbing Goober Peas." McCarthy's "suffering while a prisoner crushed his spirit so that he rarely smiled, and I think he returned to Ireland in 1867," Hubbard remembered. In the same vein, Irish-American Daniel Decatur Emmett of Ohio immortalized the Southland as the "land of cotton" when he wrote "Dixie's Land" in 1859. By popular acclaim, "Dixie" was adopted by 1861 as the song of the South, a beloved tune that became a Southern national anthem of sorts. Here was another Irish minstrel tune embraced by the Confederacy. Look away, Dixie Land, your song was written by an Irishman. The music of McCarthy and Emmett are just two examples of how Irishmen and other Southern immigrants, and not just Anglo-Saxon natives, took leading roles in the communities and in the cause of the South.

On a more serious note, this book reveals a newly-found portrait of the Irish Civil War soldier. So often seen in the blue of the Union legions, the Irish soldier should as often be remembered in the gray or butternut of the Confederacy. Indeed the "wearing of the gray" was a transformational experience for the Irish immigrants of the South. Their assimilation into Southern and American society was accelerated by the war and consecrated by the blood of battle. This is most apparent in a study of the postwar achievements of Irish Confederates, which is offered in the book's conclusion, "Irish Confederates After the War: A Nation Once Again."

*Clear the Confederate Way!* offers grist to help mill some other provocative issues. In the course of my research an interesting but inexplicable pattern was discovered among Irish companies in the Confederate army. Regiments that included Irish companies often designated them as the color company—the guardians of the regimental colors in battle. Examples include the Irish Volunteers, Company K, of the 1st South Carolina; the Jackson Guards, Company B, of the 19th Georgia; and the Virginia Hibernians, Company B, of the 27th Virginia. The new picture of the Irish Civil War soldier should include the gallant Southern Irish color companies. Irishmen proudly held the center of many Confederate battle lines.

It seems a soldier in the field in either army could not travel far without meeting an Irish comrade. In numerous battle narratives, Irish Confederates often reported they had fought, and usually defeated, Meagher's Irish Brigade. The reports were almost always mistaken. One explanation for this phenomenon might be that Irish Confederate units hoped to share the limelight Meagher's troops garnered from the New York press. Another explanation is that Confederate Irishmen often fought against the myriad Irish companies in the Union armies—companies more often than not unassociated with the Irish Brigade, a fact few of the Southern Irish realized. Battle accounts also reveal another recurring theme: the camaraderie between Irishmen in the Southern army and even between Hibernians in the contending armies. Captain John Keely of the 19th Georgia Infantry hailed fellow Irishmen manning heavy artillery at the very beginning of the war at Manassas. "Here we found several large earth forts manned by a body of Irishmen from Louisiana, from whom we received much kindness. Indeed they instantly fraternized with our company (all of whom were Irish too) and right here sprang up an acquaintance which continued till the surrender," he wrote. From that first meeting at Manassas, Irishmen met Irishmen at White Oak Swamp, Fredericksburg, Chancellorsville, Gettysburg, and in Union prisons, and always there was a "hail fellow well met" story to tell. The comity between Irishmen, North and South, is a story within the story of the war.

I ask the casual reader and the reader unschooled in Irish history and literature to indulge my penchant for Irish allusions. Irish and Confederate allusions seem to fit well together. The struggle for Irish independence has been described as a poet's dream, in recognition of the heroic ideas and actions of Padraic Pearse, the Irish poet turned rebel soldier in the Easter Rising of 1916. Understanding Irish political poetry, with an ancient lineage stemming from the Irish bardic tradition, is key to understanding Ireland's history. Southern war poetry is no less evocative of the Irish poet's dream. In fact, there is a distinct convergence of ideological and emotional themes in Irish and Confederate literature. Examples of verse and prose from both Confederate and Irish sources introduce each topic of the book. These verses emphatically illustrate the parallel hopes for Irish and Southern independence. Civil War scholars may find it surprising that even obscure Southern sources often hint at Irish-Confederate alliances. South Carolinian Robert Wallace Shand, a member of the 2nd South Carolina Volunteer Infantry, wrote that when a secessionist committee in Columbia, South Carolina, needed rebellious mottoes for recruiting posters, "We got up a splendid collection, taken largely from Irish ballads." By borrowing from Irish ballads, the South Carolinian revealed an understanding of the rebel fraternity of the Irishman and the Confederate.

The intertwining of Irish and Confederate experience also is found in a historical context. Metaphorically speaking, both countries' histories were written on tattered pages burned by fiery trial, but the Irish-Confederate nexus does not end there. One key allusion to Irish

# Preface

history strikes at the heart of one of the Irish Brigade's proudest legends—the wearing of the green by its soldiers at Marye's Heights. The Irish Confederates who watched the approach of the green flag of the 28th Massachusetts Infantry at Fredericksburg wondered how the Northern Irish could support "so foul a tyranny" as the Union. Ideology alone should have led the Irish to ally themselves with the Southern rebels. Likewise a 17th century Irish observer of the most infamous of Irish battles, at the Boyne River in 1690, would be quite confused if through time travel he came upon the field at Fredericksburg in 1862. A committed Irish nationalist would inevitably cheer on the Confederate line as it poured in the fire on the ranks of invading bluecoats—the ranks that included the Irish Brigade. We can assume this because of some observations made by military historian Gerard A. Hayes-McCoy, who reminds us that it was James II's Irish Catholic army at the Boyne that wore broadcloth and buff uniforms. Hayes-McCoy likened these Irish uniforms to the gray and butternut of the Confederates in the Civil War. Thus, by uniform identification alone, the 17th century Irishman might have taken the side of the men in Confederate garb as they fought off the Irish Brigade.

But yet another clue would attract the attention of our Irish observer—the famous sprigs of boxwood worn by the Irish Brigade soldiers at Fredericksburg. This detail certainly would lead the loyal Irishman to believe that the men in blue were the unprovoked aggressors in the battle. At the Battle of the Boyne, it was the invading army of King William III, anti-Irish forces, that donned identification greenery for the battle—the fight that led eventually to the subjugation of Ireland! In retrospect then, the Yankee Irish Brigade mangled its Irish history and, by emulating King William's army, committed a sort of historical faux pas at Fredericksburg. The wearing of the green by the Union men was a muddled attempt to prove the "Irishness" of the brigade, but the Yankee uniform, even with its ersatz Irish adornment probably did not make Meagher's soldiers more committed Unionists.

Even with the green flag and the boxwood sprigs, the ideological issue still persisted in the minds of the Confederate Irish. How could the Northern Irish fight for "so foul a tyranny" as the Union? The time traveling observer likely would have asked the same question. After all,

# CLEAR THE CONFEDERATE WAY!

Irishmen in history consistently have fought against the forces that seek to impose centralized government on a weaker neighbor. The Irish people as a whole had for eight hundred years rebelled against the concept of union. In this context, the Irish Brigade in the Civil War was an aberration. The stand of the Confederate Irish was a continuation of the rebel tradition. A discerning student of Irish history and literature will recognize that it was the Confederate experience—"the wearing of the gray," both metaphorical, political, and literal—that more resembled the Irish experience.

Beyond the legacy of the Boyne River, the wearing of the green, if not boxwood sprigs, is indeed a symbol of Irish nationalist solidarity. John Esten Cooke, the erudite Confederate officer, novelist and historian, must have realized this Irish allusion when he chose to title his postwar book about J.E.B. Stuart and Confederate miscellany *The Wearing of the Gray.* Cooke's title was wordplay on "The Wearing of the Green," a well-known 18th century Irish political song. But for the enduring popularity of his book, I would have borrowed his paraphrase of the Irish title for this work.

Oh that the memory of thousands of Irish Confederate soldiers had endured as long as Captain Cooke's works. Too many gallant Southern Irishmen "died well" in the battles of the Civil War, only to be ungratefully neglected by posterity. In the North and in Ireland their sacrifices were quickly forgotten, mainly for the political reasons already visited in this preface and perhaps because of regional prejudices. In the South, these men often were relegated to the footnotes of history because of their immigrant status.

This book will unabashedly recall the Southern service of some of these gallant Irishmen. Many readers will be introduced to men like Maj. John Dooley of Limerick, Ireland, and Gen. Patrick T. Moore of Galway, the leaders of Richmond's Irish soldiers at Manassas. As officers in the 1st Virginia Infantry, these two immigrants were inheritors of the American army unit once commanded by George Washington. Also highlighted are Southern Irish colonels William Feeney, William Monaghan, Michael Nolan, and Henry Strong. Here were four bold Confederate leaders, strong Confederate Irish voices who never explained their Rebel allegiance because all were killed in battle.

# Preface

Their ultimate sacrifices, newly examined, make eloquent statements about their Confederate service which they were never able to make in life. Colonel Robert McMillan of County Tyrone is the forgotten Irish hero of the Battle of Fredericksburg. He commanded Thomas Cobb's Brigade after Cobb was mortally wounded and with it repulsed the Union Irish Brigade at the Sunken Road. His steady hand directed the Confederate defense at a critical point of the battle. This book details his heroism.

John Mitchel, the premier Irish nationalist of the 19th century, came to the Confederacy by way of exile from British Ireland. A farmer in Tennessee, he moved to Richmond in 1862 to write blistering editorials for Jefferson Davis. He was imprisoned by Union authorities for his recalcitrant and defiant support of the South even after the war. His sons, John C., James, and William, were all in the Confederate army. John and William were killed, and James lost an arm fighting for the Mitchels' adopted homeland. A pair of Irishmen were crack artillerists for Robert E. Lee. Majors Joseph McGraw and James Reilly both pounded the Northern enemy with practiced skill and Irish aplomb. Anthony M. Keiley fought in the 12th Virginia Infantry, held statewide and later national offices, established several Southern newspapers, and subsequently became Richmond's first Irish Catholic mayor, the latter distinction achieved a full seven years before New York or Boston elected an Irishman to the same post. Captain Francis Potts is one example of the many thousands of Irish immigrants who enlisted as privates in the Confederate army. Potts rose through the ranks and became the corps paymaster for James Longstreet. He provided history with a poignant word portrait of Lee's surrender at Appomattox. Potts, like many Irish Confederates, fought for the South to the end. Many others fought for the South to the death. Those readers enamored by the war tales of the Union Irish and especially Thomas F. Meagher will find these alternative Irish heroes just as worthy of honor. There is, within their heroic stories, the echo of a soldier's voice still waiting to be heard by Southern and Irish patriots.

Reviving the truth of the service of these forgotten Irish Confederate heroes is an attempt to remember the past properly—and not an attempt to rewrite history. The purpose of this book is to resurrect the past, not revise it. Certainly my intent is not to denigrate the noble service of any soldier on either side in the war. *Clear the Confederate Way!* is an attempt to bring a truthful balance to the story of Irish participation in the war, and after more than one hundred thirty-five years that task entails the first comprehensive chronicle of Irish participation from the Confederate perspective.

Captain Keely, by all accounts one of the true Irish heroes of the war, said it best in his memoirs when he noted: "Irish soldiers in both armies made for themselves during the late war a record second to none."

## Acknowledgments

Keeping in mind that cursory acknowledgments hardly begin to repay the heavy debt an author owes to so many people, I wish to thank and acknowledge a splendid troop of family, friends, and colleagues. Without their help and encouragement this book would not have been possible.

As always, the mainframe source of anything on the Army of Northern Virginia, even things Hibernian, is Robert K. Krick, Chief Historian of the Fredericksburg and Spotsylvania National Military Park. He was the big gun in a Confederate arsenal of sources, and helped provide me an opening salvo in this battle for a book.

Likewise, the entire history division at Fredericksburg provided me a steady skirmish line of seasoned researchers and talented readers. I am greatly indebted to Don Pfanz, John Hennessy, Noel Harrison, Greg Mertz, Janice Frye, Elsa Lohman, and Keith Alexander, and particularly to those who read the manuscript, Frank O'Reilly, Mac Wyckoff, Eric Mink, and Beth Getz. Each provided me with new insights on the work, suggesting both historical and literary improvements. Any errors or omissions, however, are my own.

A phalanx of other Fredericksburg colleagues helped close up the ranks. These included volunteers, interns, coworkers in other departments, and the staff at Eastern National Bookstore. Most were amused by me and my odd project, but they continued to dutifully ask about the book's progress and encourage my efforts. Farther afield, I

# Acknowledgments

wish to thank others who helped in many different ways. Keith Bohannon, for his help with Irish Georgians; John Bigham, of the South Carolina Confederate Relic Room and Museum, for his help with South Carolina troops; Michael Musick, for his help with National Archives records; John Dove for his map-making talents; Anna Howland, for her flag drawings; Timothy Bottoms of the Cape Fear Museum; author Kirk Mitchell; Anne C. Edwards, Chancellor of the Catholic Diocese of Richmond; Fergus Galvin and Eamon McEneany of the City of Waterford Museum in Ireland; the Library of Virginia, the Virginia Historical Society, the Valentine Museum, the Museum of the Confederacy, and the Maymont Foundation. Thanks also to Dr. Art Tracy of Mary Washington College, who provided the initial encouragement to publish.

Last, but most important, I wish to thank my wife, Laura, whose editorial contributions to this project were surpassed only by her loving patience with an often preoccupied and out-of-sorts author.


Kelly O'Grady
Fredericksburg, Virginia

# Introduction

The Confederate Medal of Honor Roll includes about twenty men
clearly of Irish descent, which shows that 'Pat' took both sides of the
argument in our war, as well as of all others of modern times.

— John C. Stiles, in *The Victoria Cross of the Confederacy*

On March 1, 1866, almost one year after Robert E. Lee surrendered the Army of Northern Virginia at Appomattox Court House, Capt. John P. Keely of Atlanta wrote to his father in Ireland:

The war is over, and I do not feel ashamed of my course, for I advocated...
the cause of a noble and honest people. And while honorable war was
being conducted, God knows I fought for the cause with my whole heart.[1]

Keely, an officer in an all-Irish company in Lee's army, was one of thousands of Irish immigrants who cast their lot with the Confederacy in the American Civil War.

About 40,000 Irishmen served as soldiers in Southern armies. This generally accepted number was reported by Irish nationalist John Mitchel to the Irish newspaper *The Nation* in 1863. Other estimates more than double that figure. A postwar study reported by Michael Cavanagh, who wrote a short biography of Mitchel and edited the memoirs of Irish nationalist and Union general Thomas Francis Meagher, puts the figure at 83,000. While the exact number of Irish Confederates will never be known, it is clear that significant numbers of Irish served in Confederate armies. These men made a substantial contribution to the Southern war effort—an Irish contribution to the Confederacy that has largely been ignored, or, at best, chronicled in a piecemeal way. One of only a handful of studies of Irish Confederates, John Lewis Garland's essay "Irish Soldiers of the American Confederacy," noted almost fifty years ago that "Very few histories of these organizations [Irish Confederate companies] have yet been written."[2] This is still the case today. More than forty-five distinctly Irish companies of infantry troops served in Lee's Army of Northern Virginia. If mustered as one force, these companies, a sustained force of as many as 4,000 men, would have formed several Confederate Irish brigades.

Irish companies in Confederate service usually adopted distinctive titles, often borrowing from the names of Irish nationalist leaders such as Robert Emmet and Daniel O'Connell. Seeing the South's struggle as a revolution for independence, many companies chose the name of the first Irish rebel in America, Gen. Richard Montgomery, who died in the service of the Continental Army during the American Revolution. Raised in six states, the army's Irish companies came from Southern port cities such as Mobile, Charleston, Savannah, and New Orleans, and from growing western settlements or railroad centers such as Macon and Atlanta, Georgia, and Lynchburg and Alexandria, Virginia.

Irish units and their leaders distinguished themselves in almost every major battle of the war. In the Eastern Theater, Confederate Irish troops and leaders at least figuratively flew the green flag at Manassas, in Thomas J. "Stonewall" Jackson's Shenandoah Valley Campaign, in the Seven Days' Battles, at Sharpsburg, Chancellorsville, Gettysburg, and to the very end at Appomattox. One battle though, the Battle of Fredericksburg, holds a special place in Irish memories of the war. The Fredericksburg engagement, fought December 13, 1862, did more to shape Irish opinion on the meaning and course of the war than any other single battlefield event. Historians to date have inordinately concerned themselves with a study of the famous Union Irish Brigade at Fredericksburg, but at the brigade, regimental, and company level, Irish soldiers also were an integral part of the Confederate defense on the Rappahannock. This book specifically discusses the presence of Irish troops and leaders in the Confederate army at Fredericksburg. While no study of the Irish at Fredericksburg could be complete without a study of the Union Irish Brigade and its celebrated charge at Marye's Heights, this investigation of the Irish Brigade will dispense with the usual

# Introduction

hagiography associated with the unit and its leader, Thomas F. Meagher. Instead it will examine the Irish Brigade largely through the eyes of the Confederates who witnessed the Union unit's destruction in the battle.

On another level, the personal experiences of Irish Confederates in the war tell a larger story of the transformation of Irish immigrants into Southern patriots and finally American citizens—an assimilation process accelerated by the war and baptized in the blood of battle. For Captain Keely battle was a frightful experience he dubbed a "feast of death." If Keely's war experience is any guide, the Southern Irish soldier's story is one of patriotism, physical courage, duty, honor, and sacrifice for his adopted country—the Confederate States of America.

Here, at last, is that story.

# Irish Green and Confederate Gray

## From the Old Sod to the Old First:
## Irish Immigrants in the American South

In all the Southern states the Irish element outranked all others
[foreign-born] except in Texas where the Germans topped the list.

— Ella Lonn, *Foreigners in the Confederacy*

John Dooley had a passionate love for the land where he had found the
opportunity to live out his life in freedom; this land was the South.

—Joseph T. Durkin, in *John Dooley Confederate Soldier*

In 1885, President Grover Cleveland nominated former Confederate officer Anthony M. Keiley to be United States Minister to Italy. Keiley, an Irish-American lieutenant in the 12th Virginia Infantry during the war, had enjoyed a stellar career in Petersburg and Richmond since the "late unpleasantness." Before the war, this son of an immigrant attended Randolph-Macon College and co-published *The Southside Democrat* newspaper. After his wounding at the Battle of Malvern Hill in 1862, Keiley returned home and established the *Petersburg Express*, a pro-Confederate newspaper. After the war, he founded the *Petersburg Index* and wrote a book about his wartime experiences. Keiley became an attorney in Richmond, served three terms in the Virginia General Assembly and was mayor of Richmond for five years, 1871 to 1876. He was one of the capital city's foremost Catholic leaders and as mayor spoke against the government of King Victor Emmanuel II when the Italian kingdom annexed papal territory by force in 1870.

# CLEAR THE CONFEDERATE WAY!

Because of Keiley's high profile in the former Confederate capital, the *New York Herald* took note of his ambassadorial appointment in 1885. After the United States Senate approved his ambassadorship to Italy, the paper reported that Keiley had reproached the Italian government fourteen years before, and the Italians refused his portfolio. According to one report, a new nomination to the Austro-Hungarian court also was refused because Keiley's wife, Rebecca Davis, was Jewish. Keiley's pro-Catholic politics and his Semitic wife had afforded him no problems in his public life in Richmond; but now the former Irish Confederate faced the opprobrium of two of Europe's most cultured nations.

Keiley's high-profile "Irishness," his outspoken Catholicism, prominent political activity, and successful law career in Virginia, would not have been tolerated in some parts of nineteenth-century America. Yet Keiley stood astride Richmond's political and social establishment. His leadership role indicates that the population of the nineteenth-century South was more diverse, and Southern society more cosmopolitan, than generally recognized. This ethnic diversity was reflected in the faces of Southern soldiers. Ella Lonn's fascinating *Foreigners in the Confederacy* was a seminal work in describing the ethnic makeup of the Confederate armies. Lonn's study found not only Irish Southern soldiers, but German, Polish, French, English, Scottish, and Jewish Confederates. Italian, West Indian, Mexican, Portuguese, Swiss, Canadian, Spanish, and Scandinavian natives also fought for the Confederacy.[1] The largest immigrant group in the South, Irish and first generation Irish-American stock like Keiley, formed a strong broth for this Southern ethnic melting pot. The story of the Irish in the American South was a long-standing and complicated recipe.

There is evidence of incipient Catholic Irish settlement in the Southern states as early as the 1700s, even before the founding of the Republic. Historian Dennis Clark noted the presence of native Catholic Irishmen in the South from the country's earliest times. There were no great concentrations of Irish in America during this period, concentrations that would be seen later in New York, Boston, and Philadelphia. Yet, New Orleans and Charleston boasted significant Irish communities as early as the Revolutionary period. Before the

Revolution, settlement of Irish Catholics was forbidden by law in many colonies, and laws prohibiting Catholics were especially harsh in New England. Irish immigrants also formed a small part of the trans-Appalachian migration as well. Clark asserted that Irish Catholics together with Ulster Irish Protestant backwoodsmen pioneered early Piedmont and mountain settlements. For instance, fifty families from County Tipperary, Ireland, settled farms one hundred-fifty miles inland in Taliaferro County, Georgia, early in the 1800s.[2] Irish immigration to America increased after 1820, evidenced by the Irish labor used in the period of great canal building. Irish workers were responsible for many of the five hundred miles of transportation canals built in the South before 1860.[3]

These examples of early Irish settlement in America foreshadowed the massive Irish migration that was to come. Generally, the Irish came to this continent in two distinct waves. The first from both North Britain and Ireland swept over America from approximately 1717 to 1775. Many of these immigrants, chiefly Ulstermen from the north of Ireland, came to colonial America for economic opportunity and religious freedom. The British government in Ireland had dispossessed them of their lands and persecuted them for their Presbyterian religion. The descendants of these early American settlers are often referred to as Scots-Irish, though in actuality they might have been Scot, Welsh, English or Irish.[4] The Southern back country was the destination of most of these early immigrants, and many of their descendants filled the ranks of Confederate armies.

But these back country inhabitants, even with distinctly Irish surnames, were far removed from Ireland and culturally distant from native Irishmen by the war period. They are not the subjects of this study. The Irish of the Civil War came to the American continent after the turn of the nineteenth century. Most native Irish people—that is Gaelic-speaking, Catholic Irish—emigrated to America in the middle of the nineteenth century, just in time for America's Civil War.[5] A truer gauge of Irish participation in the war in America confines itself to this group, and to the easily identifiable concentrations of immigrants in the South by the time of the war.

# CLEAR THE CONFEDERATE WAY!

Even with the Irish exodus of the eighteenth century and subsequent migrations by the middle of the nineteenth century, the small island of Ireland teemed with nearly 8,000,000 people—or 2,500,000 more than the white population of the South. The small agricultural British province, suffering economic hardship, political oppression, and religious persecution under the Crown, needed a relief valve for its burgeoning population. These conditions triggered the second wave of Irish immigration to America. If the first wave was significant, the second Irish immigration was a cataclysmic flood. Earlier Scots-Irish Protestants had assimilated quickly in North America (in Canada as well as in the United States). In the second migration, codified religious tolerance in the United States drew many Irish to its shores. The Irish migration of the mid-century was largely a Catholic one, and these immigrants found greater acceptance in the United States than in other parts of the English-speaking world. Historian Rowland Berthoff contends that "after the 1830s [Irish] Catholics were more apt than Protestants to go to the United States" rather than Canada or other English speaking countries.[6]

Economic opportunity also spurred the Irish exodus to America. When the Irish potato crop failed in 1845, the subsequent famine, known as the Great Hunger, sent another 1,800,000 of Ireland's people to North America between 1845 and 1855. About 250,000 more Irish immigrants landed in the United States from 1856 to 1860, bringing the total count of Irish immigration to North America since 1815 to approximately 3,000,000.[7] In the Victorian century, the Celtic migration to the United States irrevocably changed the nation—in politics, in economics, and in social and religious realms. Irish participation in the war was one aspect of these changes.

In the context of a long-standing Irish presence in America, and with the colossal migration here in the prewar period, it is not surprising that there was an identifiable Irish presence in the South at the start of the Civil War. Although most Irish immigrants settled in the North, the South also became a haven for thousands of the exiled children of Ireland. The Southern states offered the Irish an agricultural society like they had known in Ireland, religious tolerance that was often lacking in the North, and economic opportunity in the form of cheap land,

# Irish Green and Confederate Gray

especially in its frontier areas. One example of Southern Irish landfall was seen in Richmond in the 1830s. When 22-year-old Limerickman John Dooley stepped on a Baltimore dock in 1832, he knew little about North and South, Union or secession. He knew only that a new world of opportunity was open to him in America. His experience in the South contrasts sharply with the lot of thousands of Irish immigrants trapped in Northern Irish ghettoes with little hope of escape and advancement. John Dooley's eventual accomplishments as a Richmond businessman and Confederate officer chronicle the story of nineteenth century Irish immigration to the American South.

John Dooley met his future wife (who incidentally

An Ulsterman for the Confederacy. The English gentlemen who erected this monument in Richmond's Capitol Square claimed Lt. Gen. Thomas J. "Stonewall" Jackson as their own, but his forbears were Irish. Jackson came from Scots-Irish stock—Northern Irish Protestants who migrated to America's backcountry in the eighteenth century. The Scots-Irish contribution to the Confederacy, with Jackson as its epitome, was enormous, but Gaelic Irishmen also fought gallantly for the South. Jackson's great grandfather, John Jackson, was born near Coleraine, County Londonderry, Ireland, in 1715 or 1719. *Author* was his distant cousin), Sarah Dooley, on the passage to Baltimore from his native Limerick, Ireland, and they married in 1836 in Alexandria. The Dooleys settled in Richmond and the immigrant's prospects flourished in Virginia's capital city.[8] According to his biographer, the Dooley home "was the recognized center of a social group whose importance has never been sufficiently appreciated—the Irish-Americans of the prewar South."[9]

In Richmond, Dooley worked as a clerk in a mercantile establishment, and later started his own business as a hatter and furrier in the city. By 1860, Dooley's Great Southern Hat and Cap Manufactory and Depot provided the Irish family with a net worth of $93,000, a fortune that included three slaves.[10] The Catholic Dooleys raised a large family that included five daughters and three sons. (The eldest son, George Dooley, died in 1860.)

The Dooleys were proud of their Irish Catholic heritage, but more often assimilation into the American mainstream meant economic and social advancement. Many immigrants did not want to identify themselves as anything but Americans. Other immigrants were misidentified by the natives who processed and naturalized them. Thus it was sometimes difficult to identify an Irish immigrant in the nineteenth century. Berthoff argued that "Many persons who appear in the American immigration and census reports as Englishmen, Welshmen, or Scots would better have been called Irish" because of parentage, religion and a way of life that identified them with Catholic Ireland.[11] Sometimes immigrants downplayed or misrepresented their Irish national origins by calling themselves British. Some native born Irishmen even claimed to be English, an assertion that was technically incorrect, but plausible in practical terms since Ireland was then a part of the United Kingdom of England, Ireland, Scotland, and Wales. However, within the United Kingdom, Ireland stood aloof, geographically and culturally. It was best described as a nation of "mixed people," and offered the world a surprisingly large and diverse population in the mid-1800s.[12] For centuries Ireland had absorbed foreign invaders while maintaining its own Celtic culture, making surnames and religious affiliation unreliable indicators of Irish birth or heritage. Thus determining the "Irishness" of an immigrant from Queen Victoria's United Kingdom was a complicated effort. Perhaps the best indicator of "Irishness" during this period was self-identification with and support for an active and increasingly militant Irish nationalist movement. This Irish nationalist struggle for an Ireland independent of the United Kingdom came to America with millions of Irish immigrants.

Certainly Irish nationalist partisans existed in great numbers in America by the outbreak of the war. These men were easily identified high profile Irish leaders, and they lived in the South as well as in the North. By one estimate, 1,600,000 natives of Ireland lived in the United States in 1860, most confined to the Northern port cities.[13] But almost every Southern city and town had its "Irish element" as well. Estimates of Irish natives living in the South in 1861 range from 85,000 to 175,000. Ella Lonn identified about 40,000 in just seven Southern cities.[14] Lonn also reported that "In all the Southern states the Irish element outranked all others [foreign-born elements] except in Texas, where the Germans topped the list."[15]

Simply stated, the South was home to many people who identified themselves as Irish regardless of their nation of birth. Some of these may have been interstate migrants who left east coast ports for western settlements, or Berthoff's "misclassified Irishmen." By mid-century, the South also counted thousands of first generation Americans of direct Irish descent. It was from all of these groups that self-identified Irish companies were raised for Confederate armies.

John Dooley's American military experience began about 1850, when he helped organize an Irish militia company in Richmond. The unit chose to name itself the Montgomery Guard, after Irish-born Continental Army General Richard Montgomery, who fell while leading a charge at the Battle of Quebec during the American Revolution. Dooley was elected captain of the company in 1860, and there was no question that the Dooleys would follow their state at the outbreak of the Civil War. The pater Dooley and two of his sons served in the Confederate army. Dooley rose to the rank of major in the 1st Virginia Regiment. By late 1862, at age fifty-two, Major Dooley retired from the army and commanded the Richmond Ambulance Corps.

At the Battle of Williamsburg, May 5, 1862, James Henry Dooley fell wounded when he was shot in the right forearm. James was the Irish family's oldest son and a twenty-year-old graduate student at Catholic sponsored Georgetown College in Washington. He was thought to have been part of a group of students who burned Abraham Lincoln in effigy in February 1861. The group of rebel Georgetown students later petitioned the Catholic college's president for permission to leave school for war service. "Our presence here any longer would be attended but with little good to us for . . . there is not one amongst us who is now able to devote that time, interest, energy, and requisite spirit to the pursuit of our classes. . .while all we have dear on earth, our country (the South), our parents and our brethren call loudly on our presence at our respective homes."[16] Dooley and the others left Georgetown shortly, and he enlisted as a private in his father's company. James was taken prisoner after falling at Williamsburg. His arm almost was amputated by Union surgeons, but in the end it was left to heal. Exchanged by August 1862, he returned to Richmond and took a lieutenant's commission in the Reserve Corps attached to the Ordnance Department. James Dooley served there until the end of the war.

## Irish Green and Confederate Gray

About the time of James' exchange, the younger Dooley son, John Edward, age nineteen, also enlisted in the Montgomery Guard. He joined the 1st Virginia Regiment at Gordonsville in August 1862, thereby replacing his older brother as a fighter in the service of the Confederacy. The younger Dooley also studied at Georgetown and planned to become a Catholic priest. His memoirs about the Irish company's war experience are filled with Irish wit and gritty campaign tales. Dooley and the Montgomery Guard were in the sunken road on the night of December 13, 1862, after the Battle of Fredericksburg, and Dooley vividly describes his part in the heroic charge of Pickett's Division at Gettysburg the following summer. At Gettysburg, Dooley was shot through both thighs and captured after lying on the field for two days. He was taken to the Union prison camp at Johnson's Island, Ohio, where he remained for twenty-one months.

On the homefront, the Dooley daughters were accomplished models of Victorian and Southern womanhood. Mary, Florence, and Josephine married and started families of their own. Alice remained single and cared for her semi-invalid mother. She also became an active suffragette. Another daughter, Sarah, served as a cloistered nun and rose to head the Monte Maria Convent of the Nuns of the Visitation on Richmond's Church Hill.

The Dooleys were an Irish-American success story. Their stature in Richmond, the capital of the Confederacy, served as an inspiring example of the transformation of modest Irish immigrants to American respectability in the nineteenth-century South. Not long out of Ireland, they quickly established themselves in America and in the South—in church and family life, in business and educational pursuits—and as ardent Confederate partisans in the American Civil War.

## The Politics of Southern Allegiance:
## Why the Irish Supported the Confederacy

*Virginia was the first state to hurl aside the tide of Know Nothingism
and maintain the rights of Irishmen.*
— A Virginia newspaper, 1861

*We cannot but recollect that in the South our countrymen were safe
from insult and persecution, while 'Nativeism' and 'Knownothingism'
assailed them in the North.*
— In The Nation newspaper after First Manassas.


The Dooley family portrait presents a happy story of Irish immigration to Southern climes. The experience of many immigrants was not as exemplary. Foreign immigration to the United States, especially of Catholics, was a major social concern of the mid-nineteenth century. The social upheaval and the impending sectional crisis found Irish Catholic immigrants, North and South, near the center of the storm. Ireland and the Irish public were greatly interested in the American Civil War because of the large numbers of recent Irish immigrants in the United States. Historian Joseph M. Hernon Jr. points out that Irish participation in the war made the crisis the main topic of Irish public interest in the period.[17] Confederate General Richard Taylor went so far as to hold immigration in part responsible for the political strife that led to the war. "The vast immigration that poured into the country between the years 1840 and 1860 had a very important influence in directing events of the latter year," Taylor wrote. "The numbers were too great to be absorbed and assimilated by the native population. States in the west were controlled by German and Scandinavian voters, while the Irish took possession of the seaboard towns."[18]

It is accepted generally by historians and reinforced by popular opinion that the Irish sympathized with the Union war effort because a majority of Irish-Americans lived in the North and many fought in the Union army. Hernon, though, convincingly concludes that most of the Irish people here and abroad were primarily antiwar, often pro-Confederate, and latterly became wholly disillusioned with the war aims propounded by the Union leadership.[19] Irish opinion in the prewar period was largely influenced by an immigrant alliance with the Democratic Party.

An ugly nativist movement greatly affected the political allegiance of Irish immigrants before the war. Persecuted immigrants found refuge with the Democratic Party, which historian Eric Foner contends was the political representative of both the Irish immigrant and the white South.[20] Thus, the party joined with Irishmen, North and South, and native Southerners against nativist Whigs and later Republicans (those who coincidentally would lead the Union war effort). With over 2,000,000 mostly Catholic immigrants (Irish, German, and others) landing on American shores in the 1850s, a long-standing but smoldering nativist movement gained momentum in the United States before the war. Part of native resentment against immigrants was based in socio-economic tension. Unlike the Dooleys, many Irish immigrants were poor, unskilled, illiterate laborers who lived in urban slums. Because of this, nativists associated all Irishmen with crime and pauperism.[21] Economic and social unrest, and the tensions between nativism and new immigrants, directly affected the country's political course.

Although nativism was widespread and was not confined to one section of the country, its political manifestation—which came to be called the Know-Nothing movement—saw its greatest gains in the North. By 1854, the Know-Nothings had captured the legislatures of several Northern states, elected most of the anti-administration (that is anti-Democratic Party) congressmen, and threatened to supersede the Whigs as a major party.[22] The most virulent anti-immigrant feelings manifested themselves in the North. Northern cities saw several serious incidents of anti-foreigner riots before the war. One of the worst occurred in Philadelphia, where an attack on Irish Catholics left sixteen dead, many more wounded, and two churches and dozens of other buildings destroyed.[23] This kind of nativist violence was attributed to the Republican Party in the war period. S. C. Hayes, a Southerner who had relocated to Philadelphia, asserted that the "native American and

Know-Nothing were identical with the Black Republican Party." Hayes said that "the Know-Nothing Party had proscribed every man who had a Mc or an O to his name during the winter of 1857 and 1858, driving many thousands of families into starvation. . ."[24]

These nativist attacks, as General Taylor suggested, may have been the first skirmishes of an American social revolution if not of the war itself. In the same period, Massachusetts disbanded its Irish militia regiments after they were called out by the governor to quell Abolitionist mobs.[25] The same level of civil violence against Irish immigrants did not occur in the South. Irish patriot Thomas F. Meagher, later a Union general, noted before the war that there were "no convent-burners, no addlepated ranters, no Know-Nothings" in the South. Meagher's nationalist compatriot John Mitchel took this argument one step further when he likened Know-Nothingism to Northern abolition. He believed that most abolitionists were also Know-Nothings.[26]

Aside from these political considerations, blatant religious intolerance in the North was no small part of the direction Irish allegiance took in the war—especially in light of the Irish Catholic experience in Protestant Britain. Outspoken Catholic Virginian Anthony M. Keiley, the son of an Irish immigrant, noted dryly while in a Northern prison that "The clerical world in Puritan-dom [the North] has not changed altogether from the happy days of Quaker whipping and Papist hanging. . ."[27] Keiley, who had fled New Jersey for Petersburg, indicated that many Irish Catholics found more acceptance for their faith, if not for its ritual, in the South. And yet to many it seems incongruous that a strong Irish Catholic presence could have so peaceably existed in the Protestant evangelical South of the mid-1800s. One explanation for this may be that Catholic leaders tailored the Church's public perception to fit its minority niche in Southern society. Historians Randall M. Miller and Jon Wakelyn have argued that "The Church recognized its minority status in an overwhelmingly Protestant society and assumed a low political and social profile for much of the ante-bellum period."[28] Then too, Southern Catholicism and American Protestantism agreed on many important social issues. Miller and Wakelyn indicate that Southern Catholicism and evangelical Protestant experience converged in many ways, especially in the realm of education and social concern for the poor. Perhaps most importantly, Catholic leaders, many of them Irish, supported the institution of slavery—the litmus test of Southernism.

How could historically downtrodden Irishmen support or at the least ignore the slavery issue? Indeed, the Catholic Liberator, Daniel O'Connell, had been a strong Irish abolitionist in the 1830s. There were several reasons why slavery was not the overriding issue for the Irish in America and abroad. A chief reason was the expedience of survival for many poor Irishmen. Embattled immigrants, many little more than newly freed slaves themselves, tolerated the Democratic Party's stand on slavery in exchange for desperately needed political patronage and economic opportunity. Irish nationalist leadership and a historic antipathy toward Great Britain likewise affected Irish allegiance in America. Irish nationalists, who drove the public debate in American Irish communities, identified with the Democratic Party because it was seen as an adversary of Great Britain. This anti-British stance fit nicely with the Southern position on slavery. Great Britain, after all, was the world's chief abolitionist state and as such was the moral darling of American abolitionists and the radical Republicans. The Irish in America had little in common with the political groups that would lead the Union war effort. The Northern cabal of Yankee Puritans, radical abolitionists allied with the world's leading abolitionist state, Great Britain, and nativist Whigs and Know-Nothings represented the historic enemies of the Irish people.

Economically, the Irish in America saw black freedom as a dire threat to their survival. Unskilled, uneducated Irish immigrants competed directly with America's blacks for menial jobs. Emancipation meant more black competition. The Black-Irish labor competition led to racist and cultural hatred on all sides. The Irish displayed a racist hatred of blacks that was repugnantly apparent in the random lynchings of New York blacks during the draft riots of 1863. On the other side, blacks in the North thought of their Irish competitors as "white niggers." No one less than the great black abolitionist Frederick Douglass acknowledged the tension between blacks and the Irish when he said that the Catholic Irish were "the enemies of human freedom, so far, at least, as our humanity is concerned." Douglass no doubt had noticed that Irishmen, willing workers and a source of cheap labor, were replacing black workers in many instances.

Ironically, the new immigrants sometimes replaced slave labor if the task was dangerous. Slaves were purchased at premium prices, and slave owners sought to shield their costly "investments" from perilous duty. An Irish day laborer could be had for a pittance, and there was no employer responsibility if he was injured on the job. A common use of Irish labor in the South was in loading cotton bales onto ships. Blacks were used at the top of the gangway while Irishmen were stationed below, in the path of the ponderous cargo. "The niggers are worth too much to be risked here; if the Paddies are knocked overboard, or get their backs broke, nobody loses anything," explained one cotton broker of this division of labor.[29]

Irishmen, valued less than some slaves, saw no reason to champion the antislavery position. There was other evidence that the Irish were at the very bottom of the socio-economic ladder. Even some avowedly egalitarian abolitionists held racially prejudiced views toward the Irish. In 1857, Hinton Helper, a North Carolina abolitionist who fled to New York during the war, wrote that the Irish "are a more brutal race and lower in civilization than the negro."[30]

Even moral imperative did not necessarily affect Irish thinking on slavery. In the religious realm, Catholic church doctrine did not preclude slavery. The church taught that "slavery, thought of theoretically and apart from specific abuses to human dignity, was not opposed to the divine or natural law."[31] The church, like Southern Protestant denominations, was more concerned that slaves were well-treated. Abolition, it contended, was a dangerous threat to societal order. Indeed, the church itself owned slaves, as had some of the founders of American Catholicism including the Carrolls of Maryland and Supreme Court Chief Justice Roger Taney. Northern Irishmen did not favor slavery, but they also did not see abolition of the peculiar institution as an overriding moral goal. In the South, Miller and Wakelyn believe, Irish support of slavery was key in staving off nativism and anti-Catholic attacks. The Catholic Church in America came under Irish leadership by the 1850s, and in the South there seems to have been a concerted effort by Church leaders to assimilate politically as a means of gaining social acceptance

# Irish Green and Confederate Gray

The Right Reverend John McGill, third bishop of Richmond, was an Irish immigrant and as the Confederate capital's wartime bishop was a staunch Southern nationalist.

*Catholic Diocese of Richmond*

and economic opportunity. Catholic bishops in the South seemed to have been in lock step on Southern nationalist issues as sectional tempers began to flare. A Catholic newspaper in New Orleans in 1856 proclaimed, "We have never yet met a Catholic who was not true to his Southern rights."[32] The wartime sympathies of the Irish Catholic Bishop of Richmond John McGill "were entirely with the Confederacy and he strongly urged his people to fight for their beloved Southland."[33]

In practical political terms, the solidly Democratic South on balance settled against Know-Nothingism, seeing it as part of the new Republican Party that replaced the Whig Party with the election of Abraham Lincoln. Indeed Millard Fillmore, who as a Whig had served as president, ran as the Know-Nothing American Party candidate in 1856.[34] As sectional tensions heated up in the prewar era, Irish loathing of the nativist Know-Nothing movement and its allegiance with Northern politicians drove many more Irish immigrants into the Democratic Party fold. Irish Confederate general Patrick Cleburne was the most prominent example of an immigrant who changed from Whig to Democrat. He made the switch after a Know-Nothing shot him in the back.

*A Georgia Anti-Know Nothing*

Governor Joseph E. Brown attacked Know Nothing nativism because of "its secrecy, its religious proscription, its warfare against foreigners." Like Brown, most Southern Democrats decried the anti-immigrant rhetoric of the Whig and Republican parties. Many Irish immigrants who had settled in the South saw little difference between nativists and abolitionists.

*Avery's History of Georgia, 1881*

In the South, the stand of Governor Joseph E. Brown of Georgia exemplified the region's attitudes toward nativism and immigrants. The Georgia governor was "a decided Anti-Know-Nothing" because of the movement's "secrecy, its religious proscription, its warfare against foreigners. . ."[35] In prewar Virginia, Democrat Henry A. Wise, running for governor in 1855, also declared against the Know-Nothings. "With all my head and all my heart and all my might, I protest against this secret organization . . . to proscribe Roman Catholics and naturalized citizens."[36] In campaigning at Richmond, Virginia Senator Robert M. T. Hunter, later the Confederate Secretary of State, charged the Know-Nothings with "proposing to destroy the liberty of conscience itself, by proscribing the members of the Catholic Church from all offices."[37] Wise, later a Confederate brigadier general, won the governorship over the Know-Nothing candidate and served in that office from 1856 to 1860. Virginia's election results were a model for the rest of the South. Georgia, Alabama, Louisiana and Mississippi also defeated nativist candidates in elections that year.[38]

Thus, because of political, economic and religious reasons, Irish opinion was solidly in the Democratic Party camp at the outbreak of the

# Irish Green and Confederate Gray

war. In the South, Irishmen were reliably in the Confederate camp as well. In 1861, a Virginia newspaper illustrated the South's political stand on nativism while explaining the local Irish community's move to support the Confederate banner: "Virginia was the first [state] to hurl aside the tide of Know-Nothingism and maintain the rights of Irishmen. They now gratefully lay down their lives, if necessary, to protect and vindicate her rights."[39]

While most evidence indicates that the Irish in Virginia and the South were ready to fight for the Confederacy, not all Southerners were of one mind on the nativism issue. John Beauchamp Jones, a xenophobic government clerk, had a different opinion on the Irish place in the Confederate nation. He questioned the appointment of Irish nationalist John Mitchel to the editorship of the *Richmond Enquirer*, an organ of the government of Confederate President Jefferson Davis. "There is no Irish element in the Confederate States. I am sorry this Irish editor has been imported," Jones wrote in his wartime diary.[40]

Jones' rantings can be easily discounted as a minority viewpoint. As early as November 19, 1861, important Confederate politicians recognized an Irish constituency worth pursuing in the South. In a

*A Governor
with Irish Sympathies*

Democrat Henry Wise was a staunch anti-Know Nothing, a friend of the Catholic immigrant, and an ally of Irish nationalist John Mitchel. Wise was governor of Virginia from 1856 to 1860, and later served as a Confederate general.

*William A. Turner Collection*

# CLEAR THE CONFEDERATE WAY!

*A Sympathetic President*

Confederate President Jefferson Davis understood Irish aspirations for national independence. Davis briefly attended Catholic school as a boy, was a good friend of Irish nationalist John Mitchel, and placed much trust in Irish native William Montague Browne, whom he named interim Confederate Secretary of State in 1862.

*I. W. Avery's History of Georgia, 1881*

letter to Davis, William Porcher Miles, a powerful Confederate congressman and former anti-Know-Nothing mayor of Charleston, described the Irish element in Kentucky:

Mr. President,

The Germans and Irish are very different people in Kentucky. The Irish are naturally democratic, and were in times past generally with us, whilst the Germans could never be relied upon in any emergency and have been therefore latterly abandoned, but not so with the Irish. They did some time ago falter, but they are latterly returning to our standard. They are a peculiar and singular people. I know them well. They have heart, which neither the German nor the Yankee proper has in this sense of the term. And with these properties, they are fond of attention and compliment, and even flattery, and consequently are very sensitive, and easily offended by neglect. Now with this disposition of these people and under these circumstances, I am sure that the appointment of a native Irishman to the high position of Brigadier General in our army would have a most happy effect in Kentucky and elsewhere among this population. I am assured that the promotion of Col. Moore of the gallant 1st Virginia Regiment would be a good appointment in a military view. His gallant conduct at the battle of Bulls' Run, and the fact that he was there severely wounded, would certainly make his appointment popular with the soldiers and add to their courage. . .[41]

Congressman Miles, who admitted that he had a "feeling for the race" because "half my blood is Irish," sought a promotion for Patrick T. Moore, a native of Galway, Ireland, who had commanded Maj. John Dooley's Montgomery Guard for ten years before being appointed colonel of the 1st Virginia—Virginia's oldest and most prestigious regiment.

Miles recognized there was an Irish constituency in the South. Some Southern Irishmen, on the other hand, came to realize that they had an important political stake in the outcome of the war. Many Irish nationalists saw parallels between the South's secession from the Union and Ireland's struggle for independence from Great Britain. If the South succeeded in asserting its independence from the United States, a powerful precedent would be set in favor of Irish independence. Ireland's independent parliament had been abolished by the Act of Union in 1800, making Hibernia little more than an agricultural colony of the British Empire. Since that time, Irish political debate revolved around those in the Unionist camp, many of whom wanted a separate Irish legislature within the empire, and Irish nationalists, who agitated for complete independence from the empire. The clash between nationalist and unionist came to a climax with the Great Famine of 1845-48, when the country lost one-third of its population to starvation and emigration. The famine years were seen by many as proof that Ireland was at best misruled under the Union, or at worst was the object of a premeditated genocidal clearance of the land. Southern Irish leaders likened the American war to the Irish struggle they left behind. In their minds, the Civil War was another opportunity to win independence by dissolving a tyrannical union.

Even while Southern Irishmen pledged their lives to defend the Confederacy as a kind of surrogate Ireland, Northern Irishmen and Irish nationalists hesitated to take up the Union cause. It is evident in retrospect that there was never much of an Irish impulse to fight the war or to defend the American Union, especially in Ireland. Dublin's *The*

*Nation* newspaper, noting the nativist problem in the North, looked for a peaceful resolution early on in the conflict. The paper's editors wrote after the fall of Fort Sumter:

> Our countrymen in the Northern States desire to defend the Union to which they swore allegiance; on the other hand, we cannot but recollect that in the South our countrymen were safe from insult and persecution, while 'Nativeism' and 'Knownothingism' assailed them in the North. There are friends of ours on both sides of this quarrel. It is a strife between brothers. We cannot desire to see either party beaten down in blood. We shall look out anxiously for news, not of victories and defeats, but of peace and reconciliation.[42]

After the disastrous retreat of the Federal army at First Manassas, another Dublin nationalist newspaper, *The Irishman*, saw a paradox in Irish-American support of the Union. The paper chastised the "noisy 'Native American' regiments running home to their mother's apron strings as fast as they could." The Irish, the paper reported, fought "with desperate bravery, under 'Native American' generals of astounding incompetence, for that very people who, a year or two before, burned their convents, insulted their priests, and threatened to rob themselves of all lawful rights of citizenship."[43]

The *Memphis Argus* took the opportunity to court the Irish of the North by praising Colonel Michael Corcoran's 69th New York Regiment:

> No Southerner but feels that the Sixty-ninth maintained the old reputation of Irish valor—on the wrong side through misguidance, not through treachery to the old cause; and not one of us but feels that the day must come when a true understanding of the principles at issue will range their fearless hearts in line with their brethren of the South.[44]

As the civil struggle intensified, Irish feeling for the Union, never strong, weakened even more. Indeed nationalist Ireland and a majority of the Irish people came to vehemently oppose the war aims of the North. This Irish constituency helped comprise the "peace Democrats," a group contemptuously called "Copperheads" by pro-war factions. Union Maj. Gen. George B. McClellan, the dandy of the Army of the Potomac and darling of the Irish in the North, ran for the presidency as a Democrat while flirting with a peace platform in 1864. Whatever sobriquet was used to describe the peace politics of the Irish, it was clear that most of them desired peace at any cost—even at the price of Southern independence. The nationalists especially wanted the war to end if only to conserve Ireland's male population for its own war of rebellion. An unnamed "Kilkenny Man" expressed this sentiment in *The Nation* as early as September 7, 1861:

> Enough! enough! Your blood was given,
> As might beseem, a grateful band—
> But mightier is the claim of heaven,
> And urgent that of motherland.[45]

Early in the war, Irish nationalism was still united in its struggle for a free Ireland, though it was seemingly split over the American crisis. The 69th New York's Thomas F. Meagher displayed the continuing Irish unity at a gathering after First Manassas. Surrounded by Irishmen who had chosen the Federal banner, Meagher magnanimously urged his Union comrades to cheer the gallant sons of John Mitchel, fighting with the Confederate army by 1861. Despite Mitchel's Rebel allegiance, the applause for the Mitchel name was deafening. Meagher and his New Yorkers had not forgotten Mitchel's contribution to Ireland's cause; likewise, the Confederate Irish nationalist still dreamed of the coming fight in the old country. He wrote:

For the sake of the island that bred them I am rejoiced that the 69th Regiment did its duty in the bloody day of Manassas—They have seen some service at last, and of the sharpest; so that I imagine the men who faced Beauregard's artillery and rifles until Bull Run ran red, will not be likely to shrink on the day (when will it dawn, that white day?) that they will have the comparatively light task of whipping their weight of red-coats.[46]

## The Rebel Church:
## Irish Priests in Confederate Service

"No, General, that is not my home. I belong to the South and there I am
bound to go."
—Father James B. Sheeran, 14th Louisiana Regiment,
C.S.A., in reply to General Philip Sheridan's
offer to parole him to Baltimore

"Arm! arm!" he cried, "For I've come to lead you, For Ireland's
freedom, we'll fight or die!"
—Father John Murphy in Boolavogue

Ireland is a predominantly Catholic country, and historically the Catholic Church has exercised tremendous influence over Irish public opinion. It was no different during the Civil War. Irish allegiance to the Southern cause was never more evident than in the actions and statements of Irish Catholic leaders. Indeed, the Irish leaders of the Church in the South were some of history's truest Confederates. At the same time Irish Protestants in the South were apt to cleave to the Confederacy out of common

IN MEMORY
OF CATHOLIC
CONFEDERATE SOLDIERS
ERECTED BY
RAMAR CARAVAN NO. 86
ORDER OF THE ALHAMBRA

*Catholic Confederates*

The Confederate battle flag and the rook of the Order of the Alhambra, a Catholic fraternal organization, combine to acknowledge the Catholic presence in the Confederacy. Most Catholic Confederates were Irish immigrants.

*Author*

# Irish Green and Confederate Gray

religious and cultural heritage and similar political sympathies. Thus Southern Irishmen, Catholic and Protestant, were united in their Confederate allegiance. Rebellion had always effected a united front among the factions in Irish nationalism, whether Catholic, Presbyterian or Protestant.

Indeed the Confederacy may have provided the best vehicle for uniting Irish Protestants and Catholics since the United Irishmen mustered in the eighteenth century. In the War period, religious differences were downplayed in nationalist, republican circles in Ireland. The United Irishmen, the nationalist group that led Ireland's rebellion in 1798, had attempted to solidify Irish Protestant and Catholic forces against Britain. In an 1848 rising, Irish Catholics and Protestants again were united in a rebellious cause. By mid-century, their union was symbolized by the new Irish national flag, which combined the old green colors of Gaelic Ireland with the orange banner of Protestantism. In 1848 no less a nationalist leader than John Mitchel implored the Protestants of Ulster to "give over your terror about the bugbear of Popery, and to join with your countrymen in taking possession of Ireland for the Irish."[47]

In the Civil War period, Irish religious opinion tipped in favor of the South. Catholic clergy in the North, such as Archbishop John Hughes of New York, eventually took a stand for peace and if possible, Irish neutrality in the war, while Southern Catholic leaders were stridently pro-Confederate. The Catholic Church in America, after all, was historically a Southern church. Historian Raymond Schmandt has pointed out that American Catholicism began in the South. By 1850, the Catholic Church in America was an immigrant church led almost entirely by Irishmen. The greatest concentration of Catholics at that time was in the South in New Orleans, which counted a Catholic population of 170,000.[48] Although the numbers of new Catholic immigrants to Northern ports were beginning to supplant the Church's Southern base, Irishmen still controlled the American organization and the Irish leaders of the Church had an especially strong presence in the South.

The Church's Irish leaders in the formative years included men such as John England, born in County Cork in 1786. He became Bishop of Charleston in 1820. The Southern diocese was a large one that included

Georgia and both Carolinas. England, whose name belied his Irish ancestry, was an active Church missionary, a traveling lecturer, an able administrator, and most importantly for the Church's acceptance in the South, a respected ecumenist.[49] As the preeminent leader of the American Church, he established in 1822 *The United States Catholic Miscellany*, the first Catholic newspaper in the United States.

No Southern Church leader was more a rebel than England's successor, Patrick N. Lynch, a native of Clones, Ireland, and the wartime Bishop of Charleston. Lynch laid out his Confederate sympathies in an exchange of correspondence with his New York counterpart, Archbishop Hughes, in 1861. Lynch wrote to Hughes on August 4, 1861, presenting the South's case for its right of secession. Hughes reprinted Lynch's letter and his own reply to it in the September 7, 1861, *New York Metropolitan Record*. Lynch blamed a "fanatical party spirit" in the North for starting the war. "Taking up antislavery, making it a religious dogma, and carrying it into politics, they have broken up the Union," Lynch wrote. He believed that the war had been forced on the South.[50] The Southern Irish bishop called on Northern Republicans, whom he blamed for the war, to fight it themselves. "Let them not send Irishmen to fight in their stead, and then stand looking on at the conflict, when, in their heart of hearts, they care little which of the combatants destroy each other."[51]

After this public tirade, Bishop Lynch followed up his fiery words with deliberate action. On September 17, 1861, he led Charleston's Irish population into the war with a public display of Southern allegiance in the city's Roman Catholic Cathedral of Saint John the Baptist and Saint Finbar. In an elaborate presentation service, Lynch blessed the Confederate flag of the city's Irish Volunteers company of the 1st South Carolina Infantry. The banner, made by Charleston's Sisters of Our Lady of Mercy, gave "to the breeze and light of the sun the emblems of Erin—the shamrock and the harp—with the palmetto of Carolina and stars of our Southern Confederacy."[52] The flag was a perfect union of Irish and Southern symbols. Ireland's harp, encircled by a mingled wreath of shamrock, oak, and palmetto, was displayed on one side. The banner's other side bore the symbols of South Carolina; a large palmetto tree and the crescent moon. During the convocation, Lynch told the Irish company, "You come of a race that has ever made brave, valiant, and chivalrous soldiers—one that has given distinguished men to every civilized nation, that have won imperishable honors and military glory on many a well-fought field."[53] The Confederate bishop continued with an unabashed call to patriotic duty. "To you, then, I commit this banner. In your hands I know it will never be stained by cowardice, or by any act that will disgrace you as a body of gallant Christian soldiery. Receive it then—rally around it! Let it teach you of God—of Erin—of Carolina!"[54] At the conclusion of the rousing ceremony, Color Sergeant Francis L. O'Neil raised high the Irish Confederate banner and the company presented arms as the Cathedral choir chanted the Hallelujah Chorus. After this distinctive recessional, the consecrated company marched to a military air toward Charleston's Hibernian Hall presumably for further libations. Lynch's Confederate Catholicism was striking, even strident, but it was not unique.

Cork County native Bishop John Quinlan of Mobile, Alabama, was another Irish church leader with strong states' rights proclivities. He joined the chorus of Southern bishops advocating secession in 1861. "We must cut adrift from the North in many things of intimate social conditions—we of the South have been too long on leading strings," he wrote.[55] With a patriotic ceremony similar to the one in Charleston, Quinlan bestowed the church's blessing on Mobile's Irish company, the Emerald Guards, as they marched off to Virginia in 1861. He was in Montgomery, Alabama, when the Confederate Provisional government authorized chaplain appointments for the Confederate forces. The bishop immediately offered the services of another Irish priest, Patrick Francis Coyle, who was dispatched to the command of Maj. Gen. Braxton Bragg at Pensacola, Florida. Quinlan also called on the Daughters of Charity of Mobile to care for the Confederate wounded at the Battle of Corinth.[56]

Other Catholic bishops in the South were equally pro-Confederate, including Augustin Verot of Savannah, Augustus Martin of Natchitoches, Louisiana, and William Henry Elder of Natchez, Mississippi. Verot, in an 1861 pastoral letter, espoused Southern nationalist aspirations and spoke out against abolitionist activities.

Bishop Martin advocated secession when he proclaimed in August 1861 that he and his Catholic flock agreed with the Southern values and beliefs of Louisiana.[57] Elder also openly supported secession and justified the institution of slavery. Like most Southern religious leaders, Catholic and Protestant, he was concerned mainly with social order and increasing his diocesan flock. An end to slavery was not part of Bishop Elder's evangelism. He was more interested that Catholic slave-holders knew it was their duty to furnish slaves with religious instruction.[58]

This position had at least one ironic result in history. James Augustine Healy, America's first black Catholic bishop, was a product of the odd mixture of Southern Catholicism and slavery. Healy was born in Macon, Georgia, in 1830 of an Irish slaveholding father and a black mother, who was probably a former slave. Healy's father provided him with a Catholic education and the opportunity led Healy to the episcopate. After the war, Healy was bishop of the Diocese of Maine. He later served as a papal assistant in Rome. Healy was by no means a typical Southern Irish bishop, and he was not a Confederate. But generally in the South, the Irish princes of the Roman Catholic Church set the tone for a Catholic-Confederate alliance. Subsequently, the secessionist charge of the church's leadership found its way into the Confederate ranks.

In Irish history, Father John Murphy is the most famous example of priestly rebellion. He led a force of pikemen at the Battle of Arklow in 1798. In Confederate service, priests were not fighting men, but many worked for the South as spies, diplomats, poets, propagandists, and chaplains. The Catholic chaplains in the Confederate armies were almost always Irish, and they did not minister only to Catholic soldiers. Father John Teeling, a firebrand secessionist priest from Richmond, was named chaplain of the 1st Virginia Regiment in June 1861. Teeling had been chaplain of the Irish company of the regiment, the Montgomery Guard. When Catholic Col. Patrick T. Moore, a graduate of the same company, became the regiment's commander, he tapped Teeling for the regimental post—even though there was an overwhelming Protestant majority in the regiment. Later Teeling was assigned chaplain to all Roman Catholic Confederate troops at Manassas.[59]

## Irish Green and Confederate Gray

No church leader was more strident in his Southern partisanship than Father Matthew O'Keefe, a native of Waterford, Ireland. His obituary in 1906 named him the chaplain of William Mahone's Brigade in the Army of Northern Virginia and a close personal friend of Gen. Robert E. Lee and Jefferson Davis.[60] O'Keefe's prewar career typified the life of an Irish Catholic priest in the South, but the Irishman was an extraordinary person and a loyal Confederate. He was an energetic church builder before the war in Maryland and in Norfolk and Portsmouth, Virginia. No stranger to the pervasive nativist threat to Catholics, O'Keefe once escaped a Know-Nothing plot to murder him by drawing twin revolvers on his assailants. According to his obituary, O'Keefe was proud of his connections with the Confederacy and bore an intense love for the Southern people and Rebel leaders. With the onset of the war O'Keefe petitioned Bishop McGill for permission to join the infantry. While the bishop would not release him from his priestly vows, he did grant that O'Keefe could take up arms to defend against a direct attack. O'Keefe interpreted this order rather liberally and attempted to lead a 500-man expedition against a Federal camp threatening Norfolk. Unhappily, his unnamed Confederate army superior allegedly drank away this opportunity to attack and Southern reinforcements changed the assault plans. Unable to fight, O'Keefe still served the army for the duration of the war and was among several progressive voices who urged President Davis to free the slaves and arm them to defend the South.

In 1864, Union Maj. Gen. Benjamin F. Butler, occupying Norfolk with his Army of the James, contacted O'Keefe: "General Butler sends his compliments to Father O'Keefe and desires to know if he prays for the Federal authorities at the vesper service." The Irish priest's reply was probably not what Butler expected: "Father O'Keefe does not return his compliments to General Butler. I do not pray for the Federal authorities at the vesper service, nor do I intend to do so. Furthermore, I never heard of such a thing!"[61] After the capture of Jefferson Davis at war's end, O'Keefe visited the fallen executive daily at Fortress Monroe. When Davis died in 1889, O'Keefe was invited by Varina Davis to accompany her husband's body to Richmond for burial. When O'Keefe died in

*Rebel Priest*

Father James Sheeran of the 10th Louisiana Infantry in a post-war picture.

*Tulane University Library*

1906, he was afforded a military funeral "in accord with his position in the Confederate Army." The former Irish Confederate chaplain "wished it to be known that he died as he lived, an unreconstructed Confederate."[62]

James B. Sheeran, a native of County Longford, Ireland, was one of the war's most noted diarists. A Redemptorist priest, he was a chaplain with the 14th Louisiana Regiment. Sheeran's story was another example of the Southern Church's overwhelmingly pro-Confederate stance in the war. In 1862, Sheeran wrote of a conversation with Union prisoners who claimed they fought only to preserve the Constitution, not because they promoted the other goals of the Lincoln Administration. Sheeran roundly disputed the contention that Lincoln and the Constitution could coexist in the same country. "My very good man," the Irish priest replied, "before going to bed every night try and recall to your memory the number of times Abe Lincoln has perjured himself by violating the Constitution since his introduction into office; then put your hand to your breast and ask yourself in the presence of God, if in fighting for your perjured President, you are fighting for the Constitution of your country."[63]

Indeed, Sheeran seems to have spent as much time proselytizing Northern partisans about Southern grievances as he did ministering to their souls. At the Second Battle of Manassas, Sheeran engaged a New York officer who "came to fight for the Union, to put down this rebellion, and . . . fight till I die for the flag of my country!" Sheeran told the prisoner that "such talk was mere nonsense; there was No Union to fight for, nor was there a rebellion to put down, for the people of the South were merely defending their national and constitutional rights."[64] At Harpers Ferry two days before the momentous Battle of Sharpsburg, Sheeran conversed with captured Yankee soldiers, taking time to "disabuse their minds of many wrong ideas they had entertained with regard to the war and the people of the South."[65] A prisoner himself by 1864, Sheeran continued his political battles by writing to New York's Irish nationalist paper, the *Freeman's Journal*, about Maj. Gen. Philip H. Sheridan's depredations in the Shenandoah Valley. Writing from a military prison at Fort McHenry, Baltimore, Sheeran chronicled his mistreatment at Federal hands. "Let it be known, then, to the Catholics of the United States, that Gen. Sheridan had gained another victory, not [only] over the defenseless women and children of the valley, but by throwing a Catholic priest into a dirty prison to be the companion of drunken and disorderly soldiers, and this, too, when some of his own Catholic soldiers are dying without the sacraments."[66]

Given the zeal of Sheeran's Confederate partisanship, as well as his hearty ego, it is difficult to gauge how factual and fair his narratives on Irish attitudes about the war are. What is clear is that he was a singularly influential and dedicated Irish Confederate. His agitation while a prisoner finally won him an audience with General Sheridan, who refused to release him or to send him back to Richmond. Instead Sheridan offered him refuge in Union-controlled Baltimore. Sheeran's reply was unequivocal: "No, General, that is not my home. I belong to the South and there I am bound to go."[67] Sheeran returned to his Redemptorist house in New Orleans after the war. He later overcame his aversion to the North when he left the order and became a pastor in Morristown, New Jersey, in 1871. He died of a stroke in 1881.

Further up the ladder of Southern chaplaincy was Father John B. Bannon, who has been called the "Fighting Chaplain of the Confederacy." Bannon, a native of County Roscommon, Ireland, was educated at Ireland's venerable Maynooth College, and became a priest by 1853. He came to America and was assigned to the burgeoning archdiocese of St. Louis, an area estimated by the Church to have a native Irish population of 10,000 by 1850. In St. Louis, Bannon was associated before the war with an Irish militia company, the Washington Blues, commanded by Capt. Joseph Kelly. During the war, Bannon served as chaplain for the First Missouri Confederate Brigade under Gen. Sterling Price. He was present at numerous battles in the West, including Pea Ridge and Port Gibson, and he witnessed the suffering of Vicksburg, Mississippi, under Union siege. Bannon, like other Irish churchmen in the South, was strongly pro-Confederate and linked the right of self-determination for the South to Irish nationalism. He was tapped by the Confederate high command to be the government's first representative to Pope Pius IX. At the Vatican, he sought papal influence to curtail Union recruitment in Ireland. Bannon spoke to the Pontiff "about the righteousness of the Confederate experiment in rebellion and the unscrupulous recruiting methods of the North."[68] Later, Bannon worked with others in Ireland to prevent Union recruitment there.

After the war, Bannon moved back to Ireland and settled in Dublin. His thoughts in a postwar letter to an ex-Confederate express his feelings about his Southern service:

> Tis a sad memory, that "Lost Cause" and all its varied incidents. Yet, tho' sad I would not blot it from my memory or expunge it from my life, for it made me acquainted with brave and honorable men, of high spirit, great endurance and generous natures, whom I am proud to remember as companions and friends.[69]

While most Irish Confederates were Catholic, the South counted as least one Protestant Irish clergyman as a chaplain. The Rev. Francis Patrick Mullally, a native of Tipperary, Ireland, was chaplain of the 1st South Carolina (Orr's) Rifles from November 10, 1863, until the end of the war. Mullally was a Presbyterian minister who served as secretary to William Smith O'Brien, the leader of the 1848 Irish rising. Mullally fled Ireland with a price on his head and settled in Georgia.[70]

One of the South's most beloved religious leaders was another Irish Catholic Southerner, Father Abram J. Ryan, known as the "Poet Priest of the Confederacy." Ryan was a simple parish priest with posts that included churches in New Orleans and Mobile. Ryan also was a noted lecturer and a freelance chaplain to Confederate troops. Much of his poetry written after the war dwelt on the defeat of the Confederacy. He remained an unreconstructed Confederate until 1878, when Northern charity aided Southern victims of a yellow fever epidemic. The Northern help softened Ryan's heart and compelled him finally to put the bitterness of the conflict behind him. Ryan commanded a special celebrity in the South and gained a widespread following that was exceptional for a Catholic priest. Tennessee Governor Robert L. Taylor characterized Ryan as the "Tom Moore of Dixie, whose spirit shall keep watch over the Stars and Bars until the morning of the Resurrection."[71] (Thomas Moore, 1780-1852, was an Irish poet whose songs and poetry exemplified an Irish national character.) An example of Ryan's Southern poetry remembers the sacrifice of his younger brother, a Confederate soldier killed in the war.

> Young as the youngest who donned the Gray,
> True as the truest that wore it,
> Brave as the bravest he marched away,
> Hot tears on the cheeks of his mother lay,
> Triumphant waved our flag one day—
> He fell in the front before it.

—From "In Memory of My Brother" by Abram J. Ryan[72]

Pere Louis-Hippolyte Gache of the 10th Louisiana Regiment proved himself another articulate Confederate Catholic chaplain. Gache was a French-born Jesuit who took his marching orders from Father Anthony Jourdan of Spring Hill College in Mobile, Alabama. The Jesuit college was the alma mater of Confederate Secretary of the Navy Stephen Mallory. In Confederate service, Gache proved to be a vehement Southern nationalist. In choosing words to chastise one of his Jesuit colleagues he attacked him as a "treacherous, kindless Yankee villain," and an "Unadulterated Yankee! Double-dyed Yankee!"[73]

Gache, like other Catholics in the South, saw abolitionists as anti-Catholic, and linked a pro-Catholic stance with the Southern position in the war. During the Seven Days' Battles, he asked a wounded

Union soldier at White Oak Swamp if he was Catholic. "'Oh, yes, Father, I am,' he answered, pitifully attempting the sign of the cross, 'I'm a Catholic and I'm a Democrat too'—meaning that he wasn't an Abolitionist and had done nothing to merit Southern wrath."[74] No doubt Gache realized there were thousands of antislavery Catholics in the Union army, but perhaps he thought them misguided or coerced into Yankee army service. On the home front, he worked against any Catholic dissension within the Southern cause. "Dear Father," he wrote to one of his wavering colleagues in Mobile, "the Yankees are just no good. I cannot abide them, neither those of the North nor those of the South. Make haste to become once more a true and loyal Southerner."[75]

In October 1862 Gache wrote to Jefferson Davis with a plan to convert Union Irish prisoners of war to the Confederate side. "I understand that there are now in our hands a large number of Irish Catholic prisoners of war, who I think may be induced to enlist in the Confederate Army." By 1864, the chaplain was able to get Brig. Gen. Zebulon York, commander of the Second Louisiana brigade, to set up a separate prison camp for about 700 of these soldiers near Salisbury, North Carolina, but few availed themselves of Gache's offer of Confederate redemption.[76]

The phalanx of clerical Confederates left no doubt as to which side the Catholic Church in the South was on. Although most priests in the war were army chaplains, Catholic priests served the South in other ways as well. At times the Catholic clergy formed a fifth column for the Confederate army. Dr. James I. Robertson's exhaustive biography of Thomas J. "Stonewall" Jackson makes mention of the general's use of the Catholic priests in Martinsburg as spies during his Romney expedition in early 1862.[77] One of Jackson's priestly spies was Father Thomas A. Becker of Saint Joseph's in Martinsburg. Becker was a convert from the Episcopal church and a graduate of the University of Virginia. Under the direction of the Richmond diocese, he passed "valuable military intelligence" to Jackson on numerous occasions.[78] Becker inevitably was placed under arrest and thrown in prison, reportedly for refusing to recognize the right of Federal authorities to dictate what prayers he offered in his church. The Martinsburg church building was for a time used as a Union prison, and Union scouts also used the sanctuary to stable horses. His wartime exploits did not hamper his ecclesiastical career. Becker later became bishop of Wilmington, Delaware, and then Savannah, Georgia.

Aside from using Church property as stable and prison, it is clear that Union forces did not afford the stridently Rebel priests of Virginia or their religion much respect. Major General Nathaniel P. Banks ordered the little stone mission church in Winchester burned after its usefulness as a cavalry stable ended.[79] At Harpers Ferry, Saint Peter's Catholic Church stood on the rocky crags of the town and often was the only place of refuge for townspeople as the indefensible village changed hands many times during the war. Saint Peter's pastor was Father Michael Costello, a native of Ireland. Though offered the chance to return home during the conflict, Costello stayed at his post protecting Church property—sometimes with help from fellow soldiers in Christ, Union and Confederate. Most threats to the Catholic Church came from Union occupiers, but on at least one occasion Union troops protected it. Once under Federal occupation, a church historian remembered, "a Massachusetts regiment, inheriting from their saintly Pilgrim ancestors a holy horror of Popery, prepared to make an attack on it [Saint Peter's]." However, the Union Irish Brigade under Thomas F. Meagher, which happened to be in the neighborhood, deterred the Puritan regiment's wicked plan.[80]

A similar incident occurred during the war in Alexandria. Father Peter Kroes, an elderly Jesuit priest at Saint Mary's Church there, was described as a "staunch friend of the South." When the town fell under Union occupation Kroes refused to take the oath of allegiance and would not honor the military commander's order to offer public prayers for the "restored government." Other obstreperous clergy in Alexandria had been physically maltreated by Yankee troops. The Episcopalian minister had been dragged from his pulpit and thrown into prison. To prevent the same treatment intended for the Catholic priest, an unnamed Union Irish regiment cordoned off Kroes' residence to protect him. On Sunday, when a provost guard was sent to Saint Mary's to enforce the "prayer order," the Irish protectors marched up the aisles and, "to the relief of the

*A Southern Irish Edifice*

Saint Mary's Church, Fredericksburg, about 1900. Saint Mary's was built in 1858 as an Irish church for railworkers in the town. The brick building with Romanesque lines was used as a hospital and storehouse for much of the war. *Author*

congregation, knelt down and crossed themselves as the would-be assailants withdrew."[81]

Saint Mary's Catholic Church of Fredericksburg also suffered an awful fate during the war. The small red brick church had been dedicated in 1858, and the original building still stands on Princess Anne Street, its modern stucco exterior painted green—perhaps in commemoration of its Irish founders. During the Battle of Fredericksburg in 1862, the church, like almost every building in the old town, was used as a hospital. "The floors and walls . . . were literally bespattered with the blood of the wounded and dying soldiers brought there for treatment."[82] From that battle in 1862, when the pews were removed and probably burned for firewood, until the end of the war in 1865, the church was used either as a hospital or for commissary storage. No religious services were held in the building until 1865, and it was not until 1869 that new pews were installed.

The Catholic churches in the South suffered terribly because of their Confederate allegiance and Southern location. The experiences of

## Irish Green and Confederate Gray

Virginia's Catholics chronicle the depredations inflicted by the war. As the fighting wore on, the Catholic congregations of the state's Diocese of Richmond dwindled. Soon the only active members of Virginia's Roman congregations were old men, women, and children. The diocese historian's comment on the "insignificant" membership left to the churches of Virginia was in itself an indication of the Irish contribution to the war effort. "The soil of the Old Dominion," he wrote, "was drenched with the blood of perhaps more Catholics than had ever lived previously within its limits."[83]

## Hot Lead and Cold Steel:
## The Press and Pike of John Mitchel

The Republican Party will not make peace! That party will not cease fingering the profits of war contracts as long as Irish and German Democrats can be found as food for Confederate artillery and musketry.

—John Mitchel, Richmond Daily Enquirer, 1862.

"Why let 'em fight," says Mr. Bright, "those Southerners, I hate 'em,
And hope the Black Republicans will soon exterminate 'em;
If freedom can't rebellion crush, pray tell me what's the use of her?"
And so he chuckles o'er the fray as gleefully as Lucifer.

—England's Neutrality: A Parliamentary Debate by
John R. Thompson of Richmond

In 1848, the new tricolor flag of Irish nationalism—a green, white and orange banner surmounted by an Irish pike—was presented in Dublin to a nationalist group, the Irish Confederation. At the meeting John Mitchel, the most influential Irish nationalist of the century, called for violent rebellion. "Brighter days are coming to us; this noble weapon glittering above us, this majestic banner, are of good omen to us. Ah! the gleaming pike head rises through our darkness like a morning star; this magnificent Irish tricolor, with its orange, white and green, dawns upon us more glorious than ever Sunburst flashed over the field . . . or blazed

# CLEAR THE CONFEDERATE WAY!

*John Mitchel in the 1840s*

In 1848 Mitchel was Ireland's leading rebel—one of the few nationalists who openly called for violent revolution against the British government. He brought his militant fervor to the Confederate cause twelve years later.

*City of Waterford Museum*

thro' the battle . . . My friends, I hope to see the flag one day waving, as our national banner, over a forest of Irish pikes."[84] Fourteen years later, John Mitchel's pike-sharp rhetoric slashed across America—in strident support of Confederate rebellion.

As a writer, John Mitchel has been compared to Jonathan Swift, Thomas Carlyle, Ralph Waldo Emerson and Charles Baudelaire. *Jail Journal*, the epic story of his exile from Ireland and triumphant return to freedom in America, has been called the Odyssey of Irish woes, the Bible of Irish nationalism. Padraic Pearse, the idealistic poet who led the 1916 Easter Rising, wrote: "Mitchel's is the last of the four gospels of the new testament of Irish nationality, the last and the fieriest and the most sublime."[85] By many twists and turns of fate, Confederate President Jefferson Davis and the South were well served by this caliber of polemical author during the Civil War.

Mitchel was a nationalist star among the Irish constellation of Confederate leaders. In Ireland, he was one of the greatest political writers of his age. In a three-year period, 1845 to 1848, the iconoclastic Ulsterman used the hot lead of the press to exhort the Irish to violent revolution. Mitchel was the first leader of his generation in Ireland to openly advocate armed rebellion against Great Britain. Only the cold steel of the pike, he believed, would win Irish national independence. But he was not merely an extremist ideologue. During a public career that spanned thirty years, "he put duty . . . before self-interest . . . did what he believed to be right and said what he believed to be true," according to one of seven Mitchel biographers, Brendan O'Cathaoir.[86]

John Mitchel's Confederate service was an interlude in a life of Irish agitation. Born in 1815 near Dungiven, County Derry, Ireland, Mitchel was the son of a Unitarian minister. His father also was a member of the United Irishmen, the group that organized the Irish Rebellion of 1798. John Mitchel was educated at Trinity College, Dublin, trained as a solicitor, and was practicing law in Banbridge, County Down, when he joined the staff of the nationalist newspaper *The Nation* in 1845. The paper, headed by Thomas Davis, founder of the Young Ireland nationalist movement, and Charles Gavan Duffy, was at the center of Irish nationalist politics, and soon Mitchel gave up his village law practice to become a full-time Dublin journalist. Duffy, recognizing his rhetorical skills, quickly made Mitchel the paper's chief writer. It was as a strident and aggressive political writer that Mitchel would take his place among Ireland's greatest republican visionaries. During the same period Mitchel came to accept the political ideals that would be represented later by Southern nationalists in America. Among these ideals were self-determination and local control of government, an economy free from taxation and regulation by a distant and powerful central government, and trade policies that favored agricultural interests over industrial lobbies. While Ireland and the Confederacy traveled similar political paths, Mitchel's journey to the American South was an arduous one.

As it had most Irishmen in the mid-nineteenth century, the Great Famine affected Mitchel personally and deeply. Ireland lost a quarter of its population to death and exile in just six years. Mitchel's political ideology evolved during the famine years. He was for mere constitutional reform in 1846, but two years later called for the violent overthrow of British rule. He judged the famine an act of genocide by British authorities—the apocalyptic end to 800 years of English oppression in Ireland. In anguish over the mass starvation and depopulation of the countryside, Mitchel increasingly began to call for physical force against the mismanagement and insensitivity of the regime. "It is indeed full time that we cease to whine and begin to act . . . Good heavens, to think that we should go down without a struggle," Mitchel wrote in the pages of *The Nation*.[87] He broke with the most powerful Irish leader of the day, Daniel O'Connell, by calling for the destruction of Ireland's modern railways, if necessary, to prevent the movement of British troops within the country. Mitchel, ever reckless and brave, saw O'Connell, a Member of Parliament who was attempting reform from within the system, as a "conspirator" with the government. "Speeches," Mitchel said, "or resolutions here never will avail or do one bit of good unless we all have arms and are ready to turn out."[88]

By early 1848, Mitchel's rebellious rhetoric was too hot even for Gavan Duffy, *The Nation's* editor, who started to remove the most inflammatory sections of Mitchel's essays. In reaction to Duffy's censorship, Mitchel quit and began his own newspaper, which he called *The United Irishman*, an allusion to the rebel group of 1798. Mitchel openly advertised his new journal as an "organ of revolution." His revolutionary writings were instrumental in gaining support for the nationalist Young Ireland movement, Mitchel's group of Young Turks who planned a war against British rule, if necessary. O'Cathaoir believes Mitchel almost single-handedly revived the republican movement in Ireland in the midst of the Famine. The movement's overall accomplishments were not as praiseworthy. The Young Irelanders, led by William Smith O'Brien, Thomas Francis Meagher, Patrick O'Donoghue, Terrence Bellew McManus, John Martin, and Kevin Izod O'Dogherty, among others, attempted a halfhearted, ill-conceived and poorly executed rising later in 1848. By that time Mitchel, the most infamous member of the group, had already been arrested, found guilty of treason and exiled to Tasmania for fourteen years.

It was during his passage to the South Pacific that Mitchel crafted his political masterwork, *Jail Journal*, published in 1854. On his voyage to Tasmania, Mitchel first saw the black face of slavery in Brazil, the world's largest slave state. From Mitchel's observation while in the Brazilian port of Pernambuco, one gets a glimpse of his early attitude toward slavery and the Irish context of his ideas about the institution.

After seeing the starving millions of Ireland, Mitchel was not appalled by the condition of the average slave, although "he did not altogether like the sight." He asked the question, "Is it better, then, to be the slave of a merciful master and a just man, or to be serf to an Irish land-appropriator? God knoweth."[89]

True to his revolutionary ideals, Mitchel acknowledged the right of slaves to gain their freedom by force. He commented on a recent insurrection in Brazil, noting his skepticism of the right of the Portuguese to hold others in slavery. "The moment the black and brown people are able, they will have a clear right to exchange positions with the Portuguese race," he wrote.[90] Most notable among Mitchel's comments on slavery was his negative reaction to the inherent hypocrisy of Britain's abolitionist stance. The empire, Mitchel contended, had grown wealthy from the slave labor in its colonies while abolishing the slave trade at home. Mitchel's thoughts on slavery and his observation of the hypocrisy of the slave trade were shaped by his world experience during his exile. He carried this philosophy to the center of the slavery crisis—America—in 1853.

That year, with help from nationalist compatriots, Mitchel escaped from Tasmania and landed at New

*Thomas F. Meagher*

The Union Irish Brigade leader was a follower of John Mitchel in the 1840s. Meagher was a pro-South Democrat until April 1861.

*Leib Image Archives*
*York, PA*

York to a hero's welcome. On the dock to greet him was his rebel compatriot,Thomas Meagher. Meagher had been convicted for his part in the rising of 1848. In America he already had achieved a certain celebrity. He proudly bore the sobriquet "Meagher of the Sword" which he had earned in the 1848 rebellion. Following Mitchel's lead, he had refused to renounce the use of armed force to win Ireland's liberty. "I look upon the sword as a sacred weapon," Meagher told the Repeal Association in 1847. He saw the sword as a symbol of the armed rebellion that would set Ireland free.[91] Meagher initially received the death sentence for his part in the rebellion, but the sentence was commuted to transportation for life to Tasmania. He escaped and fled to America before Mitchel.

With Meagher, Mitchel began a New York paper, *The Citizen*, which soon had an astounding circulation of 50,000. Both men settled into their new American lives in New York, enjoying exciting, busy routines that included journalistic pursuits, public appearances, and Democratic Party politics. As prewar tensions rose, both men announced their sympathies for the Southern position. The two Irishmen adhered to the Irish nationalist orthodoxy that believed the South's claim to the right of secession was tantamount to Ireland's attempt to sever ties with Great Britain.[92]

Meagher, by all accounts an extraordinary orator, was perhaps the more eloquent in his sympathy for the South. As an Irish personality, he was a popular lecturer below the Mason-Dixon line before the war. In Charleston he delivered a speech that raised $800 to help build a monument to states' rights hero John C. Calhoun.[93] (Calhoun himself was the son of Irish immigrant Patrick Calhoun of Donegal, Ireland.) A staunch Democrat, Meagher publicly stated as late as April 1861, "I tell you candidly and openly that in this controversy my sympathies are entirely with the South." At that time, Meagher also felt the South had a right to secede. "You cannot call eight millions of white freemen 'rebels,' sir. You may call them revolutionists, if you will," he told a Republican Party acquaintance.[94]

Mitchel also traveled the South, speaking on the sectional issues of the day. He once received an enthusiastic reception at the University of Virginia in Charlottesville when he delivered an impassioned defense of

Irish Green and Confederate Gray

Southern rights and the peculiar institution. On the question of slavery, Mitchel thought it "the best state of existence for the negro, and the best for his master; and if negro slavery in itself be good, then taking the negroes out of their brutal slavery in Africa and promoting them to a human and responsible slavery here is also good."[95]

Mitchel's view of slavery was one widely held by most Southerners of the period—a rationalization that since slavery existed in the world, American slavery was preferable to the African variety. At that time, Mitchel was more concerned with what he saw as industrial slaves in American factories, and with the Know-Nothing assault on Irish-Americans. He connected the Northern abolitionists with Know-Nothings and linked them with unscrupulous industrial barons in the North. The Northern industrialists, he contended, had no compunction about slavery when they purchased cheap raw materials produced by Southern slave labor. At the same time, he argued, many mill owners exploited their own workers, especially immigrants, as if they were slaves. Mitchel believed the mill workers of New England were more in need of emancipation than the slaves of the South.[96]

By 1854, the same year his masterful *Jail Journal* was published in New York, Mitchel had moved his growing family to Tennessee, settling near Knoxville as a back country farmer. In 1857, he resumed his journalism career when he founded the Knoxville *Southern Citizen*. Mitchel advertised the *Southern Citizen* as an organ of extreme Southern sentiment, its charge to warn the "indolent and good-natured Southerners" of the danger from the North. In an April 10, 1859, letter to his sister, Mitchel summed up his prewar, pro-Southern activities. "As for me, I am 'saving the South' with all my might—indeed so violently, that a great part of the South (besides the whole North) thinks me mad."[97]

Soon world affairs induced him to leave Tennessee, and after moving his Knoxville paper to Washington, he left for Paris hoping to influence some advantage for Ireland in the aftermath of the Crimean War. When he returned to America in the fall of 1862, Mitchel remained consistent in his support for the South. The pall of war hung over the country, and the South's position on the battlefield looked promising.

*A Rebel Writer*

John Mitchel in 1860. His poor
eyesight kept him out of the
Confederate army, but three Mitchel
sons served the South as soldiers.
Two were killed in battle and the
third lost an arm. The elder Mitchel
was a leading Southern nationalist
editorial writer.

Arthur Griffith's
*Meagher of the Sword,* 1916

The Mitchel clan was
uncompromising in its support
for the Confederacy. Three
Mitchel sons joined the Confederate army. The elder Mitchel,
disqualified from army service because of severe nearsightedness, went
to Richmond and joined the Ambulance Committee, an armed city guard
that transported the wounded from the battlefront to and around the
Confederate capital. Perhaps his most enduring contribution to the
Southern cause was as the most widely read intellectual spokesman in
the South. President Jefferson Davis tapped the Irishman to be editor of
the pro-Davis Administration newspaper in Richmond, the first of two
important editorial positions Mitchel held from his arrival in 1862 until
his arrest by Union authorities in 1865.

In supporting the Confederacy John Mitchel sacrificed much for his
political ideals. He first lost the allegiance of his old rebel friend
Meagher. Mitchel's Southern experience contrasted sharply with
Meagher's Union allegiance. When Mitchel returned to America in
1862, he found that Meagher was by then the commander of the ill-fated
2nd Brigade of the 1st Division in the Second Corps of the Army of the
Potomac, a unit popularly known as "the Irish Brigade." The man who
had loyally followed Mitchel's fiery lead when both agitated for Irish
independence in the 1840s, and had supported the Southern position

only one year earlier, had undergone a political conversion while Mitchel was out of the country. It was a strange and abrupt turn of events—and a seeming betrayal of a lifetime of resistance against central authority. Back in October 1848, Meagher and Smith O'Brien languished in the Clonmel Gaol. Both men had been sentenced to death for their roles in that year's rising. Awaiting the queen's justice, the two signed a blood pact, pledging to go to the gallows rather than renounce their rebellious actions. It seems implausible that Meagher, the same man who had signed his death sentence with his own blood, could have so totally renounced his Southern sympathies in so short a time. Indeed Meagher's nineteenth century biographer, Michael Cavanagh, could not "comprehend the cause of so sudden and radical a change."[98] Meagher's conversion may have been a nationalist scheme to hedge Irish bets over the outcome of the war. The Irish independence movement may have shrewdly taken both sides in the conflict to position itself for any eventual outcome. There does not seem to be any convincing proof of this strategy, however. For whatever purpose, Meagher's break with his nationalist leader Mitchel over the American Civil War is one of the sorrowful mysteries of Irish history.

Mitchel was undaunted by Meagher's change of loyalty. However, he apparently could not understand the logic Meagher and the Irish of the North applied to the situation. Mitchel wrote from Richmond:

> As for the Northern Irish, who seem to have got themselves persuaded that the enfranchisement of Ireland is somehow to result from the subjugation of the South, and that repeal of one union in Europe depends on the enforcement of another union in America, our friends here do not well understand the process of reasoning which leads to that conclusion, nor do I.[99]

By late 1862, Mitchel was the principal writer for the pro-Davis Administration *Richmond Daily Enquirer*. His rhetorical skills were sharp, his political commentary incisive, his personal style stinging. On Wednesday, October 1, 1862, Mitchel commented on Lincoln's decision to issue the Emancipation Proclamation after the Battle of Sharpsburg. His interpretation of Lincoln's greatest political coup was as haughty and contemptuous as any Southern fireeater's opinion on the matter. In an editorial headlined "Lincoln and His Proclamation," Mitchel viewed the device as an incitement of Southern slaves. Returning to his own interpretation of the Great Famine in Ireland as a genocidal war on the Irish, he opined that Lincoln wanted that same kind of race war in America. He wrote: "Abraham Lincoln's Proclamation ordaining servile insurrection in the Confederate States has not been for a moment misunderstood either North or South." Mitchel condemned Lincoln for taking the race war route and predicted dire consequences. "A servile war is necessarily one of extermination, and the peculiar character of the negro, adds to its inevitable horrors." Lincoln, the Irish editor said, "is the common enemy of both white and black."[100]

Mitchel also drew on his understanding of European history to chastise the British government when it became clear after the proclamation that Britain would withhold recognition of the Confederacy. His Irish nationalist contempt for the Crown and England's self-serving economic interests was illustrated in a December 11, 1862, editorial titled "Recognition Historically Treated." Mitchel asked the question, "Has the 'British Empire,' the foundations of which were laid by her Edwards and Henries, and the maturity crowned by the genius of Shakespeare and Newton, the conquests of Nelson and the triumphs of Wellington, terminated at last in the selfishness of pleasure and the timid spirit of mercantile opulence?"[101]

Mitchel's editorial reaction to the Battle of Fredericksburg that year was muted. He declined to criticize directly his old friend, Irish Brigade commander Thomas Meagher, whose command had made notorious headlines at the battle. Instead Mitchel kept a broader perspective on the engagement. Three days after the battle, on December 16, the *Enquirer's* lead editorial attacked the *New York Herald* for an article that Mitchel believed was incorrect in asserting that there was much Union sentiment in the South. He drew on an old Irish fairy tale to illustrate his point. Union " 'feeling,' which it says exists here, is like the bag of gold at the end of the rainbow. It has never been seen. It can never be found. It is a pleasing fable."[102] By December 20, Mitchel, again without mentioning the celebrated Meagher, noted the "butchery of Union generals."[103] Later that week, on December 27, the Irishman attacked the monied interests of the North for prolonging the war. After Fredericksburg, talk of a peace settlement in Northern papers intensified, especially in Democratic Party and immigrant circles. Mitchel skillfully addressed an attack on the radical Republicans to those Northern Democrats and immigrant groups. "The Republican Party will not make peace!" Mitchel proclaimed. "That party will not cease fingering the profits of war contracts as long as Irish and German Democrats can be found as food for Confederate artillery and musketry."[104]

As powerful as his writings for the *Enquirer* were in 1862, by the fall of 1863, Mitchel had moved to another Richmond journal, the *Daily Examiner*, formerly edited by John M. Daniel. At the *Examiner*, Mitchel seemed to exercise even more control on editorial content. Mitchel defined his duty as the paper's chief writer: "I point out diligently and conscientiously what is the condition of a nation which suffers itself to be conquered . . . such as we have experienced in Ireland, and endeavor to keep our good Confederate people up to the fighting point."[105]

On January 6, 1864, Mitchel wrote at great length about the economic, social and political history of the slave trade. The cornerstone of his argument, true to form, was an attack on Great Britain and its abolition of trading slaves. Abolition by Britain, he wrote, was not done out of moral imperative but to ruin Britain's chief rival, Spain, and its colonial economies, which were based on slave labor. Mitchel believed Great Britain's example had influenced the North to do the same to the South. He also believed that though the South would use English help to win independence, the Confederacy, "in her inmost soul," despised England.[106]

In an elaborate theory—a theory that only a practiced rhetorician like Mitchel could devise—he drew parallels between the war in America with what had happened in Ireland at the hands of Great Britain and in Poland at the hands of Imperial Russia. Mitchel believed that the Civil War, as the wars in Europe had been, was an economic and military conquest couched in religious and moral terms. In the American conflict, the North's conquest targeted the South. The result, he wrote, would be the economic, political and religious subjugation of an entire land.[107]

## CLEAR THE CONFEDERATE WAY!

The subjugation of Ireland by Britain had led the Society of United Irishmen to armed rebellion in 1798. The rebellion's Battle of Arklow, presaging later forlorn charges by Irish soldiers, saw a force of pikemen get within thirty yards of British guns before it was destroyed by canister and musketry. John Mitchel, in 1847, had recalled the Irish pikemen of the Rebellion of 1798 by extolling the pike as "the queen of weapons . . . the weapon of the brave."[108] Indeed, if the sword was Meagher's symbolic weapon of rebellion, the pike was one of Mitchel's favorite historical allusions—the symbol he used to exhort the Irish populace to armed resistance. By 1798, the year of the Battle of Arklow, the term "pikeman" was synonymous with rebel in Ireland. Today, the Irish pike is the symbolic weapon of 18th and 19th century rebellion in Ireland—"the weapon . . . traditionally associated with rebel Irishmen," according to military historian Gerard A. Hayes-McCoy.[109]

The Irish soldiers of the Civil War were the sons and grandsons of the generation that gave Ireland the Arklow pikemen. The war's Irish-American rebels, with Mitchel's pike and press as inspiration, became the spiritual successors of the Arklow insurgents. Indeed viewed in the context of Irish insurrection, the enlistment of thousands of Southern Irishmen in Confederate armies represented the largest "rising out" of Irish rebels since Hugh O'Neill's Nine Years War, which lasted from 1595 to 1603. In 1861, as war ignited in Virginia, a band of Confederate Irishmen in Richmond remembered the pike's rebel Irish symbolism.

# Irish Confederates in Battle

## The War Before Fredericksburg

As a general thing. . . the South has ever found true friends in Irishmen.

—*The Richmond Dispatch*, 1861

My grandfather fell on Vinegar Hill
And fighting was not his trade.
But his rusty pike's in the cabin still
With Hessian blood on the blade.

—Joseph I. C. Clarke, in *The Fighting Race*

## Pikemen in the Cathedral: The War Begins

In the spring of 1861, Richmond's Irish community celebrated Saint Patrick's Day and secession with equal enthusiasm. On March 17, Richmond's Irish militia company, the Montgomery Guard, paraded through the capital city in high spirits in honor of the patron saint of Ireland. The Guard carried the Stars and Stripes on a green flag that featured an Irish harp. One month later on April 17, Virginia, the South's leading state and the cradle of American liberty, seceded from the Union. Almost immediately the city's Irish soldiers took up the Confederate cudgel. As a long-standing state militia company the Guard had marched for years each Saint Patrick's Day adorned in bottle green uniforms, with buttons sporting the Virginia state seal and hat brass insignia encircled by shamrocks. Now the Irish company pledged its allegiance to the South and proclaimed itself a Confederate army unit.

The Irish cadre assembled at Saint Peter's Church, the Roman Catholic Cathedral of Richmond, for a solemn ceremony officiated by ardent Southern nationalist Bishop John J. McGill. Bishop McGill publicly and with elaborate rite bestowed his blessing on the Irish Confederate guardsmen commanded by Capt. John Dooley, a native of Limerick, Ireland. Part of the bishop's consecration involved the blessing of the Guard's ceremonial pikes, the ancient shaft and spearhead weapons that were the symbol of Irish rebellion. These Richmond pikemen soon traded in their ancient battle-axes for rifled muskets and their Irish green trews for Confederate gray.

On April 22, the Irish company paraded through Richmond for a second time that spring. The Limerickman John Dooley was still dressed in a vivid green uniform "with gorgeous gold stars and bars," but the color guard bore a new secession flag.[1] The marching Irish militia, reincarnated as a new Confederate army company, trumpeted the Southern loyalty of the local Irish element in the war. The *Richmond Dispatch* noted the Southern allegiance of the Irishmen of the Confederate stronghold city. "The Montgomery Guard under Captain John Dooley is composed mainly, if not entirely, of citizens of Virginia of Irish birth, who have espoused the cause of their adopted state with the devoted earnestness characteristic of the generous-hearted people of which they are representatives. As a general thing, nowhere located, the South has ever found true friends in Irishmen."[2]

Richmond Irish Catholic leaders emphasized the Church's support for the Confederate cause. Four days after Virginia voted for secession, Father John Teeling, from the pulpit of Saint Peter's, appealed to the faithful "to stand firm in the assertion of their rights." Father Teeling, the chaplain of the 1st Virginia Regiment, omitted the usual prayer for the president of the United States and substituted a reverent petition for the governor and people of Virginia and for victory in the impending war.[3]

From Saint Patrick's Day to secession, events tumbled quickly toward battle that spring. In May 1861, the Montgomery Guard moved toward the front, marching out of Richmond and north to the region's

# Irish Confederates in Battle

*Saint Peter's Church*

This unprepossessing white stone church was Richmond's first Roman Catholic Cathedral. Church leaders delivered some of the South's most strident secession rhetoric from its pulpit.

*Author*

Central Fairgrounds, where the unit boarded a train to Manassas Junction. The Guard's Irish members, the *Dispatch* noted, were "bade adieu to by hundreds of relatives and friends. While soldiers went off with cheerful spirits and light hearts, in all directions among the crowd, assembled in the grounds about the cars, could be seen evidence of a painful separation, in the shape of grief and tears. The heartfelt, tearful words, 'God Bless You' were mingled with the hope of a safe return."[4] The Guard's Irishmen already had been present at John Brown's execution at Charles Town, Virginia, in 1859. Other Irish troops had captured Castle Pinckney in the opening hostilities near Fort Sumter in Charleston Harbor. But these incidents would pale in comparison to the carnage of the war's first major battle, which was developing in the Northern Virginia countryside.

John Dooley's actions on the morning of July 18, 1861, indicate he was one soldier who realized the full import of what was to happen that day. His grave concerns were laid down for posterity when the Irish captain hastily made out his will in anticipation of a full-scale engagement at Manassas:

> I, John Dooley, of the city of Richmond, but now at Bull Run River, (hourly expecting a battle with the Northern enemy), knowing at all times, but particularly under present circumstances, the uncertainty of life, do

now make this my Will, which is all in my own handwriting. Having the fullest confidence in the sound discretion of my wife, Sarah, I do hereby give, devise, bequeath and dispose of unto her all my property. . . It is especially my wish and desire that my mercantile business shall be carried on as usual if it is at all practicable, but of this my wife must be the judge.[5]

Dooley's simple will was one of thousands written on the battlefields of the war. It was perhaps one of the first so written. Although largely a bland legal document, the will offers a personal glimpse into the Irishman's trust in his wife and her competence, his concern for his children, and his hopes for the future of his business. In retrospect, Dooley's battlefield will emphasized the seriousness of what was about to happen to him and his Irish company in the initial strike of a long, miserable war—a war many at the time thought would end within the month. With personal details settled, the Irish leader, his company, and the 1st Virginia prepared for a serious test of fire. These Irish Confederates met the enemy on the banks of a narrow Virginia stream called Bull Run.

The regiment, commanded by Galway native, Col. Patrick T. Moore, forded Bull Run at Blackburn's Ford on July 17 to reconnoiter, and the next morning crossed again to establish a line. The Irish colonel formed his line of battle on the south side of the run. The Irish company, topped conspicuously in black 1858 "Jeff Davis" hats, took up a reserve position. The Blackburn's Ford line was but a small portion of the Southern army's defensive position. Confederate Brig. Gen. Pierre G. T. Beauregard organized his army into seven brigades and arrayed them in a six-mile line paralleling Bull Run with forces massed at four crossing points. Brigadier General James Longstreet's Brigade, with the 1st, 11th and 17th Virginia and 5th North Carolina regiments, covered Blackburn's Ford on the right center of this line.

On July 18 the vanguard of Brig. Gen. Irvin McDowell's Union army attacked at Blackburn's Ford. An artillery duel ensued about eleven in the morning, with the Washington Artillery of New Orleans supporting Longstreet's Brigade. The thundering barrage lasted until about one that afternoon, when Longstreet's reserve force moved forward to meet the Union attack of Col. Israel B. Richardson's brigade, part of Brig. Gen. Daniel Tyler's division. Colonel Moore inspired his

# Irish Confederates in Battle

*In the Confederate Pantheon.* Often overlooked Brig. Gen. Patrick T. Moore of Galway, Ireland, (top left) takes his place alongside Southern celebrities like William Mahone (pictured below Moore), George Pickett (bottom center) and two of Robert E. Lee's sons, George W. C. Lee (bottom left) and William H. F. Lee (second down, center column). Moore almost certainly bellowed the first Gaelic battlecry of the war—Faugh a Ballagh!—at Manassas. *Confederate Military History, 1899*

men, Irish and native Virginian alike, by telling them that they were all free born Americans, and "that the sacred soil of their mother Virginia was polluted by the foot of the invader." Leading the way, Moore shouted the Irish war-cry, "Faugh a ballagh and charge!"[6] Clear the way and charge! It was probably the first Gaelic battle call of the war.

The 1st Virginia's attack came under furious enemy fire. "The storm of lead and iron passed through our ranks for the first time, but the men stood it like they were used to it all their lives," wrote regimental historian Charles Loehr. "But many a poor fellow was laid low," Loehr remembered, not the least of whom was Colonel Moore, struck in the head, left arm and side while leading his force toward Bull Run to counterattack the enemy's main line.[7] Moore, who had trained for that moment since 1850, was wounded seriously and never took the field again.

Command of the regiment fell to French-educated Maryland native Maj. Frederick Gustavus Skinner. According to diarist Francis Potts, an Irish private in the Montgomery Guard, Skinner rode into the fray on a chestnut mare, "cursing like a trooper and brave as a bear," and waving his sword, yelled "Charge, boys, and drive the dogs back!"[8] Instead, it was the Virginia regiment that was thrown back. The Union line hesitated and seemed content to snipe at the attackers from a hilltop. While the Virginia regiment was momentarily pinned down by rifle and artillery fire, the Irish company was chosen as a skirmish line for the next Confederate attack. Potts remembered that Skinner "took a particular fancy to our company, [and] was all the time calling for Capt. Dooley." Skinner told the Montgomery Guard that "We Irish were the very boys to fight, and to do him justice. He certainly gave us all the honor he could, and put us in as much danger as possible," Potts wryly wrote. The Irish scrivener, later the paymaster for Longstreet's First Corps of the Army of Northern Virginia, compared Skinner and the Montgomery Guard to the Connaught Rangers, an Irish regiment famous for its service in the British army. "The major was like Captain O'Shaughnessy," Potts wrote. "He would storm the very gates of hell with a company of the Rangers, and the old fellow served to think that we were as good at it as our Connaught brethren."

# Irish Confederates in Battle

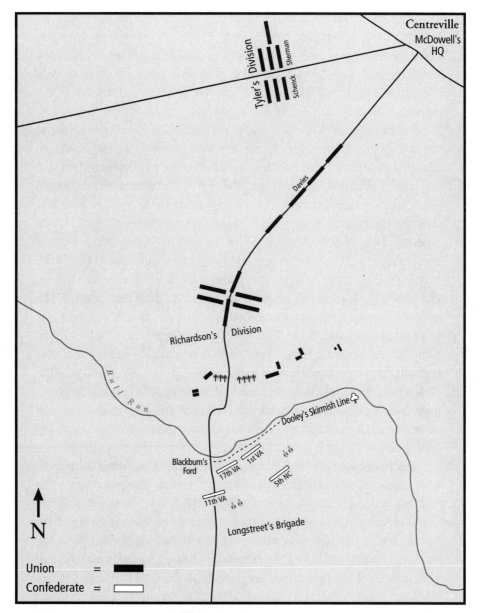

## Bull Run - July 18, 1861

**Faugh a Ballagh!** – The 1st Virginia, led by Irish Colonel Patrick T. Moore, "clears the way" for Confederate victory at the Battle of Manassas. Captain John Dooley, a native of Limerick, Ireland, commanded the skirmish line.

## CLEAR THE CONFEDERATE WAY!

With the Irish black hats in the van, Skinner called for a second assault across the stream, roaring out, "Now, charge with a cheer and make the thieving crew fly!" Potts remembered the advance of his Irish company, and a second Gaelic cheer. "In we went, our company with 'Faugh a Ballagh,' which means 'Clear the Way'. . . the war cry of the gallant 88th on the [Spanish] Peninsula under Wellington." The Confederate regiment drove back an unsteady 12th New York Infantry, but received a galling fire in the advance. Eventually, the Southern attack stalled and then faltered. John Dooley, in command of the regimental skirmish line, directed the fire fight "with a pistol in each hand, his lips compressed and his eye as stern an eye ever shone; standing right out in an open place disdaining the shelter of a tree," Potts reported. Dooley's field orders, as chronicled by Potts, sounded like a combination of raw Irish brogue and aristocratic punctilio. "That's the way, boys. Fire at the hilltop," commanded Dooley. "Come from behind that tree, ye blackguard. Now, me boys, do thus so again." The company's three lieutenants sheathed their swords, "picked up muskets, and blazed away like brave fellows as they all are," according to Potts. Still, the Confederate force made little headway. During a lull in the fighting, Dooley gave the Montgomery Guard an impromptu homily. "Keep cool, men and fire low. Should they attempt to cross [Bull Run], jump over the ditch and give them the bayonet. Let each of us commend ourselves to God and pray to Him for courage, and with our hopes and confidence in Him we cannot be beaten."

The Irish captain was called away to report to Longstreet during the next clash in what had settled into a seesaw confrontation. The Confederate force, advancing to the top of a hill, came under killing fire in his absence. Leaderless, the Irish skirmishers seemed destined for destruction. Potts betrayed his despair with the murderous situation until, he reported, "I saw Capt. Dooley coming toward us and at [the] same time a cheer rose from our left where the Old Dominion Rifles were stationed. The Capt. roared 'Come on Montgomeries!' and we were beside him in a moment." The old militia officer Dooley quickly seized control of the situation. "Take shelter, men," he told the Guard. Turning to Corporal Patrick Duffy, Dooley said, "Duffy, run down and tell Gen. Longstreet that they have the range of us with grape, and ask him what we shall do." Although the enemy fire was hot, the captain's order was "given as coolly as on parade," Potts recorded.

Dooley reformed his troops in a safer position behind a hill. With neither side willing to commit to an all-out assault, Dooley's skirmish line proved an effective and resistant pawn along Blackburn's Ford—but little more. Some of the bolder Irishmen in the regiment made their frustration with the unit's inconclusive role known to General Beauregard, who rode past during the fight and inquired which regiment he attended. "'Tis the Richmond Regiment," replied Irish Lieutenant Michael Seagers. Fearing the army commander would not know the regiment by that name, Seagers specified, "'Tis 1st regiment, Virginia volunteers, Colonel Moore.' The general turned around in his saddle and with emphasis told us, 'And a glorious regiment it is,' " Potts reported. Another Irishman of the regiment, Cpl. Samuel McRichards, a twenty-eight-year-old carpenter in the Montgomery Guard, addressed the general directly. As gray-clad troops surrounded Beauregard's horse, McRichards said, "General, we are soldiers of the 1st regiment. Your approval is very gratifying to us. And we hope you will give us a chance where we can use the bayonet. We don't like this bush fighting. All we want is a clear field and no favor and we will make you proud of us." Beauregard replied with calming words before moving on to reconnoiter the enemy.

The "bush fighting" at Blackburn's Ford lasted about two hours before Federal forces fell back. In retrospect Bull Run was but a large skirmish, the first baby step of battle for both sides. It was not without its casualties, however. Longstreet's Brigade lost 15 killed, 53 wounded and two missing. The Union counted 19 killed, 38 wounded and 26 missing. On the Confederate side, the 1st Virginia bore the brunt of the fighting with 13 killed and 27 wounded.[9] The heaviest losses were among the "pikemen" of the Irish company—the Montgomery Guard—and Company G. Major Skinner permanently replaced the Old First's Irish colonel, Patrick Moore. John Dooley, the brave Irish captain, cool and stern at Bull Run, was promoted to major.

Union chroniclers said later that Richardson's advance to the ford was merely a reconnaissance in force; Beauregard wrote that it was an attempt to cross the run in force. In either case, the fight along Bull Run

# CLEAR THE CONFEDERATE WAY!

*Rallying the Troops at Manassas.* The troops of Gens. Barnard Bee, Francis Bartow and Nathan Evans rally behind the Robinson House in the First Battle of Manassas. Irish troops from Louisiana helped hold the line until Confederate reinforcements arrived. *Battles and Leaders, 1889*

was an important strategic victory for the Southern army. As events unfolded, the Confederate resistance at Blackburn's Ford disconcerted Union commander McDowell and affected the entire Union army's strategic plan at Manassas. The Bull Run battle should have proved the Union's strength in numbers and position. Instead it foreshadowed the faulty leadership that would plague Northern arms for much of the war.

It is clear that Gen. Daniel Tyler mishandled the episode. Longstreet's Brigade of 3,500 faced Tyler's 12,000-man division and would have been swept from the ford if Tyler had attacked en masse. The 1st Virginia fought from a weak position with no entrenchments, but its "Clear the Way" intensity literally bluffed the Union attackers into retreat. Although Tyler was under orders not to engage the enemy, once in contact with the Southern army at the ford, he should have perceived the weakness of the Confederate position. A concerted and timely Union attack could have been successful and decisive. Instead, Tyler was cowed by effective and convincing Confederate resistance and retreated all the way to Centreville. By the time Tyler reported to McDowell the retreating general was demoralized by his performance along Bull Run Creek. McDowell was angry and disgusted with his subordinate's behavior. He ordered the division back to the front, but Tyler's defeatism and McDowell's anger threw the Union high command into chaos. In the face of Tyler's setback—and with unrelated supply problems—McDowell took two days to reorganize and plan a full-scale attack. This delay gave Beauregard time to garner a stronger force. He counted just 24,000 men on July 18; the arrival of 11,000 reinforcements under Brig. Gen. Joseph E. Johnston on July 19 and July 20 gave the Confederates a host almost equal to McDowell's available force. Johnston and the units that arrived July 19 and 20—particularly the brigades of Barnard E. Bee, Francis Bartow, and Thomas J. Jackson—were crucial to the Confederate victory at First Manassas.

The general engagement of the Manassas Campaign was joined July 21. When McDowell finally attacked that day, the Confederate army's stubborn defense, although sluggish at first, proved that the Confederate leadership had used its time wisely. Ultimately, Johnston and Beauregard were prepared for the Northern assault. McDowell's main thrust was aimed at the Confederate left near Groveton. A secondary attack went forward nearby across a stone bridge that spanned Bull Run along the Warrenton Turnpike. With the Confederate right at Blackburn's Ford secure and no longer threatened, Beauregard and Johnston were able to shift troops to the left to counter the concentrated Federal envelopment there. Johnston, who arrived July 20, was responsible for successfully coordinating the reinforcements that defeated the Federal right on July 21. Among those reinforcements was Jackson's Brigade, the lead element of Johnston's Army of the Shenandoah, which had arrived from Winchester on July 19. With Jackson, Johnston and an organized Confederate force, the Union attackers met stiff resistance as the Manassas mêlée ensued. In late afternoon, the pitched battle culminated in a Confederate counterattack that sent McDowell's army scrambling for cover behind the defenses of Washington.

The victorious Southern sweep of the field was anchored by Jackson, who earned his famous nickname "Stonewall." His "Stonewall Brigade," which included Irish companies in the 27th and 33rd Virginia regiments, turned the tide of the battle with a bold counterstroke from Henry house hill. The brigade's units were among those counting the highest casualties in the battle.[10] The Irish soldiers of Wheat's Battalion, under Maj. Chatham Roberdeau Wheat, helped hold the Confederate left until Bee, Bartow, and Jackson arrived to shore up the line. Wheat's Louisiana Tigers, composed mainly of Irish dock workers from New Orleans, were part of Brig. Gen. Nathan G. Evans' 1,100-man brigade. The Irish Tigers held the left of the brigade's line with devilish, hand-to-hand fighting when McDowell's main attack turned the Confederate flank. The Tigers were deployed forward of Evans' main line, and the Irish zouaves caught the hardest blows from the Federal turning movement. Even so, the Louisianans counterattacked Brig. Gen. Ambrose E. Burnside's brigade and broke the 27th New York. The Tigers lost eight killed, while another 28 were wounded, including the seriously injured Major Wheat.

Southern forces scored a tactical rout at Manassas, but gained little from the victory. The Confederate army, exhausted and disorganized, did not pursue the fleeing and defeated Yankees. The South was unable to achieve the lasting objective of the total destruction of the Union force in Virginia. Just as John Dooley's first taste of battle at Blackburn's Ford was merely prelude to the major fighting around Groveton on July 21, Manassas was merely prelude as well. The battle was a fiery omen that dispelled previous misconceptions of a short war. Overall, McDowell's army of 39,000 lost 2,896 men in the battle; the Confederates suffered 1,982 casualties.

After the war, James Longstreet remembered the 1st Virginia at Blackburn's Ford. "The old First Regiment was with me at Bull Run on the 18th of July, and made the first fight of Bull Run," he wrote. "This. . . was their first battle, and I can say that its officers and men did their duties as well, if not better, than any troops whose service came under my observation."[11] In another respect, the Irish defense at Blackburn's Ford also helped create a Confederate legend—Stonewall Jackson. When the former West Pointer and Virginia Military Institute professor arrived on the field, he posted his troops behind the ford saved by Longstreet, Dooley, and the Irish black hat skirmishers. Jackson launched his legendary career from Blackburn's Ford, a position purchased with the blood of the Irish soldiers of the 1st Virginia Infantry.


## Steady as Clocks, Chirpy as Crickets: The Irish in Stonewall Jackson's Shenandoah Valley Campaign

> Southern Irishmen make excellent 'Rebs,' and have no sort of scruple in killing as many of their Northern brethren as they possibly can.
>
> —Lt. Col. Arthur Fremantle

> We'll sing a song, a soldier's song with cheering, rousing chorus.
> As 'round our blazing fires we throng, the starry heavens o'er us.
> Impatient for the coming fight, and as we wait the morning light,
> Here in the silence of the night, we'll chant a soldier's song.
>
> —From Soldier's Song, The Irish National Anthem

General Thomas J. Jackson and the Stonewall Brigade had turned the tide at Manassas, but no military campaign before or since can match the triumphant march of Jackson in the Shenandoah Valley of Virginia in the spring of 1862. A large contingent of Irish soldiers were part of that unparalleled effort. In raw numbers, perhaps ten percent of the Army of the Valley as it existed in the campaign was invested in men in Irish or predominantly Irish companies. These included, in Jackson's Division: the Virginia Hibernians, Company B of the 27th Virginia; the Emerald Guards, Company E of the 33rd Virginia; both part of the famous Stonewall Brigade; the 1st Virginia Battalion Regulars, better known as the Irish Battalion; and in Brigadier General Richard S. Ewell's Division, Taylor's Brigade: Wheat's Battalion; two Irish Brigade companies of the 6th Louisiana Regiment; the Calhoun Guards, Company B of the 6th; the Sarsfield Rangers, the Virginia Guards, the Virginia Blues, and the Irish Volunteers of the 7th Louisiana; the Cheneyville Rifles, Company H of the 8th Louisiana; and the Emerald Guards, Company E, of the 9th Louisiana. Thus Jackson's swiftly marching infantry, dubbed "foot-cavalry," counted among its ranks nineteen companies of Irishmen. Brigadier General Richard Taylor especially cited the Irish qualities of the 6th Louisiana, which he called the Irish regiment. "The 6th were Irishmen, stout, hardy fellows, turbulent in camp and requiring a strong hand, but responding to justice and kindness, and ready to follow their officers to the death," Taylor remembered.[12] Taylor's Irishmen made their mark as Confederate fighters when Stonewall ranged over Virginia's Valley in 1862.

Above all, Stonewall's Irish Confederates were happy Southern warriors. In his memoirs, *Destruction and Reconstruction*, Taylor relates that during the Valley Campaign while on a strategic retreat up the valley, his Irish regiment was the rear guard, fighting enemy cavalry along the Valley Turnpike at night. The Irish guardsmen performed admirably "as steady as clocks and chirpy as crickets, indulging in many a jest whenever the attentions of our friends [the enemy] in the rear were slackened," remembered Taylor. "It was a fine night intirely for divarsion," drawled one Irishman of the turnpike soirée.[13] Taylor, a patrician Virginian and son of former President Zachary Taylor, came to respect the Irishmen in his command that night. The troops had heard they were opposed by forces that included perhaps the most famous Irish leader in the Union army at that time, Brig. Gen. James Shields, whose command included Irish regiments. "Them Germans is poor creatures, but Shields's boys will be after fighting," one Irish Confederate predicted.[14]

In a starry setting prefiguring the soldiers' scene in today's Irish national anthem, Taylor related the Irish throng's talk around a campfire in the Valley:

> Expressing a belief that my "boys" could match Shields's any day, I received loud assurances from half a hundred Tipperary throats: "You may bet your life on that, sor." [and ] "We are the boys to see it out." As argyles to the tartan, my heart has warmed to an Irishman since that night.[15]

Other Irish units in Jackson's army also drew the attention of their native officers. In the Stonewall Brigade, the Emerald Guards company of the 33rd Virginia "was composed chiefly of Irishmen who had migrated to the Valley to obtain employment in the Manassas Gap Railroad."[16] One native born company commander, Capt. George R. Bedinger, wrote affectionately about the Irishmen in his charge: "I am very much pleased with the conduct of my Irishmen. They are enthusiastic and brave and at the same time obedient. I think they are fond of me, at least they are very attentive to my comfort."[17] Bedinger's attentive Irish charges were not always perfect soldiers though. Another report of the company described it as the "problem child" of the brigade "because of the fondness of its members for liquor and brawling."[18]

The Stonewall Brigade's other Irish company, the Virginia Hibernians, also was composed of Irishmen who had come south to work on the expanding railroad system. The Hibernians originally were a light infantry company raised in Alleghany County, and the unit was the color company of the regiment. The Irish soldiers from Louisiana and Virginia made their presence felt in camp as well as on the battlefield. It seems the impression they made on fellow Confederates was out of proportion to their actual numerical strength. John O. Casler, a private in the 33rd Virginia, wrote that there were "several Irish companies in the 27th Virginia" and because of this the regiment was nicknamed the "Bloody 27th."[19]

Another Virginia unit, the Irish Battalion, officially called the 1st Virginia Battalion of the Provisional Army of the Confederate States, fought under Jackson in the Valley army in 1862. Four of the battalion's five companies were composed of Irishmen. The battalion was recruited in the largest cities of Virginia—rail centers and ports—where Irish laborers congregated for employment. Recruits hailed from Norfolk, Alexandria, Richmond, Lynchburg and Covington.[20]

In Richard Taylor's brigade, the 1st Special Louisiana Battalion was composed of the waterfront workers of New Orleans, many of whom were rough and ready Irishmen. This Tiger battalion was commanded by the "wild, uncouth" Chatham Roberdeau Wheat. The Virginia native seemed to be the only officer who could control the Tigers, and when he was killed at Gaines' Mill on June 27, 1862, the battalion disbanded, ostensibly because the Louisiana rapparees were unmanageable in camp. Upon disbandment, battalion members were drafted into other regiments of the Louisiana Brigade. Perhaps their extra-battlefield behavior is the reason Chaplain Louis-Hippolyte Gache reported, "Louisiana soldiers have gained a reputation for pilfering and general loutishness that as soon as anyone sees them coming they bolt the doors and windows."[21] Reuben Conway Macon, the adjutant of the 13th Virginia Infantry, related meeting a New Orleans "Tiger" at Fredericksburg later in 1862:

> This battalion was made up principally of Irishmen from the wharves, brave fighters, but equally noted for their love of plunder. As these fellows came up, one of our men said: "Pat, look over yonder. The whole face of the earth is covered with Yankees." "Faith," said he, "if they come this way, I will have an overcoat before night." He evidently had visions of stripping a dead man before night fell.[22]

The 8th Louisiana also included an Irish company, the Cheneyville Rifles, organized in Rapides Parish and led by Irish-born Capt. Patrick F. Keary. The 9th Louisiana boasted the Emerald Guards, also known as the Milliken Bend Guards, from Madison Parish. They were originally commanded by Capt. William R. Peck but were under the hand of Capt. George D. Shadburne in the Valley Campaign.

The four Irish companies of the 7th Louisiana included the Sarsfield Rangers, named after Patrick Sarsfield, a seventeenth-century Irish cavalry general who successfully defended Limerick during the Irish

# Irish Confederates in Battle

Jacobite War against William III. Military historian Gerard Hayes-McCoy called Sarsfield the Jeb Stuart of Ireland, or if historical allusion is a slave to chronology, Stuart was the Sarsfield of the Confederacy. Richard Taylor, under whose command the Rangers were brigaded, must have recognized the Louisiana company's allusion when he noted in his memoirs that Sarsfield's "brilliant" defense of Limerick was the only Irish "domestic struggle in which they [Irish soldiers] have shown their worth."[23]

Swift strikes and inscrutable maneuver characterized Stonewall Jackson's Shenandoah Valley Campaign. Its main objective was a strategic one—to divert Union strength away from Richmond during Maj. Gen. George B. McClellan's spring offensive on Virginia's Tidewater Peninsula. The clash in the Valley opened at Kernstown on March 23 when Jackson's diminutive force of 6,000 men struck elements of a 38,000-man army under Union Maj. Gen. Nathaniel P. Banks. The David and Goliath confrontation seemed a desperate attempt by Jackson to sting the Union giant hard enough to keep his attention in the Valley. Not surprisingly, Kernstown was a Confederate tactical defeat, but Jackson's bold attack convinced Federal authorities to keep

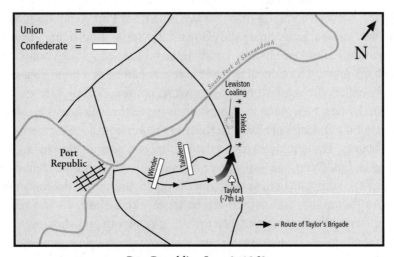

**Port Republic - June 9, 1862**

**Taylor's Irishmen flank Shields.** The Confederate brigade marched through heavily wooded and rocky terrain before striking the Union left flank.

Banks in the Shenandoah. At the same time, a Federal corps of 40,000—a force promised McClellan for his Richmond offensive—was held at Washington because of the Confederate threat in the Valley.

In April Jackson's force was bolstered by the addition of 8,500 men under Brig. Gen. Richard S. Ewell. The reinforced Confederate army repulsed a Union attack at McDowell on May 8. Jackson then directed the destruction of a small Union detachment at Front Royal May 23. The Confederate fury continued its rampage through the Valley on May 25 with another rout of lumbering Union army elements at Winchester. After that defeat, the enraged Federal Goliath converged on its vexing antagonist. Union columns under Maj. Gen. John C. Fremont and Brig. Gen. James Shields pursued the Confederates up the Valley with Jackson skillfully using his knowledge of the mountainous terrain to his advantage. The Southern army's elusive maneuvers included more than one "fine night of diversion" for Jackson's Irish troops.

One hundred-seventy-one years after the defense of Limerick, Richard Taylor learned the worth of the Irish soldier when Stonewall Jackson's defining campaign reached its climax at Cross Keys and Port Republic. On June 8, Ewell's wing of 6,500 blocked the approaching 15,000-man force under Fremont. This success allowed Jackson and Taylor to overwhelm the Irish Yankee Shields at Port Republic June 9. In the campaign's final showdown, Taylor's Louisiana Brigade successfully flanked Shields' Union line and harried it long enough for the hard-pressed Stonewall Brigade to regroup in front. Union guns on a knoll called the Lewiston Coaling were pouring killing fire on the Confederate attack when the Louisianans broke through heavy brush on the Union left. Colonel Henry B. Kelly of the 8th Louisiana remembered the attack. The enemy across a ravine opened fire on the advancing brigade, but "With one volley in reply, and a Confederate yell heard far over the field, the Louisianans rushed down the rough declivity and across the ravine, and carried the batteries like a flash."[24] The rebels were described as "an exultant crowd . . . rejoicing and shouting over their victory."[25] Though the victory was not yet complete, with steady and coordinated Southern attacks and Jackson's personal rallying of his old brigade, the Union force was thrown into a "wild retreat." The victorious Confederates pursued Shields' broken line for several miles.

## Irish Confederates in Battle

Among his many campaigns, Taylor remembered his Irishmen at Port Republic:

> I thought the men would go mad with cheering, especially the Irishmen. A huge fellow, with one eye closed and half his whiskers burned by powder, was riding cock-horse on a gun, and, catching my attention, yelled out, "We told you to bet on your boys." Their success against brother Patlanders seemed doubly welcome. Strange people, these Irish! Fighting everyone's battles, and cheerfully taking the hot end of the poker, they are only to be found wanting when engaged in what they believe to be their national cause.[26]

Taylor's comment on the seeming paradox between the unfulfilled Irish national cause, an independent Ireland, and the otherwise sterling achievements of the Irish soldier was not entirely original. The classically educated Virginia planter paraphrased the specious conclusion of the eighteenth-century philosopher Voltaire, who in typical scoffing skepticism said of the Irish soldier: "The Irish whom we have seen to be such good soldiers in France and Spain have always fought badly at home."[27] A foreign observer of the Civil War, British officer Arthur Fremantle, saw no need to fall back on such sophistry. He later observed a seeming paradox among Irish soldiers in America's war. "Southern Irishmen make excellent 'Rebs,' and have no sort of scruple in killing as many of their Northern brethren as they possibly can," he wrote with some apparent satisfaction.[28]

Jackson's celebrated Shenandoah Valley Campaign ranks among the most brilliant operations in military history. His small army of about 16,000—stocked with almost 2,000 Irish troops—stymied the strategic plans of 64,000 Federals and all but paralyzed the Union high command during the Peninsula Campaign. The Union colossus in the Valley suffered 7,000 casualties, while the Confederates lost but 2,500 men. Jackson's leadership of the Valley army's "foot-cavalry" would be the stuff of legend if it were not gloriously true. And though history has forever linked the Shenandoah with the Union Irish general Phil Sheridan, who devastated the region in 1864, the contribution of a "flying column" of Confederate Irishmen in defense of the Valley stands as a nobler Irish achievement.

ℬ. Howland 1998

*Under the Green Flag.* This artistic rendering interprets from a written description the Irish Confederate flag of the 8th Alabama's Emerald Guards (Company I). The flag was green on one side, displaying Gaelic inscriptions and Irish symbols. The other side was the Confederate national flag, popularly known as the Stars and Bars (see facing page). Banners like this were usually parade ground or presentation flags, and were rarely used in battle. They probably were furled for storage early in the war. *Drawing by Anna Howland*

Although there were numerous Confederate green flag units, the author has been unable to locate any remaining Irish Confederate flags. Only brief descriptions exist for most of these lost flags. Like the Emerald Guards' banner, they often combined Irish nationalist symbols, such as the harp and shamrock, with the Confederate colors or battle flag. The Emerald Guards' unique flag included a portrait of George Washington, the Southerner who defeated the British in the war for American independence.

*Drawing by Anna Howland*

## CLEAR THE CONFEDERATE WAY!

### Clear the Way!
### The Green Flag At Gaines' Mill

Dominick Spellman, one of the heroes of our war, a member of the
Irish company, raised the colors and gloriously
bore them for the rest of the day.

—Col. Edward McCrady

Aye, aye, said Kelly, the pikes were great
When the word was Clear the Way!

—Joseph I. C. Clarke, in *The Fighting Race*

Irish troops were wantonly sacrificed on the battlefields of Virginia
in 1862. One Irish unit destroyed in a futile frontal assault was organized
under a distinctive green flag. The banner displayed the harp—the
national symbol of Ireland, encircled by shamrocks—the Irish national
flower. It was emblazoned with the Irish war-cry, "Faugh a ballagh!" or
Clear the Way! and "Erin go Bragh," which means Ireland Forever.[29]

On a Virginia battlefield in 1862, these Irish infantrymen bore their
regimental colors into battle—the banner conspicuous and proud among
a line of the red, white and blue standards of the nation. The Irish
alferezes marked the center of the line as the order was given to advance
against a strongly entrenched foe. The soldiers knew their attack was a
desperate attempt to break the well-placed enemy line, but the Irish unit
bravely, dutifully followed its banner into the fray. The Irish infantry
force had suffered tremendous casualties before, losing about fifty
percent of its effective strength less than a month earlier in a deadly
charge against a similarly entrenched enemy. This engagement
promised to be just as devastating. Predictably, the Irishmen were
decimated again and in short order fell back while other units continued
the foolhardy advance.

As these defeated troops left the front, the color company still
defiantly bore the regimental flag; and likewise the national banner was
still held high. But the Irishmen's original green flag was not waving. As
a company flag, it did not merit a place on the battlefield; indeed it was

not at the battle at all because it had been sent home for safekeeping. For the unit's green flag was more than a mark of martial protocol; it symbolized the dream of an independent Ireland. In more ways than one, it was an Irish Rebel flag. It was a proud Irish flag with the nationalist slogans, the golden harp and emerald shamrocks of Erin on one side. Its Rebel symbols were displayed on the other—the Stars and Bars of the Confederacy complete with a central portrait of George Washington—the American rebel who had whipped the British in another American war of independence. For these Irish troops were the Emerald Guards of Mobile, Alabama—Confederate troops, Company I, the regimental color company of the 8th Alabama Infantry, brigaded under Brig. Gen. Cadmus Wilcox.

The Alabamans had fought with the Army of Northern Virginia since the battle at Yorktown. A few weeks earlier, the company's highly regarded Irish-born captain, Patrick Loughry, had been killed at the Battle of Seven Pines, fought May 31 through June 1, 1862. Now Maj. Gen. George McClellan's 100,000-man Union army was poised just seven miles outside Richmond, the Confederate capital. A new Confederate army chieftain, Gen. Robert E. Lee, opposed this formidable Federal threat. Lee, who took command after the wounding of Gen. Joseph E. Johnston June 1, inherited a scattered force of some 75,000 men. With McClellan menacing the capital, the Southern leader prudently called for Stonewall Jackson's 18,000 men of the Shenandoah Valley army to race to Richmond to reinforce him. Although McClellan had skillfully directed his army to the gates of Richmond, once there, the Union general displayed an almost craven command style—a style that would become his trademark as the army chief. Although in place to strike Lee before Jackson arrived, McClellan seemed reluctant to initiate a full-scale engagement with the Confederate army, no matter how small and scattered it seemed. Thus Southern forces, led by bold and even impetuous men, opened the campaign.

On June 26, Maj. Gen. A. P. Hill's Confederate division precipitately attacked elements of McClellan's force at Mechanicsville. Hill was to have waited for Jackson's arrival before beginning the fight, but when Jackson did not appear as scheduled, Hill attacked without support. The uncoordinated Southern assault across Beaver Dam Creek stung the 30,000 men of the Fifth Army Corps of Brig. Gen. Fitz-John Porter but was of limited success. Porter withdrew to a stronger position at Gaines' Mill. The following day, General Lee quickly seized the initiative after Hill's attack and moved to concentrate his Confederate forces on Porter. Although Porter had withdrawn from Mechanicsville, the Fifth Corps was still separated from the rest of McClellan's army by the flooded Chickahominy River. Even so, Porter held the high ground south of Cold Harbor and was protected on most of his front by Boatswain's Creek. It was across this swollen creek at the bottom of a substantial wooded ravine that Confederate troops were asked to attack.

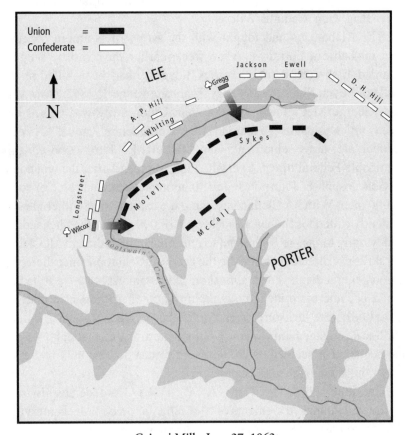

**Gaines' Mill - June 27, 1862**

**Clear the Way!** – The Emerald Guards carried the colors of the 8th Alabama as Wilcox's Brigade struck the Federal left. The Irish Volunteers were the color company of the 1st South Carolina when Gregg's Brigade attacked the Union center.

# Irish Confederates in Battle

*An Irish Volunteer*

Colonel Edward McCrady, an Irish-American from Charleston, was the first company commander of the Irish Volunteer company in the 1st South Carolina Infantry. McCrady led local Irish troops in capturing Castle Pinckney in 1861. McCrady's Irish company was the 1st South Carolina's color company.

*Cyclopedia of Eminent and Representative Men of the Carolinas, 1892*

It was a difficult, almost suicidal mission—a forlorn hope for the Irishmen of the Emerald Guards as well as for Brig. Gen. Maxcy Gregg's South Carolina brigade. Gregg's Brigade included another Irish unit, the Irish Volunteers of Charleston, which attacked on the Union right flank.

According to Confederate officer and historian Clement A. Evans, the South Carolina Irish company "formed the nucleus of . . . Maxcy Gregg's [original] regiment."[30] Evans was speaking of the color company of the 1st South Carolina Infantry, Company K, and this famous Army of Northern Virginia command had a Southern Catholic connection. Its regimental flag of blue silk with white embroidery was designed and sewn by the Catholic Ursuline Nuns of Charleston. Colonel Edward McCrady, the first company commander of the Irish Volunteers, described the banner as a "great blue flag with palmetto." It was the first regimental flag unfurled in Virginia, McCrady boasted after the war. "The whole Army of Northern Virginia was gathered and organized around its folds," he remembered.[31] McCrady had led Irish troops in Charleston at the start of the war, capturing Castle Pinckney, one of the harbor forts, as part of the Fort Sumter siege. By 1862, he was a field officer of the 1st South Carolina. At Gaines' Mill, he chronicled the charge of Gregg's Brigade and the exploits of the color-guard as it

*The Nuns' Flag*

The blue and white Palmetto flag of the 1st South Carolina Infantry was designed and embroidered by the Catholic Ursuline nuns of Charleston. That city's Irish Catholic community prominently supported the Confederacy.

*South Carolina Confederate Relic Room and Museum*

defended the nuns' flag. "None but the best soldiers are detailed for this duty," McCrady said of the 1st South Carolina color guard.[32]

The guard's conduct at Gaines' Mill proved this statement true. Gregg's Brigade led the first assaults at Gaines' Mill, bursting out of pine woods around New Cold Harbor and attacking the strong center of Porter's line. As the color company, the Irishmen of Company K held the center of the attacking line and were charged with protecting the color guard. The force had to cross several hundred yards of open fields. Exposed to deadly fire, "the whole color guard went down," remembered McCrady in 1897.[33] The palmetto flag was at first carried by Color Sergeant James "Jimmy" Taylor, who was killed instantly. "His blood was still to be seen upon its folds" in 1889 when the flag was presented to the state of South Carolina to be displayed in the capitol. When Taylor went down, Col. Daniel H. Hamilton rescued the banner and handed it to Cpl. Shubrick Hayne, who also was killed. Next it was carried across the killing field by Alfred Pinckney, and when he fell, by Gadsden Holmes. Then, remembered McCrady, a stout lad of the color company stepped forward. "Dominick Spellman, one of the heroes of our war, a member of the Irish company, raised the colors and gloriously bore them for the rest of the day," the colonel fondly remembered.[34]

Gregg's attack became a "soldier's fight" on the hillside opposite Boatswain's Creek. The South Carolina brigade lost half of its force after hand-to-hand fighting with the 5th New York Zouaves of Col. Gouverneur K. Warren's brigade. The Irish hero Spellman, only one of the cadre that McCrady memorialized as the "Boy Heroes of Cold Harbor," was promoted to color sergeant but was killed at the Second Battle of Manassas two months later. Like the ill-fated charge of the Emerald Guards, the slaughter of the boy heroes of the 1st South Carolina accomplished little.

In the end, after the late arrival of Stonewall Jackson's force of three Confederate divisions, most of the Confederate army, some 56,000 men, was brought to bear against Porter. That evening the Union Fifth Corps withdrew from the field, but its 6,800 casualties had bought time for the orderly withdrawal of McClellan's army to Harrison's Landing on the James River.

Gaines' Mill was a Confederate victory. Richmond was saved in the process, but at the exorbitant price of almost 9,000 Confederate casualties. Gaines' Mill was by no means the end of this bloody campaign. For the next four days, June 28 to July 1, Lee desperately attempted to destroy McClellan's retreating force. On June 28, McClellan moved toward the James River in what was called a "strategic withdrawal." On June 29, the armies fought piecemeal engagements at Savage's Station. There were further disjointed Confederate efforts to crush the retiring but potent Union army at White Oak Swamp and Glendale, but the Federal lines held. On July 1, the last of the bloody Seven Days' Battles was waged at Malvern Hill, where Union forces held a high plateau surrounded by protective creeks and clear fields of fire. McClellan concentrated his army at this Masada where, with the help of Union naval guns on the James, he fended off disorganized and poorly coordinated Confederate attacks.

In the sennight of fighting around Richmond, the Confederates lost 20,141 men while inflicting almost 16,000 casualties on McClellan. At Gaines' Mill, Lee won his first substantial victory as army commander, suffering the enormous casualties that often accompany a bold and aggressive leader. Gaines' Mill offered a glimpse into the future of the Confederate war effort under Lee. Among the Confederate units sacrificed to save Richmond under Lee's bloody leadership were the Emerald Guards. The Guards literally were decimated at Gaines' Mill and would incur heavy losses as well at White Oak Swamp on June 30. There, the regimental force—down to only 180 men—was cut in half after an engagement with a Union Irish force. The 8th Alabama's regimental historian reported that this enemy was the Irish Brigade of Thomas F. Meagher, but this was highly unlikely.[35] The 8th Alabama may well have encountered Irish troops, but these would have belonged to Brig. Gen. George A. McCall's division on the Union left near Frayser's Farm, Pennsylvanians of Brig. Gen. John F. Reynolds' brigade under the command of Col. Senaca G. Simmons. Perhaps the error was documented in the heat of battle or confused by the haze of memory. The chronicler may have remembered the distinctly Irish units they fought and assumed they were the most celebrated Irish unit of all. A more important conclusion from the report is the little-studied fact that there were many distinctly Irish units in both armies—the green flag of the Emerald Guards of the 8th Alabama and the Irish units of Philadelphia near Frayser's Farm being but two examples.

Yet another tale exemplifying the ubiquity of Irish troops can be found in the same campaign. At the Battle of White Oak Swamp, Meagher was on the Union right at White Oak Bridge. In that sector, far from Wilcox's Brigade, Louisiana Irish troops who were not engaged nevertheless were singled out for their battlefield heroics. Father Louis-Hippolyte Gache, chaplain of the 10th Louisiana Regiment, praised his Irish regiment for the great kindness shown to the Union troops wounded by Jackson's desultory shelling across White Oak Swamp Creek. After the battle, the summer heat of Virginia was the most pressing enemy for wounded Federals. As the Confederate army marched past the former Union positions on the way to the final showdown with McClellan at Malvern Hill, some stopped to help their stricken enemies. Father Gache remembered:

> The Irish lads of my own 10th were especially outstanding in this respect. Each time the brigade came to halt, dozens of men broke ranks and ran to cut down branches to provide shade for the wounded. Sometimes they would fix those branches into the ground beside the poor unfortunate Yankees; sometimes they would even gather up four muskets and bayonet them into the ground as a framework to support the branches. They would then give the men water, biscuits, and other bits of food that they happened to have...The Federals generally reacted with surprised gratitude.[36]

These grateful Federal Irishmen probably were members of Meagher's brigade—fighters of the 69th and 88th New York—who were heavily engaged in the fighting around White Oak Swamp and Savage Station.

## Irish Cops and Mutineers:
## The Irish Battalion and Other Culprits

They are in good spirits and are having a good time generally.

—The *Alexandria Gazette*, 1861, reporting on the Irish companies of Alexandria.
For where there are Irish there's loving and fighting,
And when we stop either, it's Ireland no more!

—Rudyard Kipling, *Ireland No More!*

By the summer of 1862, naive hopes for a short, tidy war turned to sober disillusionment at home and in camp. As the war began its second year, many soldiers, Irishmen included, began to question their service in the army. Some Irish troops openly displayed an unwillingness to fight (the enemy at least), while others violently balked at serving in the army at all. Between campaigns, even the minatory atmosphere of routine military life was no check on the high spirits of young Irishmen.

One example of recalcitrant Irish soldiers occurred during the Peninsula Campaign of 1862, during which the Emmet Guards (Company F of the 15th Virginia) was detailed to build breastworks at Grove Landing near Williamsburg. The company of about eighty men was composed of Irishmen from Richmond. The episode indicates that the company was unhappy with its native leadership, or perhaps the Irishmen were upset because they had been chosen before other companies—native companies—for the hard labor of engineering work. The company's Cpl. James F. Russell circulated a petition to force the resignation of Capt. William Lloyd, and a majority of the Irish company, incited by Corporal Russell, refused Lloyd's order to build the breastworks. The impasse was settled when the unpopular captain transferred command to Lt. James Collins. Russell was eventually court-martialed and convicted of mutiny. He was reduced to the ranks and was sentenced to thirty days of the hard labor he had sought to avoid—but now his work would be attended with ball and chain. However, Brig. Gen. John Magruder generously suspended the sentence, and the company completed its duty at Grove Landing. By June the unhappy Irish company was disbanded when many of its members claimed exemption from service under the Conscription Act, which dismissed non-citizens from service in the army.[37]

General Magruder reportedly had another run-in with an Irishman in his command. The humorous and perhaps apocryphal story of Tommy Logan, "the typical son of the Emerald Isle," is the sort of stereotypical tale often told of the Irish in both armies. Logan, a common laborer, had joined the Confederate army at the first call for troops from Mississippi. The gentlemanly General Magruder, although a hard drinker himself, ordered that no intoxicants be sold or given away within Confederate ranks. Logan was on guard one evening at Magruder's tent in camp near Fredericksburg when the commander noticed the man had been drinking and demanded to know where he got the liquor. Logan, never at a loss for an answer, said: "O, Gineral, I'm afraid you will put me in the guardhouse, I think the damn Yankees are thinking of taking Fredericksburg, and I would hate to tell some of my good friends in town

I did not fire a shot in their defense." Wanting to get to the bottom of the matter, more than punish his Irish guard, Magruder promised clemency if Logan told him the source of the contraband poteen. But Old Tommy, as he was called, demurred a bit longer. He began a long story about how he had taken a walk earlier and had spied some hitched horses. Being a former jockey in Kentucky he noticed a beautiful bay, and could not resist admiring it. Upon closer inspection, the Irish Confederate discovered a canteen of whiskey and drank the entire contents—though "not more than three fingers," Old Tommy said. "Whose horse was the canteen on?" asked the general, leaning forward for the culprit's name. "Ah! my kind Gineral," Logan replied, "I do not know the owner; but I have for the last six months seen you ridin' the noble animal." So went an old Confederate's story of Irish wit.[38]

Although Private Logan seemed willing to soldier in between libations, the example of the 15th Virginia's Emmet Guards revealed that the Conscription Act was used by some Irishmen to avoid service. Substitution, whereby a conscript could pay a fee for another to serve in his place, was an avenue of avoidance Irish immigrants usually could not afford. Waterford, Ireland, native Martin Connell of the 17th Virginia was one such Confederate discharged under the act when he claimed to be a non-citizen of the Confederate States of America and in fact a British subject—a desperate admission for any true Irishman to make.[39] No such opportunity to avoid service seemed to be available to Northern Irishmen. On a trip to New York during the war, British officer Arthur Fremantle was approached by Irish waiters, who upon discovering he was English complained to him "in hoarse Hibernian accents" about being drafted by the United States. "These rascals have probably been hard at work for years, voting as free and enlightened American citizens, and abusing England to their hearts' content," Fremantle wrote.[40]

Once part of the Confederate army, some disgruntled Irishmen sought to shoot their way out of the service. The Tiger Bayou Rifles of the 14th Louisiana Regiment mutinied when the unit was on its way to Virginia in 1862. Captain Nathan J. Rawlings of the regiment remembered that the company of Irishmen refused to complete the trip when its pay was delayed. At a stopover at Grand Junction, Tennessee, "We had quite a little battle," Rawlings remembered. Several of the

Irishmen were killed and all except nine men of the company were disarmed.[41]

There is much evidence that some Irishmen, North and South, did not serve willingly from the start, or at best exhibited rapid cases of "soldier's remorse" once in the ranks. After the Battle of Cedar Mountain in August 1862, Father James B. Sheeran of the 14th Louisiana spoke to a wounded soldier of the 73rd New York, who summed up much of the Union Irish attitude to the war.

"What's your name?" asked Sheeran of the man.

"P. Sullivan," came the answer.

"Are you Catholic?"

"Yes, I am."

"Pat, what brought you here?" Sheeran asked, guessing at his Christian name.

"O! Misfortune," was the poor fellow's wry and bitter answer. His leg had been broken by a musket ball.[42]

Desertion, a more serious symptom of "soldier's remorse," also was reported among some Irish troops, just as it was in the general population of the army. In the 17th Virginia, records account for twenty-two desertions between June 1864 and February 1865. Six of these were from the O'Connell Guards, Company I. One of the deserters was 66-year-old Irish native James Hagerty, one of the oldest deserters in the army, if not one of its oldest private soldiers.[43] In his defense, war-weary soldiers like Hagerty simply deserted to the enemy near the end of the war in hopes of getting better treatment from the inevitable victors.

There are many colorful, comical stories of the nefarious actions of the Irish soldier in camp. Elijah Henry Sutton of the 24th Georgia remembers the antics of company clown Henry Holbrooks of the McMillan Guards, the regiment's Company K. Holbrooks had been detailed by the Irish Col. Robert McMillan to carry the guidon for the regiment in drill and so was quite pleased when he was told he was not required to carry a rifle. The company commander, however, ordered the sergeant to furnish Holbrooks with a weapon. Sgt. Calvin J. Allen ordered Holbrooks to take the rifle or he would be arrested. Holbrooks answered, "I'm damned if I do it, Sergeant. If you want that gun carried, carry it yourself, by God!" The Irishman then struck Sergeant Allen over the head with a piece of rail, knocking him down, and ran off. Nothing was ever done about it, Sutton said.[44]

A more serious incident of camp intrigue involved the infamously undisciplined Wheat's Battalion from New Orleans. Captain (later Colonel) William Monaghan of the 6th Louisiana Regiment reported in October 1861 that "Private James McCormick of this company was murdered by Private John Travers of the Tiger Rifles, Wheat's Battalion." The murder occurred on October 20, and five days later a squad of ten men under Lt. Michael O'Connor tracked down and arrested Travers at about two in the morning.[45]

Another serious incident of camp horseplay involved the Irishmen who ironically became the Provost Guard for the Army of Northern Virginia—the 1st Virginia Battalion, popularly known as the Irish Battalion. These "Irish cops of the army" learned how to police some of their own before they filled the provost role for the rest of the army. The Irish laborers of the battalion, recruited in Virginia's railroad centers and ports, exhibited a rough edge at times. The unit's arrival in Richmond in the spring of 1861 was followed by drinking, fighting and some desertion—transgressions common to all volunteer forces when given liberty in a tempting city.[46] The unit's first serious brush with the law came in June that year, when Privates William Looney and William Sexton mutinied against their native Virginian officer corps. They were placed in the guardhouse but somehow acquired muskets and charged the guards, Looney wounding Lt. John Heth. Both prisoners were subdued by other officers, who drew their sidearms to restore order. The Irishmen were convicted of mutiny and sentenced to three months of hard labor with ball and chain.

Even with such troubles, the Irish Battalion continued to serve the South. After an uneven performance on the battlefield, the battalion was detailed in late 1862 to be the provost guard for Stonewall Jackson's Second Corps. In winter camp in 1862-63, it was an Irish guard of the battalion who failed to recognize General Jackson as he returned late one night to his headquarters—a small wooden outbuilding at Moss Neck near Fredericksburg. Jackson's noted staff officer, Lt. James Power Smith, wrote in 1898 that the battalion furnished Jackson's quarters an Irish guard who "marched to and fro before the door." The Irishman "took his duty of protecting the general with great pride and seriousness," Smith remembered. When the general himself was caught outside one night, "no persuasion could induce the guard to believe" the intruder was Jackson. The guard's strict attention to his duty must have pleased the dour absolutist in Jackson, while at the same time frustrating the tired general.[47]

By the winter of 1862, the battalion's leadership had found some stability under Maj. David B. Bridgford. Bridgford was a swarthy shipping broker and merchant, the son of a British diplomat. He was also

a seasoned militia officer who for several years before the war had been a member of the Richmond Light Infantry Blues, an elite volunteer militia company first organized in 1793. Under Major Bridgford, the battalion admirably performed its military police function. "I am most happy to state I had no occasion to carry into effect the order to shoot all stragglers who refused to go forward," reported Bridgford after Fredericksburg.[48]

*In the Irish Battalion*

Private Henry Kelly, a native of Ireland, enlisted in Company A of the Irish Battalion, a unit of Confederate Regulars composed of Irishmen from across Virginia. At age 23, Kelly joined the army at Richmond in February 1862. He was captured at Mount Jackson in June 1862, and sent to Fort Delaware prison, where he took the Oath of Allegiance on August 10, 1862. *William W. Turner*

# Irish Confederates in Battle

*Irish Battalion Leader*

Major David B. Bridgford commanded the 1st Virginia Battalion, a unit popularly known as the Irish Battalion. He also served as Thomas J. "Stonewall" Jackson's ordnance officer. Bridgford accompanied Jackson's corpse to Richmond in 1863.

*William W. Turner*

Prior to Bridgford, the unit had seen a steady stream of temporary leaders. There were five battalion commanders in all in less than two years. Besides Bridgford, these included John Dunburrow Munford, a political appointee with no military experience; John Seddon, the brother of the Confederate Secretary of War; Benjamin W. Leigh; and Charles A. Davidson. This rapid turnover of commanders did not bode well for the battalion's Irishmen. Munford, described as a poet and scholar, only dabbled in military service. Davidson said he "knew as much about military matters and is as capable of managing a battalion as a school boy."[49] Leigh used the post as a stepping stone to regimental and staff positions. He later became a member of A. P Hill's staff, and at Chancellorsville steadied the hospital litter of Stonewall Jackson when an artillery shell decimated Hill's entourage.[50] Davidson was a company commander who filled in as battalion commander for a short period in 1862 after Seddon resigned for health reasons. From the start, Seddon protested that he was unqualified for field service. "I beg leave to decline the position. I am not qualified for the command," he wrote to General Lee in July 1861.[51] Munford was appointed in his place when Seddon met him in the street one day and recommended the lawyer merely out of expedience.[52]

The lack of experienced and steady leadership was evident at the battalion's debacle at Cedar Mountain on August 9, 1862. The reluctant and unqualified Seddon was in command of the Irish Battalion when Stonewall Jackson's corps encountered a Federal force under Maj. Gen.

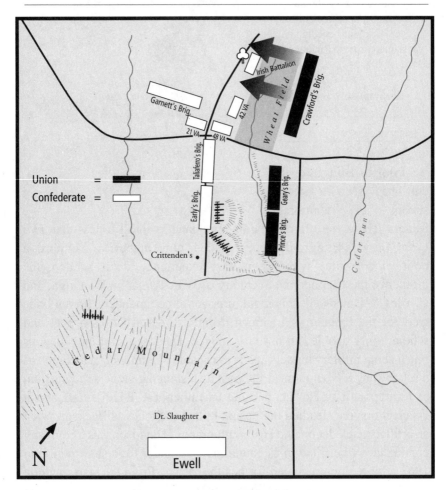

**Cedar Mountain - August 9, 1862**

**The Irish Battalion skedaddles.** A faulty troop alignment and poor field leadership led to the collapse of the Irish Battalion at Cedar Mountain.

Nathaniel P. Banks. The battalion was formed at the left flank of Brig. Gen. Charles S. Winder's command. Attacked by Union Brig. Gen. Samuel W. Crawford's brigade, Winder's left quickly collapsed and the Irish Battalion fled ignominiously after firing three ineffective volleys at the approaching Federals. According to artillery officer Lt. John Hampden "Ham" Chamberlayne, "The Irish Battalion broke disgracefully & could not be rallied, to the untold humiliation of its officers."[53] The latter part of Chamberlayne's observation was especially telling. The retreat was humiliating to the officers because the battalion exhibited the battlefield behavior of troops who lack total confidence in their leadership.

The battalion's lack of discipline at Cedar Mountain was the result of faulty leadership of the infantry at every level. Major Seddon had not deployed a skirmish line even though he faced an open field—the quickest avenue of approach for any Union advance.[54] A more serious failure of deployment rested at the brigade level. A fatal gap was left between the battalion's right flank and the left of the 42nd Virginia Regiment, and two other regiments, the 21st and 48th Virginia, were deployed at a right angle from the front and thus out of position to meet an enemy advance.[55] When General Winder was mortally wounded early in the battle, his replacement, Brig. Gen. William B. Taliaferro, rode forward but did not find any enemy on the battalion's front. He ordered the 10th Virginia to reinforce the battalion, but this regiment aligned itself on the Irishmen's left. Once the battle started the 10th broke first, according to official reports.[56] The rout of the 10th Virginia left both flanks of the battalion in the air and the Irish unit in jeopardy of being surrounded. Sensing their impending destruction, the Irishmen prudently ran for cover. Father James B. Sheeran went so far as to defend the battalion's action in the battle:

> The Irish battalion of Jackson's old Brig. and a few regiments were in the advance on the Left, and the remainder of our forces were concealed in the woods some two hundred yards to the rear. The Yankees pressed upon our advance with overpowering numbers. The Irish Brig. (sic), soon abandoned by their companions who were unable to withstand the terrible fire of the advancing enemy, for some time boldly withstood the unequal

# CLEAR THE CONFEDERATE WAY!

*The Good Fight*

John Seddon, brother of Confederate Secretary of War James Seddon, led the Irish Battalion at Cedar Mountain in 1862. His tombstone in the Fredericksburg City Cemetery memorializes his service with the Irish Confederate unit.

*Author*

contest, and only returned when their ranks were weakened by the loss of many of their bravest members.[57]

In fact, the battalion's losses were minuscule. It took the appearance of Jackson himself on the broken line and reinforcements sent up by A. P. Hill to rally the mishandled men. Historian Robert K. Krick blames the crisis on the Confederate left at Cedar Mountain on Jackson's and Winder's preoccupation with the artillery fight at the expense of infantry deployment.[58]

The hasty retreat at Cedar Mountain aside, there is no evidence that the battalion was a rabble of Irish poltroons, as some alleged. The unit had too often been valorous in other mêlées. General Winder reported after Gaines' Mill and Malvern Hill: "I cannot speak too highly of the officers and men of my brigade, in which, for a time, I must include the Irish Battalion, Captain [Benjamin Watkins] Leigh. Their coolness, bravery, and discretion entitle them to my warmest gratitude."[59]

The difference at Cedar Mountain, however, was leadership—or the lack of it. During the Seven Days' Battles, the battalion was ably commanded by Leigh, who was later killed at Gettysburg. At Kernstown the Irishmen were commanded by Bridgford. In that Shenandoah Valley battle, the battalion found itself in a fix similar to what it faced at Cedar Mountain—out of ammunition and cut off—as the Confederate right fell back. One Irish company displayed the typical gallantry of the battalion when it executed a courageous bayonet charge. It was led in this forlorn effort by Capt. J. Pembroke Thom, a self-proclaimed "Gaelic Celt" descended from the highlanders who fought with Bonnie Prince Charlie at Culloden in 1745.[60] What transpired next was the kind of fighting that made up for the pervasive Irish shenanigans in the Army of Northern Virginia. Ordered by Jackson to "Give them the bayonet!, Captain Thom . . . brandishing his sword . . . gave a wild rebel yell, and followed by the men of the Irish Bn, charged toward the enemy." Thom's charge was selfless, brave, and. . . lucky. Musket fire struck the Celtic captain three times: in the right hand, in the thigh, and in a testament protecting his heart. The Gaelic Celt collapsed unconscious only to be awakened by Jackson himself, whose victorious forces possessed the field. "The general spoke words of praise for Pembroke's courage and promised him that in the next fight he should lead the van," wrote the captain's sister, Catherine Thom Bartlett.[61]

The Irish Battalion, alongside other Irish troops of the army, would demonstrate even greater courage in combat when the opposing armies in Virginia clashed again on the plains of Manassas.

## A Battle of Rocks:
## In the Railroad Cut at Second Manassas

Throwing down their empty guns they attacked and drove back the
enemy with rocks which they found in abundance on the roadside.
The other regiments as they got out of ammunition followed
their example and soon it became a battle of rocks.

—James B. Sheeran

Farewell to Tipperary, said the Galtee Mountain boy. . .
To the men who fought for their liberty
And died without a sigh.
May their cause be ne'er forgotten. . .

—*The Galtee Mountain Boy*

## CLEAR THE CONFEDERATE WAY!

Desperate and courageous Irish leadership helped the Confederates hold a tenuous defensive line in late August 1862. Lieutenant Colonel Michael Nolan, a 41-year-old native of County Tipperary, Ireland, was in command of the 1st Louisiana Regiment when brigade leader Col. Leroy A. Stafford reported, "The men fought with rocks and held their position."

Nolan was an unlikely candidate for such heroic and determined duty. He operated a small grocery store in New Orleans before the war and enlisted as a sergeant. One of his New Orleans friends remembered:

> When I was a little boy around New Orleans, I used to collect bills for sugar at a small grocery, right opposite Charity Hospital in that city. The owner of the store was a young, blue-eyed, light-haired Irishman named Mike Nolan. Mild and polite and friendly in his manners; and I am sure it is no shame to my foresight that at that time I did not recognize him to be the best, bravest and grandest soldier I ever met."[62]

Nolan first exhibited the courage that earned him this praise at the Second Battle of Manassas.

The Second Manassas Campaign came about as a result of an aggressive Confederate strategy to prevent the Union armies in Virginia from joining forces. Called in from the West, Maj. Gen. John Pope took command of the newly constituted Army of Virginia, some 63,000 soldiers situated outside Washington, D.C. George McClellan's 120,000 men of the Army of the Potomac, meanwhile, remained inactive below Richmond at Harrison's Landing on the James River. If the two Union armies united, Lee's odds of defeating the enemy would tumble. Since Pope's smaller force presented the most vulnerable target, Lee determined to move elements of his army north and engage him before McClellan could react.

Jackson swiftly led 24,000 men moved north and on August 15, stole a march on Pope and cut the Northern supply line at Manassas Junction. The wily Jackson then took up a strong position in an unfinished railroad bed and waited for Pope to spring the Southern snare. At the same time, the remainder of the Confederate army, a 31,000-man host under James Longstreet, with Robert E. Lee hovering beside, marched to join Jackson's unholy convocation. Late in the day on

*A Battle of Rocks.* William Starke's Brigade fighting with stones near the "deep cut" at the Second Battle of Manassas. Louisiana troops under Irish colonel Michael Nolan stubbornly defended the Southern line with rocks after running out of ammunition. *Battles and Leaders, 1889*

August 28, the battle opened when Union forces led by the elite Iron Brigade marched past Jackson's position. The hero of the Shenandoah Valley sprung his trap, but after heavy and indecisive fighting, darkness ended the action at Brawner's Farm near Groveton.

The next day, as Longstreet and Lee marched to join Jackson, Pope launched a series of piecemeal attacks against Stonewall's well-placed line. The first effort unsuccessfully struck at the Confederate center with only two regiments. Next, five regiments under Maj. Gen. Philip Kearny attacked the left with some success, but fell back when reinforcements failed to arrive. A third Federal attack was launched about 3:00 p.m. Unlike the prior efforts, this assault was a determined and heavy thrust against a portion of the unfinished railroad cut held by Lt. Col. Michael Nolan's 1st Louisiana Regiment. Nolan's 1st Louisiana, organized in New Orleans by Irish Maj. James Nelligan, was part of Brig. Gen. William E. Starke's Brigade. Under the command of Col. Leroy Stafford, the brigade held the right center of the line.

Father James Sheeran described the ensuing critical close-quarter fight led by Lieutenant Colonel Nolan and his Irish regiment:

> The 1st La. R.[egiment] was out of ammunition and in fact nearly out of strength as they had been fighting for several hours against ten times their number. Col. Nolan, who commanded the 1st, was expecting reinforcements every moment. To abandon his position on the bank of the R.R.[railroad] would have turned the tide of victory against us. The gallant boys of the 1st were not long in deciding what to do. Throwing down their empty guns they attacked and drove back the enemy with rocks which they found in abundance on the roadside. The other regiments as they got out of ammunition followed their example and soon it became a battle of rocks. It may appear strange, but it is nevertheless true that our men did as much execution with these new missiles of war as with their musket balls, for after the battle many of the Yankees were found on the field with broken skulls.[63]

Against heavy odds, Starke's Brigade of Louisianans (known informally as the Second Louisiana Brigade) staunchly held the right front of Jackson's line. Though Chaplain Sheeran often overstated the gallantry of Irish Confederate troops, the "battle of rocks" at Manassas indeed helped turn the tide toward Confederate victory. The exhausted Louisianans held out long enough for Lee to unite the two wings of his army, and Longstreet's divisions arrived to aid Jackson's endangered right late that afternoon. The combined Army of Northern Virginia launched its own turning movement the next day, fell upon Pope's exposed left flank, and drove the Union army back to Washington.

The bizarre stone-throwing defense led by Nolan occurred along a section of the line known as "the dump"—a part of the rail bed that was not filled in—which left a break in the natural defensive works the rail embankment provided. "The dump" was a point of relatively easy entry into Jackson's line and thus had to be held. Indeed, the integrity of

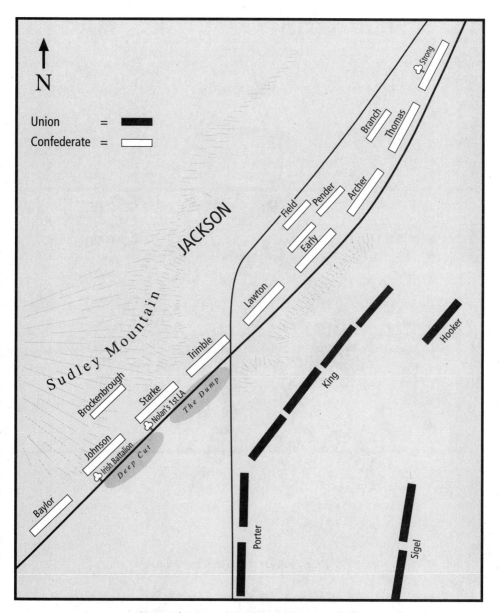

**Second Manassas - August 30, 1862**

**A Battle of Rocks.** This detail shows "the dump" where Michael Nolan and Starke's Brigade conducted the "Battle of Rocks." At the "Deep Cut" the Irish Battalion also fought with stones when its ammunition ran out. On the left of Jackson's Corps, Irish Colonel Henry B. Strong commanded Hays' Brigade.

*The Best, Bravest and Grandest Soldier*

Michael Nolan, a forty-one-year-old native of County Tipperary, Ireland, led the 1st Louisiana Infantry at Second Manassas in 1862. A New Orleans grocer, Nolan took command of Starke's Brigade at Sharpsburg, but was killed in action at Gettysburg.

*Lawrence T. Jones*

# Irish Confederates in Battle

Jackson's right flank had to be preserved since it would form the anchor or hinge of Lee's line of battle once Longstreet's wing arrived on the field.[64]

Lieutenant Robert Healy of the 55th Virginia, part of John Brockenbrough's (Charles Field's) Brigade, described how the two wings met. Brockenbrough's Virginians initially were held in reserve, but were ordered forward about 2:30 p.m. to reinforce the crumbling front. They took up a position behind the railroad cut on a hill presumptuously called Sudley Mountain, leaving the cut as a dry moat in their front. According to Healy, Nolan's troops formed a production line, with some collecting the stone ammunition and others projecting the deadly rain of rocks down upon the attackers. "The troops occupying this place [the railroad cut] had expended their ammunition and were defending themselves with rocks . . . which seemed to have been picked or blasted out of the bed of the railroad, chips and slivers of stone which many were collecting and others were throwing."[65]

---

*Saint Mary of Sorrows*

This little Catholic church near Fairfax, Virginia, is aptly named Saint Mary of Sorrows. Built in 1858 for Irish railworkers, the church was ravaged by the war. The modest frame structure was used by Clara Barton, the founder of the American Red Cross, as a field hospital for Union casualties during the Second Manassas Campaign. Funeral services for Union General Philip Kearny were held here after Kearny was killed at the Battle of Chantilly.

*Author*

Union troops had infiltrated the cut and were advancing up Sudley Mountain when help arrived. The reinforcements drove the attackers down the hill and across the valley of the cut. Healy's Virginians, richly accoutered with twenty musket rounds per man, chased the Federals back into the tree line. The Irish Confederate defenders of "the dump" in Starke's Brigade included Nolan's original Irish company, the Montgomery Guards, and James Nelligan's Emmet Guards, both in the 1st Louisiana; Capt. Patrick O'Rourke's Orleans Light Guards and Maj. Michael Grogan's Moore Guards of the 2nd Louisiana; the Emerald Guards of the 9th Louisiana, five Irish companies of the 10th Louisiana, and a significant number of Irishmen in the 15th Louisiana.

On August 30, yet another Confederate Irish unit made a noteworthy stand alongside Starke's Brigade in an area of the line called the "deep cut." These gray-mantled heroes were the seeming poltroons of the Irish Battalion, part of Col. Bradley T. Johnson's Brigade. The battalion was deployed in the cut on the left side of Johnston's line and just to the right of Starke's men. When Union Maj. General. Fitz-John Porter's Fifth Corps attacked, the Irish Battalion and the 21st Virginia counterattacked in an effective bayonet charge which cleared the rail cut of Federals.

As the fighting continued, Pope threw a substantial number of his men into the action. Ten thousand Federals advanced against the Confederate entrenchments. The railroad cut clash was described as "most obstinate," according to Colonel Johnson, who reported that "The men fought until their ammunition was exhausted and then threw stones. Lieut. Lewis Randolph of the [Irish] battalion, killed one [Federal] with a stone, and I saw him after the fight with his skull fractured."[66] Lieutenant James M. Garnett corroborated the desperate stand of the Irishmen. "The Irish Battalion. . .fought with stones after their ammunition gave out, and it is credibly stated that my friend and old college-mate, Lewis Randolph, a lieutenant in the Irish Battalion (First Virginia battalion), killed a Yankee with a large stone."[67]

After the ignominy of its precipitous retreat at Cedar Mountain, the Irish Battalion redeemed its reputation at Second Manassas. The battalion's leader, Maj. John Seddon, likewise distinguished himself in the battle by leading the unit in the capture of a field gun from retreating Federals on August 29. On a grander scale, Lee cleverly orchestrated the final curtain call of the Second Manassas Campaign. The Confederate chieftain countered Pope's last attack with a 30,000-man advance that shattered the Union offense and drove the Northern army back to Henry House hill. The campaign cost the Federals 9,931 killed and wounded and another 3,895 missing, while Confederate casualties totaled 8,353.

Mike Nolan, the New Orleans grocer, took command of the Louisiana Brigade at Sharpsburg in September 1862, when General Starke was killed. He was one of several largely unsung Irish brigade leaders in Lee's army. The "best, bravest and grandest soldier" was killed in action at Gettysburg, just short of a promising bid to become a Confederate Irish brigadier general.

Arguably, the Confederacy reached the pinnacle of its military power that summer. After his triumphant campaign in Northern Virginia, Lee was emboldened to move his victorious army north of the Potomac River. The next campaign would occur away from Virginia, in the Maryland hills around a little village called Sharpsburg.


## The Riderless Horse of Henry B. Strong:
## Sharpsburg's Bloody Day

'Neath Erin's flag with its glad sunburst
Was Emmet, who stands in that martyr-van,
Whose blood sanctified the gibbet accursed,
Where he died for the rights of man.
There was Light-horse Harry, the first in the fray,
There was Marion leading his cavaliers,
And Washington too, whose grave today
Is the shrine of patriot's tears.

— *The Hero Without a Name*, by Col. William S. Hawkins, C.S.A.


And in the midst of bloody fights
Don't let your courage lag.
For I'll be there and hovering near
beneath the dear old flag.

— *Wrap the Green Flag 'Round Me, Boys!*

One of the most forlorn and haunting photographs of the war is the image of a dead horse, which, to all appearances is merely resting on the Sharpsburg battlefield. It is believed to be the steed of Col. Henry B. Strong, an Irish native and regimental commander of the 6th Louisiana Infantry—the Irish Regiment—as Richard Taylor termed it.

Strong was a clerk in New Orleans before the war. At age forty, he enlisted and was elected captain of the Calhoun Guards, Company B, of the 6th. This Irish company chose its name well—its title and men were a perfect match between Ireland and the South. The Calhoun Guards took its name from John C. Calhoun, the states rights Congressman from South Carolina and son of Patrick Calhoun of County Donegal, Ireland.

By September 1862, Strong commanded the regiment, then brigaded under Brig. Gen. Harry T. Hays. As senior regimental commander, Strong had taken temporary command of the brigade at Second Manassas when Hays' replacement there, Col. Henry Forno, was wounded. After Lee's army swept the Northern enemy from the fields of Manassas for the second time, he chose to press his advantage with an offensive campaign into Maryland. The Confederate chieftain hoped his bold raid into a border state would retain the initiative in the Eastern Theater. The Confederacy also hoped Lee's gambit would win over the people of the state to the Southern cause while relieving Virginia of her burden as the war's most ravaged battleground.

The Maryland Campaign was characterized by the usual audacity of Lee as well as by the routine malingering command style of George McClellan, who reprised his role as the uninspired commander of the 75,000-man Army of the Potomac. The march north did not begin well for the Confederates. On September 9, Lee decided to split his 40,000 men into two wings, a risky move brought about by his desire to capture strategically important Harpers Ferry while continuing the march into Maryland. A copy of Lee's directive outlining the two-pronged movement, Special Order 191, was lost near Frederick, Maryland, and subsequently discovered by Union soldiers. McClellan was thus handed the key to Lee's invasion plan. Even with this intelligence windfall however, McClellan moved slowly. Amazingly, he did not capitalize on the information by immediately attacking one of the two vulnerable Southern columns. Instead, it was Lee—deep in enemy territory and

# Irish Confederates in Battle

*In the East Woods*

This dead white warhorse was the mount of Irish-born Col. Henry B. Strong of the 6th Louisiana Infantry. Both Strong and his mount were killed in a charge at Sharpsburg, Maryland, on September 17, 1862. The East Woods is visible in the background. *Library of Congress*

with his army divided—who continued to assume the initiative in what was perhaps his most daring campaign of the war.

As the Confederates fought to hold the passes slicing through South Mountain on September 14, Stonewall Jackson's force, like fine clockwork, captured Harpers Ferry the following day. Lee, meanwhile, positioned at Sharpsburg with only 19,000 men, decided to stand and offer battle to an enemy army that outnumbered him almost two to one—and those odds would only be offered after the Harpers Ferry force rejoined him. Lee's decision led to the bloodiest single day of the war in the ensuing Battle of Sharpsburg, waged along the undulating hills surrounding Antietam Creek. On the Confederate army's march into Maryland, Maj. William H. Manning remembered that the 6th Louisiana "crossed the Potomac to the tune of Dixie."[68] The Irish Louisianans would soon be singing a more somber tune.

McClellan opened the action at first light on September 17. Moving south along the Hagerstown Pike, Maj. Gen. Joseph Hooker's First Corps struck the Confederate left, commanded by Stonewall Jackson. The carnage was swift, the killing efficient. By noon, almost 13,000 men had been killed and wounded. The Irish 6th Louisiana was "hotly engaged in the bloody fight," according to Lt. James O. Martin of Company F. Colonel Strong's Louisiana regiment was in the line of battle early that morning, and before long would be ordered forward in the direction of a large field of corn and the advancing enemy.[69] As usual, Strong would put duty before caution as he guided his men into action on that fateful day.

Hooker's attack dealt heavy losses to the Confederate front line, which stretched across the 30-acre cornfield of David R. Miller. Hays' Louisiana Brigade was held in reserve in the West Woods behind Alexander Lawton's Brigade, under the command of Col. Marcellus Douglass. By 7:00 a.m., Hooker's wave had killed Douglass and his brigade was falling back in some disorder. The Louisianans were called up, covered a 300-yard distance under artillery fire, and plowed into Brig. Gen. George L. Hartsuff's Union brigade. Hays drove back the Federals and closed within 250 yards of a second Union line drawn up in the East Woods. Colonel Strong, mounted on a large white mare, was in the lead and made an easy target. Federal muskets quickly cut down the colonel and his mount near the edge of the timber. Captain George P. Ring was hit four times trying to aid his fallen Irish colonel.[70] Ring's heroics were to no avail: Strong had been killed instantly—another promising Irish voice silenced by a dutiful death.

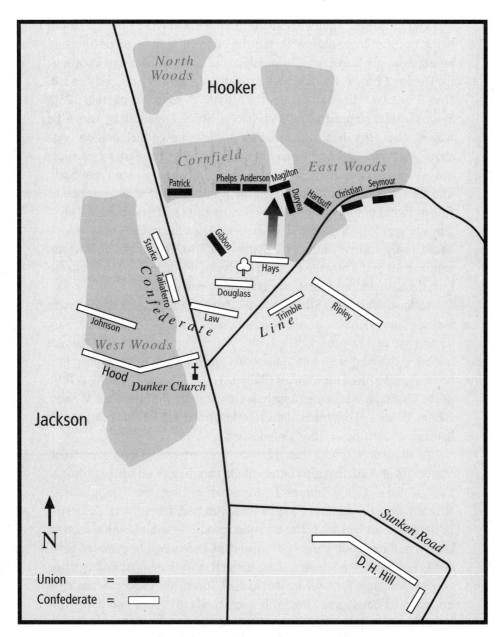

**Sharpsburg - September 17, 1862**

**Sharpsburg's Bloody Day** – Colonel Henry B. Strong was killed when he led the 6th Louisiana of Hays' Brigade across the cornfield and to the East Woods tree line.

The Louisiana Tigers held their ground a few more minutes before being ordered to withdraw in the direction of a little white meeting house, a simple frame establishment of the German Brethren known as the Dunker Church. The Federals pursued them across the bloody sward. One Unionist, thought to be the gloating adjutant of the 125th Pennsylvania, stopped to pick up one of Strong's gauntlets, which he waved over his head in triumph.[71] His showy celebration was short-lived. Indicative of the day's seesaw fighting, the Federal pursuers ran into Brig. Gen. John B. Hood's division, which drove them back. The East Woods attack devastated the Louisianans. Strong was one of fifteen Rebel colonels who fell at Sharpsburg. Sixty percent of Hays' Brigade was killed, wounded or missing after the engagement, which lasted only thirty minutes. Every staff officer and regimental commander of the brigade fell, and twelve of the officers of the Irish 6th Louisiana, including Strong, were killed or wounded.[72]

Colonel Henry B. Strong and the Irish regiment—so joyous with Jackson and Taylor in the Shenandoah Valley—were practically annihilated at Sharpsburg. The Irish colonel's men managed to recover his body the next day and temporarily buried their fallen leader in a hollow just south of the Dunker Church. Today, history remembers little of the Irishman who impetuously led the charge into the East Woods. But the famous photograph of the riderless horse is a morbid reminder of his heroic sacrifice for the Confederacy.

A more celebrated but perhaps less heroic example of Irish leadership at Antietam also involved the shooting of an officer's horse. Federal Brig. Gen. Thomas F. Meagher ordered the Union's Irish Brigade forward against Southerners who had taken up a defensive position in a sunken road. The infamous position—which would soon be known as the Bloody Lane—afforded the Confederate brigades of Brig. Gens. George B. Anderson and Ambrose R. Wright almost impregnable cover. Marching forward in the face of foolhardy orders, Meagher's brigade was devastated; two of his regiments, the 63rd and 69th New York, lost sixty percent of their troops. Meagher, who had not been part of the fighting war since the Seven Days' Battles, fell when his horse reportedly was shot out from under him. He did not remount. Meagher was carried from the field in a stupor, and it was rumored that he had been killed.[73] The Irish general, however, was alive and unscathed, and his fall probably saved his life. Some reports cast doubt on the circumstances of his unhorsing and subsequent retreat. Staff officer Lt. Col. David H. Strother reported that the general's fall was due to drunkenness. "Meagher was not killed as reported, but drunk, and fell from his horse," Strother wrote in his journal.[74] Was Strother correct in his assertion? It was the sort of allegation too often applied to an officer, especially an Irishman, who failed to live up to expectations. The truth of Meagher's conduct at Sharpsburg may never be known, but it was a stitch in a pattern of questionable incidents surrounding him for the rest of his life.

In any event, the contrast between Strong's and Meagher's conduct under similar battle conditions is striking. Strong led his Confederates into teeth of the enemy's guns; Meagher found safety behind the lives and limbs of sixty percent of his New Yorkers. Their unequal treatment by historians with Irish sympathies is disappointing. Meagher's uneven battlefield service has been celebrated often and is well-remembered, while the heroic Strong, albeit only a regimental leader, was quickly forgotten—too cheaply forgotten. Granted, Strong did not hold a brigade command, but his actions on the field were of the highest rank.

The casualty count for Sharpsburg exceeded 26,000 killed, wounded and missing, or 12,410 Federals and 13,724 Confederates. Despite his army's precarious position and heavy losses, Lee considered going over to the offensive the next day. Instead, during the night of September 18 he withdrew and led his army back into Virginia. Militarily, the campaign in Maryland was inconclusive. Politically, it was perhaps the most important of the war. European powers, including France, Spain, and Great Britain, had looked for a Confederate victory on Northern soil in the hopes of offering formal recognition to the Confederacy. It was not to be. On September 22, Abraham Lincoln used the Maryland standoff to introduce his Emancipation Proclamation, which promised freedom to black slaves in the territories in rebellion. Although unenforceable, the proclamation changed the focus of the war. Overnight Lincoln transformed the war's purpose from maintaining the Union to a moral crusade to free America's slaves. Many in the North, particularly Irish immigrants, did not concur with Lincoln's new moral initiative for the war. The introduction of the slavery issue caused Northern Irish spirit for the war to wane. Internationally, Lincoln's proclamation issued a bold political statement to the world that effectively dissuaded foreign assistance for the South. Great Britain, for instance, an activist abolitionist state, was compelled to support Lincoln in this crusade, and could no longer entertain any notion of siding with the Confederacy. The Emancipation Proclamation, compounded by the dreadful results of the Battle of Fredericksburg seven weeks later, would greatly affect Northern Irish opinion about the war.

# The Fighting Race at Fredericksburg

## Irish Tragedy and Northern Defeat

There were blossoms of blood on our sprigs of green.

— From The Fighting Race, Joseph I. C. Clarke

For death has often stared me in the face. Oh! how fearfully often.

— John Keely

**P**rivate Henry Holbrooks, an Irishman in the McMillan Guards of the 24th Georgia Infantry, was "spilin' for a fight" in the winter of 1862; so were President Abraham Lincoln and Maj. Gen. Ambrose E. Burnside, the new commander of the Union army in Virginia. General Robert E. Lee and the Confederate army prepared to oblige their Northern nemeses.

Although not a Southern victory, the Maryland Campaign had struck a fearful blow against the Union. The battle tallied the war's highest casualty count for a single day of fighting. More importantly, the ghastly struggle in western Maryland for the first time splashed the civil conflict's blood over Northern territory. The campaign shocked many Northerners with the realization that the rebellion's most powerful army could endanger Northern homes. Antietam hinted at an escalating, spreading war no longer confined to Southern soil. After the Confederate incursion into Maryland, pressure mounted in the North to check the Southern threat by winning a decisive victory over Lee.

To accomplish this, on November 7, 1862, Commander-in-Chief Lincoln tapped Burnside to lead the 120,000-man Army of the Potomac. The new army leader mounted a simple, practical campaign to take the war south again. Richmond was his objective; the destruction of Lee's army was his overarching goal. Burnside's force moved quickly toward the Confederate capital using the shortest land route—the main road through the central Virginia city of Fredericksburg. This avenue offered not only an efficiently short trip, but strategic protection for Washington. Logistically, it allowed for supply by water of the Union army on the march. Once before Fredericksburg, however, things unraveled quickly for Burnside and his Federal force.

Logistical problems delayed the army's crossing of the four hundred-foot wide Rappahannock River. The vanguard of Burnside's army arrived at Falmouth across the river from Fredericksburg on November 19. The army could not cross the treacherous water in force without bridges. Confederate troops had destroyed the civilian crossing points. Burnside had allowed for this contingency by ordering the timely delivery of bridge building equipment. Army engineers were adept at transporting and building pontoon bridges, sturdy floating structures supported by heavy wooden boats. However, the Federal pontoon bridges, borne by wagon trains, were dispatched tardily. Once on the road, the heavy trains rolled south slowly, and eventually became mired in the mud of Northern Virginia's rural byways. Finally, the pontoon trains reversed course, returned to a river port in Maryland, and were sent to the Fredericksburg region by water. Although initially planned to arrive at the river ahead of the army, the bridges were delayed until December 11.

This delay allowed Lee to divine Burnside's strategy and the Southern army, 74,000 strong, arrived in full force to block Burnside's march. The Confederates used the time to build a seven-mile defensive line across Burnside's path southwest of the town. Southern engineers and artillery turned the Fredericksburg line into an almost unassailable Confederate stronghold. Undaunted by the Confederate presence however, on December 11 and 12, a determined Northern army spanned the river with six pontoon bridges and crossed some 100,000 men to attack Lee.

Burnside's tactical plan December 13 was as uncomplicated as his overall campaign strategy. Northern assaults concentrated on two points of the Confederate line. A series of piecemeal attacks went forward near

# The Fighting Race at Fredericksburg

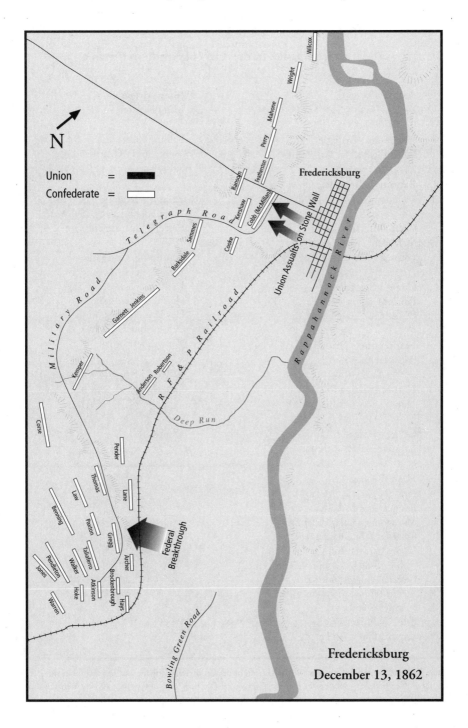

## The Irish Companies in the Army of Northern Virginia.

**Archer's Brigade**
Jackson Guards, 19th Ga.

**Anderson's Brigade**
Emmet Rifles, 1st Ga. Regulars

**Benning's Brigade**
Montgomery Guards, 20th Ga.

**Cobb/McMillan's Brigade**
McMillan Guards, 24th Ga.
Lochrane Guards, Phillips Legion

**Corse's Brigade**
Emmet Guards, 17th Va.
O'Connell Guards, 17th Va.

**Featherston's Brigade**
Jasper Grays, 16th Ms.

**Garnett's Brigade**
Montgomery Guards, 19th Va.

**Gregg's Brigade**
Jackson Guards, 19th Ga.

**Hays' Brigade**
Emerald Guards, 9th La.
Emmet Guards, 1st La.
Montgomery Guards, 1st La.
Orleans Light Guards, 1st La.
Moore Guards, 2nd La.
Irish Brigade (2 Companies), 6th La.
Calhoun Guards, 6th La.
Sarsfield Rangers, 7th La.
Virginia Guards, 7th La.
Irish Volunteers, 7th La.
Virginia Blues, 7th La.

**Jones' Brigade**
Irish Battalion

**Kemper's Brigade**
Montgomery Guards, 1st Va.
Jeff Davis Guards, 11th Va.

**Paxton's Brigade**
Virginia Hibernians, 27th Va.
Emerald Guard, 33rd Va.

**Pendleton's Brigade**
Shepherd Guards, 6th La.
Derbigny Guards, 6th La.
Hewitt's Guards, 6th La.
Hawkins' Guards, 6th La.
Orleans Blues, 6th La.
Tiger Rifles, 14 La.

**Wilcox's Brigade**
Emerald Guards, 8th Al.

**The Battle of Fredericksburg** saw the destruction of the Union Irish Brigade and marked the turning point of Northern Irish support for the war. The Confederate Irish units of the Army of Northern Virginia played an integral part in the Southern defense on the Rappahannock River.

the center of the Confederate defense by brigades from twelve divisions of the Union Second, Third, Fifth and Ninth Corps. The heavy fighting here focused along the main thoroughfare called the Telegraph Road, which at that point was lined by a stone retaining wall. The assaults along this sunken road and its sturdy stone wall, which were defended by James Longstreet's First Corps, were initially meant as a holding action while the main Federal attack went forward about four miles south against a more vulnerable section of the line at Prospect Hill. There, Maj. Gen. William B. Franklin's wing of some 60,000 men sat poised for the attack. As opportunity beckoned, Franklin faltered. Misinterpreting poorly written orders, he erred on the side of caution and committed little more than ten percent of the Federal force to the fight. Brigadier General George G. Meade's division spearheaded the Union thrust at Prospect Hill. The Southern defenders, Stonewall Jackson's Confederate Second Corps, eventually repulsed Meade's attack on the Southern right, even though a faulty disposition of troops allowed an initial Federal breakthrough. The futile frontal assaults on the stone wall, meanwhile, continued for four and one-half hours before nightfall ended the slaughter.

The Battle of Fredericksburg was a skillfully executed Confederate defensive victory—and a terrible Union defeat. The battle stopped in its tracks Burnside's march to the Confederate capital, inflicted terrible losses upon the attacking Federal columns, and crushed the spirit of the Northern army in the Old Dominion. The Union campaign to end the rebellion in the winter of 1862 splashed back across the Rappahannock. Southern losses were about 5,300 casualties, while Burnside's Federals counted an astounding 12,800 killed, wounded, and missing—8,000 of them along a few hundred yards of the line at the stone wall.

The dreadful results of the battle were widely reported. Press reports of the Federal fiasco at Fredericksburg galvanized contemporary public opinion as few other battles had done. The Union effort on the Rappahannock reflected poorly in this glaring spotlight of public scrutiny. The North, with advantages in almost every category of warfare, had suffered another horrendous defeat. In retrospect the forlorn attempts to break the Confederate line at such an imposing and seemingly impregnable point—the Sunken Road—seemed to strike at the heart of Northern anxieties over the war's purpose and the competence of its prosecutors. The Union tragedy at Fredericksburg was amplified in the public's mind by contemporary press accounts of the destruction of the Irish Brigade, which had participated in the disastrous sunken road attacks. But the Irish Brigade's annihilation was not the only Irish experience in the battle.

Southern Irish soldiery was equally conspicuous in the battle. At the brigade, regimental, and company level, Irish soldiers were an integral part of the triumphant Confederate defense on the Rappahannock River. In fact, Southern Irishmen enjoyed a smug victory at the Battle of Fredericksburg. Collared by one of many news-hounds baying about the Union defeat at Fredericksburg, Henry Holbrooks, one of the Confederate Irishmen fighting in the sunken road, remembered the battle with picaresque glee. "If ever in this world I do spile for a fight, it'll be jist sich a fight as we had behind that stone wall under Maries [sic] Heights."[1]

## Feast of Death: John Keely at Prospect Hill

Sixty thousand muskets. . . groaned their ghastly welcome to those
visitors who had come unbidden to this feast of death.

—John Keely

And every field the island through
Will show what Irishmen can do!
A soldier's life's the life for me—
A soldier's death, so Ireland's free!

—A Song for the Irish Militia by Thomas Davis

Although attention focused on the slaughter at the stone wall, the Battle of Fredericksburg opened with a sweeping infantry assault on the Confederate right flank at Prospect Hill. Lieutenant John Keely, a member of the 19th Georgia Regiment, part of Brig. Gen. James J. Archer's Brigade, was caught in the Federal onslaught. Keely was a member of the regiment's all-Irish color company, Company B, the

# The Fighting Race at Fredericksburg

*A Prince Among Men*

Irish-born Captain John Keely served in the 19th Georgia Infantry, but kept his Confederate service a secret from his family until the war was over. "I fought for the cause with my whole heart," he later wrote. Keely's Atlanta dry goods business flourished after the war. His Southern neighbors called the Irish Confederate "a prince among men."

*Atlanta Constitution Magazine, 1931*

Jackson Guards. In his memoirs written to his parents in Ireland, he would dub the Prospect Hill carnage "a feast of death." A veteran of the fighting at Seven Pines, Second Manassas, and Sharpsburg, Keely initially was pleased with the Confederate position on the crest of Prospect Hill. He witnessed the advance of Brig. Gen. George Meade's division across the Richmond, Fredericksburg and Potomac Railroad at the foot of his post: "On they came in three full lines of battle, 100 yards apart, looking magnificently, every man clad precisely like his neighbor; the jaunty looking Yankee cap set rakishly on the side of the head, muskets at a slope arms."[2]

The awe-inspiring martial array quickly turned to life-threatening horror for the Confederate Irishman. Keely remembered that the enemy's line struck "with the precision of a battering ram opening a breach."[3] But the Confederate line did not need opening; a breach already existed on an undefended 500-yard stretch of ground along a marshy area near the edge of Prospect Hill. Confederate commanders left the marsh undefended because they considered the area impenetrable by an organized force. This faulty deployment left Keely's regiment positioned for defeat. The 19th Georgia occupied a small swale to the right of this marsh, its left lazily resting in the air. The 19th Georgia's role was to anchor the left of Archer's brigade. Instead, its vulnerability to attack made the regiment the Achilles' heel for the rest of the brigade.

As the Federals swept against Prospect Hill, attackers quickly found the undefended area, funneled into the marsh, and swung around behind Archer's Confederates. With this swift Union maneuver, Keely's defensive pit on Prospect Hill became a trap. Federals of the 2nd Pennsylvania Reserves poured through the opening in the line and approached the Southerners from the left rear. The 19th Georgia was quickly surrounded when the 7th Pennsylvania Reserves moved across the field to engage them in front. Although the Confederate regiment tried to hold its position, it took little more than ten minutes for Union troops to overwhelm the Georgians.[4] Lieutenant Colonel Andrew J. Hutchins, commanding the regiment, reported: "We held our position some fifteen or twenty minutes, and could have continued to do so, but seeing the enemy advancing in our rear down our lines, and no reinforcements at hand, we gave way—all who had not already been cut off."[5]

The magnificent Federal assault had broken Stonewall Jackson's defensive line at Prospect Hill. As some of Keely's Georgians began to run, Federals shouted and pleaded for the Confederates to surrender.[6] Many of the helpless Southerners did capitulate when offered the chance by 2nd Reserves' Adjutant Evan M. Woodward. Woodward later earned the Congressional Medal of Honor for capturing the 19th Georgia's colors, of which Keely was in charge. It was the only Confederate flag captured at Fredericksburg.[7] The 19th lost not only its colors but suffered 87 killed and wounded and 107 captured.[8] These heavy losses indicate the ferocity and speed of the Union attack. Even so, some of the Georgians shared moments of comity with their foes. Several shook hands with their Federal captors as they passed to the Union rear.

Keely somehow escaped capture and made it to friendly ground unscathed. Curiously, the Irish lieutenant mistakenly believed his regiment had been defeated by a bayonet charge carried off by the famous Union Irish Brigade, commanded by Thomas F. Meagher:

> The enemy found a weak place in our line on our left, and Meagher's brigade of Irish troops charging it with empty muskets and fixed bayonets forced their way through it, and were upon us before succor could reach us.[9]

Meagher's brigade, of course, was part of the attack several miles away against the sunken road position. Keely's Georgians were not defeated by a brigade of Irishmen but by two regiments of Pennsylvanians. It is possible that he thought the Irish Brigade had attacked him because the 2nd Pennsylvania Reserves, commanded by Col. William McCandless, contained several solidly Irish companies raised in Philadelphia.[10] In his memoirs, Keely may have mistaken the Irish troops from Pennsylvania for the famous Irish Brigade. In a recurring phenomenon seen after the war, Keely may have been trying to establish a connection with the Irish who had fought for the Union. The bond of the old sod explains the magnanimity of the Union soldiers pleading for surrender and the affability of the handshaking Southern prisoners as well. Although other Confederate troops on the field were

# CLEAR THE CONFEDERATE WAY!

*Irish Troops on the Flank.* Hays' Louisiana Brigade, with a majority of Irish troops, held the Confederate right at Fredericksburg. If any Confederate brigade deserved to be called the Irish Brigade, it was this Louisiana unit in the Army of Northern Virginia. Here Hays' Brigade lays on its arms at Hamilton's Crossing on the Richmond, Fredericksburg and Potomac Railroad. *Battles and Leaders, 1889*

furious at the Georgians for bolting, Lt. William H. Johnson, acting adjutant of the 19th Georgia, reported: "General Archer said to us next day that he had no complaint to make of our regiment, that we had fought as bravely as men could fight, and that he was well pleased with our actions."[11] Confederate Irish troops stood out among Georgia's brave fighters. Corporal Daniel Rogan of the Irish company garnered mention in the official report of Lieutenant Colonel Hutchins. Rogan was "cool and collected, and joined me in several attempts to rally the men on the hill back of our original line to meet the advancing columns of the enemy," Hutchins wrote.[12]

Caught as they were by Meade's strike, Archer and Hutchins well knew the perilous situation the Southern army suddenly found itself in at Prospect Hill. For the better part of an hour, the Battle of Fredericksburg hung in the balance as Meade stubbornly held his position awaiting Federal reinforcements to exploit his success. But the initial achievement of Meade's division was squandered by the Union high command when no supporting troops were sent to reinforce the Prospect Hill attackers.

While the Pennsylvanians were left to fend for themselves on the Confederate ridge, Southern counterattackers surged forward to seal off the incursion. While Hutchins tried to rally the men of the 19th Georgia, General Archer personally led the 5th Alabama Battalion into the line, shoring up the crumbling 7th Tennessee. Colonel John M. Brockenbrough's Brigade left the security of a rail embankment and selflessly ran to the sound of the contesting guns. Like clockwork, the brigades of Cols. Robert F. Hoke, Edmund N. Atkinson, and Brig. Gen. Harry T. Hays, all part of Brig. Gen. Jubal A. Early's Division, linked up and secured the crest of Prospect Hill. Farther up the line, the hard-pressed Southern brigades of Brig. Gens. James Henry Lane and W. Dorsey Pender were rescued by precision movements engineered by Col. James A. Walker's Brigade and the Georgia Brigade of Brig. Gen. Edward L. Thomas.

In contrast to the halfhearted attack and fumbling maneuver of the Union left, the Confederate army's execution to recover its imperiled position at Prospect Hill was nearly flawless. Stonewall Jackson's Second Corps successfully sealed off the Federal breakthrough, stopped the Union advance, and repulsed its Yankee enemies with a vicious though short-lived counterattack. After this convincing Confederate rebuff, the fighting in that sector subsided. As the battle line stabilized, Keely watched the grassy field catch fire and burn the dead and wounded. He witnessed one wounded Union fellow torn to pieces when his cartridge box exploded from the heat of the flames. "Sickening in the extreme" is how Keely described the scene. "Thousands of such heart rending incidents were occurring under our very eyes, yet we dare not move to their assistance as the plain was being swept by grape and canister," the Irishman remembered.[13]

After the Prospect Hill fighting, what was left of Keely's regiment spent a restless night in the repaired line of battle. "The very atmosphere stunk with gunpowder and created a burning thirst which was hard to satisfy. . .Our dead comrades we had buried in their blankets and the wounded had been carried off to hospital," wrote Keely.[14] Among the wounded was Maj. James H. Neal, the former captain of Company B and Keely's close friend. The Irishman later married Neal's sister. Lieutenant Peter Fenlon, another Keely comrade from Wexford, Ireland, died from complications after the amputation of a shattered leg.

## A Gallant Irishman at Fredericksburg: Robert McMillan's Forgotten Victory

He was a full-blooded Irishman and a brave soldier.

—Joseph White Woods on Colonel Robert McMillan

The English strove with desperate strength,
paused, rallied, staggered, fled—
The green hillside is matted close with dying and with dead.
On Fontenoy, on Fontenoy, like eagles in the sun,
With bloody plumes the Irish stand—the field is fought and won!

—The Irish defense as described in Fontenoy 1745 by Thomas Davis

When the Prospect Hill fighting ended with Confederate victory, for all intents and purposes the Battle of Fredericksburg was over. Nevertheless, one of the most dramatic contests of the war took place closer to Fredericksburg in the 500 yards of the Confederate defensive line along the sunken road. There, Confederate riflemen securely ensconced behind a stone retaining wall smashed the relentless Federal

*The Fighting Race at Fredericksburg.* A. C. Redwood's timeless drawing of Confederates in the sunken road shows the end of the stone wall held by Phillip's Legion Infantry, a Georgia regiment that included the Lochrane Guards, an Irish company from Macon. Irish-born Col. Robert McMillan commanded the Georgia brigade in the Sunken Road, while command of the Phillip's Legion fell to another Irish native, Maj. Joseph Hamilton. *Battles and Leaders, 1889*

assaults of Burnside's holding force. The cool-headed performance of an Irish-born Rebel officer of the line during a critical part of the fighting behind the stone wall has largely been forgotten, but it was his courageous leadership of a Georgia brigade that helped ensure success on that front.

Robert McMillan, an ardent secessionist, had settled in Georgia after emigrating from Antrim, Ireland. At the outbreak of war, he raised the McMillan Guards, a company of infantry from Habersham County. Political machinations soon resulted in his being named regimental commander of the 24th Georgia Infantry. The McMillan Guards, although not wholly Irish, had a distinctly green tint with McMillan and his fighting clan at its head. In the regiment with Colonel McMillan were his sons Robert Emmet, Garnett, and Wofford.

At Fredericksburg, command of the Georgia brigade of Brig. Gen. Thomas R.R. Cobb fell to McMillan when the general was mortally wounded early in the battle. By every account McMillan rose to the occasion, operating the killing machine of the Confederate line with cool efficiency. "Col. McMillan of the 24th Georgia took command of General Cobb's Brigade during the day. He was a full-blooded Irishman and a brave soldier," wrote Joseph White Woods, a fighter in Company D of the 16th Georgia.[15] After the battle, McMillan was lionized in print. A December 30, 1862, *Charleston Daily Courier* article titled "A Gallant Irishman at Fredericksburg" hoped to prove that "Meagher met his match at Fredericksburg in a gallant son of the Emerald Isle, Colonel Robert McMillan, of the Twenty-fourth Georgia. We should like to see McMillan at the head of the lamented Cobb's brigade, pitted against Meagher or Corcoran in an open field. . ."[16] A *Richmond Enquirer* article likewise touted McMillan as the next great Confederate brigadier. "Long may Col. Robt. McMillan live to lead a brigade to such glory. His mature judgment, high order of talents, and quick perception, eminently fit him for it. His own men would die by him to a man."[17]

McMillan's conduct behind the stone wall was documented in what the editors called a private letter:

> Col. McMillan directed the small arms to cease until the enemy should come within musket range. . . The Colonel passed along the lines surveying the movements of the enemy, when, suddenly, at his command,

the brigade rose and sent a volley into the ranks of the foe which carried
ruin in its way. . . For the troops the position chosen was an admirable
one, but on the part of the officer who did his duty there was required the
utmost coolness and courage. This Col. McMillan certainly manifested.[18]

An account from Elijah Henry Sutton of the 24th Georgia's
Company K revealed the calm Irishman collecting a good luck charm
while under fire. "Colonel Robert McMillan was passing up and down
the line all the time exposing himself, but making the boys keep down
behind the wall. At last a spent ball struck him about the neck. He
dodged and placed his hand to his neck. His son, Garnett, saw it and
called out, 'Pa, are you hurt?' 'Hit, but not hurt,' came the answer, and
stooping down he picked up the ball and placed it in his vest pocket."[19]

Although he was not a professional soldier, McMillan was a
hands-on leader who could find compromise with his troops if the need
arose. Sutton captured the unorthodox command style the Cincinnatus
from Georgia exhibited in the heat of battle:

> We had orders not to fire without command. Colonel McMillan cried out:
> "Hold, don't fire yet. Wait till I give the order." And thus we were made to
> hold our fire until they were within fifty yards of our line, when someone
> cried, "Colonel, we must fire, they are coming too close." The Colonel,
> seeing he could not restrain us longer, cried, "Men, if you do shoot, shoot
> low."[20]

This flexibility of command seems to have won McMillan the
respect of the brigade, as evidenced by a letter written presumably by a
Georgia soldier and published in a Charleston paper:

> While he was passing along the line, waving his sword and encouraging
> his men, they seemed to catch the spirit of their leader and redouble their
> efforts, while his own regiment turned in the thickest of the fight and gave
> him three hearty cheers. He possesses the confidence of his troops. They
> love him, and if need be will follow him to the death. In the battle of
> Fredericksburg he won a laurel wreath to which fresh leaves will doubtless
> be added when the tocsin shall again summon him to the field.[21]

The laurel wreath designated the rank of brigadier general. While
McMillan did not achieve promotion, he certainly demonstrated the

physical courage necessary for an effective field commander. The official reports corroborate the heroic leadership of Colonel McMillan. When Brig. Gen. Joseph B. Kershaw arrived at the position well after 1:00 p.m., he reported that "Cobb's brigade, Colonel McMillan commanding, occupied our entire front, and my troops could only get into position by doubling on them."[22] By this time McMillan and the Georgia brigade had held out against the most concerted attacks of the Union Second Corps, and the Irish colonel had directed the repulse of Meagher's Irish Brigade. But the Georgians were not yet ready to retire even with the arrival of reinforcements.

Once his South Carolina brigade was in place, Kershaw noticed the "Coolness of the command." In his report he commented on how well his Palmetto-staters and McMillan's Georgians meshed: "I may mention here that, notwithstanding that their fire was the most rapid and continuous I have ever witnessed, not a man was injured by the fire of his comrades."[23] Kershaw also commended the dutiful conduct of McMillan in his official report. "Colonel McMillan . . . rendered valuable assistance, and when offered the alternative of being relieved Saturday night, gallantly claimed the honor of remaining."[24] The next day, December 14, McMillan still held the sunken road line, and he did not want to give up his hard-fought position on the 15th either. "When it was proposed to relieve Cobb's brigade, these brave fellows begged to be allowed to remain and hold the spot they had done so much to immortalize."[25] Division commander Maj. Gen. Lafayette McLaws also took note of the single-mindedness of the Georgia brigade leader. "Cobb's brigade was relieved by that of General Semmes on the night of that day, against the wishes, however, of Colonel McMillan, commanding . . . who objected to relinquish such an honorable position."[26] McLaws' report acknowledged that McMillan "behaved with distinguished gallantry and coolness."[27] In his report to General Lee, corps commander James Longstreet reiterated this praise for the Irish colonel.

In turn, the Georgia Irishman showered credit upon his officers and men: "I cannot speak in too high terms of the cool bravery of both officers and men, and the promptness and cheerfulness with which they obeyed and executed all orders," McMillan wrote. "The heaps of slain in our front tell best how well they acted their part."[28]

## The Irish Brigade at Fredericksburg: A Confederate Perspective

> Give it to them now, boys! Now's the time! Give it to them!
>
> — The orders of Irish Confederate Col. Robert McMillan, upon seeing
>
> the Irish Brigade at Fredericksburg.

> Wrap the green flag 'round me, boys!
> To die were far more sweet
> With Erin's noble emblem, boys
> To be my winding-sheet.
>
> — *Wrap the Green Flag 'Round Me, Boys!*

Robert McMillan's brave conduct at Fredericksburg—and other Irish Confederate heroics—may have come to represent Irish allegiance in the war if not for a concerted campaign to showcase the equally courageous actions of the Union Irish Brigade. The story of the battle at Fredericksburg is replete with romantic accounts of the Union Irish Brigade's assault at Marye's Heights. Many of the accounts of the brigade's charge, however, were simply the postwar paeans of Irish nationalist writers and poets. Their well-publicized narratives and popular verse usually bear little resemblance to the actual events of the battle or to the true conduct of the Irish Brigade. Indeed the Irish Brigade's popular history is mostly myth.

Initially there was a political purpose behind Irish Brigade mythology. During the war, Northern Irish leaders propounded many of these heroic tales to counter Irish allegiance with the South. After the war, more legends of the Union-Irish alliance were devised and developed by an Irish independence movement still hoping for United States assistance in its national struggle. Historian Joseph Hernon concludes that these Irish Brigade myths were needed immediately after the war by Irish nationalism to mask the movement's momentary lapse away from the American government. "The pro-Southern sympathies of Irish nationalists," writes Hernon in his book *Celts, Catholics and Copperheads*, "... were all but forgotten as the Irish in turn absorbed the myths later generations would make of the war."[29]

Even into this century, Irish nationalists consistently repeated patriotic Civil War stories that exclusively showcased the Union Irish. This propaganda campaign attempted to capture the hearts and minds of the majority of the American people for support for Irish home rule and independence. Over time the politically motivated legends about the Irish Brigade were accepted as historical fact. Through almost religious recitation, the battle tales told about the exploits of the Irish Brigade have become emeralds in the crown of Civil War legend—precious beads in a rosary of Irish-American dogma. The irony is that the gallantry of the Irish Brigade did not need its legendary embellishment. The truth of the Irish Brigade's glory would outshine its calculated myths if the facts of the fight could be found under the patina of legendary lies about the Battle of Fredericksburg. Finding the truth may be an impossible task for historians today, however, because the Irish Brigade legend is so intertwined with factual evidence.

The charge of the Irish Brigade at Fredericksburg was not all glory and green flags. For all of the romanticized attention it has received, the Irish Brigade's role in the Battle of Fredericksburg was notable, but not unusual. Five other Union brigades suffered more casualties than Thomas Meagher's brigade. The Irish Brigade lost 545 killed and wounded. By way of comparison, John C. Caldwell's brigade lost 952; Conrad F. Jackson's, 681; Albert L. Magilton's, 632; John H. Ward's, 629; and Peter H. Allabach's, 562. Ten other Union brigades counted almost as many killed and wounded.[30] Looked at in the context of casualties suffered, the assault of the Irish Brigade was no more heroic than many other Union attacks that day. Even so, numerous press accounts and memoirs of the battle took special note of the Irish attack.

The Irish Brigade legend began almost as soon as the slaughter ceased. William H. Russell, an Irish correspondent for the *London Times*, used historical allusion to describe the brigade's attack. The journalist, perhaps in an effort to ingratiate his countrymen with his British editors, touted the Irish Brigade as an American reincarnation of the European exile forces of old. "Never at Fontenoy, Albuera, or at Waterloo was more undaunted courage displayed by the sons of Erin than during the frantic dashes which they directed against the almost impregnable position of their foe," wrote Russell.[31] This rather tenuous link to the traditions of the European Irish Brigades inaugurated the glorification of the Irish attack in the minds of a world-wide audience.

Russell's pronouncement was followed in the great cities of the North with religious requiems, patriotic pageants, and Bacchanalian banquets, all dedicated to the glory, real and imagined, of the Irish Brigade. The brigade's legend was further reinforced by the fictional accounts of various Irish poets who wrote of the charge after the war. One such fictional source was John C. Hoey's poem, "That Damned Green Flag Again," wherein Confederate Gen. A. P. Hill allegedly noted the Irish assault with special disdain. Hoey's poem may have influenced historian Robert G. Athearn to attribute the report of Hill's retort to Robert E. Lee. But General Hill's division was heavily engaged at Prospect Hill, four miles away from the fighting at Marye's Heights, and thus it is highly unlikely that he commented on the green flag at Fredericksburg.

Another Irish poet, James J. Bourke, reiterated the line in a poem about Thomas Meagher after the general's untimely death. A third reference to the statement was reported by Irish Brigade member and novelist Capt. David P. Conyngham, who attributed the line only to "a rebel colonel" at Malvern Hill.[32] Other versions of the tale allude only to a Confederate aide-de-camp who allegedly made the remark to his brigadier.[33] Yet another account claims Thomas F. Meagher himself concocted the story in a recruiting speech after the Peninsula Campaign.[34] The most egregiously ridiculous attribution is to Stonewall Jackson, who is alleged to have lapsed into unlikely and uncharacteristic profanity in reaction to the green flag. A seventh source to report a rebel cursing the green flag was penned in the 1870s by Pvt. William McCarter of the Irish Brigade's 116th Pennsylvania Infantry. By then, McCarter must have heard the tale repeated a hundred times. His version is part of a reported dialogue between a captured Confederate soldier of the 3rd South Carolina Infantry and Irish Brigade members at Charles town, West Virginia. This rebel's remark alluded to the flag's appearance with the Irish Brigade at Sharpsburg's Bloody Lane fight. McCarter's version is suspect since the 3rd South Carolina was not on the same part of the field as the Irish Brigade at Sharpsburg.[35] The remark, or a similar one, very likely could have been made by a Confederate soldier, but there are so many variations on this tale's theme that the story no longer rings true. And it is logical to observe that the Confederate soldier who might have spoken the fateful words hazarded insulting his own compatriots; certainly there were many "damned green flags" in the Confederate army as well.

John Boyle O'Reilly, in his poem, "At Fredericksburg—Dec. 13, 1862," romanticized the role of the Irish on both sides of the attack. He incorrectly noted the presence of a Confederate Irish Brigade on Marye's Heights and its horror at having to shoot fellow Irishmen in the Union army. Medal of Honor winner St. Clair A. Mulholland probably started this benign and kindly embellishment. He wrote in his memoirs, without direct attribution, that the Confederate Irishmen behind the wall exclaimed, "Oh, God, what a pity! Here come Meagher's fellows!" However, no authentic reports have come to light to corroborate any Irish Confederate remorse at the stone wall. More authentic—but no less fictional—is Joseph I. C. Clarke's "The Fighting Race," which remembered the grim reality of the battle and its gory effect on the Irish ranks:

> Up Marye's Heights, and my old canteen
> Stopped a rebel ball on its way.
> There were blossoms of blood on our sprigs of green,
> Kelly and Burke and Shea—[36]

Perhaps the most entertaining example of Irish nationalist battle embellishment was the fanciful account of the rescue and return of a green flag at Fredericksburg. The flag was allegedly brought to General Meagher by a Confederate Irishmen, ostensibly a Fenian. The story was first published in the March 28, 1914, *Freeman's Journal*, a nationalist newspaper.[37] As the story goes, a certain Michael Sullivan of the "Georgia Irish Brigade" noted the fall of the Irish flag during the battle.

## The Fighting Race at Fredericksburg

Later that night Sullivan retrieved the flag under cover of darkness and wrapped it around his body under his shirt. This particular detail must certainly have alluded to the chorus of a popular Irish nationalist folk song of the early twentieth century titled "Wrap the Green Flag 'Round Me, Boys!" The Southern Irishman then swam across the Rappahannock River, at which time he was wounded in the leg by Confederate sentries who supposed him to be a deserter. The Georgian found the Irish Brigade camp and presented the symbol of aspiring Irish nationhood to Meagher, who had the soldier's wound dressed and offered him his freedom on Union soil. In perhaps the only believable part of the story, the Confederate was true to his cause and asked to return to his own lines, which Meagher agreed to allow.

This tale was a boldly amusing attempt to romanticize the role of the Irish nationalist in the Civil War, but none of the narrative even remotely squares with reality. The compiled Confederate Army roster lists five possible Michael Sullivans in Georgia regiments—the 1st Georgia Local Defense Troops (Augusta), 1st Georgia (Olmstead's) Infantry, the 5th Georgia, the 47th and the 63rd Georgia. None of these outfits were part of the Army of Northern Virginia at Fredericksburg.[38] Furthermore, there was no "Georgia Irish Brigade," although Thomas Cobb's Brigade boasted the Irish leadership of Col. Robert McMillan and included two companies of Irish troops in Phillips Legion and the 24th Georgia Regiment. It is fully evident that the tale's author had no concept of the post-battle situation at Fredericksburg and was not aware of the broad expanse of the field. The alleged Sullivan would have had to elude thousands of Union soldiers in front of the town and most certainly would not have found Confederate pickets on the waterfront. He would have had quite a bracing swim across the 400-foot, swiftly flowing river in subfreezing weather. Did the soldier's leg wound take his mind off the Herculean task at hand and warm his weary bones? Likewise, finding Meagher's command would not have been a simple matter in the dark of the night and with the chaos of the aftermath of the battle. Once ready to return, the fictional Sullivan faced a two-mile hike and swim back to Confederate lines, all this after four and one-half hours of heavy fighting in the afternoon. The nearly impossible logistics of the mission make the tale patently absurd, and yet it has been repeatedly related in histories of the Irish Brigade as fact.

Another stark problem gets in the way of this story: although there could have been other green company flags, there was only one recognizable green flag at Fredericksburg. This banner was the regimental banner of the 28th Massachusetts Infantry—and it was not captured. A guidon flag of the 69th New York was reported captured in front of the stone wall, but there are no details as to its color in the official records.[39] Yet another question looms. Given most evidence that Confederate Irishmen saw their Northern countrymen as fighting alongside what John Dooley compared to "the envenomed Puritan," why would the loyal Confederate Sullivan return the sacred green flag to those misguided souls in the Union Irish Brigade? It is painfully obvious that the story, like many Irish tales of the war, was not based in fact, but was composed well after the war by a political writer with little knowledge of the people, terrain or events at Fredericksburg. In a peculiar twist of irony, the story may have been authored by Confederate Irishman John D. Keiley Jr., who edited the *Freeman's Journal* after the war!

Authentic eyewitness Confederate accounts of the battle were just as likely to question the political motivations of Union Irish troops as they were to cheer the courage of the brigade in its forlorn hope against the stone wall. Confederate Henry H. Baker, a soldier in the Washington Artillery, which was posted atop Marye's Heights, remembered the attack:

> With them comes [Thomas] Meagher's Brigade, holding aloft the green flag of Ireland, and upon its folds is gleaming the golden harp of the Emerald Isle. . . The traditions of their country should have warned them to take the side of the oppressed. If they had done this they would not have suffered the humiliation of defeat and have had their cherished standard trailing in the dust.[40]

One Confederate argument against the existence of the Irish Brigade in the Union army was dear to the hearts of the Irish people. John Edward Dooley wrote of the Irish Brigade at Fredericksburg:

## The Fighting Race at Fredericksburg

The field on which they fell was at the foot of Marye's hill, and was the property of Col. [Morton] Marye, an officer in our brigade. In 1848 or '49 when famine was inflicting such distress in Ireland, the whole crop of corn raised upon this identical field had been sent in contribution for the relief of that starving and oppressed people. That people [the Irish Brigade], invigorated and under infamous leadership, have now done far more than the envenomed puritan to rob us of our property, devastate our lands, starve the pleading orphan and the broken hearted widow, trample in the dust every principle of right, and crush out completely our identity as a free people.[41]

Another Confederate reaction was even more vitriolic than Dooley's anti-Yankee screed. J. J. McDaniel of the 7th South Carolina believed the Irish Brigade got its bravery from the bottle. He painted a grotesque picture of the Irishmen emboldened by liquor, prodded by Meagher's charisma, and baited by Yankee flattery:

Meagher's Irish Brigade passed through the city going into the fight. They were greatly applauded and cheered as they went by the masses of skulking Yankees along the streets, saying, "Here goes the rebel batteries, in ten minutes the Irish Brigade will have them hills." Meagher made them a fiery war speech, at which they lustily huzzaed, telling them that all who had tried had failed, but he knew they could take them. The Irish, half drunk with liquor, flattered by the cowardly Yankees, and elated by the harangue of their leader, no doubt thought as they entered the plain, that they would see the rebels running. It must be said in credit of their valor, or liquor possibly, that a few of them came nearer than any others to our batteries, some lay within fifty yards of our lines at the foot of the hill. The citizens [of Fredericksburg] say that about an hour after they passed through with such boastful threats, about eighty of them came running back, and the pontoon bridges were cut to stop them at the river. Out of the whole brigade only about 200 escaped unhurt. Their liquor had led them into the "slaughter pen." May theirs be the fate of all the beastly, drunken, thievish foreigners who pollute our Southern soil in company with their employers, the Yankees.[42]

In a February 25, 1863, reprint of a *Richmond Enquirer* editorial on the battle, an Irish Confederate partisan noted simply that the "Irish Brigade shared the same fate that day of their Federal comrades; and their green flag, with its 'laurels,' trailed in the dust." And, "Down went standards and standard-bearers, harps, sunbursts and all, before the deadly storm of Lee's artillery."[43]

Private William T. Shumate, a 34-year-old Greenville, South Carolina, merchant, expressed a resigned sadness over the hopeless Hibernian assault. Shumate, a South Carolinian of Irish extraction, was a soldier in the Butler Guards of the 2nd South Carolina. The South Carolinians reinforced the Phillips Legion in the Sunken Road after the Irish attack had failed. He witnessed first hand the horrible aftermath of the Irish defeat. He remembered, "The last charge was made . . . o'er the bloody field by Meagher's celebrated Irish Brigade which was almost destroyed. The gallant fellows deserved a better fate."[44]

Not all Confederate accounts were negative. One Confederate general who supposedly did not curse the green flag was division commander George E. Pickett. He wrote to his sweetheart the day after the battle with special praise for the brigade. "Your soldier's heart almost stood still as he watched those sons of Erin fearlessly rush to their death. The brilliant assault on Marye's Heights of their Irish Brigade was beyond description . . . cheer after cheer at their fearlessness went up all along our lines."[45] Pickett's cheering division included Irish companies in James Kemper's, Richard Garnett's and Montgomery Corse's brigades. Specific accounts of Pickett's Irishmen taking note of the Irish Brigade or its distinctive green flag, however, have not been found. It is also not clear how Pickett, stationed near the center of a seven-mile front, was in a position to see the Irish attack to his left. The Lochrane Guards (the Irish company in Phillips Legion) was much closer to the fighting, yet not a single account from a member of the company mentions anyone recognizing or cheering the Irish flag. This company was directly in the path of the assaults on the stone wall and may have been substantially responsible for the destruction of the Irish Brigade. Company E of the Phillips Legion Infantry was commanded by another Irishman, Capt. Joseph Hamilton, a native of County Tyrone, Ireland. The Legion lost so many field officers that day that Hamilton took command of the regiment and was promoted to major as a result of the battle. Although a literate man and a schoolteacher after the war, Hamilton apparently did not leave any accounts of the fighting or of the charge of the brigade of men from his native land.

## The Fighting Race at Fredericksburg

Perhaps the most important account of the Irish Brigade at Fredericksburg was the reaction of the Confederate Irishman who stood between the attackers and victory—Col. Robert McMillan. In contradiction of Mulholland's lachrymose report of the fighting, there was not the slightest hint of remorse from the Irish commander. McMillan acknowledged the "large dark green flag . . . floating over the heavy reinforcement," according to a soldier's account published in the *Athens Southern Watchman*.[46] The sight of the flag did not cause the Irish colonel to flinch from his Confederate duty. "That's Meagher's Brigade," McMillan is said to have cried, and "instantly drawing his sword, his countenance lighted up, as his friends have often seen him in the political arena, and dashing along the line among men, amid him a shower of balls, and waving his sword around his head, shouted—'Give it to them now, boys! Now's the time! Give it to them!' And never did men better respond to a call."[47]

The portrait of the dutiful Confederate Irish officer of the line contrasts sharply with the picture of McMillan's celebrated Union counterpart, General Meagher. In fact, Meagher did not even take part in the assault of the Union Irish Brigade on Marye's Heights.[48] It was a murderous day for many other Union brigade leaders. In the battle where the Irish Brigade was all but destroyed, nine other Union brigade commanders were killed, wounded, or injured. Brigadier Generals Conrad F. Jackson and George D. Bayard were killed. The wounded and injured men of Meagher's rank or level of command included Brig. Gens. John C. Caldwell, Nathan Kimball, A. Sanders Piatt, John Gibbon, Francis L. Vinton, and Cols. John W. Andrews and William Sinclair. Brigadier Generals Thomas R.R. Cobb and Maxcy Gregg were lost to the Confederacy. In addition, three of Meagher's five regimental commanders were wounded.[49] But as the Irish Brigade moved onto the open field to make its immortal charge, Meagher returned to town to retrieve his horse.[50] The Irish general did not expose himself to enemy fire at Fredericksburg. In his memoir, Confederate artillery commander E. Porter Alexander noted the gallantry of the soldiers of the Irish Brigade, as well as Meagher's absence:

# CLEAR THE CONFEDERATE WAY!

A popular impression has seemed to prevail that the Irish Brigade of Thomas Francis Meagher exceeded all others in its dash & gallantry. But while it may be true that his men went as far as the farthest, Gen. Meagher's official report of the battle shows that personally he was not in the charge, but that as it began he "being lame" started back to town to get his horse & he was soon joined in town by the remnants of his brigade whom he led back to the river bank.[51]

A Yankee officer, Thomas Francis Galwey, an Irish captain in the Hibernian Guard of the 8th Ohio Infantry, also loosed an accusatory arrow at the leader of the Irish Brigade. Writing in 1889, Galwey betrayed revulsion at the slaughter of the Irish unit and anger at the absence of competent brigade leadership on the front line. Galwey's unit was at the front at Marye's Heights where the Irish captain "looked off to the left and front, and there . . . lay a line of men in blue overcoats. Was it the Irish Brigade? No, it was the Irish dead. Their brigade had been withdrawn at last by whatever officer was then in command of it."[52] Francis Walker, in his Second Corps history, called Meagher's separation from his command "strange and unaccountable."[53]

Meagher's official report of the incident is an exercise in damage control. Meagher complicated matters when he took the remnants of his brigade from the field and retreated across the river without being granted permission to do so by his division commander, Winfield Scott Hancock. There is evidence that Meagher's precipitous retreat abandoned the bravest part of his command at the front.[54] While Meagher reported he was only able to muster 280 of his 1,200 men the next day, it was not because so many had perished in the charge as his report implies. In fact, portions of his regiments stayed on the front line—either pinned down by Confederate fire or unwilling to give up hard-won ground. These men did not report to Meagher's muster because he had left them stranded on the field. Perhaps concerned about how Hancock might characterize his conduct in the battle, Meagher went over the division commander's head. Seeking out Fifth Corps leader Daniel Butterfield, Left Grand Division commander Edwin V. Sumner, and even Burnside, Meagher answered questions about his role in the attack seemingly before any had been asked. In retrospect,

Meagher's report not only greatly overstated his casualties, but was hysterical in tone.[55]

Meagher's performance at Fredericksburg, more than strange and unaccountable, bordered on dereliction of duty. And the episode was not unique in its ignominy. A critical analysis of the Irish general's overall war service reveals a deep divide between Meagher's true conduct in battle and the politicized panegyrics often heaped upon his memory. The embellishment of Meagher's battle record presents a central example of the mythologization of the Irish Brigade. In his varied career, Meagher proved himself a committed Irish nationalist, a brilliant orator, and an unparalleled inspiration to the Irish exiles in America. His record as a field commander in the Union army was, by objective measures, undistinguished. Evidence of this can be found in the *Official Records*, often in Meagher's own unabashed words.

At First Manassas, as acting major of the 69th New York, Meagher was carried from the field when his horse was shot from under him. In that battle, the regiment's Col. Michael Corcoran was captured and Lt. Col. James Hagerty was killed. The "Fighting 69th" retreated with the rest of the Yankee army at Manassas. Meagher's opportunity to shine in battle was ended when his horse was felled. His performance in stepping into the leadership breach was less than spectacular. Captain James Kelly gave the regiment's report as acting colonel.[56]

At the Battle of Seven Pines or Fair Oaks in the spring of 1862, Meagher headed the brigade of Irishmen he recruited in Northern cities. At that battle, the 69th's Col. Robert Nugent and Lt. Col. Patrick Kelly of the 88th New York were commended for their actions. Meagher, though, was not at the front. His report was long on platitudes and short on details. "For further particulars, of which I cannot pretend to be personally cognizant, I refer you with pleasure to the reports of the officers commanding the two regiments of my brigade engaged," he wrote.[57] In the Seven Days' Battles that followed a few weeks later, artillery officer Lt. Rufus King Jr. reported that Meagher was with his battery "exposed to the hottest fire" at White Oak Swamp—but not for long. "He kindly volunteered to ride to Gen. Richardson and have ammunition sent to me as soon as possible. . ." It seems odd that a brigade commander, in the heat of battle, would offer to ride back to divisional headquarters for ammunition instead of sending an aide. The ammunition never arrived.[58]

Meagher's own Peninsula Campaign report narrative was interrupted by a puzzling and embarrassing circumstance. The brigadier wrote: "Being temporarily placed under arrest until 8 o'clock the following day, I respectfully refer the general commanding the division to the report of Col. Nugent," who was commanding the brigade at Savage's Station. No mention is made of the cause of the general's arrest, but whatever the reason, the ignominy of his absence from his command is indictment enough.[59] At Malvern Hill, the last of the Seven Days' Battles, Meagher reported the reason he went to headquarters for ammunition for Colonel Nugent's regiment was that he had no aides present—a reprise of Meagher's well-timed exit to fetch ammunition for Lieutenant King's artillery.[60]

Meagher also drew adverse reports at Chancellorsville in early May 1863. Colonel Edward E. Cross of the 5th New Hampshire reportedly saw the Irish general flee during an artillery barrage on the afternoon of May 6. "Brig. Gen. T. F. Meagher lay among the enlisted men of Company G of my regiment—evidently badly scared. As soon as the firing ceased, he ran as fast as possible to the left and rear where he had a private fortification constructed."[61] Given New England's nativist reputation, the New Hampshire Yankee may not be the best source for a report on Irish behavior. Still, given Meagher's conduct on several other fields Cross's report has a certain veracity about it. The general's suspicious conduct at Sharpsburg has already been chronicled, as has his excuse for returning to town as the Irish Brigade gallantly advanced across the plain toward Marye's Heights.

Meagher's charismatic leadership was key to the Irish Brigade legend. His career in the American army, though, was as tragic as the brigade's destruction at Fredericksburg. Meagher's true conduct in battle after battle was whitewashed by most of his contemporaries. In the face of so much evidence of Meagher's failure in battle, a loyal segment of the Irish community—even the uncharacteristically reticent John Mitchel—closed ranks around the Irish celebrity to protect his reputation. The Irish Brigade's shining achievement came not in its attack at Fredericksburg or Antietam but in its defense of Meagher's good name. There is an understandable explanation for this. No true Irish patriot wanted Meagher to give his life in the American war when Ireland still needed his political leadership for an anticipated rebellion in Ireland. Therefore Meagher was allowed to avoid the hottest fire of battle. Likewise, no one was willing to ruin the reputation of one of the country's most celebrated Irish nationalists by pointing to his pattern of questionable battlefield behavior. Meagher's continuance as a senior field commander, however, unnecessarily endangered the lives of his men. Their survival also was important to Ireland's future. It was perhaps Meagher's personal confrontation with this reality that seems to have destroyed his will to fight—in America or for Ireland.

Meagher's commitment to the struggles in America and Ireland waned after Fredericksburg. He resigned from the army in the spring of 1863, returned to staff posts in the Western Theater in 1864, and in 1865 accepted a political appointment as secretary of the Montana territory. Meagher declared his intention to become a United States citizen in 1852 and took an American wife, Elizabeth Townsend, four years later. Both steps distanced him from Ireland and from its independence movement. Meagher never returned to Ireland, and there is "little evidence that he was ever actively engaged in Fenian military affairs."[62] This is an important point. The Fenian movement, also known as the Irish Republican Brotherhood, was founded in Dublin in 1858. The precursor of the Irish Republican Army, it was heavily financed by Irish-Americans and openly advocated the violent overthrow of British rule in Ireland. The group provided the only potential military threat to the Crown. Indeed, several thousand American Fenians attempted to invade Canada in 1866, and about 150 Union and Confederate Irish veterans were part of a Fenian rising in Counties Dublin, Limerick and Cork in 1867. These Irish rebellions were utter failures, chiefly because they were led by jackadandies with no military training. Meagher's celebrity and military experience could have been invaluable in recruiting and training a larger Irish force, and in planning and leading an Irish rebel insurgency. His lack of interest in the Fenian movement may confirm that his fervor for the Irish struggle was dampened by his disappointing American war experience. On July 1, 1867, Meagher fell overboard in the Missouri River and drowned. His body was never recovered.

## The Wild Geese in Gray:
## The Confederacy and the Irish Brigade's Glorious History

The Irish green shall again be seen
As our Irish fathers bore it,
A burning wind from the south behind,
And the Yankee route before it!

—Song for the Irish Brigade (Confederate)

Farewell, Patrick Sarsfield, wherever you may roam,
You crossed the seas to France and left empty camps at home.
To plead our cause before many a foreign throne
Though you left ourselves and poor Ireland overthrown.

—Anonymous c. 1690

In America, the Union Irish Brigade's comparison to European Irish Brigades of old bolstered the Yankee unit's legendary status. Civil War historians have used the romantic title almost exclusively to describe Meagher's Union unit. The Union held no monopoly on the use of the title. Confederate units also dubbed themselves the Irish Brigade. In fact, the good name of the Irish Brigade cannot be exclusively claimed by either Union or Confederate partisans. As a title and a concept, the Irish Brigade now belongs to the world, but it is rooted in European history and its continental wars. The Irish Brigade moniker always has carried with it a magical, talismanic quality. It is part of a mythology centered on the sometimes glorious, but oftentimes vainglorious, Irish military tradition.[63]

The Irish Brigade mystique began well before the Civil War in military service for France. Its origins trace back to the early seventeenth century. In 1607, recalcitrant Irish nobles and their extended clans in

## The Fighting Race at Fredericksburg

*An Irish J.E.B. Stuart*

Patrick Sarsfield, a 17th-century Irish Catholic cavalry general, has been called the J.E.B. Stuart of the Irish Jacobites. One Louisiana Irish Confederate unit called itself the Sarsfield Rangers.

*Author*

Ulster fled the country after years of warfare with the English crown. Boasting bold Irish names like O'Neill, O'Donnell, Maguire and MacMahon, they offered their military services to France because the Catholic continental power was the avowed enemy of their British nemesis. This "Flight of the Earls" led to the first Irish military presence on the continent. But the warrior earls were merely an Irish cadre. In 1691, after the Treaty of Limerick ended the Irish Jacobite War, wholesale numbers of Irish Catholic soldiers and officers left Ireland for French soil. These so-called "wild geese" formed the first Irish Brigades in the French army. These permanent Irish units were allied with the French for over 100 years.

The descendants of these first Irish military exiles were prominent in European affairs by the mid-nineteenth century. General Leopoldo O'Donnell was prime minister of Spain during the Civil War, and Bernardo O'Higgins fought against Spain in the liberation of Chile. Eduard Graf von Taafe became prime minister of Austria, and Marie Edme Patrice Maurice MacMahon, known as the Comte de MacMahon as well as the Duc de Magenta in France, became president of the Third Republic and a Marshal of France. The Irish Brigades in Europe catapulted their leaders to continental and world prominence.

## CLEAR THE CONFEDERATE WAY!

It is thus no surprise that American Irish leaders sought to reignite the Irish Brigade legend here. Thomas F. Meagher harked back to the legend early in the war. "Think of Ireland and Fontenoy!" was the battle cry Meagher used to exhort the 69th New York Regiment at First Manassas.[64] This alluded to the charge of a 5,000-man Irish Brigade of the French army during the War of Austrian Succession. The French victory at Fontenoy, near Tournai, Belgium, on May 11, 1745, was credited by Irish accounts to the presence of the French Irish Brigade on the field that day. The American Irish Brigade Meagher subsequently raised for the Union made him the most prominent Irish leader of the war.

Apart from the political power the Irish Brigades gave their leaders, a look at the history of these European units gives some perspective on the proud symbol the Irish Brigades became in the Civil War. The European Irish Brigades, at least initially, were composed of exiles who hoped to return to Ireland to win its independence. Eventually these units became standing forces of professional soldiery. Irish soldiers were highly prized and Irish units often garnered battlefield accolades on the continent. This kind of professional military service boasted a long history in Ireland. Even before the Flight of the Earls and the Wild Geese, foreign military service had been an important facet of Irish tradition from medieval times. Appearing in the thirteenth century, the first professional Irish troops were called in Irish Gaelic kerne, carousing soldiers of fortune who roamed the Irish countryside fighting for the highest-bidding lord or chieftain.

In the same period, foreign (usually Norse-Scottish) mercenaries were hired by Irish leaders as professional soldiery. These alien mercenaries, well-equipped and drilled, were called gallowglass. They were the Gaelic world's answer to invading Norman knights. These mercenaries were often given land in Ireland as payment for war service, and settled as hereditary clans in allegiance with Irish lords. Professional native Irish mercenaries, called bonnaughts, were later established to bolster clan militias in Ireland. By the seventeenth century, it was common to see Irishmen fighting for other European armies in distinctively Irish units as well as for the British Crown. Periodically Irish insurgent forces also challenged British troops at home.[65] In the nineteenth century Irishmen served in South America, Europe, and South Africa as well as in the Civil War. In the 1860s, an Irish Brigade, really only a 1,000-man force called the Battalion of St. Patrick, served at the pleasure of the Pope, and another Irish Brigade fought for France in a war with Germany. With this ancient and interesting past, is it any wonder that American Irish troops claimed the Irish Brigade title in the Civil War?

Still, service in these historical Irish brigades was not always glorious. In foreign service Irish soldiers often were sacrificed as assault or shock troops to soften up the enemy and conserve highly trained Regular forces. And an Irish unit did not necessarily have to be made up wholly of Irish soldiers. Napoleon's Irish Legion, as an example, filled its ranks primarily with German and Polish prisoners of war.[66] In Europe, the size of a unit had little to do with the use of the brigade title. Indeed throughout history some Irish brigades "had a strength which was little more than that of a company."[67] This seems to indicate that recruitment of Irish soldiers was not always a simple task. The Irish Brigade cachet alone often did not induce men to enlist. The previously mentioned Papal Irish Brigade, for instance, had planned to recruit 10,000 Hibernians, but even the Pope could raise only a fraction of that number.[68] The most pitiful example of a unit calling itself an Irish Brigade was 55 Irish prisoners of war held by the Germans in World War I. Of thousands of Irish war prisoners, only this handful agreed to renounce British allegiance to join an Irish force organized by Sir Roger Casement. They ostensibly were to be used to wrest Ireland from Great Britain with German and Irish-American help.[69] At the same time more than 130,000 Irishmen were fighting against the Germans in the British army.[70]

It was sometimes confusing during the Civil War, with both sides trying to capitalize on the distinction inherent in the "Irish Brigade" title. Numerous Irish units, from company to brigade level, called themselves the Irish Brigade. Thomas Meagher's brigade of New Yorkers, Bay Staters and Pennsylvanians is only the best known example. Brigadier General James Adelbert Mulligan's 23rd Illinois Regiment also claimed the venerable name in the Union camp. In the Confederate armies, a unit in the 6th Louisiana Regiment used the "Irish Brigade" title, as did the

1st Louisiana Cavalry. An unspecified unit under the Army of Tennessee's Irish General, Patrick Cleburne, carried the Irish Brigade banner in the fighting at Missionary Ridge during the 1863 Chattanooga Campaign.[71] True, none of these Confederate units were technically brigades, but the Union Irish Brigade itself did not exist as a fully manned brigade of Irish troops for long. It was later bolstered by the addition of German and native-born troops.[72] It is clear there were enough Irish soldiers in the South to form a fully manned Confederate Irish Brigade. Indeed the estimated 40,000 Irishmen who served in Confederate armies would have constituted a force that rivaled the Army of Tennessee, the Confederacy's principal army in the west.[73]

Why was there no true Irish Brigade in the Southern army? Part of the answer lies in the fact that there were no large concentrations of Irishmen in any one Southern city—a single place that could provide the necessary numbers of troops. Another explanation lies in how the Confederate army was organized. A Confederate Irish Brigade could have been formed with soldiers from multiple states, as was the Union's Irish Brigade. However, the Southern army tended to organize its brigades by state, and no single Southern state contained a large enough Irish population to field a true brigade. Of the thirty-nine brigades of the Army of Northern Virginia at Fredericksburg, for instance, only seven of them intermixed regiments from different states. By contrast, forty-one of the fifty-one brigades in the Army of the Potomac reached full strength by mixing regiments from multiple states.[74]

Interestingly, both governments seemed to have had an aversion to fielding ethnically segregated units. The Union Irish Brigade might never have been formed except for political considerations. Meagher's proposal to form an Irish brigade was initially denied by Gen. George McClellan. Meagher had enthusiastically written to Secretary of War Simon Cameron in September 1861, with a promise to raise a 5,000-man brigade "ready to march in 30 days." Army headquarters, however, initially did not approve of a single command of Irishmen. "The sentiment of Union that has brought them [Meagher's Irish recruits] into rank shoulder to shoulder with the natives of this and other countries is inconsistent with the idea of army organization on the basis of distinct nationalities." A unit based on nationality was unwise and inexpedient, McClellan wrote.[75]

On the face of it, McClellan's objection to ethnic segregation in the army was a stroke of typical American egalitarianism. Group politics, however, won out over the inherent fraternity of the military. Political pressure was brought to bear on army headquarters and the decision was reversed. Thereafter, there is evidence of political influence promoting ethnic recruiting. In June 1863, President Lincoln was "very glad" to allow Meagher to raise 3,000 Irish troops as long as it was with the consent of New York Governor Truman Seymour.[76]

In contrast to Lincoln's decision to raise segregated Irish units (and later separate black units), Southern Irish and Irish-American soldiers generally were assimilated into and interspersed throughout the Confederate armies. In the Southern system, the distinguishably Irish units—"green flag" Irish troops—were limited to the company and regimental level. There is evidence that Southern Irish soldiers, already well on their way to American assimilation, were more concerned with state and local allegiances than with trying to recapture the lost glories of European exile forces.

This was not always the case. The Irish Brigade mystique still cast a spell over some Hibernian hearts in the South. An anonymous writer who signed his missive "Shamrock" wrote to the *Augusta Daily Constitutionalist* in 1862 complaining that the Irish community in that city had not gotten "credit" for the number of Irish recruits it had provided the army. This situation had occurred because the city's Irishmen had joined local native companies and had not formed more conspicuous all-Irish "green flag" units. "Shamrock" exhorted Irish readers in Augusta to join that city's Irish company. "Shall we wait to be conscripted and sent among strangers, or shall we enroll ourselves with the Banner Company of the 5th Georgia—the Irish Volunteers?"[77] The fact that Augusta's Irish enrolled in native units is evidence that the Georgia community accepted immigrants as committed Southerners, and not a group of mistrusted and "ghettoized" outsiders. Even so, some Irishmen in the South still identified with the Irish Brigades of old as evidenced by the "Song for the Irish Brigade" published in a New Orleans paper in 1861:

CLEAR THE CONFEDERATE WAY!

The Irish green shall again be seen
As our Irish fathers bore it,
A burning wind from the south behind,
And the Yankee route before it!
O'Neill's red hand shall purge the land—
Rain fire on men and cattle,
Till the Lincoln snakes in their cold lakes
Plunge from the blaze of battle! [78]

## Of Patriots and Gallowglass:
## Southern Irish Soldiers and the Mercenary Myth

From Britain Isle, from sunny France,
From Erin dear they came;
And fiercely fought the North's advance,
And for our Southern fame.

— Lt. Col. Henry Monier, 10th Louisiana Infantry

Look out for hirelings! King George of England,
Search every kingdom where breathes a slave. . .

— from Boolavogue

While the Americans who used the Irish Brigade name did so to summon up romantic historical allusions, in their concept and organization the Irish Brigades of old and the Irish Brigades of the Civil War shared few similarities. The European Irish Brigades isolated and segregated Irish exiles into foreign service. America's Irish units, especially in the South, were attempts to assimilate new immigrants into American service and society. If the European Irish Brigades can be described as mercenary forces, then the American and European brigades diverge even more in their purposes. It is a long-standing myth that Irish or even German immigrants were mercenary soldiers in the Civil War. Attempts to label foreign-born soldiers as mercenaries misunderstood the dynamics of the wholesale and permanent immigration of Irish and Germans to America in the period. Almost every Irishman in Union and Confederate service was an American patriot—not an alien mercenary. In this respect, it mattered little what side these immigrants took in the war. Statistically the numbers of Irish fighting for each side hardly differed anyway. As a percentage of their populations the Irish, North and South, provided an almost equal share of men for their respective causes.

America at the time of the war had a large pool of recent immigrants, many thousands of whom chose service in the armies as entry level employment. The exiled children of Ireland were the largest group of these immigrants. In the North, nativism ranted against these newcomers, but their service was accepted as long as it was offered. It was often Southern leaders and writers who disingenuously took advantage of the immigrant rush to the ranks for propaganda purposes. Indeed, there seems to have been a concerted effort to paint the foreigners in the Northern armies as less than honorable combatants. Curiously, the same propagandists took no such notice of the substantial numbers of foreigners in the Confederate ranks. The term "mercenary," with all its derogatory implications, often was applied to any Northern soldier of foreign birth. As employed, the expression was an allusion to the unpopular use of Hessian troops by George III during the American Revolution. Indeed these ideas about brutal Hessian mercenaries may have sprung from Irish experience as much as from that of the Revolution. King George and Ireland's Viceroy Lord Cornwallis, the same soldier vanquished at Yorktown in 1781, also used Hessians to brutally put down the Irish Rebellion of 1798.[79]

Historians have postulated that some Southerners propounded a postwar mercenary propaganda campaign to account for the South's defeat. There is much evidence, however, that anti-mercenary feelings in the South were widespread even early in the war. Even Southern immigrants jumped on the anti-mercenary bandwagon. Anthony M. Keiley, writing in 1865, said the Yankee nation had twenty million men under arms with "recruits beaten up from England, Ireland, Scotland, France, Germany, Switzerland, Asia and Africa."[80]

Foreigners in the Union army were not mercenary soldiers in the classic, disreputable sense, and they certainly were not Hessian hirelings—even if many of them were of German extraction. Keiley was like many Southern partisans who exaggerated the numbers of Irish and other foreigners in the Union army without acknowledging that the Confederate army included significant numbers of foreign born fighters as well. A soldier in the 1st Georgia Regulars, William H. Andrews, lamented at Fredericksburg that "The Confederates are now fighting the world, Burnside having German, Irish, and Italian brigades. . .Every foreigner who puts his foot on American soil joins the Northern Army, for the sake of the bounty paid, if anything else."[81] Andrews failed to recognize that his own regiment had significant numbers of Irish soldiers in its ranks, including the 1st Georgia's Emmet Rifles. Even so, on a grand scale, Confederate propaganda effectively portrayed foreigners in the Northern armies as "Lincoln's hirelings," a contemptible calumny of often destitute immigrants fighting to survive the American war.

The Union Irish Brigade, as the best-known example, was distinguishable from mercenary forces and even from European Irish Brigades, whose men often served after exile or virtual enslavement. If not for the honor of Ireland alone, why did these men fight in America's war? At the start of the conflict, the men of Meagher's Irish Brigade were motivated by their own patriotic Irish political leadership as much as by the economic incentive the Union provided new recruits. Irish leaders Meagher, Michael Corcoran and James Shields touted Union service as a means to win a place for the Irish community in America. These men clearly stated another important political goal—to train troops and win United States support for an armed struggle for Irish independence. Little came of this plan, however. Money also was a great consideration for immigrant service, especially later in the war after the initial political adrenaline for fighting ran dry. Foreigners in Union armies accepted bounties as an inducement to enlist, and probably took service in the military as the best job available for unskilled and often uneducated labor.

The same can be said of many foreigners in Confederate service, although there is some evidence that foreign service in the Confederate armies may have been more ideologically driven. Fitzgerald Ross, a British officer in the service of Austria, wrote in 1864: "The Southern Confederacy being very difficult of access, the foreigners who have taken service here have all been impelled to do so by their sympathy with the cause which is in truth a noble one."[82] One Confederate Irishman was nobly true to the South even after his capture. Prisoner of war Lawrence Fitzgerald, a member of the Emmet Guards of the 17th Virginia Infantry, told his Yankee captors he would "willingly do anything but fight against the South."[83] Jefferson Davis noted, "Our service offers but little inducement to the soldiers of fortune, but a great deal to the men of principle."[84] In the summer of 1864, some Southern leaders thought their cause alone could induce immigrant enlistments in the Confederate army. Working on that assumption, General Braxton Bragg suggested to Davis that he issue general orders "inviting foreigners in the Federal ranks to come to us and offering them protection." The Confederate president considered printing the orders in English, German and French in large numbers and introducing them into the enemy's lines.[85] There is no evidence that this measure was taken.

Even with all these considerations (money, politics, and ideology), sometimes a soldier was just a soldier. The *Tipperary Advocate* newspaper believed that Irish-Americans took the part of North or South as "a mere question of locality."[86] This would explain the large numbers of Irishmen in the Union army; their numerical strength in the ranks merely may have reflected the large Irish population in the North—a geographical circumstance created by open and convenient Northern ports. Northern seaports, after all, were open to immigrants throughout the war, while Southern shores were effectively blockaded.

Confederate propaganda and Union enlistment bounties aside, historian George F. R. Henderson noted that the Union army was at least seventy percent native born, which he believed indicated that the percentage of foreigners in the Northern armies was lower than in the Army of Northern Virginia.[87] Another source went even further in making a similar assertion, but offered no figures to back up its claim. This unnamed editorial observer at the Battle of Fredericksburg wrote in the *Richmond Enquirer* that "there are more Irish in the army of the Confederate States (in proportion to population) than in Lincoln's."[88]

Even with concrete and legitimate reasons for a foreign presence in the Civil War armies, the myth that new American immigrants somehow constituted a mercenary conspiracy was long-held and pervasive. Some otherwise reputable postwar studies played into the fiction that the

Northern armies particularly were inordinately filled by foreign mercenaries. Fred Albert Shannon's study of the organization of the Union Army stated:

> The accusation of the use of foreign mercenaries is amply supported by evidence. Most of these were simply tempted by the bounties and high wages in industry to emigrate to America, and then found their way either into wage labor or the army. . . . Yet some mercenaries were imported expressly and by official action for use in the army or at least to fill quotas."[89]

However, these men were not recruited as a paid army as the Hessians had been in the American Revolution or as the gallowglass had been in medieval Ireland. Nor were they sent home at war's end as mercenary armies often were. Certainly there were Union recruiting agents in Ireland during the war, but for all intents and purposes these agents were recruiting new American citizens as much as they were signing up Yankee soldiers. This was true at least in the eyes of the Irishmen they courted for army service. When information was made available to the Irish people that Union "employment agents" were actually army recruiters, immigration to America slackened. With this trend in mind, Confederate propaganda and diplomatic efforts—including Papal intercession—successfully worked to end Union recruitment of soldiers in Ireland.[90] Confederate emissary A. Dudley Mann, after an audience with Pope Pius IX, found hope that Union recruiting in Catholic countries and especially Ireland would diminish. He wrote to Secretary of State Judah Benjamin in 1864, "To the immortal honor of the Catholic Church, it is now engaged in throwing every obstacle that it can justly create in the way of the prosecution of the war by the Yankee guerrillas."[91]

For its part, the Confederate government did not attempt to specifically recruit alien Irishmen for army service. An idea by an Irishman in Texas in 1864 to recruit in Ireland for the South was tabled by Secretary of War James Seddon.[92] James McConaughey of Marshall, Texas (coincidentally the adopted home town of Cork-born Confederate General Walter P. Lane), offered to visit Ireland to recruit an Irish Brigade for the South. In trying to convince Seddon of the feasibility of the endeavor, McConaughey offered that he had "reliable evidence from Ireland that the South can get twenty men where the North can get one—inducements being equal."[93] Later, it became clear that McConaughey planned to arrange, through the overseas sale of abundant Texas cotton, to pay men to "emigrate" from Ireland to Texas, ostensibly to find civilian work there, but then organize them into a Confederate brigade. Seddon was unwilling to use this "bait and switch" tactic to raise troops, although it was a method often used by unscrupulous agents recruiting Union soldiers in Ireland.

In Northern recruiting practice, Irishmen were usually promised civilian industrial jobs, but upon landing in America fell prey to recruiting sergeants or substitute brokers.[94] Sometimes, new immigrants were simply intimidated into joining the Union army. One such Irish recruit, Thomas Tulley, complained he was imprisoned in Portland, Maine, on trumped-up charges of drunkenness but was promised freedom if he joined Col. Joshua Lawrence Chamberlain's 20th Maine Infantry.[95] Such egregiously unfair cases led to public outrage in Ireland over Union recruitment there.

The issue of recruitment in Ireland fomented a conflict of its own—a propaganda war. In one of many examples of foreign intrigue during the war, the Confederate government waged a clandestine anti-recruitment campaign in Ireland. Henry Hotze, a Swiss-born naturalized American citizen, directed this campaign from his office in London. Hotze was a resident of Mobile, Alabama, before the war and had attended Spring Hill College, Pere Gache's Jesuit school. He joined the Confederate army in 1861 and fought at First Manassas as a private in the Mobile Cadets company. He later founded a pro-Confederate newspaper in London, *The Index*, whose main mission was to stop Union recruitment in Ireland.[96] The British Foreign Enlistment Act forbade Union enlistment in the United Kingdom, but there was evidence that Secretary of State William Seward and Minister to Great Britain Charles Francis Adams circumvented the law. This was done mainly by "emigrating" men as the Texas Irishman McConaughey had planned. Hotze and others uncovered this scandal and worked to end it. It was sometimes surprising to see who took part in this European war of words. Edwin DeLeon, a South Carolinian in France during the war, reported in 1862 that New York Catholic Archbishop John Hughes was recruiting in Ireland in defiance of the British law.[97] DeLeon operated the *Paris Patrie* newspaper as the French arm of Confederate propaganda in Europe.

Other Confederate propaganda efforts were hard-hitting and graphic. One campaign included sending a wounded Confederate Irish soldier, Capt. James Lolar, through Irish towns and villages to show the populace the terrible effects of the war.[98] Lolar presented an effective Irish pedigree because he had been an active nationalist with Smith O'Brien and Thomas Meagher before the war. It was thought by Confederate Secretary of State Judah Benjamin that Lolar's nationalist reputation and war wounds might arouse sympathy for the South in Ireland—that Lolar's physical appearance would provide "visual evidence that native Irishmen have shed blood for the Southern cause."[99]

Benjamin also dispatched Lt. J. L. Capston, an Irish native, to Ireland in July 1863 as a special agent to operate a pro-Confederate, anti-Union recruiting propaganda campaign using handbills and newspaper articles.[100] Lieutenant Capston, a graduate of Trinity College, Dublin, traveled from Dublin to Limerick and Galway to "inform the Irish masses of the true nature of the war," and offer Irishmen reasons not to emigrate.[101] Among his Irish backers on this anti-recruitment tour were members of the Irish Patriot Party, including William Smith O'Brien and John Mitchel's brother-in-law, John Martin, who believed that America and its war were siphoning off Ireland's next insurgent army.

What effect did all this have on the Irish participation in the war? The Confederacy, of course, did not have easy access to foreign ports and otherwise did not seek to tap the seemingly unlimited market in Irish soldiers for its army. Most of the Irish in the Confederate army were settled Southerners when the war began, and their numbers were limited from the outset. A discussion of emigration to America during the war is a study of emigration to Northern ports only. Twenty-eight thousand Irish people emigrated to America in 1861, and another 33,000 arrived in 1862. These numbers would have been considered normal for the period, but the figures jumped to 94,000 in 1863 and the same in 1864. Discounting a normal emigration number of approximately 30,000 per

## The Fighting Race at Fredericksburg

year, Union recruiting might have been responsible for a two-year influx of 128,000 Irishmen and women.[102] This was not an overwhelming figure, and it was hardly enough to affect the war's outcome since most of these Irish newcomers did not participate in the conflict in any capacity. An important observation is that even with many more Irishmen available for service in the North, historian James M. McPherson noted that the Irish were the most underrepresented immigrant group in the Union army in proportion to overall population. On the other hand, the Irish were the largest immigrant group represented in the Confederate states, and the single largest group of immigrants in the Southern armies.[103]

Even with Union recruitment, by at least one measure the Irish shared equally in service for Union and Confederacy. As a percentage of the overall populations from which the armies were raised in the North and South, the proportion of Irish immigrants who served in the respective armies was almost equal; both sides counted the number of Irish troops at approximately seven-tenths of one-percent of the respective populations.[104]

## The Legacy of Fredericksburg:
## Irish Opinion Turns Against the War

The [Irish] people are at last beginning to show their disgust at the crimes of the [Union] government.

— The *Cork Examiner* in reaction to the New York City draft riots.

My brave lad sleeps in his faded coat of blue,
In a lonely grave unknown, lies the heart that beats so true.
He sank faint and hungry among the famished brave,
And they laid him sad and lonely within his nameless grave.

— From Faded Coat of Blue

The Battle of Fredericksburg is the most important battlefield event of the war for many Irish-Americans today. The Irish Brigade's role in the engagement is hailed as one of the bravest feats in the history of Irish soldiery. Indeed it was. But in the war period, the sad and salacious publicity surrounding the useless slaughter of the glorious and celebrated Irish Brigade turned Irish opinion in America and Ireland—never strongly pro-Union—openly against the prosecution of the war and Irish participation in it.

As news of the Battle of Fredericksburg filtered across the sea, "the reaction in contemporary Ireland was far from jubilant. Irish nationalists mourned the annihilation of the Brigade and became more hostile toward the Union war effort."[105] Union company commander Thomas F. Galwey, an eyewitness to the battle, cynically cut to the heart of the matter in commenting on the Irish Brigade's assault on Marye's Heights. "Were they successful?" he asked. "Only in leaving their dead closest of all to the Confederate lines."[106]

Confederate attitudes after watching the brigade's destruction were just as cynical. Joseph B. Polley of the Texas Brigade sardonically characterized the wanton use of Irish troops in the massacre at the stone wall. He wrote in bitter terms that "Meagher's Irish Brigade was selected for the sacrifice" at Marye's Heights. Polley implied that the brigade had been picked for destruction because plentiful foreign troops in the Union army were expendable.[107] There is evidence that a great body of the Irish people suspected Union leaders of holding these views.

Immediately after Fredericksburg, Irish immigrant newspapers admitted that "the Irish spirit for the war is dead—destroyed in senseless battles, under incompetent officers such as Meagher. . ."[108] New York's *Irish American* newspaper was disconsolate after the battle and perhaps reflected a widespread opinion that the Irish community had done its share in the war:

> Our correspondent gives us a sad picture of the condition to which the little band of heroes led by Meagher has been reduced by its losses in the late insane attack upon the rebel works at Fredericksburg. The brigade in fact no longer exists—the remnant that remains does not constitute even a skeleton of its former self. Under the circumstances we are justified in calling upon the Government to send the few remaining men home. . .[109]

By the spring of 1863 Meagher also realized that the Irish Brigade no longer existed. In his resignation letter dated May 8, 1863, just a few days after the close of the disastrous Chancellorsville Campaign, Meagher wrote that his command was a "poor vestige and relic of the Irish Brigade."[110] The unit had not seen much action at Chancellorsville.

Other Irish voices also weighed in with calls for peace. A more conservative element in Ireland, the Irish Unionists, generally took no notice of the Irish role at Fredericksburg, but they did seize on the opportunity to call on the North to end the war.[111] On the other Irish political extreme, the *Connaught Patriot*, a pro-Fenian newspaper, went only one step further when it urged European intervention to ensure Confederate independence.[112] The *London Times* was equally pessimistic about the Irish in the American Union. In the summer of 1863, the paper's Dublin correspondent wrote:

> Great things were expected one day from "Meagher of the Sword" and his Irish Brigade; but the brigade is now annihilated, and the *Nation* [newspaper] trusts that the treatment the Irish generally have experienced from the government of the Northern States will induce them to consider whether they have not been heedlessly precipitate in their hurry to assist in the attempted subjugation of a young nation which has taken arms in defence of its rights to choose its own rulers and form of government.[113]

Much of Irish written opinion after the battle expressed a widespread belief that "puritanical, Cromwellian and anti-Irish abolitionists forced the Irish immigrant to fight the war."[114] After all, it was the Union, not the Confederacy, that recruited and later conscripted Irishmen for army service.

Irish disillusionment with the war and distrust of the Union's leadership had been building for some time before Fredericksburg. Economic distress was one important reason for Irish unhappiness with the war. The Civil War caused even greater economic distress in an already suffering Ireland, making it more difficult to emigrate to many parts of America, to settle on its frontier where the best opportunities existed, and to avoid service in either army. For Irishmen already settled in America, the war reduced monies normally sent back to indigent relatives in Ireland, and those relatives in Ireland often did not receive pensions or other benefits for the deaths of Irish soldiers in American armies. "Economically, the Irish peasants were among the worst victims of the war," according to historian Joseph Hernon's 1968 study.[115]

The peasantry were not the only group to lose because of the American conflict. The Malcolmson Cotton Mill at Portlaw, County Waterford, Ireland, part of a planned industrial village, went into decline when contracts it had with Southern producers were breached during the war.[116] With so much hardship created in an already starving land, it is not difficult to see why a majority of the Irish people became bitterly opposed to prosecuting the American war.

Irish politics also affected Irish antiwar thought. Irish nationalist opinion was split over the participation of Irishmen in the war, but it tilted decidedly in favor of participation on the Southern side. Irish nationalist sentiment, here and overseas, became increasingly and publicly pro-Confederate as the war progressed. This was chiefly because many nationalists felt that the South was a political surrogate for Ireland—an affinity that led them to see the North as the aggressor in the war. Part of this affinity was due to personal friendships as well as long-standing political alliances. The leader of the 1848 uprising, W. Smith O'Brien, was acquainted with Confederate leaders Robert Toombs, who was for a time Secretary of State, and vice-president Alexander H. Stephens. O'Brien respected them and understood the Confederate cause, and he warned Irishmen away from emigration to America to fight in the war.[117] Another nationalist leader, Daniel O'Donoghue, sought an end to the war even if it meant Southern victory. He was more concerned with gaining an American ally—under any constitution—against the British oppressor.[118]

Other incidents also served to sour the Irish on the American war. The Irish in the North were unhappy with the "bait and switch" emigration tactics that promised civilian jobs but delivered army service. Attempts at impressment of some Irishmen into the army, as in the case of the unfortunate Thomas Tully, were distastefully reminiscent of British impressment for service under the Union Jack. Tulley's story was convincing proof to many of Yankee mistreatment of the Irish.[119] Then too, the Emancipation Proclamation and its promised result to free a large pool of unskilled labor into the marketplace did not sit well with immigrants, who were already hard pressed to make ends meet in the low-wage, unskilled job market.

Conscription, however, was the spark that had Irish communities in New York rioting in the streets by the summer of 1863. By then it was clear the Union recruitment effort in Ireland had backfired, and the new Irish-Americans in the North did not come to America to fight a war. The New York City draft riots against conscription and Republican war aims, notably Emancipation, occurred July 13-16, 1863. According to historian James McPherson, the riots—which were carried out by a mob at least two-thirds Irish—were the worst civil disturbances in United States history.[120] Irish anger over black labor competition and the draft had broken out into violent expression before, but never on the scale of what was seen that summer. Similar but smaller riots had occurred in various Northern cities in the summer of 1862. Then, a Brooklyn mob of 2,000 or more Irishmen attacked blacks with such fury that one observer, John Jay, wrote that "the minds of the Irish are inflamed to the point of absolute and brutal insanity."[121]

The 1863 riots precipitated by the Conscription Act enacted March 3, also included random brutal attacks on blacks in New York proper. The mob's fury did not always determine the background of its victims. The Irish Brigade's heroic Col. Robert Nugent had been detached from command of the 69th New York, and was the provost marshal in the city during the riots. His home was destroyed by the mob. Riots that included Irish mobs also were seen in Boston, Milwaukee, and Dubuque, Iowa, as well as in smaller towns in Pennsylvania and New York.[122] In New York City alone, more than 1,000 Irishmen, another Irish Brigade of sorts, were killed by police and Union soldiers during the disturbance.[123] The riots set off another war of words over the mission of the war, the nature of Northern society and its mistreatment of the Irish there, and the relative righteousness of the Southern position. The *Cork Examiner* newspaper contemptuously wrote that under the Conscription Act "Three hundred thousand men are to be dragged from their homes to cut the throats of their Southern brethren." The riots, the paper said, showed that "The people are at last beginning to show their disgust at the crimes of the [Union] government."[124]

Many New York newspapers blamed all Irishmen for the summer mayhem in which at least nineteen blacks were lynched in the streets. The Irish-American community in New York tried to defend itself, blaming the riots on a collective rabble, not the Irish element "as a body." In the aftermath of the episode, a majority of the Irish in New York, in a fit of high dudgeon, saw many native Northerners as ungrateful and hypocritical. The Irish in the North were further alienated from the Union cause.[125] The riots, said the *Examiner*, have "brought out the latent hatred of the Yankee Know-Nothings. . . This is the fitting expression of Yankee gratitude to the Irish."[126] The *Nation* similarly charged that "abolitionists papers, preachers, and politicians" unfairly singled out the Irish community for the actions of some Irishmen in the riots.[127] The *Dublin Morning News* was even more strident in its defense of the New York rioters, proving itself anti-North if not openly pro-Confederate. The riots, the paper said, have "a Yankee smell about them. They are redolent of the methodistical canters that pity the slave and kick the coloured man out of an omnibus. . ."[128]

If conscription was the spark that ignited Irish civil unrest, the result of the Battle of Fredericksburg was a smoldering, slow-burning fuse. Using the battle's aftermath as fuel, the draft riots provided a convenient flame that touched off a broader, sweeping conflagration of Irish resentment over the war. The destruction of the Irish Brigade at Fredericksburg gave Irish participation in the conflict a cold, hard reality. Irish anger in the North was energized by a growing awareness that the brigade was ill-used by the Union high command—that the lives of its soldiers were sacrificed for reasons that were at best unimportant to Irish immigrants—and at times at odds with Irish interests. The Irish in the South also communicated this paradox. Many of them saw Yankee Irish service as a break with the mother country and its political struggle. John Edward Dooley was indignant that his own people could fight for the Union. "When we see the Irishman supporting so foul a tyranny as ever blackened the pages of any history, our indignation cannot but be moved."[129]

Some in the Confederacy recognized the Irish unrest in the North and hoped to capitalize on it. A January 6, 1864, letter to Jefferson Davis called to the attention of Confederate leaders that the "Irish element in the Northern population" was "a weak point in the enemy's lines." Southerner S. C. Hayes, the son of Irish immigrants, was for twenty years a bookseller, publisher, and printer in Philadelphia. His letter to the Confederate president asserted that "the great body of Irish at the North feel a deep interest in our [the South's] success, more especially in Pennsylvania, where they have been subjected to bitter persecution." The letter backed this contention with a brief history of the Irish experience in the Keystone State. Hayes was reminded that when he moved to Philadelphia in the 1840s, the Irish there were the "objects of bitter and most intense persecution by an ignorant band of bigots." He had seen an Irish empathy with the South when he visited several Pennsylvania counties in the summer of 1861. He remembered that a Philadelphia recruiting speech that year by Thomas Meagher had "obtained but few recruits in Philadelphia—not more than a corporal's guard."[130]

As evidence of recent pro-Confederate Irish opinion. Hayes offered private letters from James A. McMaster of New York's Irish nationalist newspaper, the *Freeman's Journal*, as well as public editorials by Irish nationalist W. Smith O'Brien. President Davis wrote to Braxton Bragg on August 22, 1864, saying the findings in Hayes' letter were "valuable and practicable. The employment of some judicious person to operate on this class of people through our own press and that of the North would no doubt be attended with good results."[131] Confederate efforts in this regard hardly could have affected the military situation at this late date.

The antiwar sentiment, the racist riots, the disgust with Union leaders—these circumstances paradoxically led to the shining example of the Union Irish Brigade America knows today. After the war, the brigade's tragic experience in battle was conveniently forgotten by Irish nationalist leaders anxious to gloss over their antiwar rhetoric and Southern sympathies. To accomplish this political rehabilitation, Irish nationalists mounted a campaign to showcase the Union Irish Brigade's patriotic service. Meagher's brigade, not its Confederate counterparts, became the symbol of Irish participation in the war—the brigade's selfless charge at Fredericksburg became an unassailable icon that overshadowed other images of Irish gallantry. Ironically it was the martyr-like service of the Irish Brigade at Marye's Heights—and contemporary disillusionment with its slaughter—that had the greatest impact in turning Irish people against the Union.

*An Irish Soldier of the*
*Southern Confederacy.*

The grave of Daniel Leary serves as a poignant reminder of the Irish contribution to the Confederate cause. Leary is buried in Richmond's Mount Calvary Cemetery.

*Author*

# The Irish Fight Continues

## The War After Fredericksburg

I paused not because he was an enemy, nor did I assist him because he
was an Irishman—I knew only that he was helpless, and in imminent
danger, and that I could assist him—and I did.

— John Keely at Chancellorsville

They speak in trumpet tone,
To do at once what is to do
And trust Ourselves Alone.

— Thomas Davis, 1842.

### The Hero of Little Hunting Run:
### Chancellorsville 1863

After the Union debacle at Fredericksburg, the glories of the Irish
Brigade began their passage into the pages of history.[1]
Confederate Irishmen, like their Union counterparts, continued
the civil struggle to what would be a tragic, bloody, fiery end. The
glories of battle gave way to simple survival. The next major campaign
for the Army of Northern Virginia opened the following spring just ten
miles from Fredericksburg on the rolling hills and dense growth around
the quiet crossroads of Chancellorsville.

The Battle of Chancellorsville May 1-5, 1863, was another
resounding Southern victory. Such a result seemed impossible when the
campaign opened, for the South seemed destined for defeat. Major
General Joseph "Fighting Joe" Hooker, a blusterous New Englander
who had shown some promise as a division commander, ordered the

130,000-strong Army of the Potomac across the Rappahannock and Rapidan rivers in late April. General Robert E. Lee's depleted Confederate army of 60,000 men rested at its railhead around and below Fredericksburg. (Longstreet and two of his divisions had been detached for service around Suffolk, Virginia.) Hooker's strategic march, well-executed and unexpected, caught the Army of Northern Virginia flat-footed. The Federal commander's swift action placed a large Union force behind the Confederate army with open avenues of approach toward Fredericksburg. A strategic retreat offered the brightest option for Lee's outnumbered and outflanked force, and Hooker probably expected as much. Lee's brazen campaign plan, however, did not include retreat. With characteristic boldness, Lee left a small portion of his army behind Fredericksburg and quickly marched with the balance into the area called the Wilderness in an attempt to resist the Union army's eastward advance.

Heavy fighting along the narrow corridors leading out of the Wilderness toward Fredericksburg punctuated the first day of battle. The Union army steadily advanced, grinding out a path against stubborn Confederate resistance. If "Fighting Joe" expected Lee to retreat when his "finest army on the planet" appeared on the Confederate flank, he was mistaken. When Lee moved against him instead, Hooker gave up his plans of advance, relinquished the high ground already gained on May 1, and retreated back along the roads away from Fredericksburg. By May 2, Hooker's men were entrenching around Chancellorsville, and the battle's initiative swung to the aggressive Lee, his bantam Southern army, and its intrepid corps commander, Stonewall Jackson. The battle that ensued is one of the greatest feats of tactical warfare in American military history, and Jackson was its maestro. His masterwork at Chancellorsville began with a twelve-mile flank march led by a brigade of Georgians under Brig. Gen. Alfred H. Colquitt. Irishman Lt. John Keely of the 19th Georgia was one of the marching van.

Napoleon wrote that "hesitation and half measures lose all in war." In the best Napoleonic tradition, on the evening of May 1, Lee and Jackson decided to take a dangerous risk. They would split their already outnumbered army and march Jackson's 30,000-man corps across the face of the enemy in an attempt to attack its apparently vulnerable right flank. Jackson's arduous march along narrow roads in the Wilderness consumed the entire day of May 2. The Wilderness forest helped shield the army's movement, but by many accounts Union headquarters knew of the Southern march. Hooker and his subordinates, however, mistook the movement for a retreat and did not take any measures to defend against an attack. The Confederate wing, unhampered by Union cavalry, attacked down the Orange Plank Road about 6:00 p.m. and swept the Union's unprepared Eleventh Corps from the field.

Jackson, however, was not satisfied with the initial success of the flank attack. Like Lee, he sought total victory, and that meant nothing less than the complete destruction of the Federal army. "In war there is only one favorable moment," explained Napoleon, and "Genius seizes it." The genius that was Jackson attempted to seize one favorable moment at Chancellorsville. With Napoleonic dash, he called up A. P. Hill's Division of some 9,000 men to lead a Confederate camisado.

Later that night the Southern corps commander rode ahead into the smoldering dark woods in search of the soft belly of Hooker's army—a weakness in the Union line where he might strike a decisive death blow. Jackson was planning an unconventional night attack to accomplish this goal, but a Confederate fusillade ended the effort and Jackson's life. About 9:00 p.m. Jackson was returning to his own lines when he was hit by a mistaken musket volley fired by his own men. Seriously wounded in the left arm and right hand, he was taken from the field. Jackson, the stone wall at Manassas, the champion of the Shenandoah Valley, perhaps the most famous man in the Confederacy, was lost to the cause eight days later when he died of pneumonia at the Confederate railhead at Guiney Station. The night attack never went forward.

The following day, May 3, the fighting at Chancellorsville reached its climax. With Jackson's senior division commander A. P. Hill also knocked out with a painful wound, Lee tapped 28-year-old cavalryman J.E.B. Stuart to lead Jackson's Second Corps. Stuart quickly rose to the occasion and launched an all-out assault against the Union entrenchments. Keely and his Irish company were part of the desperate attempt to capitalize on Jackson's initial success. Colquitt's Brigade had been shifted to the Confederate left along Little Hunting Run. The Wilderness, Keely wrote, was "in a perfect blaze, having caught [fire]

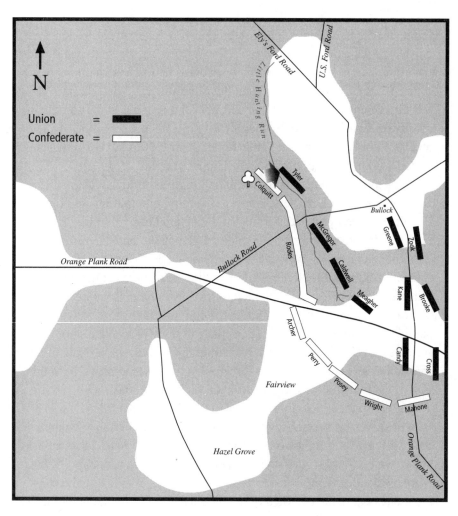

**Chancellorsville - May 3, 1863**

**The Irish Angel of Little Hunting Run** – Colquitt's Brigade tangles with Tyler's Brigade on the Confederate left. It was here that John Keely rescued a wounded Union Irishman from the burning woods.

from the myriad of bursting shells."[2] The ferocity of the Confederate assault on May 3 was captured by the Irishman's narrative. After breaking through two lines of Union defenders, Keely and his men "came upon hundreds of the enemy's wounded, left by their comrades to perish in the flames." Keely and his men "were under a terrific fire of grape, canister and musketry from the line of breastworks, which was only 100 yards from us . . . our men fell at every step; therefore we could not stop except we wished defeat or butchery from the breastworks."[3]

The concentrated firepower from these Union trenches wreaked enormous casualties on the Confederate army. The rather unimaginative Southern assaults at Hazel Grove and all along the Chancellorsville front rolled forward against what Confederate artillerist E. Porter Alexander called "probably the strongest field entrenchment ever built in Virginia."[4] Still, Keely and the army mercilessly advanced. "On we swept through these tenfold terrors, dashed like demons over the now captured breastworks."[5] By 10:00 a.m. Confederate troops seized the crossroads at Chancellorsville, Hooker's headquarters at the Chancellor house. The conjoining of the two wings of Lee's army signaled victory over the vastly larger but ill-led Army of the Potomac.

Keely and the Georgians had been fighting Union troops brigaded under Brig. Gen. Erastus B. Tyler. In that unheralded sector of the battle, a splendid thing occurred. Perhaps remembering his helplessness to aid the burning wounded at Prospect Hill, Keely risked his life to save a wounded Union soldier who had been left behind to perish in the brush fires. His recounting of the rescue must be the most powerful and poignant Irish battlefield experience of the war:

> As we tore through the flame, our hair, eyebrows and mustaches were singed off. Still, our hearts were melted with pity toward the sufferers and when we gained the breastworks and received the bugle sound "halt," every man dashed back into the flames, and did his utmost to rescue the wounded. I saw there an Irish Yankee soldier, thigh broken, with his ramrod trying to fight the flames. I took him in my arms and carried him to the breastworks, where his wounds were attended to. I paused not because he was an enemy, nor did I assist him because he was an Irishman—I knew only that he was helpless, and in imminent danger, and that I could assist him—and I did.[6]

The rescued Yankee was probably a member of the 91st Pennsylvania Regiment, a unit largely composed of Irishmen from Philadelphia. Keely wrote that he and his company knew this "mission of mercy was fraught with deadly danger. There you would find a wretch mangled, and as you started to assist him, his cartridge box would explode and blow him to atoms."[7] The Irish captain estimated that thousands of loaded muskets overheated in the flaming leaves of the Wilderness, their stocks burning until they exploded among unsuspecting Confederates. He remembered that his company lost five lives and many wounded to these ersatz land-mine muskets. "Still," he wrote to his father, "those poor fellows of the enemy received a continuance of this attention from us at the risk and even cost of lives."[8]

After the battle and the heroic rescue of the Irish Yankee, Keely sought out his own sergeant, whom he'd seen fall beside him in the charge. According to Keely, Sgt. Peter Gavan was another Irish Confederate, six-foot two, well-educated, handsome, and only twenty-one years old. He found the Irish subaltern dead, his trusted musket in his hand when he fell. More alarming, he found several other men trying to douse Gavan's burning body. "Every rag was burnt off him," Keely remembered, this soldier who was "gallant almost to rashness, the only son of a widow, with whom I was acquainted." Most of the man's body was consumed by the fire. This horror of war deeply affected Keely, who cried like a child as he buried Gavan's ashen remains. As a final, feeble tribute, he buried the sergeant's musket with fixed bayonet beside him. Keely had promoted Gavan only a few days before the battle. He kept one of the dead soldier's buttons, which he sent to Gavan's mother. He later found out that the bereaved woman "survived the sad news only two weeks."

The Battle of Chancellorsville offered John Keely two extremes of experience. In saving a fellow Irishman, he rejoiced in the reaffirmation of human kindness. The immolation of Sergeant Gavan as quickly returned Keely to the terrors of the battlefield. Matching Keely's twofold experience along Little Hunting Run was the double-edged result of the battle itself. Chancellorsville was Lee's greatest victory, a tactical masterstroke. It also was the beginning of the end for the Confederacy. The battle was merely a tactical triumph, however, for it did nothing to change the strategic balance in Virginia. If he accomplished anything, Hooker at least saved his army to fight again. The South, on the other hand, lost the services of one of its greatest heroes and generals in Jackson, a distant descendant of a Scots-Irish native of Londonderry, Ireland.

Ironically, Jackson was wounded while attempting to execute what may have been his most compelling battlefield exploit. Old Jack was attempting to end the war, not just win another battle. If his attack had succeeded, the destruction or disbursement of the largest Union army in the field may have created conditions for a peace settlement recognizing Southern independence. Of course, it is arguable whether what was left of the Confederate force could have accomplished the destruction of Hooker's army that night. When Jackson called A. P. Hill's Division forward, his tired and disorganized Confederate wing still faced a rested Federal Fifth Corps and the newly arrived First Corps. Still, Jackson's curt order to Hill "to press them" and cut the enemy off from the United States Ford telegraphed the corps leader's bold intention. The risk Lee and Jackson took in splitting their army and making the flank attack was no half-measure; neither would be Jackson's plan to trap the Union army that night. Jackson, under Lee's audacious tutelage, had placed the Southern army in a position to destroy Joe Hooker's force at Chancellorsville. Perhaps more importantly, while regrouping, Jackson grasped the greater significance of the moment: here was a chance to strike a truly decisive blow and perhaps end the war. To Jackson, certainly, the circumstances seemed ripe to destroy the Union army, and the South might never have such an opportunity again. It is this presence of mind, this grasp of meaning and situation, this focus in the midst of chaos that separates great leaders from all others. Jackson was one of the greatest of leaders—unparalleled on the field and literally irreplaceable. The opportunity Jackson glimpsed through the smoky woods that night was forever lost with his wounding. After his death eight days later, the South would never again be in the position to win a decisive, war-ending victory.

Indeed the army under Lee and Stuart failed to complete Jackson's vision for an end to the war at Chancellorsville, though not through lack of trying. The Army of Northern Virginia was irretrievably weakened at Chancellorsville, where it lost twenty percent of its force in reckless attacks on strong Northern battlements. Like Jackson, veteran field officers were irreplaceable. These losses were followed by Lee's bold decision to raid north of the Potomac River a second time, a move which triggered the Gettysburg Campaign.

# CLEAR THE CONFEDERATE WAY!

Lieutenant Keely's memory of Chancellorsville was forever tainted by his horrible experiences there. After the war he wrote to his parents in Ireland: "Thank God I am done with such scenes forever, for nothing could induce me again to suffer what I have suffered. I could relate to you facts which came under my notice . . . which would make your hearts sick."[9]

## The Confederate Irish in Pickett's Charge: Little Noted, Nor Long Remembered

The land of the Shamrock, as on other fields, contributed its quota on the strongly contested ground.

— Colonel Joseph Newton Brown of South Carolina

We know how straight into the very jaws of destruction and death leads this road of Gettysburg.

— John Edward Dooley

"The land of the Shamrock, as on other fields, contributed its quota on the strongly contested ground" at the Battle of Gettysburg, fought July 1-3, 1863. Thus did South Carolina's Col. Joseph Newton Brown note the Irish Confederate presence at the war's most celebrated battle.[10] The hallowed ground at Gettysburg is the country's foremost monument to the sacrifices of America's most tragic struggle. It was consecrated as such on November 19, 1863, just four months after the battle, when Abraham Lincoln dedicated its National Cemetery. The Irish Confederate sacrifice in Pennsylvania, mentioned only in passing by Colonel Brown, was long remembered by the words of Irish Confederate officer John Edward Dooley.

Two of history's great armies collided near Gettysburg on July 1, 1863. General Robert E. Lee's Army of Northern Virginia, now numbering about 75,000 men and reorganized from two to three corps after Jackson's death, once again faced the Army of the Potomac and its new commander, Maj. Gen. George G. Meade. The initial clash took place west of town that morning when advance elements of Confederate Lt. Gen. A. P. Hill's Second Corps struck Union cavalry and infantry on McPherson Ridge. Major General John F. Reynolds' men handily repulsed Hill's probe, but the temporary Union victory was paid for with Reynolds' life. Later that afternoon, Lt. Gen. Richard S. Ewell's Confederate Third Corps approached Gettysburg from the north, and in a concerted effort with Hill drove the Union army onto the heights south and east of town. The tactical victory netted the Confederates thousands of prisoners.

On July 2, the Union army presented a powerful fishhook-shaped line from Culp's Hill on the right through Cemetery Hill and south along the Cemetery Ridge to two hills known as the Round Tops. The Confederate army, deployed on a long exterior line, faced Meade's corps along Hanover Road northeast of town and along Seminary Ridge. After some indecision, Lee decided to strike the left flank of Meade's army with Lt. Gen. James Longstreet's First Corps and roll it up Cemetery Ridge, while Ewell's Corps struck Meade's left.

Longstreet's sweeping late afternoon assault struck the Union left at a salient centered on a peach orchard along the Emmitsburg Road and held by Union Maj. Gen. Daniel Sickles' Third Corps. The timely arrival of heavy reinforcements saved the Union left and center from collapse, and the fighting ended at nightfall. Ewell, meanwhile, launched a late and piecemeal attack against the Union right near sundown. The Confederates managed to reach the top of Cemetery Hill before being driven back, although other troops from Ewell's corps effected a precarious perch on the lower crest of Culp's Hill. For the aggressive Lee, the first two days of battle resulted in only minimal success at the cost of thousands of casualties. His newly-organized army had performed sluggishly, its maneuvers too uncoordinated to achieve victory.

Running out of fresh divisions and time, Lee decided to strike the center of the Union line on July 3. The planned attack against Cemetery Ridge would be preceded by a massive artillery bombardment, intended to soften the defenses for the infantry that would follow. Lee's cavalry under J.E.B. Stuart, which had arrived on the field the day before, would

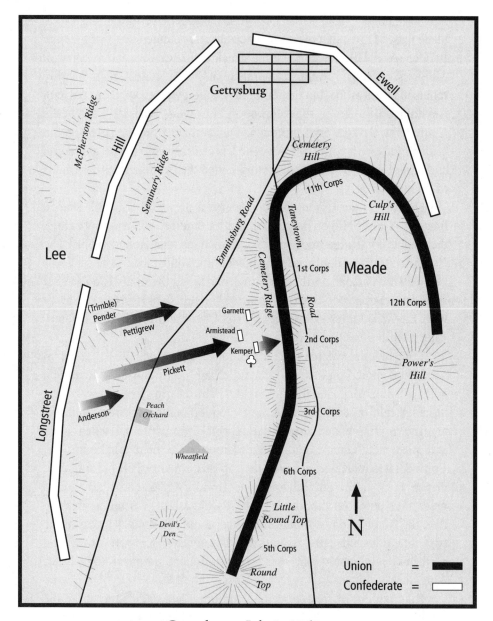

## Gettysburg - July 3, 1863

**Into the Jaws of Destruction** – John Edward Dooley witnessed the most famous assault of the war, Pickett's Charge. He was wounded and taken prisoner while leading the Montgomery Guard, part of Kemper's Brigade, at Cemetery Ridge.

harry the Union right and rear, while Ewell renewed his assault on Culp's Hill. The outcome of the campaign now hinged on the results of Lee's bold decision.

The repercussions of that decision were felt by self-possessed yet selfless Southern foot soldiers like twenty-one-year-old John Edward Dooley. Nicknamed "Gentleman Jack" for his aristocratic ways, the son of the Irish immigrant wrote eloquently of the charge of Pickett's Division on the third day of the battle. Though the most famous charge of the war bears Maj. Gen. George E. Pickett's name, his command comprised but one of the three Confederate divisions—about 12,000 men—attempting to break the Federal center. In addition to Pickett, the other two divisions were commanded by Pennsylvania-born Maj. Gen. Isaac R. Trimble and North Carolina's Brig. Gen. James J. Pettigrew. Elements from a fourth division under Richard Anderson were ordered to support the right flank of the attacking column. Pickett's three fresh brigades were led by Brig. Gens. Richard B. Garnett, Lewis A. Armistead and James Lawson Kemper. Dooley's Irish company, the Montgomery Guard, was part of the 1st Virginia Regiment brigaded under Kemper.

An artillery fight opened about 1:00 p.m. and raged for about two hours. About 3:00 p.m., with Union guns playing a punishing pibroch for the advancing Irish company, Kemper's Brigade of 1,300 men led the column of march. Lieutenant Dooley was in the van when Pickett's Virginians were pounded by Union artillery and took the first enemy rifle fire. When the Montgomery Guard's captain, James Hallinan, went down wounded, Dooley took his place and on the front rank led the blue secession flags of Virginia across the Emmitsburg Road. The 1st Virginia held a cherished position, advancing at the center of the brigade, which occupied the right wing of the march.

Kemper's thrust was the Confederacy's forlorn hope at Gettysburg—and as such perhaps it was the forlorn hope of the war. Dooley could see the first objective of the advance—a line of Union guns. He calculated the gun emplacements to be nearly one-third of a mile away on Cemetery Ridge. "Behind the guns are strong lines of infantry. You may see them plainly and now they see us perhaps more plainly," he wryly noted.[11] Dooley's narrative captured the Confederate

# CLEAR THE CONFEDERATE WAY!

*The Littlest Cap'n*

John Edward Dooley became captain of his father's Montgomery Guard company. He was wounded severely in Pickett's Charge at Gettysburg and served time in Union prison. Dooley died of tuberculosis in 1873 while studying to be a Catholic priest.

*National Archives*

struggle against well-placed Union firepower. The artillery blew large gaps in the advancing Southern line, and Dooley moved to close the "quivering melting ranks" of the Montgomery Guard. "Close up!" he ordered, and remembering the graphic horror of battle, wrote: "Close up the ranks when a friend falls, while his life blood bespatters your cheek or throws a film over your eyes!"

While volley after volley mowed down the Virginians "like wheat before the scythe," Dooley recalled that his line was within thirty yards of the enemy guns when "the well known Southern battle cry which marks the victory gained . . . bursts wildly over the blood stained field and all that line of guns is ours."[12] Dooley thought the grey-coats had won the field, but at the Irishman's perceived moment of victory he was shot through both thighs. His eyewitness account of the charge itself fell silent. Dooley and another Irish lieutenant, William Henry "Pete" Keiningham, were together on the field at the climactic moment of the charge. In fear of bleeding to death, "Gentleman Jack" saw "the dead and dying all around" while the division swept over the Yankee guns. He longed to know the ultimate result, "the end of this fearful charge." Dooley relied on his ears to tell him the outcome: "There—listen—we hear a new shout, and cheer after cheer rends the air. Are those fresh troops advancing to our support? No! no! That huzza never broke from Southern lips. Oh God! Virginia's bravest, noblest sons have perished here today and perished all in vain!"[13]

Pickett's Charge, known to history as the "High Tide of the Confederacy," was being ripped apart by the Union army's disciplined, concentrated firepower on Cemetery Ridge. Still, the mangled Confederate lines of Kemper's Brigade drifted to the left and mixed with the remnants of Garnett and Armistead, the whole pushing on as the second wave of the ill-fated charge. The attackers converged on a copse of trees. Led by General Armistead, a few hundred men stormed the Federal defenses and broke the Union line for one fleeting moment of Southern triumph. Dooley and most of the 1st Virginia did not see the final surge of the attack. Within a short time Armistead was mortally wounded, Garnett was dead, and the handful of Virginians who had made it over the low stone wall were killed, wounded, driven back or captured.

The charge never had much hope of success. In the "Old First," 120 of the 155 men engaged had fallen by the time the gallant Armistead raised his hat over the battlements. Like Dooley, General Kemper was also seriously wounded. In the aftermath of the attack, "Gentleman Jack" Dooley was taken prisoner, another sacrifice from the "Land of the Shamrock." His impassioned words of the battle captured the utter heartbreak of the vanquished Confederate army at Gettysburg. After three days of fruitless fighting, Lee and his men withdrew on July 4.

Colonel Joseph Newton Brown, writing about the sacrifices of the Irish in Pennsylvania, no doubt was alluding specifically to the Irish color bearers in the charging Confederate colossus of Pickett's Charge. He wrote particularly about the Irish color guards in his own South Carolina unit, Samuel McGowan's (formerly Maxcy Gregg's) Brigade. "In the Twelfth [South Carolina] Regiment one color bearer after another was shot dead until four were killed and two others wounded. And a scarcely less fatality attended the colors of the other regiments," Brown explained.[14] South Carolina, Louisiana, Georgia, Virginia, and Alabama all had Irish companies in Lee's army designated as regimental color companies.

Like many other Irishmen, seventeen-year-old Pvt. Willy Mitchel filled the ranks of his regiment's color guard. The boy soldier, John Mitchel's youngest son and John Edward Dooley's friend, was killed in the Virginia charge at Gettysburg. Young Willy Mitchel was the Irish nationalist's third son to gird on his father's Southern sword. He was also the first of the family to die in the war. Young Willy fell while acting as the 1st Virginia's color-bearer, after heroically picking up the regimental flag when Sgt. William H. Lawson was hit in the arm. Dooley memorialized his friend's brief service and life in verse:

> Fell mid the crash and roar of the strife,
> Gasping for Breath!
> Fell where the bravest has sacrificed life,
> Grappling with death!
>
> Died with his banner encircling his head,
> The staff by his side!
> Mid the smoke of the guns and thickly strewn dead
> His death moan was sighed![15]

## Irish Confederates After the War

Upon hearing of his son's death, John Mitchel wrote in his grief, "Our poor Willy, in that terrible slaughter of Pickett's Division, was shot through the body and at once killed. . . He could not have fallen in nobler company, nor as I think, in a better cause."[16] The so-called high tide of the Confederacy rose with blood from Erin's shore.

In the North, the public reaction to the battle was as poignant as John Mitchel's personal grief. Lincoln's dedication of the cemetery at Gettysburg, the American political scripture called the Gettysburg Address, not only expressed the president's personal sorrow for the victims of the battle—that their sacrifice shall not have been in vain—but also reached out to those on both sides of the struggle with words that recalled the higher ideals of the founders. Even passionate Confederates like "Gentleman Jack" Dooley may have yearned for a government of the people, by the people, and for the people after his painful experience at Gettysburg. But as a prisoner of war after the battle, Dooley could not reconcile the higher ideals of self-government with the people he was fighting. In one instance he could not understand why his jailer—whom he derisively called a Yanko-Irish soldier—could fight for the North. The Union man had been influenced to rebel against Britain by John Mitchel, now a staunch Confederate, in the abortive Irish uprising of 1848. Union service and Irish rebellion was an odd mixture of allegiances Dooley could not fathom. At one point Dooley confronted the Massachusetts guard:

> I began questioning him and asking him how it was possible for him who had in '48 fought or intended to fight for the same cause for which we were contending, how could he consistently turn his back on his principles and for the pitiful hire of a few dollars do all in his power to crush a brave people asserting their right of self-government. . . what, we asked, would Mr. Mitchel think of him?

Dooley, the aspiring Catholic priest, riddled the man so with guilt that he was moved to tears.[17]

John Edward Dooley recovered from his wounds, but the Irishman, the "Old First," and Confederate fortunes were devastated by defeat in Pennsylvania. Dooley was but one of 28,000 Confederate casualties at Gettysburg—a young Irish-American man who exemplified the heart of a once-proud and powerful Southern army. The Union force counted losses of 23,000. The conflagration at Gettysburg has been described as the beginning of the end of the civil struggle. While that might be true, the Confederate army in Virginia, with skilled and determined leadership, would offer resistance for almost two more years. Gettysburg, then, was but a prelude to twenty-one months of fierce fighting, bitter deprivation, and final Southern apotheosis.

## Colonel William Feeney: Lost in the Wilderness

> The minstrel boy, to the war is gone.
> In the ranks of death you will find him.
>
> — The Minstrel Boy

> Weep for him! Oh! weep for him,
> But remember in your moan,
> That he died in his pride—
> With his foes about him strown!
>
> — The Victor's Burial, Thomas Davis

After the Gettysburg Campaign, the war in the Eastern Theater moved back into Virginia. By the spring of 1864, the primary armies in the East met again in a seventy square mile tangle of undergrowth west of Fredericksburg known as the Wilderness. Like Henry B. Strong, the brave Louisiana Irishman who fell at Sharpsburg, another Irishman, Col. William Feeney, would find an all but anonymous death in the lonely woods of the Wilderness on May 5.

Not much is known about Feeney's Irish heritage. He settled before the war in Senatobia, Mississippi, where he married and worked as a saddler. In 1861, he enlisted in the Senatobia Invincibles of the 9th Mississippi Regiment, an infantry company organized near Pensacola, Florida. Feeney advanced through the ranks quickly, an indication that he may have had military experience or at least a commanding personality. He was elected 1st lieutenant, and upon the reorganization of Mississippi troops in May 1862, was promoted to captain of Company B of the 42nd Mississippi Regiment. In September 1862, he was elected major of the regiment. Two months later, Major Feeney led four companies of the 42nd Mississippi to Fredericksburg. The small battalion protected river fords along the Rappahannock until it was ordered to North Carolina just before the Battle of Fredericksburg on December 13. His diminutive detachment held an important position as the winter campaign unfolded that year. For a time, "Major Feeney and his little battalion presented the main obstacle to [Union troops] taking possession" of Fredericksburg, according to Col. Hugh R. Miller of the 42nd regiment.[18] In 1862, Feeney and his token force of Mississippians left the streets of Fredericksburg to the sharpshooters of William Barksdale's Mississippi Brigade, but the Irishman was destined to return to Virginia's riverbanks. Feeney was wounded at the Battle of Gettysburg the following summer. On December 18, 1863, he was promoted to colonel and assumed regimental command of the 42nd Mississippi. By the spring of 1864, the regiment was permanently assigned to the Army of Northern Virginia and became part of Brig. Gen. Joseph R. Davis' Brigade, Hill's Third Corps. Colonel Feeney's Confederate career reached its pinnacle in May when a new campaign opened in Virginia.

George Meade's Army of the Potomac, accompanied by the North's new general-in-chief, Ulysses S. Grant, crossed the Rapidan River with some 118,000 men in its ranks and plunged headlong into the Wilderness west of Fredericksburg. Lee's Army of Northern Virginia, about 64,000 strong, marched to intercept the advance. Fighting erupted early in the morning along the Orange Turnpike when the van of Lt. Gen. Richard Ewell's Second Corps ran into the enemy. The two-day Battle of the Wilderness (May 5-6) that followed was but the first of a series of extended bloody engagements between Lee and Grant.

While Ewell's men threw up a line of earthworks astride the Orange Turnpike and beat back a heavy Federal attack across Saunder's field on the Confederate left flank, Lt. Gen. A. P. Hill's Third Corps formed the right of Lee's army astride the Orange Plank Road. Hill's troops were especially hard pressed and fought desperately to hold and extend their

# CLEAR THE CONFEDERATE WAY!

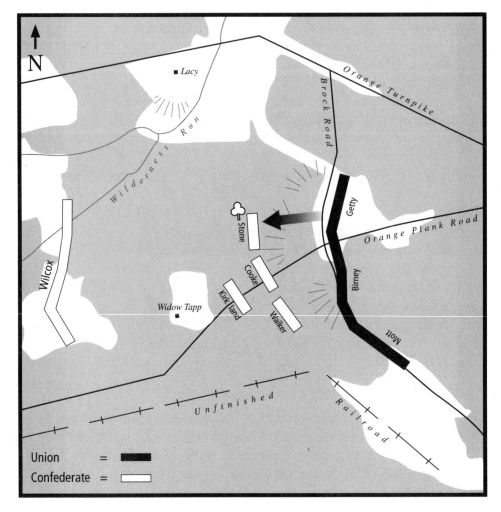

## Wilderness - May 5, 1864

**In the Ranks of Death** – William Feeney commanded the 42nd Mississippi, part of Stone's Brigade. He was killed near the Widow Tapp - Orange Plank Road front in the first half hour of fighting on May 5.

position while anxiously waiting for Lt. Gen. James Longstreet's First Corps to arrive from Gordonsville.

Colonel Feeney and the 42nd Mississippi of Joe Davis' Brigade (which was under the command of Col. John M. Stone), was dispatched to the left of the Orange Plank Road. After conferring with Colonel Stone about where to deploy his men, Feeney aligned his men on the crest of a ridge about 1:00 p.m. Within a short time the Mississippians were attacked by elements of the Union Sixth and Second corps. The fighting was especially desperate and deadly, an old-style Irish battle of plashes and ambushes. One Confederate soldier, W. S. Dunlop, called Feeney's position "the spot . . . which proved to be within the radius of what was about to become the storm center of battle."[19]

The Irishman's Mississippi command was in the thick undergrowth of the forest—the impenetrable brambles and briars which gave the Wilderness its name. "The extent of vision was not more than eighty yards in any direction, and in places not thirty," according to Dunlop.[20] Feeney's bravery made him conspicuous in a battle between soldiers otherwise rendered almost invisible by the brush and second-growth timber. Leading the Confederate advance down the slope in front of his line, Feeney was met with a hail of bullets from the opposite ridge. He probably never saw the enemy line that struck him down. The heaviest fighting raged to the right of the 42nd Mississippi, but the rapid approach of enemy sharpshooters "caused Col. Feeney to give a command sharply to take intervals" as his skirmish line of sharpshooters advanced, reported Dunlop.[21] The order was the Irishman's last. He was killed instantly just moments later and carried off the field by two men of his regiment, Richard A. Hall and Sylvanus Mitchell.[22] The soldiers who carried their fallen colonel to a hospital in the rear had been at the front only a short time. Feeney, the Senatobia saddler who had risen to field command in less than three years, was lost to the Southern cause in the first thirty minutes of fighting at the Battle of the Wilderness.

A. P. Hill's two divisions (some 14,000 men) fought throughout the day and into the evening hours, repulsing in the process the repeated attacks of five Federal divisions (about 38,000 men). A renewed Federal attack at daybreak finally succeeded in breaking Hill's thin line, but Longstreet's reinforcements arrived just in time to seal the breach and stabilize the front. The Wilderness carnage was made even more horrible by brush fires that suffocated and burned alive the helpless wounded and consumed the dead. Losses on both sides were staggering. While it is impossible to know the exact number of casualties, the Union

*Irish Confederate Artist.* Harry Arthur McArdle, a native of Belfast, presented posterity with one of the finest Confederate battle scenes of the war. "Lee at the Wilderness" depicts the dramatic "Lee to the rear!" episode at a critical part of the fighting on May 6, 1864. McArdle researched the event among the veterans who were present at the battle before rendering the painting. Lee is shown directing the Texas Brigade into the breach as it arrived on the field near the Widow Tapp farm. McArdle enlisted in the 21st Virginia Infantry in 1861, and later served the Confederate navy as a draftsman. The original painting was destroyed in the Texas State Capitol fire of 1881. *Harold B. Simpson Confederate Research Center, Hillsboro, Texas*

army probably suffered over 18,000 killed, wounded and captured in the two days of fighting. Estimates of Confederate losses total anywhere from 8,000 to 11,000 men, including Brig. Gens. Micah Jenkins, Leroy A. Stafford, and John M. Jones. Unfortunately for the South, James Longstreet was also seriously wounded and effectively lost for the war.

With so many Confederate casualties, among them three dead generals, it is no wonder the volunteer Irish colonel was not sorely missed. Nevertheless, too little is known of the Mississippi Irishman who defended Fredericksburg in 1862, was wounded at Gettysburg in 1863, and helped hold the Confederate flank in the Wilderness. His story, or his lack of one, is all too typical of many Confederate Irish who were quickly lost and callously forgotten by history. Feeney was lucky in only one respect. As a field officer, he escaped the ignominy of an anonymous grave. He is buried among his Southern comrades in the Fredericksburg Confederate Cemetery. It is a lonely grave still. Senior Irish field commanders like Feeney and the 6th Louisiana's Henry B. Strong—men who sacrificed their lives for the cause, who were struck down in the most heroic of circumstances—have not gained the full measure of acclaim from posterity. As Irish Confederates, they are lost in the pages of history—perhaps disavowed or merely forgotten by Irish historians, perhaps shunned by Northern historians because of their Southern sympathies, or neglected by Southern historians because of their immigrant status. Perhaps the countless casualties of the war rendered their passing insignificant. Their memory was given no quarter, but "in the ranks of death you will find them."

## Spotsylvania: Irish Duty and Southern Defeat

"Sir, Major Joseph McGraw returns to duty."

—McGraw, less one of his arms, to Colonel William J. Pegram

# CLEAR THE CONFEDERATE WAY!

She Trusts the Great Chieftain who stands by her side,
And the faith of her fatherland—God over us all.
Armed for the conflict, to her sisters she calls!
Back! with her red right hand,
Drives she that Northern band!

— The "Red Hand of Ireland" is raised in the Confederate cause

in Virginia by a Virginia woman.

By the end of the first week of the spring campaign of 1864, it was obvious that the nature of the war had changed. On every previous occasion, the Army of the Potomac had withdrawn after a major engagement to rest, reorganize, and move on Richmond again. After the Wilderness, however, Grant determined to push on, his objective now Lee's army rather than the capital of the South. Grant knew every battle with Lee inflicted losses the Confederates could ill-afford, while Union casualties could be replenished from the vast Northern population. The war had become nothing but a grinding and grim march of death through the rich Virginia piedmont.

Few other battles of the war exhibited man's inhumanity to man as perspicuously as did the two-week bath of mud and blood around Spotsylvania Court House. Indeed, few battles of the war demanded as much physical courage and endurance from its combatants. After the Battle of the Wilderness, the Army of the Potomac began to push south. On May 7, stiff Confederate resistance and swift marching put Lee in a strong position in front of Spotsylvania Court House, blocking the Federal army's approach to the village's strategic crossroads. Grant and Meade attacked relentlessly on May 8, 9 and 10 in an attempt to break through Lee's lines. With nothing but thousands of casualties to show for their efforts, the Union commanders, with a two-to-one superiority in numbers, hoped a grand assault against a narrow portion of the Confederate defenses would finally succeed.

The Union Second Corps under Maj. Gen. Winfield Scott Hancock spearheaded the attack in the misty pre-dawn darkness against a portion of the Southern line known as the Mule Shoe. Lieutenant General Richard S. Ewell's men held the entrenchments without supporting artillery, which had only recently been withdrawn in anticipation of a

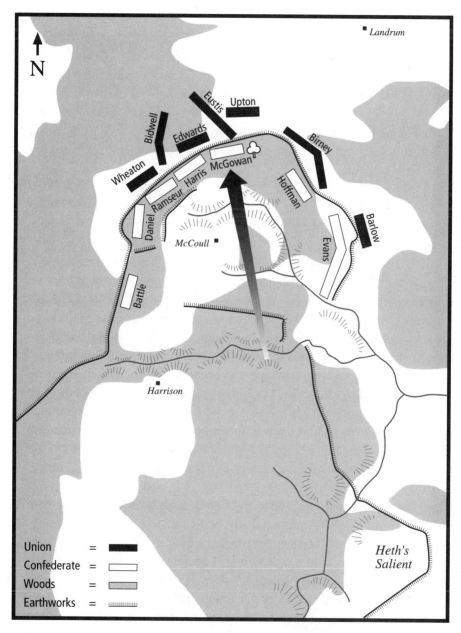

**Spotsylvania - May 12, 1864**

**At the Bloody Angle** – McGowan's Brigade fills the gap at the Bloody Angle. Major Joseph McGraw would be critically wounded during fighting at Heth's Salient May 18th.

general movement of the army. Hancock's troops swept out of the foggy darkness and up and over the outer defenses without any serious resistance. The celerity of the attack captured Maj. Gen. Edward "Allegheny" Johnson and much of his division, including much of the celebrated Stonewall Brigade. The Southern line was finally breached, but the intermingling of the Union troops and rainy darkness disorganized the attackers. The stunned Confederates, taking advantage of Hancock's inability to get his troops moving, counterattacked swiftly to repair the line.

Robert E. Lee and four division commanders, Maj. Gens. John Gordon, Robert Rodes, and Cadmus Wilcox, and Brig. Gen. William Mahone, worked feverishly to feed brigades into the fight. One of these was led by Brig. Gen. Samuel McGowan, a South Carolina son of an Irish immigrant. McGowan offered a grand display of bravery and judgment by valiantly leading his 1,100-man brigade into the salient—a killing pit known as the Bloody Angle. McGowan and his men advanced fearlessly, cheering loudly while plunging through knee-deep mud in an attempt to stabilize the line. Captain James Armstrong, company commander of the Irish Volunteers of the 1st South Carolina Infantry, witnessed McGowan leading the charge. "The gallant General McGowan, mounted on his handsome gray charger, shouted, 'Forward! my brave boys. . .'" The brigade moved forward at the double-quick under heavy fire until it reached the inner works, where McGowan fell severely wounded. "The portly form of General McGowan [was] too conspicuous a mark for the bullets . . . flying fast and furious, to miss," Armstrong reported.[23]

McGowan was succeeded by Col. Joseph N. Brown of the 14th South Carolina, who continued advancing the brigade into the Bloody Angle. The Irish Captain Armstrong, born in Philadelphia of Irish parents, went in with the 1st South Carolina. The regiment took the angle's apex and protected the eastern face of the salient while the brigade secured a section of the inner works. "There are no better soldiers in the world than these," General Rodes is reported to have exclaimed as the Carolinians, both Irish and native, advanced headlong into the angle fight.[24]

*A Confederate Lion.* Brigadier General Samuel McGowan was a first generation Irish-American. Wounded four times in the war, McGowan led his South Carolina brigade all the way to Appomattox. After the war, he served in the South Carolina legislature and on the South Carolina Supreme Court. *Library of Congress*

McGowan's Brigade drove back the Union's illustrious Excelsior Brigade and, in conjunction with other Southern units, stabilized much of the line. The close-quarter fighting, which often included hand-to-hand action, was diabolical in design and devilish in intensity. Constant rain made for a slippery mix of mud and gore. Water-filled trenches added additional misery for the men on both sides. The killing continued for almost twenty hours, with neither side willing to give ground. McGowan's personal sacrifice in the Bloody Angle was gallant, but not unusual for that killing ground. The amount of physical punishment the Irish general endured during the war, though, was extraordinary. McGowan's wounding at Spotsylvania marked the fourth time he was struck down in battle. He also was wounded in the Seven Days' Battles, at Second Manassas, and at Chancellorsville. His wounds had forced him to lead his brigade at the Battle of the Wilderness with the aid of a cane. If physical courage is any measure of a field commander, this son of Ireland was one of the finest regimental and brigade leaders in the Army of Northern Virginia.

As the Confederates in the angle fought to hold back the Federals, others worked to complete a shorter interior line well to the rear. Early the next morning, the survivors of the Bloody Angle fighting fell back to the new line. McGowan's Brigade alone counted forty percent casualties. For several days longer the armies jockeyed for position. Grant extended his left, and Lee countered to cover his right flank. On May 18, the Union army tested the Confederate line yet again with concerted attacks against the Confederate right. This time, well-placed Southern artillery helped to foil the Federal attack. Ewell's line was so closely guarded with guns that three Union corps could not even approach it.[25]

One Confederate artillery commander, Maj. Joseph McGraw, demonstrated conspicuous bravery in the May 18 attack. McGraw was "a man of enormous stature and unusual ability, possessing those rare qualities which distinguish the born commander," wrote Jennings Cropper Wise, the historian of the artillery of the Army of Northern Virginia.[26] McGraw was born in Ireland and was a lowly teamster in Sharpsburg, Maryland, before the war. He was commissioned a lieutenant in the Purcell Artillery of Lt. Col. William J. "Willie"

# Irish Confederates After the War

Pegram's Battalion in March of 1862. By 1864, the Irishman had risen to field rank in a battalion of guns commanded by Pegram. At Spotsylvania on May 18, McGraw directed his artillery in support of a part of the line assailed by Maj. Gen. Ambrose E. Burnside's command. In a prolonged artillery duel that kept the Union infantry at bay, McGraw's "courage was proverbial," lauded Jennings Wise.[27] McGraw fought on, even after being seriously wounded. According to Capt. W. Gordon McCabe, the battalion's adjutant, McGraw was on horseback in the midst of a sharp artillery duel when enemy shot tore off his left arm, leaving only a stump in the shoulder socket. Another artillery officer, Capt. John Hampden "Ham" Chamberlayne, recalled that a "large piece of shell took off his hand & shattered his arm to the elbow."[28] "For an instant his officers and men hesitated in their work to proffer aid to their much beloved field-officer," remembered McCabe. "'Don't mind me, men,' he cried, 'I'm all right—give it to 'em,' and with such words on his lips he fell forward from the saddle without a cry of pain."[29]

McGraw could not cry out because he soon passed out from the excruciating pain and heavy loss of blood. Chamberlayne quickly tied a bandage around the Irish major's upper arm and sent him to the rear. McGraw later refused anesthetic while what was left of the shattered arm was surgically removed about two inches above the elbow. The painful operation, McCabe later reported, "was done without eliciting a groan from the patient or a blink from his marvelous blue eyes."[30] Chamberlayne said McGraw "stood it [the amputation] like a hero as indeed he is."[31] The Irish major downplayed his injury although a similar wound had led to the rapid demise of "Stonewall" Jackson a year earlier. McGraw told a sympathetic officer, "I reckon I'll be off duty thirty days."[32]

The wounded McGraw was sent to a central hospital and was off duty for over five months. But his wound could not keep him from the front indefinitely. In late October, in the siege lines around Petersburg, the blue-eyed Irishman confronted Colonel Pegram. McGraw "calmly and in the most soldierly manner saluted with his good right hand and reported, 'Sir, Maj. Joseph McGraw returns to duty.'"[33] The major had slipped out of the hospital without a medical discharge, and headed directly back to his command. McGraw was soon promoted to lieutenant colonel in charge of twenty-four guns, which were captured in the subsequent retreat to Appomattox. The Irishman joked that he "held an unparalleled military record in that he had lost twenty-three guns in twenty-four days! McGraw knew that the man did not live who could justly criticize the rectitude of his conduct in battle."[34]

The fighting at Spotsylvania Court House lasted for almost two weeks, from May 8 to 21. Unable to either break through Lee's lines or draw him out from behind his entrenchments, Grant disengaged Meade's army and slipped south and east, just as he had done after the Battle of the Wilderness. Lee pulled his rapidly-thinning army out of its works and sidled southeast to keep between his opponent and Richmond. Left behind were some 18,000 Union and 10,000 Confederate casualties. The Southern army was steadily losing its ability to field an effective fighting force.

Three years of steady war were also taking its toll on the state of Virginia, as observed by Lt. Thomas S. Doyle of the Emerald Guards, Company E , 33rd Virginia, Stonewall Brigade. Doyle was captured on May 12 when Maj. Gen. David B. Birney's division broke the Mule Shoe line. The 33rd Virginia's flag was taken, as was most of the brigade. Lieutenant Doyle, penned in a "horribly muddy" cattle field with about 1,800 other Southern captives, was guarded by a regiment of Vermont cavalry and a battery of twelve-pound guns double-shotted with canister. "This information had a most wonderful effect in reconciling them to their miserable condition" as prisoners, Doyle remembered. The next morning Doyle and his comrades were marched east to Fredericksburg, where he found a most disconsolate town:

> This venerable place presented a most miserable picture of the ravages of war. All the public edifices and stores and many of the private dwellings were filled with the wounded of Grant's army, whose groans of agony filled the air. On many of the corners were standing mournful looking groups of citizens watching the passage of their friends with sad countenances. One lady, on the main street, looking from a window waved her handkerchief to the Confederates & cried, "God bless you."[35]

The twelve-pounder battery followed the prisoners in an effort to rid them of any notions of escape, the Irishman remembered. He also noted

# Irish Confederates After the War

*Immense Power on the Potomac.* Belle Plain on Potomac Creek near Fredericksburg was the Union supply base in 1864. When Lt. Thomas S. Doyle of the Emerald Guards of the 33rd Virginia was captured at the Battle of Spotsylvania Court House, his Union captors marched him to a prison ship at Belle Plain. The abundance of vessels, men, guns and stores on the creek convinced Doyle of the "immense power of the United States Government." *Battles and Leaders, 1889*

that their new guards, the 79th New York Volunteers, a New York City regiment of Scots nicknamed the "Highlanders," treated them with great kindness. The Scotsmen could afford to be magnanimous; their three-year enlistment was up and the Highlanders were on their way home. This was a type of reprieve most Confederates could only dream about.[36]

The prisoners marched twenty miles to the Potomac Creek landing at Belle Plain, where Doyle perhaps for the first time realized the hopelessness of the Southern cause. "It was not until the deep water was reached that the immense power of the United States Government was entirely evident. . . The wharf was lined with vessels of all classes from first rate river steamers to fishing smacks, loaded with men, guns & stores."[37]

For Doyle, the war was over. His prisoner group was parceled out among Federal prisons at Point Lookout, Maryland, Fortress Monroe, Virginia, and Fort Delaware, Delaware—the latter being Doyle's final place of confinement until his release on June 16, 1865. For the rest of Lee's dwindling army, Confederate heroism would beget Southern martyrdom during eleven more bitter months of America's momentous struggle.

## Three Cheers for Finegan's Brigade: General Joseph Finegan at Cold Harbor

Gen. Finegan was a born fighter, of hot Irish blood. . .

— H. M. Hamill

We're here from every Southern home.
Close the ranks! Close up the ranks!
Fond weeping voices bade us come.
Close the ranks! Close up the ranks!
The husband, brother, boy and sire,
All burning with one holy fire—
Our country's love our only hire
Close the ranks! Close up the ranks!

— Close the Ranks by John L. O'Sullivan

Joseph Finegan, a native of Clones, Ireland, "was a born fighter, of hot Irish blood, and I have a very vivid memory of how his stumpy figure and fiery horse went flashing to and fro ahead of his men."[38] So remembered Confederate veteran H. M. Hamill of one of the highest-ranking Irishmen in the Confederate army.

Brigadier General Joseph Finegan was a political general. He had no prior military experience when he was made a brigadier general and named commander of the Department of Florida for Confederate forces in April 1862. Florida Governor John Milton appointed the Irishman to organize the military affairs of the state in 1861. Finegan's rapid rise to Confederate military prominence was remarkable for an Irish

# Irish Confederates After the War

*"Finegan Me Bye."* Brigadier General Joseph Finegan of Clones, Ireland, used Florida political connections to gain the leadership of that state's Confederate forces. Finegan won a decisive victory over a Union invasion army at Olustee, Florida, in early 1864. Later that year, Robert E. Lee tapped him to command the Florida Brigade in the Army of Northern Virginia. *The Museum of the Confederacy*

immigrant. He came to America in the 1830s, and settled in Fernandina, Florida, where he operated a sawmill for a time. Before the war he was a lawyer and business partner of Florida's United States Senator David Yulee, a political powerhouse who was responsible for Finegan's military appointment.

As department commander, Finegan used his skills of organization to raise, equip, and train an adequate defense force for Florida. By early 1864, he had amassed a force of 5,200 Confederates and devised a defensive strategy for the state should the Union attempt to invade. On February 7, a Federal Tenth Corps invasion force of approximately 5,100 men under Brig. Gen. Truman Seymour landed at Jacksonville, Florida, and moved inland. Finegan, usually a methodical planner, decided to scrap his original plan to stand on the defensive. Instead, he advanced on the Federals in an aggressive campaign, without adequate knowledge of the enemy's strength and without good communication with his subordinates.

On February 20, the Irish general struck the advancing Federal column at Olustee—a bold, even impetuous gesture. Eyewitness accounts of the fight put Finegan and his son under fire. Captain James Cooper Nisbet of the 21st Georgia remembered the Finegans at Olustee. The younger Finegan was assigned to his father's staff—a seemingly safe arrangement—but "The boy, Irishman-like, plunged into the thick of the fray. His anxious father equally exposed, said to him: 'Go to the rear Finegan, me B'ye, go to the rear, me B'ye! Ye know ye are ye mither's darlin.'"[39] This account almost sounds comical, but to his credit the political general had the sense to give tactical command of the Confederate front to a more seasoned battle veteran, Brig. Gen. Alfred H. Colquitt. Overall, Finegan's offensive gamble proved a resounding success. Union forces, including a vanguard of the 7th New Hampshire and the 8th U.S. Colored Infantry, were routed. Seymour, whose heavy losses totalled 1,861 killed, wounded, and missing, withdrew to Jacksonville that evening. The Confederates also captured six guns, 1,600 small arms, and 150,000 rounds of ammunition. Finegan's Florida force also sustained substantial losses of 934 killed and wounded. His pursuit of the fleeing Yankees was desultory, and the Irish commander later was blamed for his failure to capitalize on his victory. Colquitt was hailed as the "Hero of Olustee."

Today, there is a Finegan monument on the battlefield at Olustee, Florida. Its inscription in praise of the Irish general reads, "So well did he perform his part that a signal victory over the Federals was won." Some question the sweeping credit given Finegan for the Confederate victory. Battle of Olustee historian William H. Nulty downplays Finegan's role in the campaign. "Seymour . . . was fortunate in having General Finegan for an opponent," he wrote.[40] The fact remains that it was Finegan's organization of the defense of Florida, if not his battlefield prowess, that led to the defeat of the Union invasion. The fact that Finegan recognized his inexperience as a field commander and passed command on to Colquitt's shoulders cannot be ignored.

Finegan's success in Florida captured the attention of Robert E. Lee, who tapped him for brigade command in Virginia during the summer of 1864. It was in Virginia that the political general reached his level of incompetence. Finegan led the Florida Brigade during the Cold Harbor Campaign, May 31 to June 7, a series of engagements culminating with the an infamous Northern frontal assault on June 3. The battlefield had reached within a few miles of Richmond. After a month of fighting the Army of the Potomac numbered about 117,000 men, while Lee's Army of Northern Virginia was able to field but 60,000 troops.

Finegan's Brigade, consisting of three regiments and two battalions of Florida infantry, was part of Maj. Gen. William Mahone's Division. The Floridians held a reserve line along the center of the formidable Confederate defenses, on the left side of the division. On June 3, Grant ordered a coordinated attack of the Second, Sixth, and Eighteenth Corps all along the Confederate front. The Union assault at Cold Harbor saw 7,000 Federals fall within a short time, most of them in the first hour. Finegan's Brigade was called forward to plug a gap in the Southern line when Francis C. Barlow's 1st Division of the Second Corps broke through. "Gen. Finegan, on horse, was racing up and down the line, crying: 'Get ready, men; fall into line and charge,'" reported H. M. Hamill. A Savannah war correspondent, Peter W. Alexander, wrote that "The Florida troops . . . made a magnificent charge, [and] swept the enemy before them like a whirlwind." As if to emphasize his point,

Alexander dubbed Finegan's men the "Whirlwind Brigade." The Florida attack greatly heartened Finegan's soldiers, who took up the cry: "Three cheers for Finegan's Brigade!"[41] But the battle was not yet over.

The men from the Sunshine State occupied a salient in the line only fifty yards from Union infantrymen. The official account of what happened in the Cold Harbor salient that evening holds that Finegan attacked the Federals and was repulsed. In dealing with what must have been a frustrating situation Finegan again displayed the impetuosity he had used to advantage at Olustee—but this time his aggressiveness spelled disaster. Finegan's force was not only perilously close to Federal riflemen, but situated at the base of an exposed ridge. Minie balls from Federal rifles came down like hailstones, wrote one Confederate soldier. "The fire was galling, and came so thick and fast our colors were soon riddled, and the flag staff perforated in a number of places."[42]

This deadly angle, like the salient at Spotsylvania, was a death trap for the Florida soldiers. Finegan decided to drive back the Union sharpshooters and detailed the 9th Florida and the 6th Florida Battalion to do the job. The attacking force, under Lt. Col. John M. Martin and Maj. Pickens B. Bird, was greatly outnumbered—a mere skirmish line against a Federal division. It attacked in broad daylight across an open field and was easily repulsed with heavy losses. But Finegan did not give up trying to secure his position. More importantly, and perhaps disastrously, he did not fall back in the face of superior numbers, nor did he seek additional help. Instead, he ordered three more regiments, only about two hundred troops, to try another sortie. One soldier blamed Finegan's lack of information for his foolhardy decision. "Could our brigade commander have seen the situation as we did from our plainer point of view, he never would have permitted this second sacrifice of so many brave soldiers. Indeed, I have been told that the order was all a mistake and was not so intended." But the Floridian did not completely blame Finegan. He believed that some "qualifying or optional directions were dropped" in the order's transmission.[43]

At about seven-thirty that evening, the Florida brigade's second forlorn hope, led by Capt. Seaton Fleming, went over the top and was cut down scarcely forty yards from its trench—the charge a microcosmic spectacle of the horrendous trench warfare yet to be seen in World War I. Finegan was stuck with his perilous position.

The Confederate lines held firm at Cold Harbor. Lee had won one of his last clear-cut victories of the war on much of the same ground where he had won his first great victory as an army commander two years before at Gaines' Mill. The Federals lost 13,000 at Cold Harbor, the Confederates about 5,000. The stalemate once again forced Grant and Meade to change their strategy. Lee's army was being bled, but Richmond had to be taken from another direction, in another way. To accomplish this, the Union commanders shifted their base of operations to City Point on the James River, and the next phase of the campaign to end the war in the East resumed.

In his memoirs, Grant acknowledged that his last assault at Cold Harbor was a mistake. "I have always regretted that the last assault at Cold Harbor was ever made," he wrote.[44] No such regret was recorded from the Confederate general who had vainly sacrificed his Florida soldiers at Cold Harbor. Joseph Finegan remained with Lee's army during the Petersburg Campaign until March 20, 1865, when he was detailed back to his home state. He died in Sanford, Florida, October 29, 1885, after a successful postwar law career.[45] He rests in the Old City Cemetery in Jacksonville, Florida. His grave's monument recognizes his most important allegiances. It reads, "General Joseph Finegan, Confederate States Army, Born in Ireland."

## Truly the Cause Is Lost: Anthony M. Keiley at Petersburg

No man, in all the ages, died for what he thought the right and true, in absolute fruitlessness.

— Anthony M. Keiley

Said a New England grace, "I've hastened luscious food to bring to you; Here's a dish that quite new!" "Faugh! Butternuts!" said Lincoln, and grew sick; But he revived right quick When he perceived that they were nicely cracked.

*A Catholic for the Confederacy.* First generation Irish-American Anthony M. Keiley was a lieutenant in the 12th Virginia Infantry. He was captured defending Petersburg in 1864, and served time in several Federal prisons. A newspaper publisher and state legislator, Keiley became Richmond's first Irish Catholic mayor in 1871. He later served as president of the International Court in Egypt. *Cooke Collection, Valentine Museum*

# Irish Confederates After the War

He tasted them and smacked
His lips and cried, "O, Cromwell, king of saints!
You've cured all my complaints:
These nuts are good, with blood of hearts prepared.
The fools their heads have bared. . ."

—Lincoln's Royal Reception

While the fighting raged at Cold Harbor in June of 1864, the Union Army of the James under Maj. Gen. Benjamin F. Butler attempted to take Petersburg, an important railroad center twenty-five miles below Richmond. On June 9, a ragtag collection of second class militia sacrificed itself to save the Cockade City from the campaign's initial Union onslaught. "Truly, the cause is lost," wrote Southern militiaman Anthony M. Keiley, "but no man, in all the ages, died for what he thought the right and true, in absolute fruitlessness."[46] He was captured by Federal cavalry, one of sixty-five casualties in "this trifling event" that saved Petersburg.

Anthony Keiley, the son of Irish immigrant John D. Keiley, was born in Paterson, New Jersey, and had attended Randolph-Macon College in Virginia. Thereafter he was co-publisher of *The South Side Democrat*, a newspaper in Petersburg. The New Jersey native wrote eloquently, philosophically—even comically—about the Southern cause while languishing in a Federal prison for the duration of the war. His memoirs, *In Vinculis, or The Prisoner of War*, relate two aspects of the conflict often overlooked: thousands of untrained and ill-equipped home guards desperately served the South's cities as a last line of defense; and thousands of Southrons suffered and died in Union prison camps after the parole and exchange system was all but abolished under the tenure of General-in-Chief Grant.

By 1864, Keiley was an army veteran who had served as a lieutenant in the Petersburg Riflemen, Company E, 12th Virginia Regiment. He resigned from the regular army due to wounds received at Malvern Hill, although he remained on active duty until the Gettysburg campaign. Once back home, Keiley volunteered for duty in Col. Fletcher H. Archer's Battalion, a Petersburg home guard unit. When wounded, he unsuccessfully applied for a post in the Confederate State Department. He was working in his little office in Petersburg when the town's fire alarm alerted its inhabitants of approaching enemy troops. The advancing Union force was composed of three cavalry regiments, about 1,300 troopers under German-born Brig. Gen. August Valentine Kautz, reinforced by two infantry brigades, about 3,200 foot-soldiers under Maj. Gen. Quincy Adams Gillmore.

Keiley estimated that Archer's Battalion, which was put in the town's first line of defenses, numbered only 150 men. Behind this line, former Virginia Governor Henry A. Wise, now a brigadier general, struggled to assemble about 2,500 additional men. The home guard battalion was largely made up of wrecked soldiers and old men armed, as Keiley noted, with rusty and often damaged converted flintlocks without bayonets. Hopelessly outnumbered and with little hope of regular army reinforcements, the militiamen stood their ground. Keiley wrote in his memoirs, "that morning's work showed as stout hearts beat beneath gray locks as beneath gray jackets."[47]

The home guard unit was deployed in shallow earthworks facing flat open country astride the Jerusalem Plank Road. The unit did not have any artillery support and was thinly dispersed across a 600-yard front. After a brief flurry of gunplay afforded by a Union cavalry reconnaissance, two regiments of Federals dismounted and advanced on the home guards. "The Yankees . . . became convinced that no cavalry charge would frighten these un-uniformed and half-armed militiamen from their posts," explained Keiley, "and that a regular infantry attack must be made." The tiny band of Petersburgers—tradesmen, farmers, clerks, and schoolmasters, many of them over fifty—held off Kautz's force for two hours, buying precious time for Confederate regulars to array themselves for a final defense. The stalwart defense, coupled with an incredibly inept Federal effort, saved Petersburg for the time being, but the homeguard battalion was eventually surrounded. Those not killed were captured, Keiley among the latter. "Some of the noblest . . . fell with their backs to the ground and their front to the foe, consecrating with their blood the soil of the homes they defended," wrote General Wise in his report of the action.[48] Keiley presented a more somber picture in the aftermath of the battle. That night, prodded with the points of bayonets to a prison ship, Keiley wrote, "a more forlorn set of

Confederates never trusted in 'Deo Vindice,'" the Confederate motto,
which means "God will Vindicate."[49]

"Rebellion is the name which stupidity gives to Progress," Keiley
penned during his prison odyssey.[50] He spent time at both Point
Lookout, the Union prison camp on a barren spit of sand at the lower
Southern end of Maryland, and at the infamous prison camp at Elmira,
New York. Keiley's stay at Elmira changed his perspective on Union
prisons. In September 1863, he had written to Secretary of War James
Seddon asking him to intervene on behalf of a Petersburg friend whose
brother was an enemy prisoner of war at Belle Isle in the James River at
Richmond. The man, who was not named, was "an old, honest and every
way reputable citizen," Keiley wrote. The imprisoned brother, shoeless
and almost naked, had been held in the Confederate prison without
exchange for some time. Keiley's friend had been denied the
opportunity to see the prisoner, and entreaties to Brig. Gen. John Henry
Winder, Richmond's provost marshal, went unanswered. "Such
inhumanity is, I believe, without parallel in the conduct of civilized
belligerents. . . Our soldiers in Northern prisons have hardly ever been
refused opportunity to communicate with their friends and relatives, and
. . . even parties whom they consider disloyal," Keiley wrote.[51] But after
his experience at Elmira, the Irishman excoriated Northern prisons and
even defended Maj. Henry Wirz, the Swiss commandant of
Andersonville prison in Georgia. The Elmira prison camp, explained
Keiley, was even less tolerable than Andersonville.[52] Wirz was executed
as a war criminal in November 1865 for his part in the deplorable
conditions at the Southern prison.

Although native-born and Southern-educated, Keiley often betrayed
his Irish heritage in his prison memoirs. Invoking the name of Father
Theobald Matthew, the Irish temperance leader of the 1840s, he noted
that even the good Father could not have withstood the temptations of
"liquid comfort" that starving Confederates sought in the last hard days
of the war. Although he acknowledged that Confederate whiskey was so
bad as to "make a nun swear," his cure for dysentery was to drink
"Hennessey straight." He compared the much coveted but seldom
available cup of coffee to the poteen of a Wexford man, and in his

critique of prison fare rejoiced that "Potatoes are the inspiration of Irishmen! Sourkraut is——the devil!"[53]

The Southern Hibernian also made friends with his Northern Irish guards. In one instance, the bond of Ireland may have saved Keiley's life. One Irish jailer warned Keiley of impending danger in a holding facility at Hampton, Virginia. The lower level of the prison, the guard said, held Union prisoners accused of criminal acts. There "a jolly son of Erin—a Federal soldier," explained that Confederate prisoners were garroted and robbed if they ventured downstairs.[54]

Keiley was exchanged October 11, 1864. He returned home and wrote for the *Petersburg News* until he was arrested again after the war by Federal authorities for writing anti-Northern editorials. He was held at Richmond's Castle Thunder prison until June 4, 1865.

## In the Gap of Danger:
## Major James Reilly and the Siege of Fort Fisher

He has added another name to the long list of fields on which he has been conspicuous for indomitable pluck and consummate skill.

— Maj. Gen. W. H. C. Whiting

One sword at least thy rights shall guard.
One faithful harp shall praise thee!

— The Minstrel Boy

On the North Carolina coast in 1865, a veteran artillery officer found himself in effective command of Fort Fisher at the entrance to the Cape Fear River. The earthen fort, which shielded the South's last open port at Wilmington, lay dangerously exposed to naval bombardment on three sides. The unfortunate officer was Maj. James Reilly, a native of Ballydonaugh, near Athlone, Ireland. His forlorn outpost faced an attacking force of fifty-nine Union vessels with a combined 627 guns, as well as 8,000 Union troops under Maj. Gen. Alfred H. Terry. As an officer in command of a Carolina coastal fort, Reilly was ending his

# Irish Confederates After the War

*Old Tarantula*

Major James Reilly of Athlone, Ireland, led one of the crack artillery batteries in Robert E. Lee's army. Reilly surrendered at Fort Fisher, North Carolina, and settled in Wilmington, where he helped establish a Catholic church.

*North Carolina Division of Archives and History*

Confederate service where he began the war, but with one ironic twist—the Irishman had switched sides!

Reilly's military career is intriguingly picaresque. It was apparent early on that he craved a military life when he ran away from home at the age of sixteen and joined the British army. His mother tracked the young fusilier down and, one might imagine, took him home by the ear with instructions not to try that sort of thing again. Reilly, reaching his majority at age eighteen, left home a second time to re-enlist in the Queen's service. This time, his mother had no legal recourse to retrieve her son from the army, so she did what any Irish mother hen would do—she dressed him in women's clothing and smuggled Reilly out of Ireland. Once in New York, however, where he was entrusted to the care of an uncle, Reilly joined the American army. He fought in the Mexican War as an artillery private with General Winfield Scott's army when it entered Mexico City, and thereafter fought in campaigns against the Indians. As an artilleryman, though, he spent most of his time serving in coastal fortifications, including posts in Florida, at Fortress Monroe in Virginia, and at Fort Moultrie in South Carolina.

In 1861, as a United States Regular, Reilly was in charge of a small garrison at Fort Johnston in Smithville (now Southport), North Carolina, when North Carolina state troops surrounded the place. As an ordnance sergeant with only a caretaker force, he surrendered the fort "under protest." It was probably the most courteous surrender of the war. Indeed, Reilly meticulously demanded receipts from his Rebel neighbors for the ordnance and ordnance stores of the post. He reported the next day to Washington to Adjutant General Samuel Cooper, who soon would become the Confederacy's ranking general: "I have the honor to report herewith that this post has been taken possession of this morning at 4 o'clock a.m. by a party of citizens of Smithville, N.C."[55] That morning, about twenty rebellious Tar Heels woke Reilly in the old fort's officer's quarters and demanded the keys to the ordnance magazine. "I told them I would not give up the keys to any person with my life," the Irishman related, but the men chastised him for his obstinacy and threatened to break open the storehouse. Reilly reported:

"I considered a while and seen it was no use to persevere, for they were
determined to have what ordnance stores there was at the post. I told them
if they would sign receipts to me for the ordnance and ordnance stores of
the post, I would give it up to them (There was no alternative left me but to
act as I did.) They replied that they would do so."[56]

Later in the war, Reilly would have a second chance to redeem his
capitulation at Smithville.

Perhaps because his American roots were firmly established in
North Carolina, the Irishman quickly accepted a commission as captain
of artillery in the Confederate army after the war began. As the
commander of the Rowan Artillery—known as Reilly's Battery—he
was assigned to the Army of Northern Virginia. The new battery
commander, described as "rough, gruff, grizzly and brave," was called
"Old Tarantula" by his men. Reilly's Battery was roundly praised for its
service in Virginia. At Second Manassas, Reilly was mentioned in the
official report of Maj. B. W. Frobel, who said the Irish artillerist
"sustained his old and well-merited reputation" in the battle.[57] Major
Valerius C. Giles, a staff officer of John Hood's Texas Brigade, captured
a bit of Reilly's Irish brogue, quoting the artilleryman driving Union
troops off Dogan's Ridge: "The domned skillipins [spalpeens?]
skedaddle extinsively," Reilly said of disorganized Yankee batteries
opposing him. In the battle, the gallant, gruff old Irishman rode fifty
yards in front of his battery, directing its fire with deadly accuracy.
According to Giles, "That splendid old battery passed through it all,
never losing a gun or caisson, and thundering on more than twenty
battlefields."[58] The Irishman also earned the respect of the high
command, which recognized his technical expertise. In the spring of
1863, Reilly was appointed by Army Artillery Chief William N.
Pendleton to a board to enumerate improvements in the army's artillery
force.

The Irish gunner gained a sterling reputation in Robert E. Lee's
army, but by 1865 Reilly was back in North Carolina at Fort Fisher.
There, he commanded the 10th North Carolina Regiment, a unit also
known as the 1st North Carolina Artillery. Fort Fisher was a
well-engineered and enormous sand mound fort. Located at the entrance
to the Cape Fear River, the citadel was strategically important to the

South and was thought by many to be impregnable. It was such an imposing stronghold that it was called the "Sevastopol of the South," an allusion to the fortified seaport made famous in the Crimean War. Fort Fisher was described by its commander, Col. William Lamb, as "the last gateway between the Confederate States and the outside world." Its capture would have sealed off the blockade-running port of Wilmington on the Cape Fear. General Lee, who realized that his army could not subsist should the fort fall, ordered the bastion held at all costs.[59]

The North, aware of the fort's significance, set its sites on Fisher and mounted a major campaign to capture it. The first attempt in December 1864 under Maj. Gen. Benjamin Butler ended in failure. Reilly was instrumental in defending against Butler's expedition. Major General William Henry Chase Whiting, the district commander, reported of Reilly, "I have to say he has added another name to the long list of fields on which he has been conspicuous for indomitable pluck and consummate skill."[60] The fort's Chief of Artillery, Maj. William J. Saunders, also called attention to "the skill displayed by that splendid artillerist, Maj. James Reilly."[61] Colonel Lamb, too, noted Reilly's service against the Butler expedition: "To the coolness and experience of Major Reilly we are indebted for the defense of the land face. . ."[62]

A new and more determined Federal offensive began January 6, 1865. Major General Alfred H. Terry's Provisional Corps of 8,000 men landed above the fort on January 12-13. Terry's infantry were supported by Adm. David Dixon Porter's North Atlantic Blockading Squadron. The Confederates had little with which to respond. General Lee had dispatched Maj. Gen. Robert F. Hoke's Division to North Carolina as reinforcements. However, Braxton Bragg, the Confederate department commander, failed to employ Hoke's 6,000 men efficiently. Instead of either contesting the Union landing or attempting to lift a subsequent siege of the fort, Bragg held the veteran infantry in a defensive position below Wilmington and watched as Fort Fisher fell. General Whiting, who realized the importance of Fort Fisher to the South, arrived at the citadel with 600 reinforcements. Colonel Lamb, the fort's commander, had at his disposal a garrison of only 1,200 men, the fort's forty-seven heavy guns, and the resolve not to surrender the South's last port.

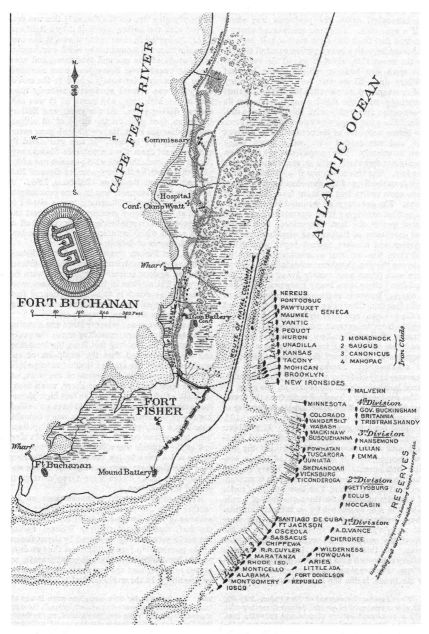

*The Sevastapol of the South.* This map of the Union naval and land attacks on Fort Fisher, North Carolina, shows the enormous effort exerted to pound the fort into submission. Major James Reilly's men initially held the fort's northern land face. Fort Buchanan, to the southeast, was Reilly's fallback position if Fisher fell. *Battles and Leaders, 1889*

On the afternoon of January 15, after more than twelve hours of naval bombardment, Terry's infantry attacked the bastion. Lamb deployed Reilly with about 600 men on the western end of the land face near the Cape Fear River—directly in the face of the attacking army. The Confederate defense of Fort Fisher began to unravel almost immediately. By 3:00 p.m., Reilly counted only 350 effectives. Part of his force, South Carolina troops preferring the safety of the fort's bombproofs to the dangers of the parapets, refused to man the ramparts. Less than an hour later, Union flags began to appear on the westernmost parapet known as Shepherd's Battery. As a bitter hand-to-hand struggle ensued, the fort's senior officers began to fall. Whiting was wounded leading a counterattack on this western salient in an attempt to reinforce Reilly, who was heavily outnumbered. Even without Whiting, the Irishman fought on with determination. "Reilly was a veteran soldier," Lamb later reported, "and showed his indomitable courage later in the day."[63]

As Reilly battled to stop Terry's advancing infantrymen, who had swept through the River Road sally port and were picking their way over the battery traverses, Colonel Lamb was fighting off a motley force of 1,600 lightly armed sailors and 400 United States Marines, who had launched a diversionary attack against the Northeast Bastion. Before long, Lamb realized the real threat to the fort was on Reilly's front, and moved reinforcements in his direction. The Federal army had concentrated Brig. Gen. Adelbert Ames' division, six brigades plus engineers and artillery, on the western face of the fort. Four of Ames' brigades, under Cols. N. Martin Curtis, Galusha Pennypacker, Louis Bell, and Joseph C. Abbott, assaulted Reilly's position. Lamb later reported that 50 men on the parapet could have held the position for reinforcements, but it seems implausible that so small a force could have defended the wall against a determined division-strength assault. Within a short time the gallant Lamb was wounded in the hip leading a bayonet charge against a Union column inside the fort, and command of the fort fell to the man who had surrendered Smithville a few years earlier—Maj. James Reilly.

By this time, the battle for Fort Fisher was a "soldier's fight," according to Lamb, "a stubborn hand-to-hand encounter." Close-range artillery fire simmered a macabre stew—the fort itself became a cauldron of chaos and death.[64] The wounded Lamb sent for Major Reilly, who "came and promised me that he would continue the fight as long as a man or a shot was left, and nobly did he keep his promise."[65] Reilly was determined that the ignoble surrender at Smithville would not be repeated. The Irish artillerist and his men fought on with "a determination that would be hard to excel," Reilly explained after the war.[66] But the Confederate position was desperate, and Reilly knew it. Union troops "were all around my gallant little band of Tar Heels, fighting from traverse to traverse, with no hope but fighting to the last ditch. It was like unto a mole and a mountain—uphill work."

Reilly was waging a losing fight, but he did not give up easily. As night fell, he led a feeble and wholly ineffective counterattack. The northeastern face of the fort had been taken, and Reilly had the wounded Whiting and Lamb removed from the area and taken to Battery Buchanan, a smaller citadel about a mile to the southeast of Fort Fisher. Reilly proposed to make a final stand at Buchanan, although by this time he commanded nothing more than a token honor guard. The major remembered the pitiable scene as the Confederacy abandoned its last conduit to the world. "I formed my brave little command of thirty-two into a column of fours, and with saddened hearts marched away from the fort we had defended with all our might."[67]

What Reilly found at Battery Buchanan dismayed him. The naval garrison there under Capt. Robert T. Chapman had abandoned the fortress and had spiked its guns. Lamb was appalled. "None of the guns at Fort Fisher were spiked," he remembered, "the men fighting them until they were destroyed or their defenders killed, wounded, or driven out of the batteries by overwhelming numbers."[68] Chapman's actions infuriated Reilly, who had foreseen the need to fall back to Buchanan and had sent word to the naval commander to prepare to hold the battery. "I thought [Chapman] too good a soldier to abandon us," he remembered sadly. The Irishman had waged a fighting retreat to Battery Buchanan, but about 10:00 p.m., with a fresh Union brigade approaching down the beach and no help in sight from Bragg or Hoke, and with no artillery to thwart the attack, he gave up the fight. By that late hour Reilly's command numbered only about 500, including those men who had escaped from Fort Fisher; most of them had no weapons. Major James H. Hill, Whiting's chief-of-staff, and Marine Capt. A. C. Van Benthuysen concurred with Reilly's decision to surrender. The three men walked out onto the beach between Buchanan and Fort Fisher toward the approaching Union skirmish line. Reilly unceremoniously took out his handkerchief, placed it on the point of his saber, and quietly awaited the end. It was a simple, sad surrender.

Lamb later reported that the garrison was not *officially* surrendered by Reilly, the senior officer on the field. Fort Fisher, Lamb explained, was surrendered by Major Hill and Lt. George D. Parker. This arrangement may have been to spare Reilly the ignominy of the episode. According to Fort Fisher historian Chris E. Fonvielle, Jr., the fort was officially surrendered by Colonel Lamb and his superior, General Whiting. Whatever the case, Reilly's "protest" at Fort Fisher can be judged quantifiably more vehement than it had been across the Cape Fear River at Smithville in 1861. Union casualties were 686 naval personnel killed and wounded; and 955 soldiers killed, wounded and missing; Confederate losses are more difficult to calculate, but at least 500 men were killed and wounded.

In addition to the dead and maimed Southerners, almost 2,000 officers and men were captured at Fort Fisher. One of them, James Reilly, was held as a prisoner at Fort Delaware until the end of the war. Major General Whiting died from his wounds while incarcerated at Fort Columbus on March 10, 1865. Reilly named one of his daughters Katherine Whiting Reilly, after General Whiting's wife. After his release from prison in May 1865, Reilly returned to Wilmington and became a farmer. After the war, Colonel Lamb and others found Braxton Bragg a suitable scapegoat for the fall of Fort Fisher. For a time after the battle though, Lamb blamed the Irishman Reilly for failing to lead his force to the top of the parapet on the western face—a failure in deployment that allowed a blind spot just below the fort's walls. Reilly's faulty defense of the western salient, though second-guessed by Lamb, was eclipsed by the Irishman's cool conduct thereafter, including the short and sharp retreat to Fort Buchanan. Perhaps Reilly's most lasting praise came from his daughter, who remembered him as "a kind, gentle and patient man."[69]

## Irish Confederates After the War

### An Irishman at Appomattox:
### The Death of the Confederacy by Captain Francis Potts

I loved the cause . . . I never despaired of the Republic.

— Captain Francis Potts

For though with angry gestures, the Yankee bid him cease.
The priest, with hands uplifted, bid his people go in peace.

—The Battle of Saint Paul's by a Louisiana soldier

"I rode to the foot of the hill on which the village is situated and where General Longstreet was. In a few moments more General Lee and staff rode down, and entered a small orchard, which will be forever memorable as the scene of the surrender of the Army of Northern Virginia."[70] So reported Capt. Francis Potts as he witnessed one of the most heart-moving scenes of the war—Gen. Robert E. Lee's surrender of the Army of Northern Virginia at Appomattox Court House in April 1865.

After Cold Harbor, the war in Virginia devolved into a terminal disease in the heart of Confederate territory. Ulysses S. Grant's ten-month siege of Petersburg, though a lengthy and bitter struggle, finally bore sweet fruit for the Union when Confederate forces abandoned the Cockade City on the night of April 2-3, 1865. The Petersburg Campaign, a grand strategic effort to capture the central Virginia communication and supply hub, was meant to strangle Richmond and throttle the Confederate government behind its palisades. The Petersburg siege, from June 1864 to April 1865, was one of the Herculean contests of the war. The investment of the city cost the Union some 42,000 casualties, with Confederates losses totaling about 28,000 men killed, wounded and captured. As Grant had foreseen, the fall of Petersburg cut Richmond's jugular and without a supply line from the south, the capital city became untenable. Robert E. Lee informed Jefferson Davis of this stark fact on April 2 and made plans to take his dwindling army south. In a desperate maneuver, Lee marched as many as 50,000 men towards the Southside Railroad in the hope of joining forces with Joseph E. Johnston's Confederate army in North Carolina. Grant vigorously pursued the escaping Southerners. After a week of exhausting rearguard fighting by the outnumbered, ill-equipped and poorly-fed Confederates, the race ended. Union cavalry blocked the Southern retreat while Federal infantry closed an inevitable noose around its quarry. The brilliant four-year campaign of the Army of Northern Virginia was over.

Francis Potts, a native of Ireland, was 26 years old when he enlisted in the Confederate army as a private in Richmond's Montgomery Guard—one of the Irish pikemen in Saint Peter's Cathedral. By the end of the war he was paymaster for Longstreet's Corps and a former assistant quartermaster. At Appomattox, with a flag of truce flying, Potts described the scene near the McLean house as the Confederate high command assembled to discuss surrender terms:

> There were present General R. E. Lee, looking grander than I ever saw him before, in full uniform . . . the handsomest man I ever saw, my old chief, General Longstreet, with slouch-hat pulled down on his brow, pulling his shaggy beard and looking as if, left to himself, he would much rather fight it out, Major General Gordon and Major General W. F. Lee, soldier-like and imposing, inferior in personal appearance only to his noble father. A crowd of staff officers made up the party and a sadder one I have seldom seen.[71]

Standing in the orchard shedding salt tears on a bitter morning, Potts saw himself as "a subjugated rebel, who has no nation, no rights, and no greenbacks."[72]

Just days before, Potts had eaten lunch with Thomas Conolly, one of the wealthiest men in Ireland, the lord of Castletown House in County Kildare and the Member of Parliament for Donegal. Conolly, "an ardent partisan of the South," had sought a fortune by running cotton through Wilmington. His plan was hampered when his ship *Emily* was damaged en route. The scheme completely fell through with the fall of Fort Fisher. Conolly had rowed ashore in Brunswick County, North Carolina, and was visiting Richmond when the capital fell.[73] After a lunch with the Irish blockade runner, Potts bade farewell to some dear friends on Church Hill in the city, rode over the Mayo Bridge, and "looked my last on our Capitol in Confederate hands."[74]

# Irish Confederates After the War

When Richmond fell that April day, Potts was a broken man. He had looked to God to extricate the South from its difficulties. Indeed he was a staunch Confederate to the bitter end. "I loved the cause and until our army was hemmed in on front and rear, and on both sides, I never despaired of the Republic," he loyally wrote.[75] It is because of the Irishman Potts, writing in a sweep of embittered emotion to his brother in Canada, that history today can bear witness to the death of the Confederacy and feel the utter ignominy of that death. "We have proven ourselves unworthy of independence," he wrote. "For no people in the history of the world ever surrendered their liberties so basely, as our people have done."[76]

Potts was not speaking of the brave men and women who had sacrificed so much for the Confederacy—of those there were many by April 1865. He excepted those few who had fought to the end at Appomattox. The final flight to southside Virginia had been a confused and frustrating one for the Irish quartermaster. He had sworn terribly at his teamsters when they created a disgraceful stampede clearing a site for Porter Alexander's artillery during the retreat. "I galloped backward and forward, reasoned with some, remonstrated with others, threatened here and struck there; but all in vain. I dare say I used language more forcible than elegant . . . for unique swearing commend me to any teamster," the Irishman wrote in one of the few light moments of his narrative.[77] It took over 112,000 Federals to hunt down and capture less than 28,000 Confederates during the headlong flight to Appomattox. Potts' cause was lost, but the tiny Southern army had not gone down without a fight. Union casualties totaled 1,316 killed, 7,750 wounded and 1,714 missing, for a total of 10,780. The Confederates surrendered 26,765 men, lost 6,266 killed and wounded, 3,800 deserted, and 13,769 were captured during the final campaign.

Lee was now expected at the home of Wilmer McLean in the little village of Appomattox for one of the most momentous meetings of the war—the surrender of his army to Ulysses S. Grant. Potts arose upon hearing a tremendous cheer in the Confederate ranks,

and there was General Lee, hat in hand, on his iron-gray charger . . . around him surging . . . a mass of men in all varieties of uniform—the buff of the staff, the red of the artillery, the yellow of the cavalry, the blue of the infantry, in Georgia tweed, in Carolina butternut, in Virginia full cloth and English gray. . . . As each pressed the hand of the matchless leader and loved friend, the big tear rolled down the sunburnt cheek, and General Lee for the first time since I had the opportunity of observing him, showed the gentle heart he held in his bosom, and the 'strong man wept.'"[78]

Potts recorded history's most poignant picture of Lee when the grand general returned to the Confederate camp after his meeting with General Grant. Upon dismounting, Lee was "soon the center of a crowd of weeping men." And still, Potts recorded, "Never in his greatest success did General Lee look more the man than in his misfortune."[79] Grant's surrender terms were generous, and Potts noted "the handsome manner in which the Yankees behaved during the whole affair, the respect shown by their officers to General Lee, and the entire absence of any word or deed calculated to wound the feelings of the most susceptible Confederate." The nation's healing began at Appomattox.[80]

Quickly paroled, Potts rode with a group including Maj. Gen. William Mahone about seventy miles to the town of Clarksville, in Mecklenburg County, Virginia. The trip took about two days. The Irishman was still holed up there when he wrote to his brother, the Reverend John Potts, about the death of his beloved Confederacy. Then, as he had done when he left Ireland for America, he resolved to start his life over again. Like many other Irish Confederates—immigrant Confederates—Potts would begin a new life for a second time after the war. He shortly returned to Petersburg, where he worked as a commission merchant before moving back to Richmond. In the capital city he established the commission house of Lee & Potts, married and had four children. Captain Francis Potts died at his home on Third Street in 1890. He is buried in the company of 18,000 other Confederate soldiers in Richmond's Hollywood Cemetery.

# Irish Confederates After the War

## A Nation Once Again

For freedom comes from God's right hand
And needs a godly train.
And righteous men must make our land
A nation once again.

— From A Nation Once Again by Thomas Davis.

The track of our beloved Confederacy through the political
firmament was fitful, like that of a meteor . . .

— John Keely

**E**arly in the war, Capt. John Hampden "Ham" Chamberlayne wrote home to his mother:

> It has never for one moment occurred to me to wish that the separation had not been tried. Rather than be under them [the North] or joined with them on any terms but as their masters or their enemies I would gladly see Virginia pacified as Ireland was by Cromwell.[1]

Unfortunately for Virginia and the South, Chamberlayne's Cromwellian scenario came to pass. Two hundred years after Oliver Cromwell and his Puritan army laid waste to Hibernia, the South saw its cities burned, its crops destroyed, and its people pacified by a hegemonic neighbor. Ireland and the Confederacy, with similar aspirations for nationhood, also shared a similar fate in a war for independence. As the ruins of the Confederacy smoldered at war's end, some Southerners held the utter defeat of the Irish as the only parallel to their own experience. Southern diarist Mary Chesnut voiced fearful concern that she and her

*Confederate High Cross.* The Irish high cross grave marker of Pvt. John Murphy touts Irish and Confederate lineage. As a young immigrant from Cork, Murphy served in all three branches of the Confederate armed services. After the war, he amassed a fortune as a Richmond hotelier and businessman. He is buried in Richmond's Catholic Mount Calvary Cemetery. *Author*

family would be reduced to the level of Irish immigrants because of the South's defeat.[2] It is telling that this was the worst horror she could imagine befalling the vanquished Southern aristocracy. One of her Irish in-laws was at once optimistic, realistic, and philosophic. "I admire the Yankees so, as a nation," wrote Dr. Mark Reynolds. "I find it difficult to quarrel with them individually, even when they come to rob me. Our girls will soon be marrying Yankees, and then the thing will blow over. And yet I was born a rebel—being an Irishman. Ireland was never conquered. We were conquered."[3]

But all was not devastation for the Irish in America. Many Irish immigrants in the South, whether they considered themselves conquered or not, found assimilation and opportunity in the postwar years. John Mitchel, famous in America as the "Irish Patriot" as well as a staunch Confederate, became editor at the *New York Daily News* shortly after the fall of Richmond. Mitchel's trial, however, was not yet over. In June 1865, General Grant ordered Mitchel arrested in New York because the Irishman publicly demanded justice for the Confederacy in the aftermath of the war and denounced the imprisonment of Jefferson Davis. The Irishman was shipped South again.

Even while being held as a prisoner with Jefferson Davis at Fortress Monroe, the unrepentant Irish Confederate still commanded respect from Irish-Americans. In prison Mitchel was given succor by one of his Yankee Irish guards, one Mike Sullivan of Fethard, County Tipperary. "We feel badly about you and the way you're used here," the Irish guard told Mitchel at Fort Monroe. Sullivan's sentiments were widely held by Irishmen, North and South. Shortly thereafter, Mitchel was released by the Union government under pressure from Fenian leaders and New York Irish politicians. Upon his release in the fall of that year, Mitchel moved to Paris and became a financial agent for the Fenian movement. Though he was the forerunner of the Fenian ideal of militant republicanism, he had little confidence in Fenian leadership at that time, and warned against an uprising that had little chance of success.[4] As if to substantiate his concerns, two Fenian rebellions that followed the war were absolute disasters.

Returning to New York, Mitchel founded yet another newspaper, *The Irish Citizen*, in 1866. Mitchel reflected on his life and seemed to have had little perspective of his notable place in history. In February 1866, he wrote to his wife: "I have been a martyr now for eighteen years, and it is quite a bad trade. I had rather be a farmer."[5] Indeed in Ireland, Mitchel had become a martyr for Irish independence—a martyr in the nineteenth century second only to Emmet, by some estimations. In 1875, all but forgotten by the South and by Northern Irishmen, Mitchel returned to Ireland where he was elected to Parliament by an overwhelming majority. The Young Irelander turned old Confederate was to be a Member of Parliament. He was unable to enjoy his victory, however. After years of exile and his sacrifices in the American war, Mitchel died just a few days after the election. He was sixty-five.

Mitchel's untimely death revived his Confederate allegiances. Virginia and the South erupted in expressions of sympathy for Mitchel's widow. Jefferson Davis remembered Mitchel as a stalwart Southern nationalist. "Together we struggled for states' rights, for the supremacy of the Constitution, for community independence, and, after defeat, were imprisoned together. . . I mourn for him and regret his death as a loss to mankind." The memorials for Mitchel came from the highest levels of the old South. Praise for him was in the loftiest of language. Robert E. Lee had described Mitchel as "a powerful and brilliant writer, a scholar of splendid ability, a gallant gentleman, and a tower of strength to the Confederate cause." Mitchel's biographer, William Dillon, called the Irish Confederate "the greatest Irishman of his generation."[6]

Many today see Mitchel as the anti-hero of Irish nationalism. Modernists have tarnished his reputation because of his pro-Confederate stance—a position often oversimplified as merely being pro-slavery. In America, Confederate partisans often overlook Mitchel, though he was an effective and loyal advocate for Southern independence. Northern Irishmen often ignore his superb nationalist career because of his Confederate dalliance. At least one historian, Mitchel biographer Brendan O'Cathaoir, forgave him for the vagaries of his political alliances and remembered him above all for his consistent stand in defense of the underdog, whether the Irish peasantry, Catholic and Protestant, the slaves of Pernambuco, or Meagher's Confederate "revolutionists." Subsequent events vindicated Mitchel's belief that England would not test the Union's power on the American continent by

# Irish Confederates in Battle

### The Irish Commander of Fort Sumter

John C. Mitchel, the Irish patriot's oldest son, died while commanding Fort Sumter, South Carolina. At eighteen, Mitchel accompanied his father in exile to Tasmania in 1848. Educated as a civil engineer, the younger Mitchel joined the garrison at Fort Sumter as an artillery lieutenant. In command of Sumter by 1864, he was mortally wounded in the third bombardment of Sumter (July 7 to September 4). His final words paraphrase those of 17th-century Irish general Patrick Sarsfield. "I die willingly for South Carolina, but oh that it had been for Ireland!"

*Fort Sumter National Monument*

---

aiding the Confederacy. Conversely, the United States government never repaid Northern Irish allegiance to the Union by helping Ireland in its struggle for independence. "I do not repent anything I have done," Mitchel cried from the dock in 1848, "and I believe that the course which I have opened is only commenced." As he predicted in 1847, the passionate desire for Irish nationhood would overcome the British Empire. Mitchel is buried in Newry, County Down, Ireland.[7]

Ironically, John Mitchel's grandson, John Purroy Mitchel, would become mayor of New York, the city that had supplied so many of the Irish troops who attacked Marye's Heights in 1862. Mayor Mitchel—who interestingly enough won election as an anti-Tammany Hall candidate—was the son of Capt. James Mitchel, an Irish Confederate officer who lost his right arm in battle while fighting to defend the Confederate capital in 1862. James was wounded again at

Marye's Heights during the Chancellorsville Campaign while acting as Brig. Gen. John B. Gordon's chief of staff. Captain Mitchel later served as assistant adjutant general for Gens. Alexander R. Lawton, Clement E. Evans, and James L. Kemper.

James was but one of three Mitchel boys who fought for the Confederacy. Willie Mitchel, the youngest son of the Irish nationalist, and John Edward Dooley's comrade in arms, was killed carrying the 1st Virginia colors in Pickett's Charge at Gettysburg. Another son, Captain John C. Mitchel, had taken part in the attack on Fort Sumter at the outbreak of hostilities. He was killed there three years later while in command of the battered garrison post. A civil engineer who built railroads before the war, John Mitchel was "a born soldier, a man of nerve, finely tempered as steel, with habits of order, quick perception, and decision," according to Maj. John Johnson of the Confederate Engineer Corps. Captain Mitchel left the world with a poignant reminder of his affection for both Ireland and his adopted state: "I die willingly for South Carolina, but oh that it had been for Ireland!"[8] This Mitchel son is buried in Charleston, South Carolina, where for a time his grave was strewn with flowers each year on the anniversary of Stonewall Jackson's death. Mitchel's epitaph links Ireland and the Southern cause for eternity. It reads: "I could not fight for Ireland, so I chose to fight for the South."[9]

Robert McMillan and his sons also sacrificed much for their adopted country. The forgotten hero of Fredericksburg's Sunken Road also performed admirably with Brig. Gen. William T. Wofford's Brigade at the Battle of Salem Church during the Chancellorsville Campaign. In contrast to Thomas Meagher's "lame excuse" at Fredericksburg, McMillan, hampered by injury at Salem Church, did not let his lameness keep him off the field. According to a newspaper account dated May 27, 1863, McMillan's horse stepped on his foot while on battalion drill, causing a severe and painful injury. But, the reporter noted, "[w]hen the order came that the enemy was to be met, the hour found him in the saddle and at the head of his command."[10] The Georgia colonel was hailed as "a rising officer" after he led his regiment during Wofford's pursuit of the retreating Unionists across the Rappahannock River.

Despite heavy lobbying by several newspapers and McMillan himself, he was never promoted to general. Even with McMillan's outstanding battlefield performance, he could not overcome his regiment's poor reputation for drill and discipline. Captain Benjamin Stiles of the 16th Georgia early on called McMillan's 24th Georgia command "a laughing stock."[11] This reputation and McMillan's lack of military experience worked against his promotion. By January 9, 1864, he resigned his commission, possibly because of poor health. His resignation may have been a consequence of his son's resignation the previous day. The younger McMillan, Robert Emmet, had been suffering the lingering effects of wounds received at Sharpsburg. After suffering for more than one year, the young major resigned his commission. Another son, Wofford McMillan, died June 29, 1865, at the infamous Union prison camp at Elmira, New York. A third son, Garnett McMillan, survived the war as the captain of the McMillan Guards and was elected to the United States House of Representatives after Reconstruction only to die of tuberculosis at the early age of thirty-two. Colonel McMillan, commenting on the war and his family's part in it, said, "No act of ours in this contest should cause a blush to mantle the cheek of any honest, true-hearted Southern man."[12] He died in 1868.

After the war, Ireland and its future still attracted a share of American public notice. Former Irish Confederates garnered their share of the American limelight as well. Old Confederates in general were concerned about Irish affairs. Hilary Herbert, the colonel of the 8th Alabama Infantry under which the green flag Emerald Guards served, proclaimed Charles Stewart Parnell to be "the wisest leader I think Ireland has ever had." Herbert hoped "Ireland's redemption from misrule may not be so distant." Colonel Herbert later became Grover Cleveland's Secretary of the Navy.[13]

The war experiences of many Southern Irishmen broadened their political horizons in the postwar United States. Irishmen gained American political experience by holding senior posts in all branches of the Confederate government. Osborn Lochrane, the organizer of the Lochrane Guards of the Phillips Legion Infantry, was a "poor Irish youth" who started his career in America as a store clerk in Athens, Georgia. He became a politically well-connected lawyer. After serving

*Georgia Chief Justice*

Irish immigrant Osborn A. Lochrane raised the Lochrane Guards, an Irish company in Macon, Georgia. He served as the Chief Justice of Georgia's Supreme Court during the war.

*I. W. Avery's History*
*of Georgia, 1881*

as Chief Justice of the State Supreme Court of Georgia during the war, he became a Macon Circuit Court judge.[14]

One of the most powerful Confederate politicians was Dubliner Edward Sparrow, Chairman of the Military Affairs Committee in the Confederate Congress. He was a congressman from Louisiana. William Lander, a native of County Tipperary, represented North Carolina in the same legislative body. County Mayo's William Montague Browne was a personal aide to President Jefferson Davis and served as interim Secretary of State in 1862. He headed Browne's Reconnaissance Cavalry Corps, a local defense force in Richmond, and was made a brigadier general by Davis in 1864. After the war Browne was a planter, newspaper editor, and a professor at the University of Georgia.[15]

Dublin born John William Mallett held an important high-level post in the Confederacy as well. At age twenty-six, he was made an officer of artillery on the staff of Brig. Gen. Robert Rodes, but by 1862, Mallett, a doctor of chemistry, was a colonel in charge of the Confederate Ordnance Laboratory in Richmond. Mallett was a graduate of Trinity College, Dublin, and earned his Ph.D. at the University of Gottingen, Germany. He taught at Amherst College but remained in the South after the war, where he taught at universities in Alabama, Louisiana, Texas

*Irish General and Presidential Aide*

William Montague Browne of County Mayo, Ireland, served at Jefferson Davis'
side for much of the war. The Irishman was interim Confederate Secretary of State
in 1862, and was awarded the rank of brigadier general in 1864. *Library of Congress*

and Virginia. He never relinquished his British (Ireland was then part of
the United Kingdom) citizenship and was a member of the Royal
Society of London.[16]

# CLEAR THE CONFEDERATE WAY!

*An Irishman Born?*

Confederate Secretary of the Navy Stephen R. Mallory was born of Ellen Russell Mallory of Waterford, Ireland, and an Irish-American father, John Mallory, from Connecticut. Under Secretary Mallory, the Confederate Navy developed the world's first ironclad warship as well as the first combat submarines.

*Battles and Leaders, 1889*

Secretary of the Navy Stephen Russell Mallory was another high-ranking Irishman in Confederate service. Mallory's mother, Ellen Russell, was born in Waterford, Ireland, and his father, John Mallory, was an Irish-American from Connecticut. Secretary Mallory was born in Trinidad, and his Irish parentage was an issue with the Rebel war clerk John Beauchamp Jones. The xenophobe Jones questioned Mallory's competence and loyalty because he suspected him of being "an Irishman born." In fact Mallory was a loyal and gifted Confederate and one of Davis' best cabinet appointments. He grew up in Florida, where he fought in the Seminole War, became a lawyer and a judge and served in the United States Senate as chairman of the Naval Affairs Committee until secession. Mallory's expertise on naval matters made him eminently qualified for the Confederate navy post. Although Jones claimed Mallory was "soundly abused for not accepting . . . plans . . . to build iron-clad steam rams to sink the enemy's navy," the Irish-American secretary's wartime accomplishments were substantial and had far-reaching effects on the history of naval warfare.[17]

Contrary to Jones' assertion, the Confederate Navy under Mallory not only built the first ironclad ship, *CSS Virginia* [also known as

*Merrimack*], but also assisted in the development of the world's first successful combat submarine. The South hoped that a small fleet of underwater vessels would cripple the Union Navy's blockade of its ports. Perhaps the best known Confederate submariner was a private investor named Horace L. Hunley, whose name is forever associated with the submarine *CSS Hunley*. Although it was not the first undersea submersible, *Hunley* was the first to successfully sink a ship during war when its torpedo rammed into the side of *USS Housatonic* in February of 1864. Unfortunately, the submarine and its crew were lost in the effort.

Today, we know that *Hunley* was but one of perhaps a dozen commissioned Confederate submarines. Southern Irishman John P. Halligan of Selma, Alabama, built a 30-foot submarine in July 1864 and employed it in Mobile Bay. Although many writers have long believed Halligan's *St. Patrick* was a semi-submersible, historian Mark K. Ragan has conclusively demonstrated the boat was in fact a steam-powered submarine. Unfortunately, bickering officers and few targets of opportunity hamstrung the boat's efforts to sink enemy ships. *St. Patrick's* most notable (and unsuccessful) effort was against *USS Octorara*, one of Adm. David Farragut's blockading squadron ships in Mobile Bay.

Although Confederate experiments in submarine warfare—which included the use of periscopes, electric batteries, steam power, and undersea divers—bore little fruit, they influenced the inventor of the world's first modern submarine, Irishman John Philip Holland. Holland, a school teacher from County Clare, Ireland, emigrated to America in 1873. He was an ardent Irish nationalist and supporter of the Fenian Brotherhood. Taking a cue from the Confederate strategy that a small submarine fleet could contend with a powerful navy, the Fenians came to the idea that Irish submarines could destroy Britain's mastery of the seas. Holland began building submarines in Paterson, New Jersey, in 1875. His project was financed by the Fenian Skirmishing Fund. By 1880, Holland launched the *Fenian Ram*, which had only limited success and does not seem to have ever been used in combat. Still, Holland's expertise in the field and perseverance finally paid off. In 1895, the J.P. Holland Torpedo Boat Company received a ship contract from the United States Navy. The *USS Holland*, launched in 1898, was the world's first practical combat submarine—a direct Irish descendant of Stephen Mallory's Confederate navy, John P. Halligan's *St. Patrick* and the *Fenian Ram*.[18]

The Dooley name also achieved national recognition. Major Dooley arrived in America a poor immigrant, served in the militia, and had even commanded the illustrious 1st Virginia between campaigns in 1862. The regiment's historian, Charles T. Loehr, called Dooley no military genius but "one of the kindest and most generous of men." John Mitchel claimed Dooley was "one of the best Irishmen" he ever met on the continent.[19] Father Joseph Durkin, John Edward Dooley's editor, wrote that the elder Dooley had a passionate love for the South—"the land where he had found the opportunity to live out his life in freedom."[20] John Dooley died suddenly in 1868. He left but a small estate since his business was ruined by the war. His epitaph sums up his life of leadership and virtue:

> Major John Dooley
> A Devout Christian
> A Brave Soldier
> The Ever Ready Friend of the Poor
> His Memory Lives in the Hearts of His Countrymen
> Requiescat in Pace

Virginia epistler "Ham" Chamberlayne wrote home September 16, 1863, from internment at Johnson's Island, Ohio: "Tell Mr. Dooley that his son is here & well of his wound tho' a little lame."[21] It was welcome news in the Dooley household. John Edward Dooley had suffered on the field at Gettysburg for two days before he was captured and given medical attention. He was shipped to Johnson's Island, where he spent the next twenty-one months. Young Dooley was not freed until the end of February 1865, when he and about 1,100 other Confederate prisoners were exchanged at Aiken's Landing on the James River. "Gentleman Jack" was greeted at the dock by his brother James, who was on a committee set up to care for wounded veterans. By Saint Patrick's Day, the Dooleys were reunited at home again, attending Mass and partaking of wine and apple brandy in honor of the feast day. During this interlude, John sported his new captain's bars earned at Gettysburg. He also bore the scars of battle and presented the stark countenance of a war survivor. At dinner one night his prison-induced wraithlike frame and short stature caught the bemused attention of a black servant. "Golly, massa! You'se the littlest cap'n I ever seed!" said the man to the laughter of Dooley and his dinner companion.[22] After the war, John Edward returned to finish his education at Georgetown. He entered the novitiate hoping to become a priest, but in May 1873 the littlest captain died of tuberculosis only a few months before taking his final vows.

In 1892, James Henry Dooley, the surviving scion of the clan, wrote a lasting testament to the lowly privates in the Confederate army: "They were the true patriots and the true heroes of the war. In life they were without honor and without reward. In death they went to unknown places. Let their memory at least be graced with women's tears and men's applause."[23] This Dooley was one of the most successful Irish Confederates. He began his Southern service as a lowly private. In the reunited nation he was a millionaire before the age of forty. Just one generation out of Ireland and crippled by the war, Dooley was one of the wealthiest men in the country by 1899. He made his fortune by investing in and developing railroads in America's Gilded Age. Dooley founded the profitable Seaboard Airline (later Coastline) Railway, worked as a Richmond attorney, and served in the Virginia General Assembly for six years, beginning in 1871. Dooley and his wife, Sallie Mae, built two of America's castles, the Victorian mansion Maymont in Richmond, and the Italian Renaissance style Swannanoa atop Afton Mountain near Charlottesville. Childless, the couple left their fortune to various Richmond philanthropies, including the Richmond Public Library, the Crippled Children's Hospitals of Richmond and Roanoke, the Medical College of Virginia, Saint Peter's Catholic Church and Saint Paul's Episcopal Church, Saint Joseph's Villa orphanage, Saint Paul's Home for the Aged, and the White House of the Confederacy. Dooley also organized Richmonders to send aid to the famine sufferers in Ireland in 1880. Maymont became a Richmond city park in 1925. James died in November 1922 at the age of eighty-one. He was interred in Hollywood Cemetery, amid thousands of other Confederate veterans. His remains have been removed to the Dooley mausoleum at Maymont.

Dooley attended church with another old Irish Confederate, Patrick Theodore Moore. After his wounding at Manassas, Moore spent a great deal of effort trying to get another field command. He wrote to Secretary of War George W. Randolph on August 8, 1862:

> Sir:
> At the very beginning of this war, as you are aware, I had the honor of commanding the 1st Virginia Regiment, which entered the service fully equipped, without cost to the Confederate or State government.
>
> I hope I may appeal confidently to the accompanying letters from my commanding officers, in proof that it is from no want of zealous effort on my part to discharge all my obligations to the Service that I now find myself without a command.
>
> If the President can consistently restore me to a position in the army, such as the best exertions of which I am capable might enable me to fill with usefulness to the Country, it will be most gratefully appreciated by
>
> Your Obt. Servant,
>
> P.T. Moore [24]

This entreaty included letters of commendation from Gens. A. P. Hill and James Longstreet, who said of Moore: "He is an active and gallant officer, and worthy of the confidence of the Government. The 1st was, at the time Col. Moore left it, one of the best Regiments in the Confederate Army. . ."[25] Moore never got his old command back. Instead, he was kept in Richmond and helped organize the Virginia Reserve force under Brig. Gen. James Kemper. In 1864, Moore was promoted to brigadier of the 1st Brigade of Virginia Reserves, local defense troops in Richmond. After the war, he began an insurance agency in the capital city and died there in 1883.

As with Dooley and Moore, the paths of postwar lives often crossed. Thirty years after the war, a heartfelt correspondence began between two old foes. It was indicative of the kind of respectful rapprochement settling over the entire country now that the war's combatants were old men. On November 3, 1893, the Wilmington, North Carolina, *Weekly Star* published a letter from E. Lewis Moore of Framingham, Massachussetts:

# Irish Confederates in Battle

Sir:

I shall be glad to know whether Major James Reilly who commanded a battalion of North Carolina Artillery during two attacks on Fort Fisher is still living and where I shall address him or if any of his living representatives can be communicated with by me. I am in possession of the sword that he wore so honorably in both those engagements and which I received from his own hand on the surrender of the fort. I shall be most happy to send it to him by express if he wishes to reclaim it. I shall be pleased to have his recollections of our brief meeting on that memorable evening.

Very respectfully,

E. Lewis Moore,
late Captain and Assistant Adjutant, Abbott's Brigade [26]

Captain Moore's "memorable evening" recalled James Reilly's surrender of the Sevastopol of the South on the beach in front of Battery Buchanan in 1865. Since his capture at Fort Fisher and his release at war's end, Reilly had settled outside Wilmington on his farm, Farmer's Turnout, near Moore's Creek in Brunswick County. His first wife, Annie, died in 1877. Reilly then married Martha Henry, with whom he founded the area's first Catholic church and school. The Saint Paul Catholic Mission was the only Catholic church between Wilmington and Fayetteville at that time. Reilly donated the land and hired the school's first teacher, an Irishwoman named Kate Sweeney. After the war, he was appointed head of several ferry services in the Cape Fear region—a plum government job that illustrates his prominence in the community. Thirty years after the war, the Irish hero of Fort Fisher was being offered his sword back. Reilly fully appreciated the gesture:

You, my brave and gallant opponent in war, fully illustrate the magnanimous character of a good soldier and a gentleman...When I surrendered my sabre to you it was with a heart of the deepest depression. As a brave soldier you treated us courteously, and showed no bravado over our defeat, for which accept my sincere thanks. . . . Captain, if you have time come to see me, and we will visit the Fort, and see its ruins.[27]

There is no evidence that the Yankee captain ever accepted the Irishmen's invitation. A year later, November 5, 1894, Major Reilly died

## CLEAR THE CONFEDERATE WAY!

*A Gallant and
Efficient Officer*

Captain Blayney T. Walshe of
Wexford, Ireland, parlayed his
Confederate service into lucrative
Louisiana public service jobs after
the war.

*Confederate Veteran Magazine, 1898*

at his home. Wilmington's
former Confederates and
Irish citizens took note of the
hero's passing. His funeral
procession was led by a
contingent of the Hibernian
Benevolent Society and the
Cape Fear Camp of
Confederate Veterans. The
large cortege marched
through Wilmington to Oakdale Cemetery, which includes an 1872
monument dedicated to the memory of 550 unknown Confederate
soldiers killed at Fort Fisher. The soldiers are buried beneath the
memorial. There in the shadow of the Confederate soldiers' monument,
shading the final resting place of his comrades, lies the Irish Confederate
hero of North Carolina's coast.

Other Irish Confederate soldiers prospered in the postwar South.
One of the company commanders of the Louisiana Irish Brigade, Capt.
Blayney Townley Walshe, survived the war to return to his adopted city
of New Orleans. A native of New Ross, County Wexford, Ireland,
Walshe was a young clerk when he enlisted in the Washington Artillery.
Later he transferred to the infantry and was wounded in the ankle at
Gaines' Mill. Detached as chief of the Passport Office in Richmond,
Walshe supervised a lieutenant and twenty-six clerks—the minor
office's large staff is evidence that the Confederacy established an

impressive bureaucracy in a short span of time. He later served as a provost marshal in Louisiana and Mississippi, and forwarded an idea to lead an independent cavalry command of invalid soldiers like himself. In approving this idea, Gen. Richard Ewell wrote that Walshe was "a gallant and efficient officer. . . From what I know of the captain, I am sure it would be a fighting command."[28] General Lee decided against the idea, but Walshe later led two companies of home guard cavalry in 1865. After the war, Walshe became a prominent New Orleans merchant, the city's administrator of finance, and a state tax collector. He also served as president of the Army of Northern Virginia Association, a veterans' group. In a speech at a banquet for the Army of Tennessee in 1896, the Wexford man gave his opinion on the demise of Lee's army: "And so it came to be regarded that the Army of Northern Virginia was invincible. At the last they were overwhelmed and overpowered by the vast armies recruited from every clime and commanded by that great soldier, Gen. U.S. Grant, who had his immense army supplied and equipped as no army has ever been in modern times."[29]

Walshe's successful postwar career was not unique. Another Irish-American success story was that of Andrew Blakely, a native of Belfast. He enlisted in the Washington Artillery of New Orleans at the age of nineteen, served in Richardson's Battery, and fought at First Manassas and in the Seven Days' Campaign. At the Second Battle of Manassas on August 30, in fighting around the Chinn house, Blakely was seriously wounded in the head. The Irish artilleryman was left in a deserted cabin near that battlefield until he was captured eighteen days later. He lost his right eye as a consequence of his wounds, was exchanged and served out the rest of the war as a clerk in the Confederate Treasury Department. After the war he took a job as a hotel cashier in New Orleans. His hotelier career reached the pinnacle in 1895. That year, after thirty years of hard work in New York and Louisiana, Blakely opened the new St. Charles Hotel, a 1,000-room luxury resort in the heart of New Orleans.[30]

Other stellar Southern Irish careers were launched after the war. On April 10, 1865, Anthony M. Keiley wrote to U.S. Army Headquarters in Richmond, Major General George L. Hartsuff, commanding:

General:

> The undersigned, citizens of Petersburg, desirous of conferring with influential citizens of Richmond on the steps proper to be taken in the existing military condition of affairs with a view to the restoration of civil government, respectfully ask a passport to visit Richmond and return for that purpose.[31]

Keiley headed a delegation of Petersburgers and Richmonders who immediately set to work to regain civilian control of their cities. This was the first step in what would be for Keiley a lifetime of leadership and public service in central Virginia. The Irishman joked that the war had made him one of "Lee's Miserables." He thought himself the literal Hibernian who refused to buy a trunk because he had nothing to put in it. Shortly after his letter to General Hartsuff, he was arrested for writing anti-Northern editorials in his newspaper, the *Petersburg News*. When Keiley was released from Richmond's Castle Thunder prison in June 1865, he quickly established the *Petersburg Index* newspaper. One of Keiley's employees at the *Index* was Ham Chamberlayne, the artillery officer who bandaged Joseph McGraw's shattered arm at Spotsylvania. Chamberlayne, who left a wealth of information on the army's campaigns, started his journalism career with Keiley and wrote for the Petersburg paper until 1873.[32]

Keiley married in November of 1865. In 1866, he published *In Vinculis*, the memoir of his capture and four months spent in Union prisons. Throughout this period, he continued to serve in the Virginia House of Delegates, a position he gained in 1863. Keiley was reelected to two more biennial terms in the legislature and served until 1871. He moved to Richmond in 1870, the year military authority ended in Virginia. With civilian authority restored, Keiley was elected in 1871 to be the first Irish Catholic mayor of Richmond, a seat he held until 1876. (The former Confederate capital elected its first Irish Catholic mayor nine years before New York elected Irishman William R. Grace to that position and eleven years before Boston elevated Hugh O'Brien to that city's highest post.) Keiley and James Henry Dooley, as the Irish aristocracy of the city, welcomed Irish leader Charles Stewart Parnell to Richmond in 1880, part of an effort to relieve famine in Ireland that year.

Keiley was the Richmond city attorney until 1885. Although powerful politicians at the state and local level, Irish Confederates like Keiley did not gain national political prominence until a Democrat won the White House again. It was almost twenty years after the war when that finally happened. In 1884 Grover Cleveland, the governor of New York, was the first Democrat elected president since the Civil War. Irish Catholic votes, traditionally in the Democratic column, figured prominently in Cleveland's election. Although the Republican Party offered as one of its campaign issues Irish freedom from Britain, some Northern Republicans chased away Irish votes when they slandered Cleveland and the Democrats as the party of "rum, Romanism, and rebellion." Although the phrase was meant as an epithet, these elements did indeed describe most of the Irish in the South—staunch Democrats, devout Catholics, loyal Confederates—and not unlikely to partake of election day cheer.

Keiley looked for a diplomatic appointment from President Cleveland. Like Keiley, many former Confederates were swept into national office with Cleveland's election. At the same time, others in the Keiley family held powerful positions in varying walks of life. Anthony's brother, Maj. John D. Keiley Jr., a former Confederate quartermaster, was coeditor of New York's *Freeman's Journal*, the country's foremost Irish nationalist newspaper. Another Keiley brother who served in the Confederate army, Benjamin, would become the Catholic Bishop of Savannah in 1900.

Though his brothers' careers were progressing, Anthony Keiley's job prospects hit a snag in 1885. After unsuccessful attempts to present Keiley as a United States ambassador to Italy and Austria, President Cleveland's Secretary of State Thomas Francis Bayard appointed Keiley to the International Court, over which he presided 1886-1902 in Cairo and Alexandria, Egypt. The tribunal was called to settle the financial claims of various nations on the Khedive of Egypt. In this prestigious position, the old Confederate Keiley became a citizen of the world. The Twainesque writer, worldly and wry, later "kept beautiful chambers" in London and Paris, according to gossipy Confederate officer William Gordon McCabe. Keiley's compelling life ended prematurely. Tragically, the Confederate militiaman—wounded at Malvern Hill, captured at Petersburg, interned at Elmira—was killed by runaway horses in Paris in 1905.[33]

Other Confederates stayed closer to home. Confederate sharpshooter Berry Benson reported the last maneuver of one of the South's bravest field commanders, Brig. Gen. Samuel McGowan. McGowan, wounded four times in the war and a survivor of eight months of siege at Petersburg, was the very portrait of despondence at Appomattox in 1865. Benson repeatedly asked the Irish-American general if the rumors of surrender were true. McGowan gave him no answer. Later the South Carolina sharpshooter found the Confederate lion "in the woods, crying, half-dressed, taking off his old dirty uniform, and putting on a newer brighter one used on state occasions. I did not then need his acknowledgment of our miserable fate. His face and the changing of his uniform were enough," Benson reported.[34] McGowan, the son of an Irish immigrant, was an attorney and a South Carolina legislator before the war. After the sad surrender, he returned to his hometown of Abbeville and embarked on a political career as illustrious as his military one had been. He was first elected to the United States House of Representatives, but as a former Confederate general officer and a Democrat, he was not allowed to take his seat in Congress. McGowan, as he had so often during the war, kept fighting. Now his battles were in the political arena, where he became an outspoken critic of the Radical Republicans and their plans for Reconstruction. In 1878, he was elected to the state legislature, and then as an associate justice of the South Carolina Supreme Court. He held that post for fourteen years until 1893. The indomitable Sam McGowan died in 1897 and is buried in the Long Cane Cemetery in Abbeville.

Southern soldiers who had served in the ranks often suffered more and greater hardships in the postwar years than educated general officers like McGowan. Like their former superiors, these soldiers carried on, often counting on the inspiration and leadership of a cadre of undaunted former Confederate heroes. Henry W. Grady, an Atlanta newspaper editor, wrote in 1886 of the defeated Confederate soldier: "What does he do—this hero in gray with a heart of gold? Does he sit down in sullenness and despair? Not for a day."[35] Grady was the son of Confederate Maj. William Sammons Grady. He was only fourteen when his father's corpse was returned from the war. Major Grady, descended from William O'Grady of Donegal, Ireland, had raised a company of Georgians and North Carolinians from the region surrounding Athens, Georgia. As a 41-year-old captain at Fredericksburg, Grady led his Company G (the Highland Guards), 25th North Carolina, Robert Ransom's Brigade, down the face of Marye's Heights. The Georgian and his men fought shoulder-to-shoulder with Thomas Cobb's Brigade in the Sunken Road. Grady was later promoted to major and was mortally wounded at the Battle of the Crater in late July 1864. He died from his wounds at his brother's house in Greenville, South Carolina, while en route home to Athens.

Grady's Confederate service and his supreme sacrifice in battle were heroic, but his legacy was even more far-reaching. Major Grady bequeathed to the country his Irish-American son, Henry W. Grady, who became famous as the orator of the New South Movement. The son helped lead the South out of the ruins of war and beyond the humiliation of Reconstruction. His speeches for economic progress, national reconciliation and racial harmony were well-received in the North and South. Grady even was urged to run as Grover Cleveland's vice-president in 1892. His oratorical skills were legendary, his wit sublime. In trying to account for his gift of oratory, Henry Grady pointed to his Irish heritage and humorously offered, "My father was an Irishman and my mother a woman."[36] On another occasion, the Irish Atlantan jocularly, yet pointedly, addressed the Union's army's Prometheus, Maj. Gen. William Tecumseh Sherman: "I want to say to General Sherman—who is considered an able man in our parts, though some people think he is a kind of careless man about fire—that from the ashes he left us in 1864 we have raised a brave and beautiful city. . ."[37]

Like Southern hero Thomas J. "Stonewall" Jackson, Henry Grady died of pneumonia at the age of thirty-nine. Some of his final words were: "I die serving the South, the land I love so well. Father fell in battle for it. I am proud to die talking for it."[38] In his famous New South speech given before the New England Society convening in New York in 1886, Grady offered: "There was a South of slavery and secession—that South is dead. There is a South of union and freedom—that South, thank God,

*My Father was an Irishman*

Henry W. Grady, the son of Confederate Col. William S. Grady, attributed his glibness as an orator to his father's Irish roots. Henry, an Atlanta newspaperman, was the leader of the postwar New South movement, an effort to modernize and industrialize the Southern states. *Georgia Department of Archives and History* is living, breathing, growing every hour."[39] The speech trumpeted the future of a new South—and a new country.

John Keely was one Irishman who heeded the call of the New South. He had entered the military service of the old South because, in his words, "It was the land I loved"—the land that "received me with open arms."[40] He was optimistic about the future after the war, an optimism that shows through in his post-war letters to his father in Ireland:

> America was visited by me in an unfortunate season. Still I have established for myself a character for integrity, which will some day prove "the nucleus" around which a fortune will, with God's blessing, be formed."[41]

Keely seemed to have little reason for such optimism. The veteran of the 19th Georgia had served from the Seven Days' Battles to the surrender of Joseph Johnston in North Carolina, where he had been severely wounded in the leg at the Battle of Bentonville, the last major Confederate offensive against Sherman's blitzkrieg across Dixie. His nest egg of gold coins was lost when he and his trunk were captured on the sandy plains of North Carolina. Keely, realizing his predicament, sarcastically related to his father what worldly possessions he had at war's end:

> I found myself possessor of the following very valuable property: two suits of Confederate uniforms, a canteen, a sword, a haversack, a wounded leg, one shirt and one pair of drawers, and the reputation of an Infernal Rebel![42]

It was Keely who had lost his regiment's colors at Prospect Hill during the Battle of Fredericksburg. He had also lost many of his Irish comrades during the war, as well as his life's savings. But the "Infernal Rebel" now called himself an American, and through his long and honorable Confederate service had proved himself in his new country. He quickly put the "ten-fold terrors" of the war behind him. "We Americans," he wrote to his father, "can adopt and throw away the thing which we call 'Military Affectation' at a moment's notice."

Keely's story is illustrative of the Irish in the South, in the Confederacy, and in its armies. Like many Irish Confederates Keely found his fortune in America. He gained acceptance from Southern leaders and built friendships with Georgia natives. After the war, he served on the staff of Georgia Governor John B. Gordon, a former Confederate major general. Keely's Southern neighbors called the Irishman "a big-hearted prince among men." When John Keely died in 1888, he owned one of the largest dry goods businesses in the city of Atlanta, a place, the Irishman said, that had "phoenix-like . . . arisen from its ashes."

# Epilogue:

## The West's Awake

And later times saw deeds so brave . . .
Oh, they died their land to save . . .

— *The West's Asleep*, by Thomas Davis

he Irish contribution to the Confederacy, though largely unexplored until now, is an enormous topic. This book has only focused on the war in the East, but the Western Theater lies waiting for another researcher interested in the Irish in the greater Confederacy. But to briefly state the case here, there were many Hibernian highlights and sterling Irish leaders in the war in the West.

Readers may have noticed that this study only briefly mentioned the most famous and highest ranking Irish Confederate, Maj. Gen. Patrick Cleburne, often called the "Stonewall" Jackson of the West. Cleburne has gained a large popular audience and has been dealt with by at least two biographers and in several anthologies. He is the only Irish Confederate of thousands not ignored by Hugh Judson Kilpatrick in his 1874 Boston speech with the promising title, "The Irish Soldier in the War of the Rebellion." (Kilpatrick's monograph misspelled Cleburne's name.) Those searching for Kilpatrick's mention of the overall and important contribution of Irish soldiers in Confederate service will be sorely disappointed.

Cleburne was born appropriately on Saint Patrick's Day, March 17, 1828, in Cork, Ireland. A veteran of the British army when he landed at New Orleans in 1849, Cleburne worked as a druggist after he settled in

Helena, Arkansas, and became a lawyer by 1856. He left the Whig Party when it was infiltrated by anti-immigrant nativists. His political conversion to the Democratic Party was a conspicuous example of the widespread allegiance of Irishmen to the party of the South. He raised the Yell (County) Rifles and was elected colonel of the 1st Arkansas Regiment in the spring of 1861. The County Cork native was a major general and division commander in the Army of Tennessee when he was killed at Franklin, Tennessee, on November 30, 1864. Cleburne was an outstanding general, winning laurels at Chickamauga, Chattanooga, Ringgold Gap and in the Atlanta Campaign. According to Robert E. Lee, "Cleburne . . . inherited the trepidity of his [Irish] race. On a field of battle he shone like a meteor in a clouded sky! As a dashing military man he was all virtue; a single vice did not stain him as a warrior. His generosity and benevolence had no limits. The care which he took of the fortunes of his officers and soldiers, from the greatest to the least, was incessant. His integrity was proverbial, and his modesty was an equally conspicuous trait in his character." Cleburne, proclaimed Lee, was a "military genius."[1] For the Irish general, this was high praise indeed from the South's most splendid soldier.

Cleburne also is remembered for committing Confederate heresy in January 1864. On the second day of the new year, he presented the officers of the Army of Tennessee with a reasoned argument for granting freedom to slaves who took up arms for the Confederacy. The meeting Cleburne convened under the auspices of Lt. Gen. William J. Hardee had all the earmarks of a military cabal the likes of which had not been seen in America since the Newburgh Conspiracy. Cleburne showed no signs of disloyalty however; it was his *solution* to the South's manpower shortage that rankled. A retrospective of Cleburne's lengthy document reveals the Irish general as an avant-garde thinker with little political sense. In his "memorial," as the bombshell was euphemistically called, he predicted the defeat of the South if conditions did not radically change. "The history of this heroic struggle will be written by the enemy . . . [O]ur youth will be trained by Northern school teachers; will learn from Northern books their version of the war," he warned.[2]

Cleburne's logic and idealism, his common sense and as well as his naive folly speak for themselves in the "memorial." Its main points:

# Epilogue

The immediate effect of the emancipation and enrollment of negroes on the military strength of the South would be: To enable us to have armies numerically superior to those of the North, and a reserve of any size we might think necessary; to enable us to take the offensive, move forward, and forage on the enemy. It would open to us in prospective another and almost untouched source of supply, and furnish us with the means of preventing temporary disaster, and carrying on a protracted struggle. It would instantly remove all the vulnerability, embarrassment, and inherent weakness which result from slavery.[3]

As between the loss of independence and the loss of slavery, we assume that every patriot will freely give up the latter—give up the negro slave rather than be a slave himself.[4]

Slavery was not the only issue to be decided by the war, Cleburne contended. "It is merely the pretense to establish sectional superiority and a more centralized form of government, and to deprive us of our rights and liberties." The issue can be neutralized by freeing slaves loyal to the Confederacy, he concluded.[5] Overarching the memorial's plan were Cleburne's sense of Southern patriotism and his belief in the universal, God-given freedom of mankind. "It is the first principle with mankind that he who offers his life in defense of the State should receive from her in return his freedom and his happiness," he wrote.[6] No one less than Irish political thinker Thomas Davis might have written these lines against central government authority and in favor of universal liberties.

The Confederate high command would have none of it. The Southern brass buzzed with negative reactions that cold winter. Some of Cleburne's colleagues tried to distance themselves from the Irishman and his egalitarian ideas. Major General William H. T. Walker wrote to Jefferson Davis on January 12, "Further agitation of such sentiments and propositions would ruin the efficacy of our Army and involve our cause in ruin and disgrace."[7] Brigadier General Patton Anderson, an attendee at Cleburne's meeting, wrote to Lt. Gen. Leonidas Polk on January 14 that the "elaborate article" was "a monstrous proposition . . . revolting to Southern sentiment, Southern pride and Southern honor."[8] President Jefferson Davis moved quickly to quash Cleburne's paper. He wrote back to Walker on January 13: "Deeming it to be injurious to the public service that such a subject should be mooted, or even known to be entertained by persons possessed of the confidence and respect of the people, I have concluded that the best policy under the circumstances will be to avoid all publicity."[9] Secretary of War James Seddon wrote to Gen. Joseph Johnston on January 24 that the scope of the initiative was beyond the Constitution, and that "Such views can only jeopard[ize] among the States and people unity and harmony, when for successful cooperation and the achievement of independence both are essential."[10]

Johnston quickly passed the word to the officers involved; fourteen had signed under Cleburne's own hand. In Johnston's memo to the army there was a special, curt note to Cleburne: "p.s.—Major General Cleburne: Be so good as to communicate the views of the President, expressed above, to the officers of your division who signed the memorial."[11] On February 2, Johnston reported to Seddon that Cleburne had voluntarily dropped the discussion. The Irishman's plan had sent political shock waves through the Confederacy. The secretary of war was reassured that Cleburne was a loyal and valuable officer.

Patrick Cleburne's departure into Confederate politics possibly thwarted his chances of advancing to corps and army command. The decision not to utilize Southern blacks as soldiers might have been one of the more important turning points of the war. Black soldiers, most of them slaves, fought side by side with whites in the Continental Army during the American Revolution. Assuming that blacks again would have joined the army in return for freedom and pay, it certainly would have relieved the constant manpower shortages the Confederacy faced later in the war. Indeed, the Confederate government only months later decided to put blacks in uniform, but by then it was too late to save the Confederacy. If Cleburne's idea had been implemented, it might have changed the course of the war; it certainly would have altered the course of racial history in this country. At the least, Cleburne's elevation to corps or army command, instead of the hapless John Bell Hood, might have changed the complexion of the war in the West.

Another Irish Confederate general in the western war was Walter Paye Lane, also a native of County Cork. Lane was at the Battle of San Jacinto in the Texas war against Mexico, was a veteran of the Mexican War, an Indian fighter and a gold miner. A confirmed bachelor and a

# Epilogue

sleepwalker, Lane settled in Marshall, Texas, in the 1850s. The Irishman was elected lieutenant colonel of the 3rd Texas Cavalry in the summer of 1861. During his Confederate career he fought under Brig. Gen. Ben McCullough and with Brig. Gen. James McIntosh at Chustenallah in the Indian Territory, in present-day Oklahoma. His horse was shot out from under him at the Battle of Wilson's Creek, Missouri, but he continued to lead the advance on foot. At the Battle of Pea Ridge, McIntosh ordered Lane to take four cavalry companies and charge a hill. At sixty yards, a thousand Union infantry rose up and with six artillery pieces opened on his command. Lane's battle commands echo a bit comically, but still must have been effective. "I hallooed to my men: 'Fall back, or you will all be murdered!' They didn't wait for a repetition of the order, but went at once, and, as Shakespeare puts it, 'Stood not on the order of their going,'" Lane reported.[12] He was thereafter promoted to brigadier. Lane was wounded at Mansfield, Louisiana, April 8, 1864, and retired to his business and community affairs in Marshall, Texas. Lane's memoir bears one of the longest of titles in an era of long titles: *The Adventures and Recollections of General Walter P. Lane, a San Jacinto Veteran, Containing Sketches of the Texan, Mexican and Late Wars with Several Indian Fights Thrown In.*

James Hagan, born in 1822 in County Tyrone, Ireland, was a Mobile businessman who became a brigade commander in the Confederate Army of Tennessee. His family moved to America and settled near Philadelphia, where Hagan grew up. He was a cavalryman in Zachary Taylor's army at Monterrey in the Mexican War. Hagan was an Alabamian at the advent of the Civil War. He first led the Mobile Dragoons, a cavalry company raised to defend the Alabama port city. As a major in the 1st Mississippi Cavalry he saw service at Shiloh in April 1862, and later that summer became colonel of the 3rd Alabama Cavalry, part of Braxton Bragg's Army of Tennessee. In early 1863, Hagan commanded Joseph Wheeler's brigade of cavalry and later commanded William Allen's Brigade. He was wounded three times during the war, was paroled May 9, 1865, and died in Mobile in 1901.

One of the most nefarious Confederate generals of the war was John McCausland, a St. Louis-born son of an Irish immigrant. Nicknamed "Tiger John," McCausland was an 1857 graduate of Virginia Military

Institute and also attended the University of Virginia. He helped organize the Rockbridge Artillery and the 36th Virginia Infantry in 1861, when he was commissioned a colonel. McCausland operated in western Virginia, Tennessee, and Kentucky, and had defiantly led his men out of Fort Donelson before it was surrendered in 1862. During the course of the war he fought under John B. Floyd, William W. Loring, John Echols, Samuel Jones, and Albert G. Jenkins. McCausland was promoted to brigadier in May 1864. He is perhaps best known in Virginia for defending Lynchburg from the depredations of Maj. Gen. David Hunter. The Irishman is known in Pennsylvania for burning and looting Chambersburg in July 1864 in a bid to extract a $500,000 ransom from the town. He earlier had extorted $20,000 from Hagerstown, Maryland, residents. McCausland fought with Jubal A. Early in the 1864 Shenandoah Valley Campaign, and was with Brig. Gen. Thomas L. Rosser at Petersburg. At Appomattox, McCausland reprised his escape act from Fort Donelson by leading his brigade through U.S. Grant's snare and returning to Lynchburg. McCausland refused reconstruction and left the country for Europe and Mexico, mysteriously returning to West Virginia with the capital to buy a 6,000 acre farm there. He died in 1927.

The Western armies also had numerous units of Irish troops. Irish companies that were not part of the Army of Northern Virginia include, from Alabama: the Emmet Guards of Mobile, Company B of the 24th Alabama; the Mobile Dragoons, first led by General James Hagan of County Tyrone, and by Colonel Theodore O'Hara, the author of the funereal poem "Bivouac of the Dead"; the Alabama Light Dragoons of Mobile; and the Irish Volunteers of Montgomery.

From Arkansas: Captain Griff Bayne commanded an Irish company of the 12th Arkansas Battalion of Sharpshooters. It was this company that is thought to have performed so admirably at Port Gibson, Mississippi, during the Vicksburg Campaign. Reported one Confederate in his memoirs, "At Port Gibson, Mississippi . . . a hand full of brave men from Erin kept back a whole regiment of Federals. In this instance their thoughts must have been of their fatherland and the oppression it had suffered."[13]

# Epilogue

From Georgia: part of the 1st Georgia Infantry of the Army of Tennessee were the Irish Volunteers of Augusta and two companies called the Irish Jasper Greens, an Irish militia force first formed in 1842. In the 5th Georgia, Company C was an Irish company called the Irish Volunteers, from Richmond County, Georgia.

From Louisiana: the Southern Celts and the St. Mary's Volunteers were part of the 13th Louisiana; and, according to historian Ella Lonn, there were four Irish companies in the 20th Louisiana and two Irish companies from Donaldsonville. A cavalry unit, Company F of the 1st Louisiana Cavalry, called itself both the Irish Brigade and the Copperheads. Louisiana had several Irish militia companies. Eight of these, including the Shamrock Guards, the O'Brien Light Infantry and the Loughlin Light Guards, under Col. P. O'Brien, formed the Louisiana Irish Regiment. The Dillon Guards in the 11th Louisiana Infantry also were an Irish company.

In Missouri, Lonn mentions but does not identify two Irish or Irish-American regiments under Col. Robert S. Bevier of the Missouri State Guard. One of these might have been the 5th Regiment, according to John Lewis Garland.[14] General Sterling Price's army included an Irish artillery battery, and a company called the Shamrock Guards.

In North Carolina, an artillery battery formed at Wilmington, Company H of the 40th North Carolina (3rd N.C. Artillery), was "composed principally of Irishmen, and no better or more loyal men, or better soldiers could be found in any company. When work or fighting was to be done, they were always ready, and would go wherever ordered," according to Capt. Edward Hill, the company commander. The Irish battery served a short stint in Virginia in 1862. It was stationed near Fredericksburg, on the Potomac River, until the spring of that year.[15]

In South Carolina, three different companies of infantry called themselves the Irish Volunteers. Two of these were part of the Army of Northern Virginia for brief periods. The first was an Irish company, Company C, of the former Charleston city militia, initially part of the Confederate 1st (Charleston) Battalion. This force was later merged with the 1st South Carolina Battalion of Sharpshooters to form the 27th South Carolina Infantry. This regiment, under Brig. Gen. Johnson

Hagood at Petersburg, also fought in North Carolina before the war's end. The second Irish Volunteer company was Company K, 1st Regiment of South Carolina Volunteers, led into service by Capt. (later Col.) Edward McCrady Jr. The third Irish Volunteer company, led by Edward Magrath and W. H. Ryan, was formed September 16, 1860, for state service. This company might have called itself the Old Irish Volunteers because of its prewar tenure; it was the progenitor of the other two. There is a monument to the Irish Volunteers of Charleston, South Carolina, in that city. According to an 1893 article in *Confederate Veteran*, the monument cost an impressive $15,000 to build. Two Irish companies comprised the Irish Artillery at Fort Sumter and a company of infantry from Charleston initially named itself the Meagher Guards until the Irish patriot chose Union allegiance. The company thereafter was known as the Emerald Light Infantry. It was disbanded in 1862.

Tennessee boasts the 10th Tennessee Infantry, an Irish regiment from Nashville immortalized in a recent book by Ed Gleeson entitled *Rebel Sons of Erin*. The 10th Tennessee is often referred to as the Irish Regiment and carried a green flag into battle. Another Irish regiment, according to Garland, was the 2nd Tennessee Infantry as well as Company I of the 21st Tennessee (later Company B of the 5th Confederate Infantry). John Berrien Lindsley, the editor of the *Confederate Military Annals of Tennessee*, believed the 5th Confederate Regiment was "an Irish regiment."[16] He wrote: "The Irish name is associated with all that is true to allegiance and gallant in arms, and while no monumental brass commemorates their deeds in the New World, their friends across the Atlantic are assured that the name and fame were upheld by the Fifth Confederate. Their bones lie on every battle-field from Belmont to Bentonville, and at the last roll-call they can proudly answer to their names."[17] According to a *Confederate Veteran* article in 1900, Confederate soldiers are buried in the "Irish Cemetery" in Tazewell, Tennessee.

In the Lone Star state, the Davis Guards, Company F of the 1st Texas Artillery, made the Irish soldiers of Texas famous at the Battle of Sabine Pass. On September 8, 1863, Lt. Richard Dowling and thirty-eight Irish gunners manned an unfinished earthwork on the Sabine River between Texas and Louisiana. A Federal invasion fleet, carrying about 4,000 troops under Maj. Gen. William B. Franklin, attacked the fort. Of four Federal gunboats, two were hit and grounded by Dowling's guns and the other two withdrew. The defense of the pass kept Federal forces out of Houston and Beaumont, and the fort was held by Confederate forces until May 1865. Also from Texas were an Irish company in the Rio Grande Regiment and a company in Terry's Texas Rangers, mustered from the Irish colony of San Patricio, Texas. Garland also surmises that the 10th Texas Infantry in Cleburne's Division was predominantly Irish. This Irish regiment captured six stands of colors at Missionary Ridge. Texas sources on Irishmen in the Confederacy are scant. An anecdote in the 1896 *Confederate Veteran* recalls an Irishman in the 5th Texas Infantry, a unit that was part of the Army of Northern Virginia. Confederate epistler Joseph B. Polley tells of a "Fifth Texas Irishman, who sent out [on] a skirmish line, came back on a treble quick, and was told by his Lt., 'I'd rather die, Mike, than run out of a fight in such a cowardly manner.'" The Irish Texan "fixed upon the officer a witheringly sarcastic look and replied: 'The hail you would, Leftenent—the hail you would, sor, whin there was only a skirmish line of us boys, an' two rigiments and a bathery of thim!'"[18]

In 1864 Union Irish prisoners of war in Georgia formed the 2nd Foreign Battalion, also known as Brooks' Battalion, and later known as the 8th Confederate Battalion. It was engaged in the defense of Savannah, attempted to mutiny and was disbanded, according to Garland.

As one can see, the list of units in the West is long indeed, and no doubt from them many western tales of Confederate Irishmen can yet be told.

*Irish Artillerist*

The Confederate battle flag adorns the stone of Thomas Byrne, an Irish gunner in the Purcell Artillery under William J. Pegram.

*Author*

# Postscript

## In Sunshine or in Shadow

No more the bugle calls the weary one,
Rest, noble spirit in thy grave unknown

*— Faded Coat of Blue*


**V**irginia's landscape is sparsely but decidedly dotted with evidence of Irish Confederate soldiers—men who were proud both of their Irish roots and Confederate service. "You'll come and find the place where I am lying," says the father to his son in the old Irish lament "Danny Boy." Readers of this book are encouraged to take notice of the archaeological evidence of those who answered the metaphorical Confederate pipers' call from 1861 to 1865.

Some Rebel kerne can be found in Mount Calvary Cemetery in Richmond, in the cemetery of Saint Mary's Catholic Church in Alexandria, in Fredericksburg's City (Confederate) Cemetery, in the Spotsylvania Confederate Cemetery, in the Hebrew Cemetery in Richmond, at Saint Mary of Sorrows Church in Fairfax, and in the famous Hollywood Cemetery of Richmond.

At Mount Calvary, which is situated on a gentle slope along the James River adjacent to Hollywood, a visitor will find a modern monument erected in 1957 by the Order of the Alhambra, a Catholic fraternal organization. "In memory of Catholic Confederate Soldiers," reads the inscription under both the Confederate battle flag and the Stars and Stripes. Nearby, in a 19th century indigent Irish section of the cemetery, lie the remains of Daniel Leary of the 4th Alabama Regiment.

The fading stone notes that Leary was a native of County Cork, Ireland, and a soldier of the "Southern Confederacy." He died February 12, 1862, evidently from wounds suffered at First Manassas. No Southern organization tends the grave, which lies forgotten in the Catholic cemetery. But Leary did not forget his country of birth or his Southern compatriots. His stone offers: "Bequethed his pay & Effects to the Sick Alabama Soldiers With whom he fought Bravely at Manassas."

More fortunate was Thomas Byrne, who rests beside his wife in the same cemetery. Amid the Celtic crosses of a more prosperous section of Mount Calvary, the Byrne stone erected by their children displays the Confederate battle flag and remembers that Byrne, born 1844, died 1909, was a private in Pegram's Battalion, Purcell's Battery 1861-65. One of the Celtic crosses of Mount Calvary is the high cross of John Murphy, C.S.A., an Irishmen who served the Confederacy in the infantry, artillery and cavalry. He was born February 15, 1842, in Cork, Ireland, and settled in Lynchburg, working as a laborer there by 1860. He enlisted May 1, 1861, in the Emmet Guard, Company F of the 15th Virginia Infantry. After this Irish company was disbanded, Murphy joined the Rockbridge Artillery, and later served in the 2nd Kentucky Cavalry. He was wounded and captured at the Battle of Cloyd's Mountain May 9, 1864, and was imprisoned at Camp Chase, Ohio. Murphy operated Murphy's Hotel, a Richmond landmark, after the war. The building still stands one block from Capitol Square, near Saint Peter's Church. Murphy, never more than a private in the army, acquired the Southern courtesy title of "colonel," and was commander of the Robert E. Lee Camp of Confederate Veterans, 1886-87. At the same time, Murphy was national president of the Catholic Knights of America, a fraternal organization that he helped found in 1877. "Colonel" Murphy was instrumental in bringing a new federal office building to postwar Richmond, and served on the committee that unveiled Richmond's grand statue of General Lee in 1890. He died February 20, 1918, leaving an estate worth almost $900,000.

Across town, more Confederates can be found in the Hebrew Cemetery, which has a section dedicated to Jewish Confederate soldiers. Beneath the Star of David an inscription reads: "To the Glory of God and in Memory of the Hebrew Confederate Soldiers Resting in this

# Postscript

*Hebrew Confederates*

A section of Richmond's Hebrew Cemetery commemorates Southern Jews who gave their lives for the Confederate cause. Monuments such as this one indicate that the old South was more culturally diverse than is generally portrayed. One of these Hebrew Confederates, Jacob Cohen, also was an Irish native. He was a lieutenant in an Irish company of the 10th Louisiana Infantry. Cohen was killed at Second Manassas. *Author*

Hallowed Spot." Thirty Jewish men are immortalized as Confederate heroes, including Jacob Cohen, a native of Ireland who led Irish troops in the 10th Louisiana Regiment. Cohen commanded the Shepherd Guards, Company A of the 10th, when he was killed August 30, 1862, at the Second Battle of Manassas. The Hebrew Confederate Monument was erected in 1866 by the Hebrew Ladies Memorial Association and was placed into a perpetual care program in 1930.

Not far from the Hebrew Cemetery is the Shockoe Hill Cemetery, one of Richmond's oldest and most historically significant burial grounds. A new stone was recently erected there to the memory of Gen. Patrick Theodore Moore, 1821-1884, and his wife, Mary Randolph Mosby Moore. Also at Shockoe, near the graves of John Marshall, the country's powerful Supreme Court justice, and Elizabeth "Crazy Bet" Van Lew, the Union spy and friend of runaway slaves, is the resting place of John Dooley, the Irish immigrant patriarch of the Dooleys of Richmond. Dooley's epitaph connects the Irish to the Confederacy. It reads, "Sacred to the Memory of John Dooley, A Native of Ireland, Major of the 1st Va. Regt. of Inf. who died on the 21st Feb. 1868 in the 57th Year of his Age." Nearby are the remains of Edward "Ned" Stephens McCarthy, the Irish-American captain of the 1st Richmond Howitzers, who, as the monument reminds the visitor, was killed at the Battle of Cold Harbor June 4, 1864. Ned McCarthy, the older brother of Confederate diarist Carleton McCarthy, entertained John Dooley and John Mitchel on the hills west of Fredericksburg in 1862. Mitchel remembered the opening salvos of the campaign. "We sat for awhile with our friends of the Richmond Howitzers, viewing the gathering hosts of the Yankees filling up the plain, and admiring their order and celerity, when, about one o'clock, I think, an aide-de-camp rode up to Ned McCarthy, and conveyed to him some order. He bowed, and turned to his men, when every artilleryman was at his gun in a moment. 'We are to open the ball,' [McCarthy] said."

Ninety miles north on the old Ox Road not far from Fairfax Station stands the prewar Catholic Church, aptly named Saint Mary of Sorrows. The little white frame building was two years in the making, built by Irish Catholic workers employed in building the Fairfax railroad pass. It was dedicated September 19, 1858, by the Rebel Bishop John McGill. During the war the church was used as a shelter for wounded Union soldiers—Clara Barton's first field hospital—during the Second Manassas Campaign. A monument outside the church, erected by the Order of Alhambra in 1961, claims that the site was where Barton developed the idea for an American Red Cross organization. The church's pews were removed for firewood in the winter of 1861-62, but later were graciously replaced by Ulysses S. Grant. In September 1862 the body of Union Irish Maj. Gen. Philip Kearney was brought to the little Irish church after he was killed at the Battle of Chantilly. His funeral Mass was held in Saint Mary's churchyard. Later, Robert E. Lee ordered Kearney's body, horse, and saddle returned to the Federal lines.

# Postscript

There are signs of Irish Confederate graves at Saint Mary of Sorrows, but no stones remain.

Across the breadth of Northern Virginia in Alexandria, another Catholic cemetery holds the remains and the memory of Irish Confederates. Saint Mary's of Alexandria was an important Irish enclave in Virginia. The parish was founded in the 1790s by Colonel John Fitzgerald, an aide-de-camp to Gen. George Washington. Its cemetery on the Potomac River is thought to be the oldest Catholic burial ground in Virginia. Two Irish companies of the 17th Virginia, the O'Connell Guards, Company I, and the Emmet Guards, Company G, were raised in Alexandria. The city also provided Irish troops for the Irish Battalion and garrisoned the Irish Volunteers, a battery of the 19th Virginia Heavy Artillery. With such a concentration of Confederate Irish service from Alexandria, it would be surprising not to find evidence of this service in Saint Mary's cemetery. James Brannon rests there. A native of County Kildare, he was twenty-five years old when he enlisted shortly after secession on April 24, 1861. Brannon was a laborer with blue eyes and sandy hair. He had gained the rank of corporal in the Emmet Guards, when he was discharged under the Conscription Act. Also at Saint Mary's, a bronze plaque marks the grave of Patrick Gorman. He is identified as a gunner in "Kemper's Battery," the Alexandria Battery commanded by Lt. Col. Delaware Kemper. Also representative of the Irish soldiers of Alexandria was John Delihunt [Delahunty?], whose worn gravestone barely rises above ground level today. Delahunt was an Irish native who came to America in 1849. He was a baker by trade and joined the Emmet Guards April 25, 1861, perhaps swept up in the emotion of secession fever pulsing through the city that week. He was on baking duty for some of his army service and deserted the army at Lexington in June 1864. He was sent to Washington and then to Philadelphia for the duration of the war, took the oath of allegiance, and now rests in his adopted hometown of Alexandria. As this book goes to press, it appears that Saint Mary's Cemetery, the oldest Catholic cemetery in the state, may be threatened by the expansion of the Woodrow Wilson Bridge over the Potomac.

The Irish of the Southern armies also can be found in more conventional Confederate resting places, such as private military cemeteries. The forgotten colonel, William Feeney, rests in the Fredericksburg Confederate Cemetery, his worn and neglected stone no different from those of a hundred other Confederate comrades. Not far afield from Feeney, a native officer's stone, that of Maj. John Seddon, proudly displays his brief tenure as leader of the Irish Battalion. In the same section of the Fredericksburg City Cemetery, the Celtic high crosses of the French family plot proclaim a more distant yet not forgotten link between the South and its Celtic, if not Irish, past.

In Spotsylvania's Confederate Cemetery a close inspection reveals a few Irishmen in the ranks of the Rebel dead resting there. In the Louisiana section lies Lt. John Fennelly, adjutant of the 14th Louisiana Regiment. Fennelly was an Irish native. He joined the Quitman Rangers, Company H, as a private. His grave marker lists him as a member of Company F, but the lieutenant was a regimental staff officer. He had settled in New Orleans and worked as a plasterer before the war. He was killed at Spotsylvania. In the same line of stones is the grave of Sgt. John Mulrooney of the 6th Louisiana's Company I, which called itself the Irish Brigade. In the Georgia section is the grave of David J. Pitts, a musician in Col. Robert McMillan's company, the McMillan Guards, Company K of the 24th Georgia. In the Virginia section of the cemetery lies M. P. Bell, one of the Irish soldiers of the Stonewall Brigade, the Emerald Guards, Company E of the 33rd Virginia.

As a private Confederate burial place, Hollywood Cemetery in Richmond overshadows all others—it is the Confederate army's city of heroic dead. In 1920, when the wealthy Irish-American philanthropist James Henry Dooley died, he was interred among the Confederate veterans in Hollywood Cemetery. Today, as befits his stature as one of America's wealthiest first-generation Irishmen, his grave is contained in a classical mausoleum near his Richmond estate, Maymont. Captain Francis Potts, the Irish pikeman who rose to be James Longstreet's paymaster, is buried in Hollywood, as are countless other Confederates of Irish birth and descent

Other Irish Confederate graves can be found in almost every wartime state. John C. Mitchel, the Irish nationalist's son killed at Fort Sumter, is buried in Charleston, South Carolina. According to Claudine Rhett, writing in Volume 10 of the *Southern Historical Society Papers*, his grave site for a time was decorated by loyal Southerners each year on the anniversary of "Stonewall" Jackson's death. To clear up some confusion found in some Confederate sources, Mitchel's father, the great Irish nationalist and Confederate editorialist John Mitchel, is not buried in the South. He rests alongside his parents in his native Ireland, at Newry, in the province of Ulster. He still awaits the province's independence from Britain.

These Confederate grave markers and memorials are many, but there are many forgotten and anonymous Confederate Irish soldiers who lie in unheralded graves. Their final resting places are often unknown. Among these are two company commanders of Mobile's Emerald Guards, 8th Alabama Infantry: Capt. Patrick Loughry, who was killed at Seven Pines, and Capt. C. P. Brannigan, who was killed leading the Irish company at Gettysburg. Colonel Michael Nolan, the blue-eyed New Orleans grocer, was killed on the third day at Gettysburg in command of Brig. Gen. William Starke's former brigade (also known as the Second Louisiana Brigade). By one account, the Tipperaryman was about to receive his general's star, but instead earned an anonymous grave. A similar fate befell Col. William Monaghan, an Irishman who commanded Harry Hays' and Robert Hoke's brigades in the Mine Run Campaign. In leading two brigades, at least temporarily, Monaghan held the highest level of command of any Irish officer in the Army of Northern Virginia. He later took command of the Louisiana Brigade at Spotsylvania when Hays was wounded. Monaghan was killed at the Battle of Reams' Station August 25, 1864, after years of selfless Confederate service; no Irish monument crowns his grave in Shepherdstown, West Virginia. Mention has already been made of the death in battle of Col. Henry B. Strong at Sharpsburg. Another Irish colonel, Peter Brenan of the 61st Georgia Infantry, was lost in action at Gettysburg. In the same titanic struggle, Capt. James Hallinan of the 1st Virginia's Montgomery Guard was mortally wounded in Pickett's Charge. No Irish monuments remember their sacrifices. Why are there so few memorials to the Irish leaders and troops of the "Lost Cause?"

Some may be surprised to learn that the old Confederacy boasts some rather fine, if obscure, examples of Irish Confederate memorials; not all of the South's Irish soldiers are forgotten. In Savannah, Georgia, the Irish Jasper Greens are memorialized in stone in the Savannah Catholic Cemetery. Charleston's Irish Volunteers monument stands in the Saint Lawrence Catholic Cemetery in that city. In Texas, four Confederate monuments with Irish connections exist. Major General Patrick Cleburne gave his name to the city of Cleburne, Texas, where the Confederate Memorial Fountain focuses attention on the Irish Confederate martyr. (Cleburne's grave monument is in the Maple Hill Cemetery in Helena, Arkansas.) Irish Lt. Richard Dowling, the hero of Sabine Pass, Texas, has three monuments dedicated to his Confederate service. The imposing, larger than life Dick Dowling Statue Monument at Sabine Pass includes the names of the handful of Irish artillerymen who fended off a Federal invasion fleet in 1863; it was unveiled in 1937. Another Dowling monument stands in Houston's Hermann Park, dedicated on Saint Patrick's Day, 1905. Dowling's grave monument is in Saint Vincent's Cemetery in Houston.

A monument stands today to the "hero" of Ocean Pond (Olustee), Brig. Gen. Joseph Finegan, in Olustee, Florida, and Finegan's grave monument is in Jacksonville, Florida's Old City Cemetery. Three Southern monuments testify to Father Abram J. Ryan's Confederate allegiance. Mobile, Alabama, is home to a Father Ryan memorial in the Children of Mary Lot of the Mobile Catholic Cemetery. There also is a Father Ryan monument in New Orleans, unveiled in 1950. Father Ryan's grave monument in Norfolk, Virginia's Elmwood Cemetery also attests to the poet priest's Confederate patriotism.

Not all memorials to Irish Confederates were cast in stone or bronze. Praise came to some Confederate Irishmen in poetry. A war poem was written for the Irishmen who served South Carolina in the Charleston Battalion, Company C, known as the Irish Volunteers. The company later was part of the 27th South Carolina and saw service in Virginia and North Carolina as well as in its native state. The paean, written by James Power, is typical of the florid, inflated rhyme and verse of the Victorian age—as such it is not great poetry—but its many Irish allusions serve to forever tie the Irishmen of the Palmetto state to the Lost Cause.

# Postscript

To the Irish Volunteers
Air— "The Soldier's Joy"

Since valiant Oscar, now two thousand years ago,
The race of brave Milesus was a terror to the foe,
The Red Branch Knights, through bloody fights,
Oft rent the air with cheers,
When vict'ry was the wonted right
Of the Irish Volunteers!

From the battlefield of Gawra, the gay Feinne fierce and true,
Their banner flaunted proudly down the road to Eighty-two.
Dungannon saw 'neath Grattan's law,
The Feinne without fears
As the breeze swept past the green flag
Of the Irish Volunteers!

Today we see the prototype of Eireann's ancient fame—
The Irish bosom swells with joy at mention of the name.
Tho' exile's chill, he feels yet still.
He hails the name with cheers—
These men of muscle, heart and will—
Our Irish Volunteers!

When country calls to arms, they are ever in the van;
In fealty to that calling you yield not to natal son.
Your banner's green, as plainly seen,
Portrayed the strife of years—
Monumental honors to the dead
Of the Irish Volunteers!

— James Power, 1877

Appendix I

# The Wearing of the Gray

## Irish Companies in the Army of Northern Virginia

The green flag seemed to exert a magnetic control over the brawny sons
of the Emerald Isle. Their fondness for their own companies is
explicable: the Irishman fights better shoulder to shoulder with Irishmen
as comrades, and always yearns to reflect the honor on 'Ould Ireland.'

—Ella Lonn, *Foreigners in the Confederacy*

## A Note on the Irish Companies in the Army of Northern Virginia

A study of Irish troops in the Confederacy is a study of the armies at the company level. In the Army of Northern Virginia, there were no Irish brigades or regiments, although Richard Taylor called the 6th Louisiana the Irish regiment. The company, then, the smallest organization in the army, was the largest unit of Irish organization in this army. Therefore, I have included regiment and brigade information for each company to help the military historian pinpoint the approximate location of Irish companies on the battlefield. Although difficult to study as a military unit, the company makes a good study for details of the war. Primary sources often focus at the company level because the company was the unit the individual soldier most identified with.

Some general observations about the Irish companies in the Confederate army are in order. Irish companies often protected the regimental colors. The Irish Volunteers of the 1st South Carolina, the Jackson Guards of the 19th Georgia, and the Virginia Hibernians of the

27th Virginia are some notable examples of this interesting phenomenon. The commander of the 8th Alabama, Col. Hilary Herbert, provided evidence of Irish service in color guards when he noted that Sgt. Michael Sexton of the regiment's Emerald Guards was the regiment's "gallant" color sergeant at Gaines' Mill. Sergeant Sexton was killed in that battle. Corporal Phelan Harris was another Irish color bearer of the 8th Alabama whom Herbert cited for gallantry at Sharpsburg and Salem Church. (See Herbert's "A Short History of the Eighth Alabama.")

Often troops serving in Confederate Regular units had a preponderance of Irish soldiers in their ranks. This is perhaps because they were recruited from statewide labor sources, i.e. Irish enclaves, often established for laying rail, or it is because Confederate Regulars were formed around a nucleus of pre-war militia companies, many of which were composed of Irishmen.

Although there were many Irish companies in the army, there were many Irish and Irish-American soldiers who joined local units that were not all Irish. Therefore a study of only Irish units and leaders probably understates the overall Irish contribution to the war effort. On the other hand, some units that were originally all Irish lost their Irish character as time wore on. This meant that their original Irish character was forgotten after the war. John Berrien Lindsley, in his *Military Annals of Tennessee*, noted that ports of immigration were closed to the South, and with a limited Irish population, a company organized as an Irish green flag unit was not easy to rebuild as such.

The companies are listed here in the brigades they were part of at the Battle of Fredericksburg. Some general reference sources consulted for this compilation include state roster books of Georgia and Louisiana, compiled rosters found in the "Virginia Regimental Histories" Series, William Frayne Amann, *Personnel of the Civil War*, Volume I, The Confederate Armies; W. Brewer, *Alabama: Her History, Resources, War Record, and Public Men from 1540 to 1872*; Joseph H. Crute Jr., *Units of the Confederate States Army*; and A. S. Salley Jr., *South Carolina Troops in Confederate Service*, Volume I. Additional pertinent sources follow select entries.

# Appendix I: Irish Companies in the Army of Northern Virginia

## ALABAMA

**Emerald Guards, Company I, 8th Alabama Regiment:** Wilcox's Brigade: Company Commanders: Patrick Loughry, killed at Seven Pines; C. P. Brannigan, in command at Fredericksburg, killed at Gettysburg; John McGrath, wounded at Wilderness and Spotsylvania. This company was formed at Mobile. Part of the 8th Alabama, it began its career with the Army of Northern Virginia at Yorktown. The unit entered Confederate service wearing a dark green uniform. The company flag featured the Confederate colors with a central portrait of Washington on one side. The other side of the banner displayed a harp encircled by shamrocks and the inscriptions "Erin go Bragh" and "Faugh a ballagh." There is evidence from the regiment's commander, Hilary Herbert, that the Irish company was the 8th Alabama's color company. At Frazier's Farm, the regiment reportedly fought Meagher's Irish Brigade, taking fifty percent casualties in the process. An Alabama Irishman defended the pulpit of Salem Church in the Chancellorsville Campaign. The Irish sharpshooter was quoted as saying he delivered "from that pulpit some of the most forcible argument any one iver sint from it before." (Ernest B. Furgurson, *Chancellorsville 1863: The Souls of the Brave*, 277.)

## GEORGIA

**Emmet Rifles, Company B, 1st Georgia (Regulars): G. T. Anderson's Brigade:** Company commanders: William Martin, to lieutenant colonel, Feb. 3, 1862. Martin died of tuberculosis while home on leave October 16, 1864. 1st Lieutenant James G. Montgomery, to captain of Company K, January 15, 1862, wounded at Sharpsburg; Robert J. Magill, 1st lieutenant; Michael L. Cass, 2nd lieutenant. Georgia rosters list no company names of the 1st Regulars, but this company is identified as such in William Frayne Amann, *Personnel of the Civil War*, Volume I, 48. The Georgia Regulars, as in other states, may have been built around prewar militia companies. This unit could have been an Irish militia company that kept its prewar name. The roster list also shows Company G of the 1st Georgia to be largely composed of soldiers with Irish surnames. 1st Georgia Companies A, D, E, F, and M also show a large number of Irish surnames in the roster lists.

**Jackson Guards, Company B, 19th Georgia Regiment: Archer's Brigade:** The Guards were an Irish company raised in Atlanta, probably named after powerful Democratic President Andrew Jackson—to proclaim the Irish company's party allegiance. The unit's original flag was green with the harp and shamrock displayed prominently, according to a May 27, 1861, *Southern Confederacy* article. The company commanders were James Henry Neal, to colonel of the regiment August 20, 1863. He was killed at Bentonville, North Carolina, March 1865; Dennis Myers, to June 26, 1862, wounded at Second Manassas; John Keely, promoted Sept. 2, 1863, wounded at Bentonville. The Guards were the color company of the regiment, and the unit lost the colors when it was heavily involved in the Prospect Hill fighting at Fredericksburg. By the end of the war, the regiment was part of Alfred Colquitt's Brigade. In his memoirs, Captain Keely tells the story of how members of the brigade visited him at his hospital window after his leg was shattered at Bentonville. "Goodbye, Capt. Keely, give us Irish soldiers always, you stayed with us as long as you could, and we won't forget you," he was told. His own company broke ranks to shake his hand, with one saying: "The honor of old Ireland . . . should never be tarnished." Keely and the Jackson Guards fought from the Seven Days' Battles to Joseph Johnston's surrender in April 1865.

**Montgomery Guards, Company K, 20th Georgia: Toombs' Brigade (Benning):** This was a predominantly Irish company from Richmond County, Georgia. Company commanders were Captain Jesse F. Cleveland, to December 31, 1861; William Craig, 1st lieutenant to captain, January 10, 1862; and to major May 8, 1864; Joseph H. Russell.

**McMillan Guards, Company K, 24th Georgia Regiment: Cobb's Brigade:** The McMillan Guards, though not entirely Irish, had a distinct Irish flavor because of its immigrant patron Robert McMillan, and the presence of his sons in the company. The company was formed in Habersham County, Georgia. The company commanders were Capt. John G. Porter, resigned February 13, 1863; and Capt. Ezekiel Fuller, captured at Deep Bottom, Virginia, August 16, 1864. The company was part of the force holding the Sunken Road at Fredericksburg. One Irishman in the Guards, Henry Holbrooks, had this to tell a reporter after his fight behind the stone wall: "Well, stranger, I've often hearn tell of men spilin' for a fight an' I've hearn some men myself a spilin' for a fight. Now Stranger, I never did spile for a fight myself because I mout get killed, but Stranger if ever in this world I do spile for a fight it'll be jist sich a fight as we had behind that stone wall there under Maries [sic] Heights." Such was the experience of the McMillan Guards at Fredericksburg. The vignette was reported in the soldier's Irish dialect. (Elijah Henry Sutton, *Grand Pa's War Stories*.)

**Lochrane Guards, Company F, Phillips Legion Infantry: Cobb's Brigade:** This was a company of Irishmen from Macon, Georgia, named for Osborn A. Lochrane, an Irish immigrant who rose to serve as the Chief Justice of the Georgia Supreme Court during the war. He was a political ally of Governor Joseph E. Brown and a prominent spokesman in the Irish-American community in Georgia. The *Macon Daily Telegraph* of July 27, 1861, reported the "meeting of Irish citizens was large and enthusiastic. A military company was at once organized and Jackson Barnes, Esq., unanimously elected captain . . . The name of the Company is a just tribute to an able and patriotic Irishman." The Guards were described as a "noble band of patriots, all natives of the 'Emerald Isle.'" Part of Cobb's Brigade, the company was directly in the path of the ill-fated Union assaults on the Sunken Road. If Confederate Irishmen had an occasion to witness and cheer the celebrated attack of the Irish Brigade at the Stone Wall, it was this unit. However, there seem to be no reports of Irishmen in the Lochrane Guards acknowledging the green flag of the 28th Massachusetts. Company commanders:

# Appendix I: Irish Companies in the Army of Northern Virginia

Jackson Barnes, resigned Sept. 12, 1862; Patrick McGovern at Fredericksburg; 1st Lieutenant James Meara, resigned Jan. 13, 1862; 1st Lieutenant Michael S. Walsh, wounded at Gettysburg. The company was later called the Lochrane Light Infantry. (Volume 244, Fredericksburg and Spotsylvania National Military Park Manuscript Collection.)

## LOUISIANA

**Emmet Guards, Company D, 1st Louisiana: Hays' Brigade:** Company commanders: James Nelligan, promoted to major June 16, 1862; Captain Albert N. Cummings. This company, named after Irish nationalist Robert Emmet, was formed in Orleans Parish.

**Montgomery Guards, Company E, 1st Louisiana: Hays' Brigade:** Company commanders were Capt. Michael Nolan, until promoted April 28, 1862; Capt. Michael B. Gilmore, killed June 25, 1862; Capt. Thomas Rice. The company was from Orleans Parish. Part of the 1st Louisiana, the unit distinguished itself at Second Manassas. According to Chaplain Joseph Sheeran, the regiment held its position even when it ran out of ammunition: "Throwing down their empty guns they attacked and drove back the enemy with rocks which they found in abundance on the roadside. . . [A]fter the battle many of the Yankees were found on the field with broken skulls." (Joseph T. Durkin, *Confederate Chaplain: A War Journal of James B. Sheeran.*)

**Orleans Light Guards, Company F, 1st Louisiana: Hays' Brigade:** This company was raised in New Orleans. Company commanders: Patrick O'Rourke, to April 28, 1862; Samuel H. Snowden, to January 1864; James Dillon. Virginian William Cabell Tavenner, later a lieutenant colonel in the 17th Virginia Cavalry, enlisted in this company and was elected lieutenant in April 1861.

**Moore Guards, Company B, 2nd Louisiana: Hays' Brigade:** Company commanders: John Kelso, to April 30, 1862; Michael Grogan, promoted to major July 1, 1862; James F. Utz. The company was raised in Rapides Parish.

**5th Louisiana Regiment, Hays' Brigade:** Louisiana historian Terry Jones counts ninety-four Irish-born in this regiment, though it had no distinctly Irish company. Irish-born John McGurk commanded the Chalmette Guards, Company B, which was fifty-nine percent foreign, according to Jones. Captain A. E. Shaw also commanded this company. An August 27, 1861, letter from Theodore Mandeville, a soldier in the regiment, contends that the regiment was mostly "uneducated Irishmen." (Terry L. Jones, *Lee's Tigers: The Louisiana Infantry in the Army of Northern Virginia.*)

**Irish Brigade (Company A), Company I, 6th Louisiana: Hays' Brigade:** The name was chosen for this unit as the South's attempt to garner some cachet from the mystique of the Irish Brigades made famous in European history. Only two companies were raised under the Irish Brigade banner. Evidently the Irish in the South felt state and local ties were more important than trying to recapture the lost glories of European exile forces. Company commanders: Samuel L. James, promoted to major December 1861; Joseph Hanlon, promoted to major Sept. 17, 1862; Blayney T. Walshe. The company was raised in Orleans Parish. (For more information, see James Gannon, *Irish Rebels Confederate Tigers: A History of the 6th Louisiana Volunteers, 1861-1865.*)

**Irish Brigade (Company B), Company F, 6th Louisiana: Hays' Brigade:** Company commanders: William Monaghan, to major June 27, 1862; Michael O'Connor. Lieutenant General Richard Taylor, who commanded the Louisiana brigade early in the war, said of the 6th Louisiana: "The 6th were Irishmen, stout hardy fellows, turbulent in camp and requiring a strong hand, but responding to justice and kindness, and ready to follow their officers to the death." (Richard Taylor, *Destruction and Reconstruction,* and James Gannon, *Irish Rebels Confederate Tigers: A History of the 6th Louisiana Volunteers, 1861-1865.*)

**Calhoun Guards, Company B, 6th Louisiana: Hays' Brigade:** This company was from Orleans Parish. It was first commanded by Henry B. Strong, who was promoted to regimental command May 9, 1862. He led the regiment at Sharpsburg, where he was killed, one of fifteen Confederate colonels who fell in that battle. Thomas Redmond is also listed as a company commander. The company took its name from states' rights politician John C. Calhoun, the son of Irish immigrant Patrick Calhoun of County Donegal, Ireland. (James Gannon, *Irish Rebels Confederate Tigers: A History of the 6th Louisiana Volunteers, 1861-1865.*)

**Sarsfield Rangers, Company C, 7th Louisiana: Hays' Brigade:** Company commanders: J. Moore Wilson, McGavock Goodwyn, and Charles Cameron. The company was raised in Orleans Parish. It was probably named for Patrick Sarsfield, the 17th century Irish Catholic general who successfully defended Limerick in the Irish Jacobite War against William and Mary. According to Richard Taylor, Sarsfield's "brilliant" defense of Limerick was the only Irish "domestic struggle in which they [Irish soldiers] have shown their worth." (Taylor, *Destruction and Reconstruction.*)

**Virginia Guards, Company D, 7th Louisiana: Hays' Brigade:** Company commanders: Robert D. Scott, Louis H. Malarcher. The company was mustered from Orleans Parish. Although only four 7th regiment companies are noted here as Irish, Thomas Benton Reed of the 9th Louisiana wrote that the 7th Louisiana "was composed mostly of Irishmen." In his memoir, *A Private in Gray,* Reed tells an amusing tale of a fight between two quarrelsome Irishmen. (*A Private in Gray,* Camden, Arkansas: T. B. Reed, 1905, 40-41.)

# Appendix I: Irish Companies in the Army of Northern Virginia

**Irish Volunteers, Company F, 7th Louisiana: Hays' Brigade:** This company was raised in Assumption Parish. Company commanders: William B. Ratliff, Thomas Gibbs Morgan, Thomas W. Kerrigan.

**Virginia Blues, Company I, 7th Louisiana: Hays' Brigade:** The Blues were from Orleans Parish. Company commanders: Daniel A. Wilson Jr., a Virginian who was promoted to colonel and appointed judge advocate for the Second Corps, Army of Northern Virginia, January 1, 1863; Captain Charles Bellinger.

**Cheneyville Rifles, Company H, 8th Louisiana: Hays' Brigade:** The Rifles, from Rapides Parish, were led by Patrick F. Keary. The company carried a flag made from the wedding dress of Mrs. T. B. Helm, a New Orleans belle. The colors were lost July 2, 1863, in the Cemetery Hill fighting at Gettysburg. A 1911 *Confederate Veteran* article reported that the flag was returned at a war reunion in Little Rock, Arkansas.

**Emerald Guards, Company E, 9th Louisiana: Hays' Brigade:** This company also was known as the Milliken Bend Guards. It was raised in Madison Parish. Company commanders were William R. Peck to lieutenant colonel April 24, 1862; George D. Shadburne, resigned October 1, 1862; Edward Owens.

**Shepherd Guards, Company A, 10th Louisiana: Starke's Brigade:** Company commanders: Alfred or Alexander Philips, resigned December 28, 1861; Jacob A. Cohen, killed August 30, 1862; Isaac Lyons. The largely Irish company was formed in Orleans Parish and is unique in that it had two Jewish company commanders. Cohen was born in Ireland.

**Derbigny Guards, Company B, 10th Louisiana: Starke's Brigade:** Company commanders: Lea F. Bakewell, resigned August 26, 1861; Edward W. Huntington, resigned December 28, 1861; Henry C. Marks, killed July 1, 1862; James Buckner, promoted October 6, 1862; Charles Knowlton, to October 31, 1864.

**Hewitt's Guards, Company C, 10th Louisiana: Starke's Brigade:** Company commanders: Richard M. Hewitt, resigned Dec. 28, 1861; Thomas N. Powell, promoted to major May 3, 1864, wounded at Spotsylvania, killed at Petersburg; James Scott.

**Hawkins' Guards, Company D, 10th Louisiana: Starke's Brigade:** Company commanders: Charles F. White, resigned December 21, 1861; Jacob H. Williams, resigned November 8, 1862, Ernest Webre, to January 10, 1865.

**Orleans Blues, Company H, 10th Louisiana: Starke's Brigade:** Company commanders: William B. Barnett, to January 13, 1863; Leon Jastremski. The company was formed in Orleans Parish.

**14th Louisiana, Six Companies, Starke's Brigade:** Ella Lonn reported six of twelve companies in the 14th were predominantly Irish. No company has the usual distinctly Irish appellation. The 14th was part of what has been called Lee's Foreign Legion, and was to have been part of a Polish Brigade organized under Col. Valery Sulakowski. Other commanders were Richard W. Jones, Zebulon York and David Zable. The regiment was predominantly German, French, and Irish, according to historian Arthur Bergeron. In 1861 en route to Virginia, some members of the regiment got drunk and rioted at Grand Junction, Tennessee, when they were not paid on time. Five men died in what was described as a mutiny. Captain Nathan J. Rawlings described the incident this way: "Then the Tiger Rifles, a company of Irishmen, refused to go further without pay. The colonel ordered them on the train; they would not obey, so we had quite a little battle. Several of the Irishmen were killed, and all of them were disabled [disarmed?] except nine men." (N. J. Rawlings, *Thrilling Experiences of Captain N. J. Rawlings.*) The company alluded to were the Tiger Bayou Rifles commanded by Field F. Montgomery, promoted to assistant quartermaster October 8, 1862; Charles R. Martin, resigned February 19, 1863; George H. Pouncey, to May 24, 1864.

**15th Louisiana Regiment, Starke's Brigade:** Although there were no distinctly Irish companies in the 15th Louisiana, Historian Terry Jones counts more than 100 Irish-born in the regiment. A cursory look at Louisiana rosters shows Irish surnames interspersed throughout the ten companies of the regiment, seven of which were raised in New Orleans.

**Wheat's Tiger Battalion, 1st Special Battalion Louisiana:** Commanded by Chatham Roberdeau Wheat. The battalion was composed of the waterfront workers of New Orleans, a large portion of whom were Irishmen. Wheat's Tigers were of part of Richard Taylor's Louisiana brigade. They distinguished themselves at the First Battle of Manassas, Front Royal and Port Republic. Wheat, described as a "wild, uncouth person," was killed June 27, 1862, at Gaines' Mill. The battalion was disbanded August 21, 1862, ostensibly because the soldiers in the unit were unmanageable in camp. The battalion members were drafted into other regiments of the brigade. Perhaps their extra-battlefield behavior is the reason Chaplain Louis-Hippolyte Gache reported "Louisiana soldiers have gained a reputation for pilfering and general loutishness that as soon as anyone sees them coming they bolt the doors and windows."

## MISSISSIPPI

**Jasper Grays, Company F, 16th Mississippi, Featherston's Brigade:** Mississippi fielded at least one predominantly Irish company. And there are hints of a larger Irish presence in the Magnolia state. Thomas Francis Galwey of the 8th Ohio's Hibernian Guard mentions a Mississippi Irishman at Fredericksburg. "Jim Gallagher told us that he met a man from the 16th Mississippi Regiment (an Irish regiment, it seems) and this man

# Appendix I: Irish Companies in the Army of Northern Virginia

assured him that it was his regiment which had given us our first fire at the edge of town." (Galwey, *The Valiant Hours*, 67.) This implies that the Irishman was part of William Barksdale's Brigade, which fought in the town. The 16th Mississippi was not an Irish regiment, and was not part of Barksdale's Mississippi Brigade. The 16th was in Winfield Scott Featherston's Mississippi Brigade. The regiment's Company F, the Jasper Grays, led by Capt. James J. Shannon, was predominantly Irish. Shannon later rose to lieutenant colonel and led the regiment. The Jasper Grays were raised in an Irish Catholic enclave in Jasper County at Paulding, Mississippi, April 27, 1861. The company's chaplain was a Catholic priest, according to Ada Christine Lightsey's *The Veteran's Story*. "Old Father Boheim . . . left his ivy-crowned church and the people he loved. Some of the boys in the company were of his faith but he was a good friend of the Protestant boys and cheered us in our life of toil and hardships. . . But he never tried to win us from our faith."

But not all the Mississippi Irish wanted a part in the American war. According to John K. Bettersworth in *Confederate Mississippi*, "Around Paulding in Jasper County there were Irish Catholics who refused to fight." The 16th Mississippi's Company D, the Adams Light Guard, also lists a significant number of Irish surnames. This company was mustered in at Natchez May 25, 1861. It was first led by Captain (later Major) Samuel E. Baker. (*Mississippi Register*, vol. 1, 1908, 460). At Chancellorsville, May 3, 1863, the regiment's Irish color-bearer, Corporal W. J. Sweeny, fell with severe wounds under a fire of grape shot. In that battle, the 16th was in Brigadier General Carnot Posey's Brigade. In the 2nd Mississippi, Company B, the O'Connor Rifles also boast some Irish heritage. The company was from Tippah County, mustered at Ripley March 4, 1861, and led by Captain (later Major) John H. Buchanan.

## SOUTH CAROLINA

**Irish Volunteers, Company K, 1st South Carolina, Gregg's Brigade:** According to Clement Evans "This company formed the nucleus of Colonel Maxcy Gregg's regiment." Company commanders were Edward McCrady Jr., Michael P. Parker, and James Armstrong Jr., "often spoken of as 'one of the best loved citizens of Charleston,' " according to Col. Joseph N. Brown. The company was organized at Charleston, the first in South Carolina to volunteer "for the war." It was first led by McCrady, who had captured Castle Pinckney with a force of local militia made up of Irishmen. As with many Irish companies, the Irish Volunteers became the color company of the regiment. The flag of the 1st South Carolina, made of blue silk with white embroidery, was designed and embroidered by the Ursuline Nuns of Charleston. The Irish company's exploits in defending the nuns' flag was chronicled by McCrady in an article titled "The Boy Heroes of Cold Harbor." In the fighting around Richmond June 27, 1862, "Dominick Spellman, one of the heroes of our war, a member of the Irish company, raised the colors and gloriously bore them for the rest of the day. . ." Major General Robert Emmett Rodes said of the 1st South Carolina: "There are no better troops in the world than these." A postwar memorial for the company noted, "The Irish Volunteers were not bound to the State by birth; but when her liberties were imperilled, they promptly rallied to her standard; and how firmly and devotedly they guarded her honor is silently but eloquently told in their long death roll." Poet James Power wrote a tribute to the Irish Volunteers of Charleston in 1877. A part of the poem reads: "Tho' exile's chill, He feels yet still. He hails the name with cheers—These men of muscle, heart and will—Our Irish Volunteers!" (*Charleston News and Courier Presses*, "To the Irish Volunteers.")

**Irish Volunteers, Company C, 27th South Carolina Infantry, Hagood's Brigade:** This company was originally part of the Charleston Infantry Battalion. It was first led by Capt. W. H. Ryan, who was killed July 18, 1863, at Battery Wagner, South Carolina. This Irish Volunteer company spent most of the war at Fort Sumter, but joined the Army of Northern Virginia in the 1864 fighting at Cold Harbor and around Petersburg. It counted eighteen killed in its short stint in Virginia. The company ended the war in North Carolina. The 27th South Carolina was formed by consolidating the Charleston Battalion with the 1st South Carolina Battalion Sharpshooters in September 1863. Its commanders were Col. Peter C. Gaillard, Lt. Col. Julius A. Blake, and Maj. Joseph Abney.

## VIRGINIA

**Montgomery Guard, Company C, 1st Virginia Regiment, Kemper's Brigade:** The fitness for duty of the Montgomery Guard at the outbreak of war can be attributed to ten years of leadership given the company by Patrick T. Moore, company commander from 1850-1860. According to regimental historian Lee Wallace, unlike other companies in the 1st Virginia, the Guard had never been threatened with disbandment through lack of interest. Each year the Montgomery Guard sponsored a St. Patrick's Day ball. On this occasion before secession the company, in green uniforms, marched through the city flying the U.S. flag, the ". . .[S]tars and stripes, the first in a ground work of green surrounding the harp of Erin." The company's distinctive uniform included brass insignia with the initials "M.G." encircled by a wreath of shamrocks, topped by an eagle. Their 1858 dress black hats were festooned with a drooping white feather tipped in green. At the outbreak of war, the company, now led by Capt. John Dooley, was composed mainly of citizens of Irish birth, "some six foot or over, and a number had seen service in the Crimea." (Lee Wallace Jr., *1st Virginia Infantry*.) Moore, a native of Galway, had been promoted to colonel and had succeeded to command of the regiment. The company was with the 1st Virginia when it was deployed in the Sunken Road at Fredericksburg about 7:00 p.m. December 13. John Edward Dooley, the son of the aforementioned commander, remembered the night: "With the moans and cries of the dying enemy in our ears, we set about providing a defense against the enemy's sharpshooters, so that we too may not be groaning and dying when the morrow's night arrives." About midnight the company captured a Union scouting party that wandered too close to their line. Company commanders: John Dooley, November 18, 1861, to

# Appendix I: Irish Companies in the Army of Northern Virginia

major; William English, April 26, 1862, resigned; James Mitchell, August 28, 1862, resigned; James Hallinan, killed July 3, 1863; John E. Dooley.

**Irish Battalion, 5 Companies, 1st Virginia Battalion: Jones' Brigade, Provost Guard:** Battalion commanders: Maj. John Dunburrow Munford, 1861-62; Maj. John Seddon, 1862 until resigned, brother of Confederate Secretary of War, buried Fredericksburg Confederate Cemetery; Maj. Benjamin W. Leigh, 1862 until reassigned; Lt. Charles A. Davidson, 1862; and Maj. David B. Bridgford, 1863-65. Four of the five companies in the battalion were predominantly Irish, the other being German, according to Ella Lonn. Regimental historians Robert Driver and Kevin Ruffner report that the battalion was recruited in the largest cities of Virginia—rail centers and ports—where Irish laborers had congregated for employment before the war. Recruits came from Norfolk, Alexandria, Covington, Richmond and Lynchburg. In 1861, Lt. John Heth, a recent graduate of Virginia Military Institute, led 200 Irishmen from Covington to Richmond, according to the regimental history. As is routine with Irish units, colorful stories of the Irish Battalion abound. A Private William Looney was found guilty of mutiny and attempted murder of a lieutenant. His counsel offered this defense: the prisoner was "an ignorant Irish recruit." The battalion was detached as provost guard of Thomas J. Jackson's Corps, and then filled that role for the entire Army of Northern Virginia, thus becoming the "Irish cops" of the Confederacy. At Fredericksburg, the unit protected the railroad terminus and road junction near Hamilton's Crossing, arrested stragglers, and detained and paroled prisoners of war. Major Bridgford was pleased to report that it had not been necessary to shoot any stragglers during the campaign. The battalion later moved to winter quarters at Moss Neck.

**Jeff Davis Guards, Company H, 11th Virginia Regiment: Kemper's Brigade:** This was a company raised in Lynchburg, which was a major rail center. The city was a terminus for the Orange & Alexandria, the Virginia & Tennessee and the Petersburg & Lynchburg or Southside lines. (Robert C. Black III, *The Railroads of the Confederacy.*) Consequently many Irish laborers were available for service. The company was commanded by 19-year-old Virginia Military Institute cadet J. Risque Hutter, and later by James W. Hord. While the company is not as "green" as some, its roster boasts a good number of Irishmen, as well as members from Germany, Italy and Switzerland. The Irish soldiers were laborers, railworkers and farmers. There was a tailor and even one reporter.

**Emmet Guard, Company F, 15th Virginia: Corse's Brigade:** Commanded by Capt. William Lloyd, 2nd Lt. James Collins. This was "a company of Irishmen from Richmond, eighty men strong. . ." The company was unhappy with the leadership of Captain Lloyd at Williamsburg and circulated a petition to force his resignation. When the company refused an order to build breastworks near Grove Landing, Lloyd transferred command of the company to Lieutenant Collins. Corporal James F. Russell, who had persuaded some in the company to disobey Lloyd's orders, was convicted of mutiny. He was reduced to ranks and sentenced to thirty days hard labor with ball and chain. The sentence was suspended by Brig. Gen. John B. Magruder, and the unit finally marched to duty at Grove Landing. The company was disbanded in June 1862, with many of the soldiers claiming exemption from service under the Conscription Act, which exempted non-citizens. (Louis H. Manarin, *15th Virginia Infantry*, 7.)

**Emmet Guards, Company G, 17th Virginia: Corse's Brigade:** This was an Alexandria light infantry unit under Capts. James Edward Towson Jr. and Robert F. Knox. The company wore a uniform of green fatigue jackets and green trousers. The regimental rosters of the Irishmen of the Guards show different degrees of Southern patriotism. Lawrence Fitzgerald as a prisoner of war told his captors he would "willingly do anything but fight against the South." Another Irish soldier claimed exemption from service under the Conscription Act when he pressed his claim as a British subject and a non-citizen of the Confederate States of America. (Lee Wallace Jr., *17th Virginia Infantry*.)

**O'Connell Guards, Company I, 17th Virginia: Corse's Brigade:** This light infantry company was from Alexandria, composed largely of railroad workers. Company commanders were Capts. Stephen W. Prestman, killed in a train accident in 1864; and Raymond Fairfax. The growing transportation center of Alexandria provided a good number of Irish troops to the army. According to Wallace's regimental history, rumors of desertions among the Irish companies, reported in the local newspaper, were untrue. They were "in good spirits and. . .having a good time generally." Alexandria supplied three Irish companies to Confederate service. The third was called the Irish Volunteers, which became the 19th Battalion of Heavy Artillery under Capts. Thornton Triplett and George T. Whittington. The 19th was not part of the Army of Northern Virginia. (Lee A. Wallace Jr., *A Guide to Virginia Military Organizations 1861-1865*.)

**Montgomery Guards, Company F, 19th Virginia: Garnett's Brigade:** Company commanders: Bennett Taylor, a 24-year-old teacher. He was wounded at Williamsburg and wounded and captured at Gettysburg. A descendant of Thomas Jefferson, Taylor is buried at Monticello; James D. McIntire, age 20, a clerk and University of Virginia student. This company was raised in the Charlottesville area. The regimental history includes a punctilious letter to Brig. Gen. Richard B. Garnett from the young company commander McIntire after Col. J. B. Strange was wounded at the Battle of Slaughter's Gap, October 15, 1862. "Brigadier-General Garnett: This regiment was acting more directly under your orders than those of its commander, Captain Brown, who was present during the engagement. I did not recognize Adjutant Wood as its commander on that day, he being only a third lieutenant. Respectfully, James D. McIntire." (Jordan and Thomas, *19th Virginia Infantry*.)

**Virginia Hibernians, Company B, 27th Virginia: Paxton's Brigade:** This was a light infantry company raised in Alleghany County. The company commanders were Harry W. (Henry) Robertson, Jacob Miley and Lt. John P. Welsh. Welsh wrote home to his mother and wife December 26, 1862: ". . .I think weel get through safe if the yankies lets

# Appendix I: Irish Companies in the Army of Northern Virginia

us alone and the prospects are very good for that I think they got anough of it at Fredericksburg." (John P. Welsh, "Letter of December 26, 1862," Volume 83, Fredericksburg and Spotsylvania National Military Park Manuscript Collection.) The Hibernians were the color company of the regiment. Welsh's brother James was a Union soldier in the 78th Illinois. War letters from both brothers have been studied by W. G. Bean, "A House Divided: The Civil War Letters of a Virginia Family," *Virginia Military and Historical Biography*, Volume LIX, 397-422.

**Emerald Guard, Company E, 33rd Virginia: Paxton's Brigade:** The Emerald Guard was raised in the New Market area of Shenandoah County. According to the 33rd Virginia regimental history, "The unit was composed chiefly of Irishmen who had migrated to the Valley to obtain employment on the Manassas Gap Railroad." The company commanders were Marion Marye Sibert and George R. Bedinger, killed at Gettysburg July 3, 1863; Lt. Thomas S. Doyle. Doyle left a graphic account of the condition of Fredericksburg in 1864. He was marched through town as a prisoner of war, captured at the Battle of Spotsylvania. "This venerable place presented a most miserable picture of the ravages of war. All the public edifices and stores and many of the private dwellings were filled with the wounded of Grant's Army, whose groanings filled the air." (Thomas S. Doyle memoir, Volume 67, Fredericksburg and Spotsylvania National Military Park Manuscript Collection.)

# Faded Coats of Gray

### Irish Officers in the Army of Northern Virginia

Soon we found that the knoll on which Major Dooley and I were
standing seemed to become a special object of the enemy's shot; they
evidently took us for two officers of distinction.

— John Mitchel, behind McCarthy's Battery at Fredericksburg.

## A note on Irish officers in the Army of Northern Virginia

T his is the first comprehensive list of Irish officers who served
under Robert E. Lee—Lee's Irish Lieutenants. The roster includes
the most prominent and well-documented Irish Army of Northern
Virginia officers. They are included here because of their connection to
the battle narratives of this book, or because of their prominence in the
army. Most are Irish-born, some may be first generation Americans of
Irish descent. Leaders who may be even further removed from the Old
Sod are included because they led distinctly Irish units. For good
measure, the general officers of the greater Confederacy—that is, not
associated with the Army of Northern Virginia—also are included.

The biographical and military information is compiled from
numerous sources including memoirs, state roster books, regimental
histories, Jon Wakelyn's *Biographical Dictionary of the Confederacy*,
*The Confederate General*, Ezra Warner's *Generals in Gray*, Bruce
Allardice's *More Generals in Gray*, and Robert K. Krick's *Lee's
Colonels*.

## CLEAR THE CONFEDERATE WAY!

**Andrews, R. Snowden:** Maj. Andrews was born in Washington, D. C., the son of Irish immigrant Brevet Brig. Gen. Timothy Patrick Andrews. General Andrews, born in 1794, served on the staff of Maj. Gen. Henry Halleck, the Union Chief of Staff. A hero of the Mexican War, the elder Andrews was named paymaster of the Union army in 1862. His son, Snowden, was an architect and builder in Baltimore when war broke out. He chose to go with the South, organized the 1st Maryland Artillery, and rose to the rank of major in the Confederate army. He was wounded at the Battle of Mechanicsville in 1862, and as commander of an artillery division at the Battle of Slaughter's (Cedar) Mountain was grievously wounded in the abdomen. He was captured and paroled and recovered to fight again. Major Andrews was wounded again at Winchester in 1863, and then was sent to Europe to procure more guns for the South. After the surrender, he spent two years in Mexico, building the Imperial railroad there, and then returned to Baltimore where he resumed his building career and was appointed brigadier general of artillery in the Maryland militia.

**Armstrong, James Capt.** Called one of the best loved citizens of Charleston, Armstrong was company commander of the Irish Volunteers, Company K, 1st South Carolina (Gregg's). Born in Philadelphia, Armstrong was harbormaster of Charleston before the war. He enlisted as 2nd lieutenant of the company and was acting captain after Sharpsburg. He was wounded slightly at Sharpsburg and Fredericksburg. At Gettysburg, he was wounded a third time while he carried the regimental colors after the color-bearer was shot down. He was wounded for the fourth time at Spotsylvania. This last wound, a shattered right leg, did not heal until 1871, according to Southern historian and Confederate general Clement Evans. Armstrong wrote about the regiment's part in the Bloody Angle fighting at Spotsylvania. "The Confederate States had in their service no braver, more loyal or devoted son." (B. F. Brown in *Confederate Veteran*, Volume III, 281)

**Atkins, Robert Goring Capt.** Described by Ella Lonn as a British knight-errant, Atkins had a short-lived career as captain of Wheat's Life Guards, Company E, 1st Louisiana Special Battalion. The largely Irish battalion was raised in Orleans Parish. There is no record of Atkins' service to the Confederacy after Wheat's Battalion was disbanded in the summer of 1862.

**Barnes, Jackson Capt.** Barnes was the original company commander of the Lochrane Guards, Company F, Phillips Legion Infantry of Georgia. The Irish company was named for Irish immigrant Osborn A. Lochrane, the wartime chief justice of the Georgia Supreme Court. Barnes, a Macon lawyer, helped organize the company but resigned his commission September 12, 1862.

# Appendix II: Irish Officers in the Army of Northern Virginia

**Barron, Patrick Lt.** Born in Ireland. Barron was a 21-year-old officer of the Shepherd Guards, Company A, 10th Louisiana in 1862. He was commissioned a 2nd lieutenant December 6, 1862, just before the Battle of Fredericksburg. Barron was 5' 8-1/2" tall, with dark hair and eyes, sandy complexion. He was a New Orleans laborer before the war. He was wounded at Monocacy and surrendered at Appomattox.

**Bellinger, Charles E. Capt.** Bellinger was a single, 40-year-old New Orleans resident when he enlisted as a private in the Virginia Blues, Company I, 7th Louisiana on June 7, 1861. He became captain of the Irish company and was captured November 7, 1863, at Rappahannock Station, Virginia. He was received at the Old Capitol Prison, Washington, D.C., and then transferred to Johnson's Island, Ohio, November 11, 1863. He took the Oath of Allegiance and was released June 12, 1865. Bellinger was 5' 6" tall, had dark hair and complexion and blue eyes.

**Boggs, James Brig. Gen.** Born County Down, Ireland. Boggs' parents moved to western Virginia in 1807. Boggs, a large slaveholder in Franklin, now West Virginia, was general of militia before the war. Boggs led the 18th Virginia Militia Brigade to Winchester in the winter of 1861. Under the command of Stonewall Jackson, the militia saw its first action against Union home guards in northwest Virginia in December 1861. In early 1862, Boggs' force guarded Jackson's left flank at Romney. Shortly after Romney was taken, Boggs, age 65, fell ill and returned home, where he died on January 28, 1862. Buried Mount Hiser Cemetery, Franklin, West Virginia.

**Brannigan, C. P. Capt.** Born in Ireland, Brannigan (alternately spelled Branegan) enlisted as a single, twenty-three-year-old merchant/clerk in Mobile. He succeeded Patrick Loughry as company commander of the Emerald Guards, Company I, Eighth Alabama. Brannigan commanded the company at Fredericksburg, and he led the Guards at Salem Church in May 1863, as part of Wilcox's Brigade. Brannigan was wounded in three places and was taken prisoner at Gettysburg. He died of his wounds and was placed on the Confederate roll of honor. The Irish captain was six feet tall, with gray eyes and dark complexion.

**Brenan, Peter Maj.** Born in Ireland. At Fredericksburg Brenan was captain of the Stark Guards or Wiregrass Rifles, Company F, 61st Georgia. The company was from Quitman County, Georgia. Clement Evans reported that at the Battle of Fredericksburg, December 13, 1862, Brenan was part of the counterattack at Prospect Hill that chased the Federals across the rail tracks. As regimental commander, he was killed in action at Gettysburg. Buried Laurel Hill Cemetery, Savannah, Georgia.

**Bridgford, David B. Maj.** Bridgford was the son of a British (probably English) officer who had served in Canada and in the War of 1812. The regimental history of the battalion counts him among the officer corps assessed to be competent enough to mold Virginia's Irish recruits into a disciplined force. Bridgford was a ship's broker and commission merchant in New York City before and after the war and a merchant in Richmond in

1860. He enlisted at age 29. For a short time he was on Stonewall Jackson's staff as ordnance officer. (Lenoir Chambers, *Stonewall Jackson*, 305-306.) He became provost marshal for Jackson's Corps and then for the army in the fall of 1862. He was among the staff contingent with Jackson at Guiney Station when Jackson died in May 1863 and with the escort of the general's corpse to Richmond and Lexington. He died February 21, 1888, in New York City. He is buried in Greenwood Cemetery.

**Browne, William Montague Brig. Gen.** Born County Mayo, Ireland, 1823. Browne, called an Englishman by war clerk John Beauchamp Jones, was born in Ireland of a family that had been in the country for more than 200 years. He was well-educated and widely traveled and is thought to have been in the British diplomatic service before coming to America in the early 1850s. He became a naturalized U.S. citizen in 1857. He was an editor for the *New York Journal of Commerce* and the *Washington Constitution*, and was involved in Democratic politics before the war. He was a friend of Georgia politician Howell Cobb and a supporter of President James Buchanan. In 1861, Jefferson Davis appointed the Irishman an assistant secretary of state to Robert Toombs, and Browne kept that position when Robert M. T. Hunter replaced Toombs. Browne was the acting Confederate secretary of state for one month when Hunter left the post, and before Judah P. Benjamin replaced him. Davis later named Browne his aide-de-camp with the rank of colonel. Browne's diplomatic experience and personal relationships with Georgia's leaders were used by Davis to persuade that state to adhere to the conscription act and send Georgia state troops for Confederate service. In 1863, Browne led the 1st Virginia Cavalry Battalion, a local defense force also known as Browne's Reconnaissance Corps, on picket duty around Richmond. By late 1864, Browne was assigned to lead a small brigade of Georgia troops to Savannah, when he joined General Hugh Weedon Mercer in that city's defense preparations. President Davis nominated Browne for promotion in November 1864. In early 1865, Browne went to Augusta where he was put in charge of conscripts and reserve troops. By late March, he removed to Athens where he was arrested May 8 and paroled. He became a lawyer after the war, and was also a correspondent for the *Louisville Daily Courier* and the *New York World*. He was editor of *The Southern Farm and Home Journal* for four years and then took a post as a professor of history and political science at the University of Georgia. He died in 1883, and is buried at Oconee Hill Cemetery in Athens.

**Burt, William Giroud Col.** Born in Ireland, Burt was a 32-year-old stonecutter in 1860. He was a sergeant in the 22nd South Carolina in December 1861; promoted to lieutenant March 12, 1863; lieutenant colonel August 18, 1864; colonel July 30, 1864. Burt surrendered at Appomattox. He was a resident of Bossier Parish, Louisiana, after the war.

**Cameron, Charles Capt.** Born in England, Cameron was appointed captain of the Sarsfield Rangers, Company C, 7th Louisiana in December 1863. He enlisted in Company K of the same regiment June 7, 1861. He was promoted to sergeant major of that company and then became its captain January 7, 1862. Incomplete records show

# Appendix II: Irish Officers in the Army of Northern Virginia

Cameron was wounded and captured sometime in the spring of 1863, and was absent from duty until his appointment to the Irish company. Cameron was a 40-year-old schoolteacher in Livingston, Louisiana, in 1861.

**Carroll, Michael Lt.** Born in Ireland, Carroll was a married laborer in New Orleans before the war. He enlisted in 1861 at age 25. A lieutenant in the Shepherd Guards, Company A, 10th Louisiana, he last fought at the Battle of Fredericksburg. He resigned his commission December 20, 1862, after serving one year.

**Cass, Michael L. Lt.** Cass was a second lieutenant in the Emmet Rifles, Company B of the 1st Georgia (Regulars). He enlisted in Company D of that regiment and was promoted February 1, 1861. He later transferred to the Irish company, then to Company K, where he earned promotion to 1st lieutenant; and finally to Company E of the 1st Georgia. Cass died of disease in Savannah on June 27, 1864.

**Cleburne, Christopher Capt.** Born County Cork, Ireland. He was the half-brother of Patrick Cleburne. He received no special treatment from his high-ranking brother, who preferred that he earn his spurs, so to speak. Christopher was a company commander under cavalry raider John Hunt Morgan. The younger Cleburne was mortally wounded at Cloyd's Mountain, Virginia, on May 10, 1864. He was 21 and before coming to America was a student at Trinity College, Dublin.

**Cleburne, Patrick Ronayne Major General.** Cleburne was born on St. Patrick's Day, March 17, 1828, at Bridgepark Cottage in County Cork, Ireland. He was a division commander in the Army of Tennessee, the highest-ranking Irish Confederate. Cleburne has been dubbed the "Stonewall Jackson of the West." In Ireland, he was afforded a good education with tutors and private schooling. He was a druggist's apprentice, but failed an apothecary examination at Trinity College, Dublin. He then joined the British Army, but left the queen's service at age 21, when he received an inheritance. He sailed for America, landing in New Orleans, and settled in Helena, Arkansas, by 1850. He worked as a druggist there and became a lawyer in 1856. In the same period, Cleburne was shot in the back, probably by a Know-Nothing adherent. He switched his political allegiance from the Whig Party, which had been taken over by nativists, and joined the pro-immigrant Democratic Party. Elected captain of the Yell (County) Rifles, he led the company to seize the Federal arsenal at Little Rock in February 1861. After secession, he was elected colonel of the 1st Arkansas Infantry doing garrison duty along the Mississippi. In July, the regiment joined a force under General William J. Hardee in an invasion of Missouri. In the fall of 1861, Hardee, at Bowling Green, Kentucky, put Cleburne in command of a brigade. He was promoted to brigadier general March 4, 1862. Cleburne performed admirably at Shiloh, was part of the Confederate vanguard in its invasion of Kentucky, and was credited with leading the Confederate victory at Richmond, Kentucky, although he was shot in the face in that battle. At Perryville, he led his brigade when it broke the Federal center, but his horse was killed and he was wounded in the leg. Cleburne was promoted to major general December 20, 1862, and fought at Stones River, Tennessee. In 1863, Cleburne's performance was praised at Chickamauga and Chattanooga. General Braxton Bragg reported Cleburne's command defeated every enemy assault, and eventually charged and routed them. He repeated his success at Ringgold Gap. The Confederate Congress and even anti-Irish war clerk John Beauchamp Jones praised Cleburne after these battles. The Irish general's idea to free and arm Southern slaves could have proved a turning point in the war. Instead, it probably stopped any further progress in his Confederate career. Cleburne fought in the Atlanta Campaign but was killed at the Battle of Franklin, Tennessee. An Episcopalian, he never married. He is buried in Helena, Arkansas.

**Cleveland, Jesse Capt.** Cleveland was the original company commander of the Montgomery Guards, Company K, 20th Georgia. This Irish company was raised in Richmond County, Georgia. Cleveland was elected captain August 8, 1861, but resigned his commission December 31, 1861. He was succeeded by Major William Craig.

**Cohen, Jacob A. Capt.** Born in Ireland. Cohen was a 41-year-old, single laborer when he enlisted in New Orleans on July 22, 1861. Although Jewish, his Irish birth evidently led him to identify with the Irish community in New Orleans. He was elected 1st lieutenant of the Shepherd Guards, Company A, 10th Louisiana, and commanded the Irish company from November 1861. He was promoted to captain January 15, 1862. He was killed at Second Manassas, August 30, 1862. Buried in the Confederate soldiers' section of the Hebrew Cemetery, Richmond.

**Collins, James Lt.** Collins was a resident of Richmond when he enlisted May 1, 1861, in the Emmet Guards, Company F, 15th Virginia. He took command of the Irish company briefly in the summer of 1862 when some soldiers threatened mutiny. He resigned his commission June 24, 1862, when the company was disbanded.

**Craig, William Maj.** Born in Ireland. At Fredericksburg Craig was a 33-year-old captain of the Montgomery Guards, Company K, 20th Georgia. A merchant in Augusta before the war, he rose to regimental rank and was paroled in May 1865.

**Cummings, Albert N. Capt.** Cummings was a 27-year-old single resident of Adams County, Mississippi, when he enlisted May 2, 1861, in the Emmet Guards, Company D, 1st Louisiana. He was elected 1st lieutenant December 1, 1861, and became captain of the Irish company June 16, 1862. Cummings was wounded in a skirmish on the opening day of the Seven Days Campaign, June 25, 1862. He was absent from the rolls until February 1864. He was captured at Fisher's Hill September 22, 1864, and was received at Fort Delaware by way of Harpers Ferry on September 27. He took the Oath of Allegiance and was released May 30, 1865. Cummings was 5' 9", had a fair complexion, auburn hair and blue eyes.

**Davidson, Charles A. Capt.** Born Lexington, Virginia, November 9, 1839, Davidson was an 1860 graduate of Virginia Military Institute and studied law at the University of

# Appendix II: Irish Officers in the Army of Northern Virginia

Virginia. He served a short stint as an aide to Virginia Governor John Letcher and was commissioned a 1st lieutenant of engineers in the Provisional Army of the Confederate States. He was assigned to Company E of the Irish Battalion October 21, 1861. Davidson was promoted captain August 14, 1862, and as senior company commander led the battalion at Sharpsburg in September of that year. In November 1864, he was assigned commandant of the Army of Northern Virginia's military prison, and Davidson surrendered at Appomattox. He was a lawyer, politician and businessman after the war. Buried Stonewall Jackson Cemetery, Lexington.

**Dillon, James Capt.** Born in Ireland, Dillon was a company commander of the Orleans Light Guards, Company F, 1st Louisiana. A 28-year-old married farmer in New Orleans, he enlisted May 2, 1861. He was wounded June 25, 1862, at the Battle of Seven Pines.

**Dolan, Thomas Capt.** Dolan was an officer in the Monroe Guards, Company K, 5th Louisiana. Born in Louisiana, he enlisted June 4, 1861, at age 24. He resigned December 1861 or January 1862.

**Dooley, John Maj.** Born about 1810 in Limerick, Ireland. Dooley came to the U.S. in 1832. He was the head of a prominent Irish Catholic family in Richmond, a wealthy businessman, and president of the city's Young Catholic Friend Society. He was captain of the Montgomery Guard, an Irish United States militia company before the war, and was the company's commander when it was transferred to Confederate service as part of the 1st Virginia Regiment. Dooley was promoted to major November 18, 1861. He later served in the Confederate Ambulance Corps. First Virginia Infantry historian Charles Loehr wrote of Dooley: "Though not much of a military genius, was one of the kindest and most generous of men." He died in 1868. Buried Shockoe Hill Cemetery, Richmond.

**Dooley, John Edward Capt.** Born in Richmond 1842. He succeeded his father as company commander of the Montgomery Guard, Company C, 1st Virginia. Captain Dooley was in the Georgetown College Class of 1862, and may have taken part in the burning in effigy of Lincoln on that campus just after his election. In his memoirs, *John Dooley, Confederate Soldier,* he relates his posting in the Sunken Road at Fredericksburg on December 14. Dooley took part in Pickett's Charge at Gettysburg and was wounded and captured there. He was a POW until 1865. After the war he became a Jesuit brother and died at Georgetown May 8, 1873.

**Dooley, James Henry Lt.** Major Dooley's older son, James Henry Dooley, was the surviving scion of the Dooley clan in Richmond. James was born in Richmond in 1841 and was a Georgetown law student (Class of 1869). His war service was brief. He enlisted as a private in his father's company, the Montgomery Guard, and was wounded and captured at Williamsburg. He was exchanged August 2, 1862, and discharged November 17 of that year. He later took a commission in the Reserve Corps and worked in the Ordnance Department. After the war, he amassed a fortune and built Maymont, a Victorian estate that is now a Richmond city park. He also established the Richmond

Public Library, the Crippled Children's Hospital and St. Joseph's Villa, a multimillion-dollar Catholic orphanage, built in the Italianate style.

**Doyle, Thomas Lt.** Doyle enlisted as a private in the Emerald Guards, Company E, 33rd Virginia. He was captured at Strasburg June 5, 1862, and was promoted to lieutenant December 30, 1863. He was captured again May 10, 1864, at the Battle of Spotsylvania. He is notable for his vivid description of the town of Fredericksburg as he was marched through it as a POW. He was held at Fort Delaware until June 16, 1865, and died October 7, 1918, at the Richmond Soldiers Home, age 76. Buried Hollywood Cemetery.

**Duffy, Patrick B. Lt. Col.** Born in Nicholas County, Maryland, circa 1840. Duffy was a graduate of Mount Saint Mary's College, a Catholic school in Maryland. He was captain of Company C, 9th Virginia Battalion in May 1861. The unit became the 25th Virginia and by May 1862 he was lieutenant colonel of the regiment. General Jubal Early did not consider Duffy an "efficient officer." Duffy resigned October 8, 1862, but later was commissioned a captain, assistant commissary supply. He married Fannie E. McConihay in 1867 and was a merchant after the war in Braxton County, West Virginia. He died in January 1893.

**English, William Capt.** English was a lieutenant in the Montgomery Guard militia company in Richmond before the war. A 42-year-old merchant, he enlisted in the Confederate army April 21, 1861 as 2nd lieutenant. He was wounded at Blackburn's Ford, part of the Manassas campaign, July 18, 1861. Promoted to captain November 19. Resigned April 26, 1862. Died in Richmond 1876.

**Feeney, William A. Col.** Feeney was a saddler in Senatobia, Mississippi, when he enlisted as a lieutenant of Company I, 9th Mississippi in 1861. He was promoted to captain of Company B, 42nd Mississippi, May 14, 1862; and promoted to major in September, 1862. He received his colonelcy December 18, 1863. Feeney's 42nd Mississippi was part of Stone's Brigade at the Battle of the Wilderness. The brigade contemplated a desperate empty rifle charge on May 5 in its attempt to hold out against the concerted attacks of the Union Sixth and Second Corps near the Widow Tapp farm. Feeney was killed in action there in the first half-hour of fighting. He was severely wounded at Gettysburg. In 1862, Feeney led four companies of the 42nd Mississippi to Fredericksburg November 14. They protected river fords along the Rappahannock until they returned to North Carolina December 13. For a time "Major Feeney and his little battalion presented the main obstacle to their [Union troops] taking possession" of Fredericksburg, according to Colonel Hugh R. Miller. (*Supplement to the Official Records*, Part II, Volume 34, 210-211). He was married to Bettie C. Feeney of De Soto County, Mississippi. A United Daughters of the Confederacy chapter in Senatobia was named for Feeney. He is buried in the Fredericksburg Confederate Cemetery.

**Fenlon, Peter 2nd Lt.** Born in Wexford, Ireland, Fenlon was a member of the Jackson Guards, Company B, 19th Georgia. He was wounded at Fredericksburg when Archer's

# Appendix II: Irish Officers in the Army of Northern Virginia

Brigade was overrun at Prospect Hill. He died of his wounds in a Richmond hospital January 16, 1863. Captain John Keely wrote: "Our dead comrades we had buried in their blankets, and the wounded had been carried off to hospital. Amongst the latter from my company was Lieutenant Fenlon from Wexford. He had had his leg broken, it was amputated and he died from mortification."

**Fennelly, John Lt.** Born in Ireland. Fennelly was a New Orleans plasterer. He enlisted July 1, 1861, in Company H, 14th Louisiana Infantry. Promoted 2nd lieutenant November 14, 1862. He was the regiment's acting adjutant by late 1863. Officially appointed adjutant to take effect October 12, 1863. Killed at Spotsylvania. Buried Spotsylvania Confederate Cemetery.

**Finegan, Joseph Brig. Gen.** Born in Clones, Ireland. Finegan came to the U.S. in the 1830s and settled in Florida. He operated a plantation and sawmill and later was a business partner with Senator David Yulee. As Army Department Commander in Florida, he raised and organized defense forces for that state. His efforts culminated in Confederate victory at the Battle of Olustee or Ocean Pond February 20, 1864, in which a Federal invasion force under Brig. Gen. Truman Seymour was repulsed. At Olustee, H. M. Hamill remembers: "Gen. Finnegan [sic] was a born fighter, of hot Irish blood, and I have a very vivid memory of how his stumpy figure and fiery horse went flashing to and fro ahead of his men." (Hamill, in *Confederate Veteran*, Volume XII, 540.) Later Robert E. Lee tapped Finegan for brigade command in the Army of Northern Virginia. Finegan's Florida Brigade plugged a gap in the line at Cold Harbor on June 3, 1864. His troops helped hold the lines around Petersburg for the remainder of 1864. Finegan was reassigned to Florida in 1865. After the war Finegan was a cotton broker, lawyer and state senator.

**Finn, John Thomas Lt.** Finn enlisted as a private in Company A, 12th Virginia Infantry, October 4, 1861. A resident of Petersburg, he was wounded at Seven Pines June 1, 1862. He spent two and a half months in the hospital until August 19, when he was detailed for hospital duty. He was discharged from the regiment November 18, 1863, but was promoted to 2nd lieutenant in the Petersburg City Battalion, a home guard unit in the state reserve forces. Finn was company commander of Company A, which was composed of Catholic men from Saint Joseph's Catholic Church in that city.

**Garrity, James Capt.** Born in St. Louis, Garrity enlisted at the age of 19. He was single and a clerk in New Orleans. He became captain of the Orleans Cadet Company B, Company E, 5th Louisiana, a regiment described as being made up of mostly "uneducated Irishmen." Garrity was wounded at Malvern Hill and Sharpsburg, but was still present on the rolls at Fredericksburg.

**Gilmore, Michael B. Capt.** Gilmore was company commander of the Montgomery Guards, Company E, 1st Louisiana. He enlisted April 28, 1861, in New Orleans and was elected 1st lieutenant. He was killed June 25, 1862, the opening day of the Seven Days Campaign.

**Grady, William Sammons Maj**. Grady was descended from William O'Grady, an immigrant from County Donegal, Ireland. He was the father of Henry W. Grady, the orator of the New South movement. An Athens, Georgia, merchant, Major Grady enlisted at age 40. At Fredericksburg he was captain of the Highland Guards, Company G of the 25th North Carolina. This company was raised in Clay and Macon Counties, North Carolina, and Athens, Georgia. The 25th North Carolina was heavily involved in the fighting along the Sunken Road at the Battle of Fredericksburg. According to division commander Robert Ransom, the 25th North Carolina "pushed forward to the crest of the hill" at Marye's Heights and then took positions "shoulder to shoulder with Cobb's and Cooke's men in the [sunken] road." Grady was mortally wounded at the Battle of the Crater in 1864, and died at Greenville, South Carolina, while en route home to Athens.

**Grogan, Michael Lt. Col.** Born in Ireland. Grogan was a machinist in New Orleans when he was commissioned a 2nd lieutenant of the Moore Guards, Company B, 2nd Louisiana. He was promoted to major July 1, 1862. At Fredericksburg, at age 27, he was in charge of the regiment. The 2nd Louisiana was involved in light skirmishing, but Edmund Pendleton's official report cites Grogan, among others, as deserving special commendation for his conduct during the battle. Grogan was promoted lieutenant colonel May 12, 1864, and was wounded November 12, 1864.

**Hagan, James Brig. Gen.** Born County Tyrone, Ireland 1822. Hagan's father was a farmer near Philadelphia during the general's childhood. At age 15, Hagan moved to Mobile, Alabama. Recognized for "conspicuous and distinguished gallantry" at the Battle of Monterrey in the Mexican War, he was a member of Hays' Texas Rangers, a cavalry unit in Zachary Taylor's army. In 1848, he was commissioned captain of the 3rd U.S. Dragoons. In Confederate service, Hagan initially captained the Mobile Dragoons doing Gulf Coast guard duty. He was promoted to major of the 1st Mississippi Cavalry and ordered to Kentucky in September 1861. Hagan fought at Shiloh, and then began an illustrious career with the Army of Tennessee. He was promoted to colonel of the 3rd Alabama Cavalry July 1, 1862. Hagan was described as a natural horseman and a reckless fighter. He led his regiment in Braxton Bragg's invasion of Kentucky in 1862. In early 1863, he was put in charge of General Joseph Wheeler's cavalry brigade, and Wheeler recommended the Irishman for promotion. Bragg, however charged that Hagan was an alcoholic and blocked the promotion. Hagan resigned in November 1863, but returned to duty in the spring of 1864. He led his old regiment in the Atlanta campaign and in August 1864 took command of William Allen's Brigade, which he led until the end of the war. He was wounded three times: in the leg at Franklin, Tennessee, in 1862; in the body near Kingston, Tennessee, in November 1863, and through the arm at Monroe's Crossroads, North Carolina, March 10, 1865. A plantation owner before the war, Hagan lost his fortune when he converted it to Confederate money. He managed a

# Appendix II: Irish Officers in the Army of Northern Virginia

plantation after the war and President Grover Cleveland gave him a government post in 1885. The Irishman was described as "courteous in the old school vein, genial, convivial and simple-minded as a child, the veteran was popular with all classes and ages in Mobile." He died in Mobile in 1901. Buried Magnolia Cemetery. (Allardice, *More Generals in Gray*, 111-113.)

**Hallinan, James Capt.** Also sometimes listed as Halloran or Hollinan. He was a 21-year-old laborer when he enlisted April 21, 1861, in the Montgomery Guard, Company C of the 1st Virginia Infantry. He was promoted to corporal January 1, 1862; appointed 2nd lieutenant April 30, 1862; wounded at Williamsburg May 5, 1862; on duty July 21, 1862; and promoted to captain August 28, 1862. Hallinan was mortally wounded in Pickett's Charge at Gettysburg July 3, 1863.

**Hamilton, Joseph Lt. Col.** Born in County Tyrone, Ireland. Hamilton was captain of Company E of the Phillips Legion from Georgia, part of Cobb's Brigade stationed behind the Stone Wall at Fredericksburg. He was promoted to major December 13, 1862, as a result of the battle, and to lieutenant colonel soon thereafter. He was wounded at South Mountain and Cold Harbor. Hamilton commanded the Phillips Legion during the Knoxville Campaign in the winter of 1863, where he was again wounded. He was captured at Sayler's Creek in 1865. He was 25 years of age upon enlistment. Hamilton was a teacher in Dalton, Georgia, and Los Angeles, California, after the war. He died October 22, 1932. Buried Marietta (Georgia) Confederate Cemetery.

**Hanlon, Joseph Lt. Col.** Born in Ireland. Hanlon was a newspaper reporter in New Orleans before the war. He became captain of the Irish Brigade Company A, Company I, 6th Louisiana. Hanlon was a lieutenant colonel by June 4, 1861. He was wounded and captured at Winchester, June 1, 1862. Hanlon commanded the Irish regiment, the 6th Louisiana, at Gettysburg. He was 5' 7", with fair complexion, brown hair and hazel eyes. He was age 30 at enlistment. Hanlon also was captured at Chancellorsville and Strasburg. He died in Rockbridge County, Virginia, July 3, 1870.

**Hanna, John Francis Lt.** Born in Philadelphia. Hanna is one of the South's and Virginia's immortal boy soldiers—one of the New Market cadets. See William Couper, *The VMI New Market Cadets* (Charlottesville: The Michie Company, 1933), number 96. A graduate of Gonzaga College, Georgetown, and the Virginia Military Institute, he was a 1st lieutenant at the Battle of New Market, VMI's finest moment. Hanna reportedly fought hand to hand and sword to sword with a Federal officer at the battle. A devout Catholic, Hanna was the sergeant of the guard when Stonewall Jackson lay in state at V.M.I. after his untimely death at Guiney Station.

**Hobbs, Richard Capt.** Born in Ireland 1825 or 1836. Hobbs was company commander of the Dougherty Grays, Company K, 51st Georgia. He was wounded September 14, 1862, at South Mountain. His left arm was amputated above the elbow. In January 1863, Hobbs was appointed by General Alexander R. Lawton to be purchasing agent for the armies of Tennessee and Northern Virginia. After the war he was a lawyer and city judge in Albany, Georgia.

**Keary, Patrick F. Capt.** Born in Ireland. Keary was a planter from Cheneyville, Louisiana. He was company commander of the Cheneyville Rifles, Company H, 8th Louisiana. Keary was absent sick at Fredericksburg. In February 1863, on special assignment, he raised a battalion of sharpshooters, about 325 men, at Alexandria, Louisiana. He served briefly under General Richard Taylor.

**Keely, John P. Capt.** Born in Ireland. Keely commanded the Jackson Guards, Company B, 19th Georgia. He was commissioned a 2nd lieutenant June 11, 1861, became 1st lieutenant June 26, 1862, and was promoted to captain September 2, 1863. Keely's company, part of Archer's Brigade, was overrun in the heavy fighting at Prospect Hill, part of the Battle of Fredericksburg. He also was involved in the heavy fighting at Chancellorsville. After the war, Keely married the sister of his regimental commander, Lt. Col. James Neal, and was on the staff of Georgia Governor (and ex-Confederate General) John B. Gordon. He headed a large dry goods business in Atlanta of which he wrote in 1866: "Atlanta, phoenix like, has arisen from its ashes. It is now larger than it ever was, which goes far to show the amount of energy and capital brought into play in this small but important 'inland seaport,' the converging point of four railroads."

**Keiley, Anthony M. Lt.** Born Paterson, New Jersey, 1833, the son of Irish immigrant John D. Keiley Sr. He enlisted on secession day, April 19, 1861, as a sergeant in the Petersburg Riflemen, Company E, 12th Virginia Infantry. He attended Randolph-Macon College and edited the *Norfolk Virginian* and later was a newspaper publisher in Petersburg. Keiley was admitted to the bar in 1859, and initially opposed secession. In late 1861, he was detailed as a judge advocate on court martial duty and was elected lieutenant May 1, 1862. He received a severe foot wound at Malvern Hill, but stayed with the army until the Gettysburg Campaign. In February 1863, Keiley applied unsuccessfully for a job in the Confederate State Department. He resigned his commission December 1, 1863. He returned home and edited the *Petersburg Express* until June 1864. He also served in the Virginia House of Delegates. In 1864, he enlisted in the state reserves, and was assigned as a private in Archer's Battalion. He was captured in the home guard defense of Petersburg on the Jerusalem Plank Road June 9, 1864. He served four months at Point Lookout, Maryland, and Elmira, New York, prison camps. He was exchanged in October 1864, when he returned home and edited the *Petersburg News* until arrested for writing anti-Union editorials. He was held at Castle Thunder by U.S. authorities until June 1865. Postwar, he founded the *Petersburg Index*, published *In Vinculis*, the memoir of his POW experience, and served in the legislature until 1871. Keiley was mayor of Richmond, 1871-76; Richmond city attorney until 1885; and president of the International Court, Cairo, Egypt, 1886-1902. Keiley was accidentally killed by runaway horses in Paris in 1905. W. Gordon McCabe remembered Keiley in a St. Patrick's Day, 1917 report of the Virginia Historical Society as "one of the most brilliant men of his day" and "a gallant soul."

# Appendix II: Irish Officers in the Army of Northern Virginia

**Keiley, John D. Jr. Maj.** Born Paterson, New Jersey. Major Keiley was the brother of Confederate diarist Anthony M. Keiley. He lived in Petersburg before the war. He enlisted as a private in Richmond's Montgomery Guard April 21, 1861. He is mentioned as John Edward Dooley's friend "Jack" in the Dooley memoir. At Bull Run, he was tented with James Mitchel, a son of John Mitchel, and Francis Potts. On September 20, 1863, Keiley was appointed quartermaster for Walker's Brigade of the Confederate Third Corps. After the war he was co-editor, with James A. McMaster, of New York's *Freeman's Journal*, the country's foremost Irish nationalist newspaper. He was made a Knight of St. Gregory the Great by Pope Pius IX.

**Keiningham, William Henry Lt.** "Pete" Keiningham was a 19-year-old clerk when he enlisted April 21, 1861, in Company D, 1st Virginia. He is mentioned in John Edward Dooley's memoir, and was the lieutenant who fell wounded with Dooley at Gettysburg. Keiningham mustered in as a sergeant, to 2nd lieutenant April 26, 1862, to 1st lieutenant July 3, 1863. He was a POW at Johnson's Island, Ohio, in September 1863, at Point Lookout, Maryland, March 21, 1865, and then was transferred to Fort Delaware, where he was released after taking the Oath of Allegiance. Died in Richmond, February 13, 1899.

**Kelso, John Capt.** Kelso briefly was company commander of the Moore Guards, Company B, 2nd Louisiana. He enlisted May 9, 1861, in New Orleans. He was on the roll through April 1862.

**Kenna, Henry R. Lt.** Born in Ireland. Kenna was in the Emmet Guards, Company D, 1st Louisiana. He enlisted April 28, 1861, and was killed at Payne's Farm, Virginia, November 27, 1863. He was single and had been a clerk in New Orleans before the war.

**Kerrigan, Thomas W. Capt.** Born in Minnesota. Kerrigan become captain of the Irish Volunteers, Company F, 7th Louisiana. He was wounded May 4, 1863, at the Second Battle of Fredericksburg. Before the war he was a laborer, 28 years old, single, residing in Ascension Parish, Louisiana. In 1861 he was on detached duty in the Torpedo Bureau.

**Lane, Walter P. Brig. Gen.** Born County Cork, Ireland in 1817. His family emigrated in 1821. Lane grew up in Ohio and Louisville, Kentucky. He met Stephen F. Austin, the Virginian who founded Texas, who persuaded him to move to the Lone Star settlement in 1836. Lane earned a lieutenant's commission after he fought at the Battle of San Jacinto in the Texas war against Mexico; the Irishman fought at Monterrey and Buena Vista and was an army scout in the Mexican War. He later was an Indian fighter, a teacher, and a privateer, and he prospected for gold in Arizona, Nevada and Peru. A confirmed bachelor and a sleepwalker, Lane settled in Marshall, Texas, in the 1850s. The Irishman was elected lieutenant colonel of the Third Texas Cavalry in the summer of 1861. In Confederate service, he fought under General Ben McCullough and with General James McIntosh at Chustenallah in the Indian Territory in what is now

Oklahoma. His horse was shot out from under him at Wilson's Creek, Missouri, but he continued to advance on foot. At Pea Ridge, McIntosh ordered Lane to take four cavalry companies and charge a hill. At sixty yards, a thousand infantry rose up and with six artillery pieces opened on his command. "I hallooed to my men: 'Fall back, or you will all be murdered!' They didn't wait for a repetition of the order, but went at once, and, as Shakespeare puts it, 'Stood not on the order of their going.'" He was thereafter promoted to brigadier. Lane fought at Corinth, Iuka, in the Indian Territory and in the Red River Campaign. He was wounded at Mansfield, Louisiana, April 8, 1864, and retired to his business and community affairs in Marshall. A colorful Irishmen of the Confederacy, Lane was called "a superior cavalry officer" by General E. Kirby Smith. His memoir bears one of the longest of titles in an era of long titles. (*The Adventures and Recollections of General Walter P. Lane, a San Jacinto Veteran, Containing Sketches of the Texan, Mexican and Late Wars with Several Indian Fights Thrown In.*)

**Leigh, Benjamin Watkins Capt.** Born January 18, 1831. Leigh was company commander of Company A of the Irish Battalion as of May 25, 1861. He commanded the battalion at Gaines' Mill and Malvern Hill during the Seven Days Campaign, and was cited by General Winder for his service there. He left the battalion to command the 42nd Virginia Infantry in November and December 1862. He was promoted to major and served on the staff of General Edward Johnson and as assistant quartermaster for A. P. Hill. Leigh was killed in action at Gettysburg. Buried Shockoe Hill Cemetery, Richmond.

**Loughry, Patrick Capt.** Born in 1817 in County Mayo, Ireland. Company commander of the Emerald Guards, Company I, 8th Alabama. At enlistment, Loughry was a married, forty-five-year-old merchant in Mobile. He was killed at Seven Pines June 1, 1862. In that battle, Loughry was wounded in the arm, but refused to leave the field, and was subsequently killed. He earned a place on the Confederate roll of honor. According to Colonel Hillary Herbert's "Short History" of the regiment, Loughry briefly took command of one wing of the regiment at Williamsburg after the death of Lt. Col. Thomas E. Irby. The Catholic chaplain Louis-Hippolyte Gache said of Loughry: "I have nothing but praise for the excellent Captain Loughry . . . a devoted and zealous Catholic. . ."

**Lynch, Michael Maj.** While his United Daughters of the Confederacy descendants claim he was born October 3, 1842, in Lumpkin County, Georgia, official records list Lynch as being born in Ireland in 1835. He ran a dairy business at Stewart, Lumpkin County, Georgia. Lynch was part of the Army of Northern Virginia as captain of the Stewart Infantry, Company I, 21st Georgia, part of the illustrious Doles-Cook Brigade. He organized this company and was promoted to major by 1864 after being wounded at Chancellorsville. "Like most Irishmen [he] was a born soldier and a very efficient officer," according to J. Cooper Nisbet of the 21st and 66th Georgia. The brigade historian Henry W. Thomas said "No more gallant officer wore the gray than dear old Major Lynch, and no man had more friends among officers and men than he." He "frequently comes . . . to see some of his 'old b'yes' as he calls them and talk over the old

# Appendix II: Irish Officers in the Army of Northern Virginia

days," Thomas wrote of Lynch in 1903. He died in Atlanta, Georgia, on November 3, 1915. (See Henry W. Thomas, *History of the Doles-Cook Brigade*, 371, and James Cooper Nisbet, *Four Years on the Firing Line*, 16.)

**McCausland, John Brig. Gen.** Born St. Louis, Missouri, of Irish parents. He was one of the most nefarious Confederate generals of the war. Nicknamed "Tiger John," McCausland was an 1857 graduate of Virginia Military Institute and also attended the University of Virginia. He organized the Rockbridge Artillery as well as the 36th Virginia Infantry in 1861, when he was commissioned a colonel. McCausland operated in western Virginia, Tennessee, and Kentucky. He was at the 1861 Battle of Carnifax Ferry. He led his men out of Fort Donelson before it was surrendered in 1862. In the course of the war, he fought under John B. Floyd, William Loring, John Echols, Samuel Jones and Albert Jenkins. He was promoted to Brigadier in May 1864. He fought with Jubal Early in the 1864 Shenandoah Valley Campaign, and was with General Thomas Rosser at Petersburg, fighting at the Battle of Five Forks. He fought at Cloyd's Mountain, Monocacy, and then led his brigade to the ramparts of Washington, D.C. McCausland is perhaps best known in Virginia for defending Lynchburg from the depredations of Union General David Hunter. The Irishman is known in Pennsylvania for burning and looting Chambersburg in July 1864 in order to extract a $500,000 ransom from the town. He earlier had extorted $20,000 from Hagerstown, Maryland, residents. At Appomattox, McCausland reprised his escape act—as at Fort Donelson, he led his brigade through Grant's snare and returned to Lynchburg. McCausland refused reconstruction and left the country for Europe and Mexico, mysteriously returning two years later to West Virginia with the capital to buy a 6,000 acre farm there. He died in 1927.

**McCarthy, Edward Stephens Capt.** Born Richmond February 21, 1836. "Ned" McCarthy commanded McCarthy's Battery of the 1st Richmond Howitzers. A soldier in his battery called him "as brave as Marshall Ney." At Fredericksburg, Irish nationalist John Mitchel and Major John Dooley were with McCarthy as the battery opened up on the Union forces approaching Marye's Heights. Mitchel wrote: "We sat awhile with our friends of the Richmond Howitzers, viewing the gathering hosts of the Yankees filling up the plain, and admiring their order and celerity, when, about one o'clock, I think, an aide-de-camp rode up to Ned McCarthy, and conveyed to him some order. He bowed, and turned to his men, when every artilleryman was at his gun in a moment. 'We are to open the ball,' he said." McCarthy was killed at Cold Harbor June 4, 1864, and is buried in the Shockoe Hill Cemetery, Richmond.

**McCrady Jr., Edward Lt. Col.** Born in Charleston, South Carolina. McCrady was captain of the Meagher Guards, a company of Irish rifles which captured Castle Pinckney early in the war. The company drew its name from Thomas F. Meagher (Meagher of the Sword), the Irish nationalist leader who later became a celebrated Union general. Since Meagher was a prominent Irish leader in the United States before the war and had often sympathized with Southern political causes, the Charleston company chose his name for its sobriquet. When it was realized that Meagher's sympathies had changed, the company changed its name to the Emerald Light Infantry. Later McCrady headed the Irish Volunteers, Company K, 1st South Carolina (Gregg's). McCrady was promoted to lieutenant colonel June 27, 1862, and was wounded at Manassas. In January 1863, he was injured in camp and subsequently assigned as an instruction camp commander in Florida. After the war he was an author/historian and later served in the South Carolina legislature.

**McCrady, Thomas Lt.** McCrady was a member of the Irish Volunteers, Company K, of Gregg's 1st South Carolina. He was breveted a second lieutenant January 25, 1862. He suffered wounds at Second Manassas August 29 of that year, and was wounded again at Fredericksburg, December 13, 1862. He was absent due to wounds for much of 1863. McCrady was promoted to 2nd lieutenant in the summer of 1864, but retired to the invalid corps November 3, 1864.

**McFarland, Robert Capt.** Born in Ireland, McFarland was briefly company commander of Company H, 4th Alabama, which was part of Law's Brigade.

**McGovern, Patrick Capt.** McGovern was company commander of the Lochrane Guards, Company F, Phillips Legion Infantry. He succeeded Capt. Jackson Barnes in September 1862. McGovern enlisted August 24, 1861, at Macon. He was captured September 13, 1862, at South Mountain. McGovern was dropped from the rolls February 24, 1864, after a prolonged absence for chronic illness.

**McGowan, Samuel Brig. Gen.** Born October 9, 1819, in Laurens, South Carolina. McGowan was a lawyer in Abbeville, South Carolina, before the war. McGowan has been called one of the finest regimental and brigade commanders in the Army of Northern Virginia. If physical courage is any measure of a field commander then this high praise is well placed with McGowan. A veteran of the Mexican War, he was present at Fort Sumter and First Manassas. He was appointed colonel of the 14th South Carolina Regiment and was wounded in the Seven Days' Campaign and at Second Manassas. McGowan succeeded to brigade command after the Battle of Fredericksburg where Brig. Gen. Maxcy Gregg was killed at Prospect Hill. He was promoted to brigadier general April 23, 1863, and was wounded a third time at Chancellorsville. With the aid of a cane he led troops in the Wilderness and was wounded a fourth time at the Bloody Angle of Spotsylvania. Captain James Armstrong of the Irish Volunteers of the 1st South Carolina saw McGowan in the van at the Bloody Angle: "The gallant General McGowan, mounted on his handsome gray charger, shouted, 'Forward! my brave boys. . .'" He described "the portly form of General McGowan" as "too conspicuous a mark for the bullets . . . to miss." McGowan was with the army when it surrendered at Appomattox. At Appomattox, South Carolina sharpshooter Berry Benson found him preparing for Lee's surrender "In the woods, crying, half-dressed, taking off his old dirty uniform, and putting on a newer brighter one used on state occasions." (Susan Benson Williams, ed.,

# Appendix II: Irish Officers in the Army of Northern Virginia

*Berry Benson's Civil War Book*, 201.) After the war McGowan was a South Carolina legislator and State Supreme Court Justice.

**McGrath, John Lt.** McGrath was an officer in the Emerald Guards, Company I, 8th Alabama. He became company commander after the death of C. P. Brannigan at Gettysburg. McGrath was cited for gallantry at Seven Pines, according to Colonel Hilary Herbert. An Alabama regimental sketch reports McGrath wounded at Wilderness and Spotsylvania.

**McGraw, Joseph Maj.** Born in Ireland, McGraw was a teamster in Sharpsburg, Maryland, before the war. He was commissioned a lieutenant March 31, 1862, in the Purcell Artillery, Pegram's Battalion. He was wounded during the Seven Days Campaign and lost an arm at the Battle of Spotsylvania. Jennings Wise relates the Spotsylvania incident: "While sitting on his horse . . . a solid shot tore Maj. McGraw's left arm from his body, leaving only a stump in the shoulder socket. 'Don't mind me, men,' he cried, 'I'm all right—give it to 'em,' and with such words on his lips he fell forward from the saddle without a cry of pain." (Jennings Wise, *The Long Arm of Lee*, Vol. II, 798.) McGraw commanded an artillery battalion at Appomattox. After the war he moved to Brooklyn, New York.

**McGurk, John Capt.** Born in Ireland, McGurk was company commander of the Chalmette Guards, Company B, 5th Louisiana. He was on recruiting duty in New Orleans early in 1862, and was absent sick in Richmond November-December 1862. McGurk was listed as a POW at Rappahannock Station, Virginia, November 7, 1863. He was interned at Johnson's Island, Ohio, until he took the Oath of Allegiance June 13, 1865. McGurk was a painter. He had a dark complexion, blue eyes and dark hair, and stood 5' 10".

**McMillan, Robert Col.** Born in Antrim, Ireland, 1805, McMillan was regimental commander of the 24th Georgia from August 30, 1861. He served in this post for most of the war until January 9, 1864, when he resigned, probably in consequence of poor health and his son's resignation the previous day due to wounds. McMillan is one of the forgotten heroes of the Confederate victory at Fredericksburg. A Georgia soldier, Joseph White Woods, remembers McMillan behind the stone wall: "Col McMillan of the 24th Georgia took command of General Cobb's Brigade during the day. He was a full-blooded Irishman and a brave soldier." McMillan, called by a Charleston newspaper "a gallant Irishman at Fredericksburg," was hailed by the *Southern Watchman* of Athens, Georgia, as "a rising officer" after his success at the Battle of Salem Church. McMillan remembered his part in these battles and in the war this way: "No act of ours in this contest should cause a blush to mantle the cheek of any honest, true-hearted Southern man." He died in 1868. Buried Old Cemetery, Clarksville, Habersham County, Georgia.

**McMillan, Robert Emmet Maj.** Born 1835. This was the son of Colonel McMillan, and a namesake of martyred Irish nationalist Robert Emmet. He was promoted to major of the 24th Georgia August 24, 1861. McMillan was wounded in the right leg at Sharpsburg and resigned because of wounds January 8, 1864. He died in 1890. Buried Old Cemetery, Clarksville, Georgia.

**McMillan, Garnett Capt.** A son of Colonel McMillan, he became captain of the McMillan Guards, Company K, 24th Georgia. Garnett enlisted as a private August 24, 1861, but was quickly promoted to 2nd lieutenant July 1, 1862. He was behind the stone wall at Fredericksburg and witnessed his father being struck by a spent ball. Garnett had a close call himself at Fredericksburg. Elijah Henry Sutton told the following anecdote: "During the day Lieutenant (afterwards Captain) Garnett McMillan obtained a long range gun and was firing, between charges, at some sharp shooters who were lying behind a railroad fill and shooting at everything that showed itself. He had loaded his gun and had his head up looking for a target for his bullet when several of us saw a flash of a rifle at the fill. We cried, 'Down,' and some one pulled at him and he dropped his head just in time, for the ball passed, as near as we could tell, right through the space occupied by his head a moment before." Garnett was elected to the United States House of Representatives in 1874. He died of tuberculosis at the age of 32. Another McMillan, Wofford W. McMillan, is listed as 2nd sergeant as of August 24, 1861. Wofford died at the infamous Union prison camp at Elmira, New York, June 29, 1865.

**Magill, Robert John Lt.** Born in Georgetown, South Carolina, Magill served as an officer in the Emmet Rifles, Company B, 1st Georgia (Regulars). He was elected 2nd lieutenant of Company E of the same regiment October 16, 1861, and transferred to the Irish company February 20, 1862, as a 1st lieutenant. He ended the war as an officer in Company E; surrendered at Greensboro, North Carolina, April 26, 1865. Died at Green Cove Springs, Florida, October 11, 1911. Buried in Evergreen Cemetery, Jacksonville, Florida.

**Mahoney, Daniel Lt.** Born in Ireland, Mahoney was in the Shepherd Guards, Co. A, 10th Louisiana. He enlisted July 22, 1861, and was appointed lieutenant December 23, 1862. He was captured at Spotsylvania May 10, 1864, was sent from Belle Plain on Potomac Creek to Fort Delaware, and was released on oath June 16, 1865. Mahoney was a single laborer, age 23 in 1861. He was 5' 11", and had a ruddy complexion, auburn hair and gray eyes.

**Mallett, John William Col.** Born in Dublin, Ireland, October 10, 1835, Mallett was made an officer of artillery on the staff of Maj. Gen. Robert Emmett Rodes and by 1862 was in charge of the Confederate Ordnance Laboratory in Richmond. Mallett never relinquished his British citizenship. He held an A. B. degree from Trinity College, Dublin, and earned a Ph.D. in chemistry at the University of Gottingen, Germany. He was a professor of chemistry at Amherst College, the Universities of Alabama, Louisiana, Texas and Virginia, and was a member of the Royal Society of London.

# Appendix II: Irish Officers in the Army of Northern Virginia

**Mallory, Stephen Russell Confederate Secretary of the Navy.** Born Trinidad, 1813, of Irish parents. His father, Charles Mallory, was sea captain in Bridgeport, Connecticut. He died when Stephen was nine. He was raised by his mother, Ellen Russell Mallory, a Roman Catholic from County Waterford, Ireland. Mallory grew up in Florida where he fought in the Seminole War. He was a customs inspector at Key West, a lawyer and a judge in Florida and served in the United States Senate, as chairman of the Naval Affairs Committee, until secession. The Confederate Navy under Mallory not only built the first ironclad ship (*CSS Virginia*), but developed the world's first combat submarines. The South hoped that a small fleet of underwater vessels could compete with the Union Navy and the Northern merchant marine. Mallory was the South's only Navy secretary, and after the war he was a lawyer in Pensacola, Florida.

**Martin, William Lt. Col.** Martin began his Confederate service as captain of the Emmet Rifles, Company B, 1st Georgia (Regulars). He was elected commander of the Irish company February 1, 1861, and was promoted to lieutenant colonel February 3, 1862. Martin died of tuberculosis at his home October 16, 1864.

**Meara, James Lt.** Meara was an officer in the Lochrane Guards, Company F, Phillips Legion Infantry. He resigned his commission January 13, 1862.

**Mitchell, James Capt.** This Captain Mitchell enlisted as a private April 21, 1861, in the Montgomery Guard, Company C, 1st Virginia Infantry. He was a 21-year-old clerk in Richmond. He was elected 2nd lieutenant August 30, 1861, and was appointed captain of the Irish company April 27, 1862. He was wounded August 30, 1862, at Second Manassas.

**Mitchel, James C. Capt.** Mitchel was one of three sons of Irish nationalist John Mitchel who fought for the Confederacy. He lost his right arm in battle in 1862 and then was appointed to the Adjutant General's Department as an assistant adjutant general assigned to various commands in the Army of Northern Virginia. Mitchel was appointed assistant adjutant general December 28, 1862, and was ordered to report to General Robert E. Lee "for such duty as he may assign him to." On January 17, 1863, he was ordered to report to Stonewall Jackson for duty with Lawton's Brigade. On October 6, 1864, he was assigned assistant adjutant general of Brig. Gen. Clement A. Evans' Brigade of John B. Gordon's division. By February 10, 1865, Mitchel was assigned to Maj. Gen. James L. Kemper's Reserve Forces of Virginia. James was the only Mitchel son to survive the war. His son, John Purroy Mitchel, became mayor of New York City.

**Mitchel, John C. Capt.** The oldest son of Irish patriot John Mitchel, he was born in Ireland. He was eighteen when his father was transported to Australia, and he accompanied him there. Educated as a civil engineer, the younger Mitchel traveled the United States building railroads. He enlisted as a lieutenant of artillery with the South Carolina Regulars at Fort Moultrie and became part of the Confederate garrison at Fort Sumter when it fell in 1861. Not liking garrison duty, he attempted to raise a company of light artillery for the Army of Northern Virginia, but his superiors objected and he remained at Fort Sumter for the war. In 1864, he assumed command of the battered fort; at that time, the citadel's flag was shot down as often as six times a day. On July 20, he was mortally wounded while standing on the parapets during an artillery barrage. He had refused shelter for a sentinel, and the captain felt obliged to assume the same risk. He died three hours later with the words, "I die willingly for South Carolina, but oh that it had been for Ireland!"

**Monaghan, William Col.** Born in Ireland, Monaghan was a 44-year-old notary public in New Orleans when he enlisted in 1861. He was commissioned captain of the Irish Brigade Company B, Company F, 6th Louisiana. Monaghan was a full colonel by 1862. He was part of a court of inquiry in October 1862, to investigate the withdrawal of Lawton's Brigade near Shepherdstown during the Maryland Campaign. Monaghan escaped capture by swimming the Rappahannock River when his regiment was overrun at Rappahannock Bridge, Virginia, November 7, 1863. He commanded Hays' and Hoke's brigades in fighting along Mine Run later in this winter campaign. In Monaghan's Mine Run report, he praised his officers and men for "their desire to encounter the enemy—a desire, I regret to add, we were not permitted by the abundance of his prudence to gratify." Monaghan took command of the Louisiana Brigade at Spotsylvania when General Harry T. Hays was severely wounded May 10. Monaghan's command was in the hottest part of the salient on May 12 at Spotsylvania. He was wounded at Ox Hill, was a POW at Strasburg, and was killed in action August 25, 1864. Buried Elmwood Cemetery, Shepherdstown, West Virginia. (James Gannon, *Irish Rebels Confederate Tigers: A History of the 6th Louisiana Volunteers, 1861-1865*.)

**Montgomery, James G. Capt.** Montgomery was an officer in the Emmet Rifles, Company B, 1st Georgia (Regulars). He was elected lieutenant of the company February 1, 1861, and was promoted to captain of Company K of the same regiment January 15, 1862. Montgomery was wounded at Sharpsburg September 17, 1862, and retired with a permanent disability due to wounds by August 25, 1864.

**Moore, Patrick T. Brig. Gen.** Born in Galway, Ireland, September 22, 1821. Moore, the son of a British diplomat, was a merchant in Richmond and from 1850 to 1860 was captain of the Montgomery Guard, a militia company. Moore was a leader in the Irish Catholic community in Richmond and was an officer in Richmond's Hibernian Society. He was appointed colonel of the 1st Virginia Regiment at the outbreak of the war. Moore was severely wounded at First Manassas, and spent months recuperating and seeking a new command. In a July 30, 1862, letter to Secretary of War George W. Randolph, A. P. Hill said of Moore: "I have served with Col. Moore and know him well, and can assure you that he is too valuable a man to be left un-employed during these stirring times." Moore was given command of local defense troops and promoted to brigadier general September 20, 1864. After the war he was a Richmond insurance agent. He died February 19, 1883, and is buried in Shockoe Hill Cemetery. Major John D. Ross of the

# Appendix II: Irish Officers in the Army of Northern Virginia

52nd Virginia described Moore as "a terrible old croaker." (Ross, *West Virginia History*, Vol. XLV, 173.)

**Morgan, Thomas Gibbs Capt.** Born in Baton Rouge, Louisiana, Morgan commanded the Irish Volunteers, Company F, 7th Louisiana. He enlisted June 7, 1861. He was a 24-year-old married farmer. Morgan was wounded at Sharpsburg September 17, 1862. He was listed as a POW November 7, 1863. He died at Johnson's Island, Ohio, January 21 or 22, 1864.

**Munford, John Dunburrow Maj.** Born Richmond, 1810, Munford was an expedient appointment for command of the Irish Battalion in July 1861. He was tapped for the post by John Seddon, who wanted to resign for health reasons. Munford was a lawyer and farmer in Botetourt County with no military experience. He was relieved of command in January 1862 and assigned to the 15th Virginia Infantry. He resigned his commission in May 1862. Charles Davidson said Munford "knew as much about military matters . . . as a school boy." He died in 1876.

**Myers, Dennis S. Capt.** Myers was 1st lieutenant in the Jackson Guards, Company B, 19th Georgia, enlisting June 11, 1861. He was elected captain of the Irish company on June 26, 1862. Myers was wounded at Second Manassas on August 30, 1862, and resigned because of disability on September 2, 1863. He died in Atlanta, Georgia.

**Neal, James Henry Col.** Neal began his Confederate career as captain of the Jackson Guards, Company B, 19th Georgia. He enlisted June 11, 1861. Neal was elected major of the regiment on June 26, 1862; was promoted to lieutenant colonel January 12, 1863; and to colonel August 20, 1863. He was killed at the Battle of Bentonville, North Carolina, in March 1865. Neal is buried in the Neal family lot at Oakland Cemetery, Atlanta, Georgia. Irishman John Keely married Neal's sister after the war.

**Nelligan, James Lt. Col.** Born in Ireland, Nelligan was a New Orleans auctioneer. He was commissioned Captain of the Emmet Guards, Company D, 1st Louisiana, and as a major at Fredericksburg "was court-martialed for leaving his regt in fight at Fredericksburg and Gettysburg, but was whitewashed." Nelligan was wounded in the Seven Days Campaign, June 25, 1862, at Chancellorsville and Mine Run. He commanded the 1st Louisiana in 1863 and until captured in 1864. He was a POW at Winchester, September 19, 1864, and spent time in Union prisons at Point Lookout, Maryland, and Fort Delaware.

**Nolan, Michael Col.** Born in County Tipperary, Ireland, Nolan was a New Orleans grocer. He enlisted as a sergeant and soon was the company commander of the Montgomery Guards, Company E, 1st Louisiana. Nolan took command of the regiment when Lt. Col. W. R. Shivers was wounded in the Peninsula Campaign. At age 41, Nolan commanded the regiment at Fredericksburg. Colonel Edmund Pendleton's report in the *Official Records* mentions Nolan for special commendation. At Sharpsburg, Pendleton reported, "Lieut. Col. M. Nolan, of the First Louisiana, though painfully wounded in the leg, remained at his post during the fight, commanding his regiment with coolness and bravery." Nolan took command of William Starke's Brigade when the brigadier was killed in that battle. For a time Nolan was responsible for the safety of the notebooks of Chaplain Louis-Hippolyte Gache, whose memoirs are widely read today. Gache's editor, Cornelius Buckley, wrote Nolan was to be commissioned brigadier general when he was killed in action at Gettysburg July 3, 1863. Nolan was described as a "blue-eyed, light-haired Irishman . . . mild and polite and friendly in his manners," and "the best, bravest and grandest soldier." The Louisiana rosters call Nolan "a most gallant officer."

**O'Brien, John F. Maj.** O'Brien attended the United States Military Academy at West Point from June 1859 to January 29, 1861. At the outbreak of the war, he sided with the Confederacy and was recommended for a commission by General William J. Hardee who knew O'Brien at West Point. O'Brien began his Confederate service at Charleston May 21, 1861, as a lieutenant of artillery. On April 17, 1862, he was promoted to captain and appointed to the staff of Brig. Gen. Charles Sidney Winder, commander of the Stonewall Brigade. O'Brien was active in the Seven Days and Valley campaigns, and was well-regarded by Winder, who seldom missed an opportunity to mention him in his official reports. O'Brien was promoted to major May 27, 1863, and reported to General Pierre G. T. Beauregard in South Carolina. His compiled service record shows O'Brien bought a "French revolving pistol with English belt and equipments" from the Charleston arsenal during this billet. O'Brien was ordered to the staff of General E. Kirby Smith in the Trans-Mississippi November 18, 1863, and was en route to a temporary billet under Maj. Gen. John H. Forney at Enterprise, Mississippi, when he was captured February 13, 1864. O'Brien was exchanged July 22, 1864, and served as assistant adjutant general in the District of Arkansas to December 24, 1864. He was reassigned to the Trans-Mississippi January 2, 1865.

**O'Connor, Michael Capt.** Born in Ireland, O'Connor was married and a storekeeper in New Orleans before the war. He enlisted at age 35 and was commissioned a 1st lieutenant of a company in the Irish Brigade, Company F, 6th Louisiana. He later was promoted to captain of the company. He was wounded at Sharpsburg and was not present at Fredericksburg. He was wounded and captured near Fredericksburg as part of the Chancellorsville Campaign. He is listed as a prisoner of war at Rappahannock, Virginia, November 7, 1863. He was paroled and exchanged February 24, 1865.

**O'Hara, Theodore Col.** Born Danville, Kentucky, February 11, 1820. O'Hara was a graduate of Saint Joseph's College. He was an officer in the Mexican War, and a captain in the 2nd U.S. Cavalry, 1855-56, fighting Indians under Robert E. Lee. O'Hara is the author of "The Bivouac of the Dead," a poem written in memory of Mexican War veterans, and now immortalized in America's national cemeteries. He enlisted as a captain of infantry in March 1861, and became lieutenant colonel of the 12th Alabama in July of that year. He later was assistant inspector general to Albert Sidney Johnston and a

# Appendix II: Irish Officers in the Army of Northern Virginia

staff officer for other western commanders. He died in 1867 and is buried in Frankfort, Kentucky.

**O'Neal, Edward A. Col.** Born in Madison County, Alabama, September 20, 1818, the son of an Irish immigrant. O'Neal headed an Alabama brigade at Yorktown and in the Seven Days Campaign. He was wounded at South Mountain in September 1862, and wounded again at Chancellorsville while in charge of Rodes' Brigade. He commanded a division at Gettysburg. Passed over for promotion to brigadier after Gettysburg, he left the Army of Northern Virginia. In a January 25, 1864, letter of complaint to Alabama congressman James Phelan, O'Neal stated: "I have fought in every battle from Williamsburg to Gettysburg except Sharpsburg and the first battle of Fredericksburg, where I was detained from wounds from the field." In response General Lee said of O'Neal: "I have a just appreciation of his gallantry and worth." O'Neal commanded a brigade in the Atlanta Campaign. He was a lawyer in Florence, Alabama, and was governor of that state 1882-86.

**O'Rourke, Patrick R. Maj.** Born in Ireland, O'Rourke became a staff officer for the 1st Louisiana, but began his wartime career as captain of the Orleans Light Guards, Company F, 1st Louisiana. He enlisted April 27, 1861, in New Orleans where he had worked as an inspector. O'Rourke was wounded at Sharpsburg September 17, 1862, and his left arm was amputated. Consequently, he was appointed to a staff position and later was transferred to the Trans-Mississippi Department.

**Owens, Edward Lt.** Born in Ireland, Owens was an officer in the Emerald Guards, Company E, 9th Louisiana. He enlisted in 1861 at age 32. He was a single laborer living in Madison Parish, Louisiana. He is present on the rolls from November 1862 to April 1863. Owens was promoted to 2nd lieutenant April 20, 1862. He was captured at Gettysburg July 3, 1863, and interned at Johnson's Island, Ohio, until he was paroled February 24, 1865.

**Parker, Michael P. Capt.** Parker was company commander of the Irish Volunteers, Company K, of the 1st South Carolina. He entered service at Charleston, June 25, 1861, as 1st lieutenant. He was promoted to captain January 23, 1862. Parker was wounded at Sharpsburg and was absent for wounds for much of 1863. He was back on duty for the start of the 1864 campaign, and later that year was provost marshal at Augusta, Georgia. He retired to the invalid corps June 2, 1864.

**Peck, William R. Col.** Born in Tennessee, Peck enlisted at age forty on July 7, 1861. He was a single planter living in Madison Parish, Louisiana. His first post was as captain of the Emerald Guards, Company E, 9th Louisiana. He was promoted to colonel October 8, 1863, and brigadier general on February 22, 1865.

**Porter, John G. Capt.** Porter was company commander of the McMillan Guards, Company K, 24th Georgia. He was elected captain of the company August 20, 1861, and resigned his commission because of disability February 13, 1863. He died in Clarksville, Georgia, April 1, 1863.

**Potts, Francis Capt.** Born in Ireland 1835. Potts enlisted as a private April 21, 1861, a member of the Montgomery Guard, Company C, 1st Virginia. He fought at First Manassas and was promoted to sergeant July 15, 1861. He was detailed from the regiment October 7, 1861, to the quartermasters' corps. He served as assistant quartermaster of Longstreet's command in the Tennessee campaign, where the corps commander commended his performance. He was later named paymaster for the corps. He chronicled some of his war experiences and wrote "The Death of the Confederacy: The Last Week of the Army of Northern Virginia," a letter to his brother in Canada about the evacuation of Richmond and Lee's surrender. "I loved the cause and until our army was hemmed in on front and rear, and on both sides, I never despaired of the Republic," he wrote. Potts was bitter in defeat. After his surrender and parole, he characterized himself as "a subjugated rebel, who had no nation, no rights, and no greenbacks." A successful Richmond businessman after the war, he died in the capital city in 1890 and is buried in Hollywood Cemetery.

**Powell, Thomas N. Maj.** Powell was captain of Hewitt's Guards, Company C, of the 10th Louisiana. He was a planter in New Orleans when he enlisted July 22, 1861. He was appointed 2nd lieutenant August 3, 1861, and was elected captain January 17, 1862. He was promoted to major May 3, 1864.

**Quinn, Andrew Capt.** Quinn was one of four documented company commanders of the Emerald Guards, Company I, 8th Alabama; the other three, Loughry, Brannigan and McGrath, were killed or wounded.

**Ratliff, William B. Capt.** Ratliff briefly was company commander of the Irish Volunteers, Company F, 7th Louisiana. He was a 32-year-old married planter residing in Napoleonville, Louisiana. He enlisted June 7, 1861 and resigned October 1861.

**Redmond, Thomas Capt.** Born in Ireland, Redmond enlisted June 4, 1861, in the Calhoun Guards, Company B, 6th Louisiana. He was sick at Lynchburg from September 1862 to October 1863. He was captured and listed as a POW at Rappahannock Station, Virginia, November 7, 1863, and was taken to Johnson's Island, Ohio. Redmond was a clerk in New Orleans before the war. At enlistment he was 25 and single. He had a dark complexion, dark hair and gray eyes, and was 5' 9" tall. Redmond took the Oath of Allegiance June 13, 1865.

**Reilly, James Maj.** Born at Athlone, County Westmeath, Ireland, 1822. Reilly ran away from home at sixteen years and joined the British Army. His mother smuggled him out of Ireland, and the army, to the states, where he joined the United States Army. A veteran of the Mexican and Indian wars, as a United States regular he surrendered Fort Johnston in Smithville, (now Southport) North Carolina, to rebel forces in 1861. He accepted a

# Appendix II: Irish Officers in the Army of Northern Virginia

commission as captain of North Carolina troops and commanded Reilly's Battery of the Rowan Artillery in the Army of Northern Virginia. According to Jennings Wise, in the spring of 1863 Reilly was appointed by Chief of Artillery William N. Pendleton to a board to enumerate improvements in the army's artillery force. In 1865, he found himself in command of Fort Fisher, North Carolina, when the fort's commander, Colonel William Lamb, was wounded. Lamb remembered, "Reilly came and promised me that he would continue the fight as long as it was possible and nobly did he keep his promise." (*Southern Historical Society Papers*, Volume 21, 287.) Reilly eventually surrendered Fort Fisher, thus perhaps becoming the only officer to surrender to both sides in the Civil War. According to Robert K. Krick in *Lee's Colonels: A Biographical Register of the Field Officers of the Army of Northern Virginia*), his men called him "Old Tarantula," and he was variously described as "rough, gruff, grizzly and brave." Once called upon to clear out an enemy sharpshooter, Reilly directed a cannon shot directly into the sniper's lair. "Old Captain Reilly [He was but forty at the time.] was so elated with the fine shot he made and the fun it created that he laughed until the tears rolled down his wrinkled old cheeks." Reilly's grandson, Lawrence Lee, related in a 1983 letter that his mother, Major Reilly's daughter, remembered him as "a kind, gentle and patient man."

**Rice, Thomas Capt.** Rice was company commander of the Montgomery Guards, Company E, 1st Louisiana. He enlisted April 28, 1861, in New Orleans as a sergeant. He was reduced to ranks November 22, 1861, but promoted to sergeant again on June 20, 1862, and to lieutenant July 11, 1862. Rice was wounded at Sharpsburg September 17, 1862, but returned to duty that December. He was wounded again May 12, 1864, at Spotsylvania. No date given for promotion to captain.

**Russell, Joseph H. Capt.** Russell served as an officer in the Montgomery Guards, Company K of the 20th Georgia. He was a sergeant in the Guards August 8, 1861, was elected 2nd lieutenant April 5, 1862, and transferred to the 6th Alabama as a 1st lieutenant June 12, 1864. He was later elected captain, but retired from field command October 29, 1864, presumably because of wounds. Russell joined the Invalid Corps December 1, 1864, and was assigned to the Bureau of Conscription in Richmond December 6, 1864.

**Ryan, Thomas P. Lt.** Ryan was an officer of the Irish Volunteers, Company C, of the 1st South Carolina. He enlisted at Charleston June 25, 1861. He resigned from the company February 28, 1862, to join the 23rd South Carolina. He was promoted to captain of Company C of the 23rd South Carolina in December 1864.

**Ryan, W. H. Capt.** Ryan was the company commander of Company C, the Irish Volunteers of the Charleston Battalion. He never fought in the Army of Northern Virginia, but is mentioned here as the organizer of this Irish company. The battalion was later consolidated in the 27th South Carolina Infantry, which fought in Virginia in 1864. Captain Ryan was killed July 18, 1863, at Battery Wagner in South Carolina.

**Scott, James D. Capt.** Born in Ireland, Scott commanded Hewitt's Guards, Company C of the 10th Louisiana. He enlisted July 22, 1861, and was on the rolls from January 1862 to August 31, 1864. Before the war he was a laborer from Donaldsonville, Louisiana. At enlistment he was single and 31 years old.

**Scott, Robert B. Capt.** The commander of the Virginia Guards, Company D, 7th Louisiana. He enlisted June 7, 1861. Born in Louisiana. At enlistment he was 32, single, and a New Orleans resident. He was on the rolls to February 1862, when he resigned.

**Seagers, Michael Lt.** Born in Ireland, and a merchant in Richmond when he joined the Montgomery Guard militia company June 12, 1859. An active Catholic leader in Richmond, Seagers was treasurer of Saint Vincent's Catholic Beneficial Society. He was elected 2nd lieutenant in the militia and took the same rank to Confederate service April 21, 1861. He was 44. Seagers fought at First Manassas, but resigned July 21, 1861. He died at Coalfield, Chesterfield County, Virginia, August 6, 1882.

**Seddon, John Maj.** Born October 8, 1826, Seddon was the brother of Confederate Secretary of War James Seddon. He was appointed captain of Company D of the Irish Battalion in May 1861. He was on detached service in Fredericksburg from September to the end of November 1861, and absent sick for the first two months of 1862. Even so, Seddon was appointed major of the battalion in May of that year. His horse was killed in the rout of the Irish Battalion at Cedar Mountain, and he resigned for disability in September 1862. He was elected to the Virginia senate, but died December 5, 1863. Buried in the Fredericksburg City Cemetery.

**Shannon, James J. Lt. Col.** Shannon resided in Jasper County, Mississippi, near Paulding, which included an Irish Catholic enclave. The area of the state was called the piney woods, and Shannon was described as "a typical piney woods country lawyer" by Private David Holt in his memoirs, *A Mississippi Rebel in the Army of Northern Virginia*. Shannon also was the proprietor of the *Eastern Clarion* newspaper. At age thirty-six, he raised the Jasper Grays, Company F of the 16th Mississippi, and was elected captain May 31, 1861. The company marched to Corinth for three months drill and was billeted in the jailhouse. Shannon was indignant over the accommodations. "We have started off to battle and it will commence right here if we are not removed from this place," he told his commander. The Irish company was moved to a church. Shannon was promoted to lieutenant colonel April 28, 1862, but resigned his commission December 20, 1862, for health reasons. According to Holt, "Shannon was tall, higher than six feet, [and] exceedingly thin. When he gave orders, he always began with 'Attention, Battalion,' and stood on his toes as if he wanted to see each one of his men."

**Shaw, A. E. Capt.** Shaw had a short army career as an officer in the Chalmette Guards, Company B, 5th Louisiana. A married New Orleans clerk, he enlisted June 4, 1861. His record simply reads: "in arrest since June 23, 1861."

# Appendix II: Irish Officers in the Army of Northern Virginia

**Skinner, Frederick G. Col.** Skinner was born March 17, Saint Patrick's Day, 1814, in Annapolis, Maryland. He was schooled in France. Skinner was appointed major in the 1st Virginia Infantry in May 1861, and took command of the regiment when Colonel Patrick Moore was wounded at Blackburn's Ford July 18, 1861. He "cursed like a trooper" and was "as brave as a bear," according to Francis Potts. Skinner took a particular fancy to his Irish company, the Montgomery Guard. He was promoted to lieutenant colonel November 18, 1861, and was wounded at Second Manassas. He never returned to field command, but was promoted to colonel July 3, 1863, and retired to the Invalid Corps February 6, 1865. Skinner took the Oath of Allegiance May 29, 1865. He died in Charlottesville May 22, 1894; buried in Westminster Churchyard, Baltimore.

**Snowden, Samuel H. Capt.** Snowden was an officer in the Orleans Light Guards, Company F, 1st Louisiana. He enlisted in that company in New Orleans April 25, 1861, as a lieutenant. He was promoted to captain April 28, 1862. Snowden was wounded at Second Manassas August 29, 1862. He was detailed to general court-martial duty in January and February 1863, and was acting regimental quartermaster by the summer of that year. He was appointed assistant quartermaster in January 1864.

**Strong, Henry B. Col.** Born in Ireland, Strong was a clerk in New Orleans before the war. He enlisted in 1861 at age forty and began his Confederate army career as captain of the Calhoun Guards, Company B, 6th Louisiana. He quickly advanced to regimental command and was killed at Sharpsburg in fighting near the Dunker Church. There is a remarkable photograph of Strong's dead horse in lifelike repose taken shortly after the Antietam battle. ( (James Gannon, *Irish Rebels Confederate Tigers: A History of the 6th Louisiana Volunteers, 1861-1865*; William A. Frassanito, *Antietam: The Photographic Legacy of America's Bloodiest Day*.)

**Sweeney, John Lt.** Sweeney enlisted at Charleston June 25, 1861, a member of the Irish Volunteers, Company K, 1st South Carolina. He was promoted to 1st lieutenant January 23, 1862. He was wounded at Chancellorsville May 3, 1863, and was absent for wounds until the end of 1863. By the summer of 1864 he was listed as absent without leave and the following October he was dropped from the rolls.

**Thom, J. Pembroke Capt.** Born Culpeper, Virginia, 1828. He was captain of Company C of the Irish Battalion. Thom was a graduate of Fredericksburg Academy, attended the University of Virginia and graduated from the Jefferson Medical College, Philadelphia. He served in the Mexican War, a lieutenant in the 11th United States Infantry, and also was an assistant surgeon in the United States Navy. His letters home constitute *My Dear Brother: A Confederate Chronicle*, a book edited by his sister, Catherine Thom Bartlett. Thom was a "Gaelic Celt," whose ancestors fought with Bonnie Prince Charlie at Culloden in 1745. He was wounded leading a charge at Kernstown. He resigned from field command and was assigned to the Ordnance Department in August 1862. He later went to Canada until 1866, and after the war was a doctor, politician and port official in Baltimore. He died in 1899.

**Walsh, Michael S. Lt.** Born in Ireland, Walsh was a 1st lieutenant in the Lochrane Guards, Company F, Phillips Legion Infantry. He enlisted August 21, 1861, at Macon, and was made a corporal before being elected lieutenant. He was twenty-three years old. Walsh had been a printer for the *Savannah Morning News* from 1858. He was wounded at Gettysburg July 3, 1863, was captured and taken to Johnson's Island, Ohio July 18. In prison, he told his captors that he gave himself up at Gettysburg by concealing himself in some rocks when the Confederate army fell back. He asked to be allowed to return to Ireland and his family. He was not released, and Walsh did not take the Oath of Allegiance until May 12, 1865.

**Walshe, Blayney Townley Capt.** Born in Wexford, Ireland, 1840, Walshe was commander of the Irish Brigade Company A, Co. I, 6th Louisiana. He was wounded in the ankle at Gaines' Mill June 27, 1862, and then detached as chief of the Passport Office in Richmond September-October 1863. By 1864 he was assigned the job of provost marshal for several Louisiana parishes by General Joseph E. Johnston. He proposed the formation of an independent cavalry command to be made up of invalid soldiers, but the idea was quashed by Robert E. Lee. Brig. Gen. Harry Hays wrote of Walshe: "Capt. B.T. Walshe is a gallant and efficient officer, and will do good service for the Confederacy in whatever position he may be placed." Walshe was a New Orleans clerk before the war. He was retired by the Medical Examining Board, presumably because of his war wound, and after the war he became a prominent merchant, New Orleans Administrator of Finance and the state tax collector for the New Orleans area.

**Welsh, John Payne Capt.** Welsh was company commander of the Virginia Hibernians, Company G, 27th Virginia. Born in Rockbridge County, Virginia, he was the son of a Scots-Irish settler. He enlisted March 19, 1862. Welsh was wounded in the hip at Gettysburg and died of his wound in a Williamsport, Maryland, hospital July 15, 1863. He is buried in the Catholic Cemetery, Williamsport. His brother, James Welsh, moved to Illinois, joined the Republican Party and was a Union soldier in the 78th Illinois.

**Wilson, Johnathan Moore Maj.** Born in Ireland, Wilson, age 30 in 1861, was a New Orleans merchant. He served as captain of the Sarsfield Rangers, Company C, 7th Louisiana. Wilson is probably the "Louisiana major" who collared Allen C. Redwood of the 55th Virginia at Second Manassas. (*Battles and Leaders*, Volume II, 535.) Trying to rally men to his command, "The major was courteous but firm," Redwood reported. "Better stay with us, my boy, and if you do your duty I'll make it right with your company officers when the fight's over. They won't find fault with you when they know you've been in with the 'Pelicans,' " the major told him. Wilson was wounded at Winchester June 14, 1863. By 1864, Wilson was in command of the Pelican Regiment, the 7th Louisiana. He was captured at the Battle of the Spotsylvania, May 10, 1864, and sent from Belle Plain landing in Stafford, Virginia, to Fort Delaware prison. He died in 1894. Buried Metarie Cemetery, New Orleans.

# Bibliography

## MANUSCRIPTS

Brooke, John R. Letter to Francis Walker, May 28, 1884. Mark Edgar Richards Collection, United States Army Military History Institute.

Confederate General and Staff Officers Compiled Service Records. National Archives, Washington, D.C.

Fredericksburg and Spotsylvania National Military Park Manuscript Collection, Fredericksburg, Va.

Herbert, Hilary Abner. Papers. Southern Historical Collection. University of North Carolina Library.

Mackay-Stiles Collection. Southern Historical Collection. University of North Carolina.

McNeill, Betty Ann. "Civil War Services of the Daughters of Charity." Compiled from Military Service, Civil War Accounts, Archives of Saint Joseph's Provincial House, Emmitsburg, Maryland, ASJPH 7-5-1-1.

Potts, Francis. "Diary kept by Francis Potts, a private in Co. C, 1st Regt. Va. Volunteers, July 14, 1861-September 21, 1861." Virginia State Library Archives.

———. The Death of the Confederacy: The Last Week of the Army of Northern Virginia as set forth in a letter of April 1865. Richmond: Private Printing for A. Potts, 1928.

Smith, James P. "Stonewall Jackson in Winter Quarters at Moss Neck." An address delivered in Winchester, Va., January 19, 1898. Jedediah Hotchkiss Papers. Library of Congress, Washington, D. C.

United Daughters of the Confederacy Bound Typescripts. Georgia Archives.

Weston, James A. Unpublished letter to Zebulon Vance, October 29, 1863. North Carolina States Archives, GP 170.

## OFFICIAL PUBLICATIONS

Davis, George B., Leslie J. Perry, and Joseph W. Kirkley. *The Official Military Atlas of the Civil War.* New York: Gramercy Books, 1983.

Hewett, Janet B., ed. *Supplement to the Official Records.* vol. 24. Wilmington, N. C.: Broadfoot Publishing Co., 1996.

*War of the Rebellion: A Compilation of the Official Records of the Union and Confederate Armies.* Washington: Government Printing Office, 1888.


## NEWSPAPERS

*Arlington Catholic Herald*
*Athens Southern Watchman*
*Atlanta Constitution Magazine*
*Augusta Daily Constitutionalist*
*Catholic World, The*
*Charleston Daily Courier*
*Charleston News and Courier*
*Confederate Veteran*
*Richmond Daily Enquirer*
*Richmond Daily Examiner*
*Southern Confederacy*
*Wilmington Weekly Star*


## PUBLISHED PRIMARY SOURCES

(includes autobiographies, diaries, journals, memoirs, and reminiscences, and unit histories)

Alexander, Edward Porter. *Fighting for the Confederacy: The Personal Recollections of General Edward Porter Alexander.* Gary W. Gallagher, ed. Chapel Hill: University of North Carolina Press, 1989.

# Bibliography

Allan, William. *The Army of Northern Virginia in 1862.* Boston: Houghton Mifflin Co., 1892.

Andrews, W. H. *Footprints of a Regiment: A Recollection of the 1st Georgia Regulars 1861-1865.* Annotated by Richard M. McMurry. Atlanta: Longstreet Press, 1992.

Baker, Henry H. *A Reminiscent Story of the Great Civil War: A Personal Experience.* New Orleans: Ruskin Press, 1911.

Bartlett, Catherine Thom. *My Dear Brother: A Confederate Chronicle.* Richmond: Dietz Press, 1952.

Beall, John B. *In Barrack and Field: Poems and Sketches of Army Life.* Nashville and Dallas: Publishing House of the Methodist Episcopal Church, South, 1906.

Bean, W. G. "A House Divided: The Civil War Letters of a Virginia Family." *Virginia Military and Historical Biography.* vol. 59., 1951.

Bernard, George S. *War Talks of Confederate Veterans.* Petersburg, Va.: Fenn & Owen, 1892.

Brown, Varina D. *A Colonel at Gettysburg and Spotsylvania: Col. Joseph Newton Brown.* Columbia, S. C.: State Co., 1931.

Buckley, Cornelius M., S. J., trans. *A Frenchman, A Chaplain, A Rebel: The War Letters of Pere Louis-Hippolyte Gache, S. J.* Chicago: Loyola University Press, 1981.

Caldwell, J. F. J. *The History of a Brigade of South Carolinians, First Known as "Gregg's" and Subsequently as "McGowan's Brigade."* Dayton, Ohio: Morningside Press, 1984.

Casler, John O. *Four Years in the Stonewall Brigade.* James I. Robertson Jr., ed. Dayton, Ohio: Morningside Press, 1971.

Cavanagh, Michael. *Memoirs of Gen. Thomas Francis Meagher, Comprising the Leading Events of His Career.* Worcester, Mass.: Messenger Press, 1892.

Chamberlayne, C. G., ed. *Ham Chamberlayne Virginian: Letters and Papers of an Artillery Officer in the War for Southern Independence 1861-1865.* Richmond: Dietz Press, 1932.

Clark, Walter, ed. *Histories of the Several Regiments and Battalions from North Carolina in the Great War 1861-65.* 5 vols. Wendell, N. C.: Broadfoot's Bookmark, 1982.

Cockrell, Thomas D. and Michael B. Ballard, eds., *A Mississippi Rebel in the Army of Northern Virginia: The Civil War Memoirs of Private David Holt*. Baton Rouge and London: Louisiana State University Press, 1995.

Conyngham, David P. *The Irish Brigade and Its Campaigns*. New York: Fordham University Press, reprint, 1994.

Corby, William. *Memoirs of Chaplain Life: Three Years with the Irish Brigade in the Army of the Potomac*. Lawrence Frederick Kohl, ed. New York: Fordham University Press, 1992.

Donald, David Herbert. ed. *Gone for a Soldier: The Civil War Memoirs of Private Alfred Bellard*. Boston: Little, Brown & Company, 1975.

Dunlop, W. S. *Lee's Sharpshooters, or the Forefront of Battle*. Little Rock: Tunnah & Pittard, 1899.

Durkin, Joseph T., S. J., ed. *John Dooley Confederate Soldier: His War Journal*. Ithaca, N. Y.: Georgetown University Press, 1945.

————. *Confederate Chaplain: A War Journal of James B. Sheeran, C. SS. R.* Milwaukee: Bruce Publishing Co., 1960.

Evans, Clement A. *Confederate Military History: A Library of Confederate States History*. 12 vols. Wilmington, N. C.: Broadfoot Publishing Co., 1987-89.

Fremantle, Arthur James Lyon. *Three Months in the Southern States*. Lincoln: University of Nebraska Press, 1991.

Galwey, Thomas Francis. *The Valiant Hours*. Harrisburg, Pennsylvania: The Stackpole Co., 1961.

Gordon, Armistead Churchill. *Memories and Memorials of William Gordon McCabe*. 2 vols. Richmond, Va.: Old Dominion Press, 1925.

Grant, U. S. *Personal Memoirs of U. S. Grant*. 2 vols. New York: Charles L. Webster & Co., 1886.

Johnson, Robert U. and Clarence C. Buel, eds. *Battles and Leaders of the Civil War*. 4 vols. New York: Century Co., 1884-89.

Jones, John Beauchamp. *A Rebel War Clerk's Diary at the Confederate States Capital*. Philadelphia: J. B. Lippincott & Co., 1866.

Keiley, Anthony M. *In Vinculis or The Prisoner of War*. New York: Blelock & Co., 1866.

# Bibliography

Kilpatrick, Hugh Judson. *The Irish Soldier in the War of the Rebellion.* Deckertown, N. J.: Privately printed, 1880.

Lane, Walter P. *The Adventures and Recollections of General Walter P. Lane.* Austin: Pemberton Press, 1970.

Lasswell, Mary, ed. *Rags and Hope: The Recollections of Val C. Giles, Four Years with Hood's Brigade, Fourth Texas Infantry, 1861-1865.* New York: Coward-McCann, 1961.

Lee, Robert E., Capt. *Recollections and Letters of General Robert E. Lee.* Garden City, N. Y.: Garden City Publishing Co., 1904.

Lightsey, Ada Christine. *The Veteran's Story: A Story of the Jasper Greys, 16th Mississippi Regiment.* Meridian, Miss.: The Meridian News, 1899.

Lindsley, John Berrien. *Military Annals of Tennessee (Confederate).* Nashville: J. M. Lindsley & Co., 1886.

Loehr, Charles T. *War History of the Old First Virginia Infantry Regiment, Army of Northern Virginia.* Richmond: Old First Virginia Association, William Ellis Jones, printer, 1884.

Macon, Emma Cassandra Riely and Reuben Conway Macon. *Reminiscences of the Civil War 1861-5.* Cedar Rapids, Iowa: Privately printed, 1911.

McCabe, W. Gordon. "Annual Report of the Virginia Historical Society." March 17, 1917.

McDaniel, J. J. *Diary of Battles, Marches and Incidents of the Seventh South Carolina Regiment.* Fredericksburg and Spotsylvania National Military Park Manuscript Collection.

McManus, Thomas Jefferson. "Sketch of the History of the Catholic Church in Martinsburg, West Virginia." *Papers on the History of the Catholic Church in Virginia.* Published by the Fifth Annual Convention of the Catholic Benevolent Union of the State of Virginia, June 1875.

Mitchel, John. *Jail Journal or Five Years in British Prisons.* Poole, England: Woodstock Books, 1996.

———. *The Last Conquest of Ireland (Perhaps).* London: Burns, Oates & Washbourne. No date. First published in Dublin, 1861.

———. *The Poems of Thomas Davis.* New York: D. & J. Sadlier & Co., 1866.

Mulholland, St. Clair. A. *The Story of the 116th Pennsylvania Volunteers in the War of the Rebellion.* Lawrence Frederick Kohl, ed. New York: Fordham University Press, 1996.

Nisbet, James Cooper. *4 Years on the Firing Line.* Bell Irvin Wiley, ed. Jackson, Tenn.: McGowat-Mercer Press, 1963.

O'Brien, Kevin E., ed. *My Life in the Irish Brigade: The Civil War Memoirs of Private William McCarter, 116th Pennsylvania Infantry.* Campbell, CA. Savas Publishing Co., 1996.

O'Grady, Standish, ed. *Pacata Hibernia or A History of the Wars in Ireland During the Reign of Queen Elizabeth.* London: Downey & Co., Ltd., 1891.

Pickett, George E. *The Heart of a Soldier: As Revealed in the Intimate Letters of General George E. Pickett.* New York: Seth Moyle, 1913.

Polley, J. B. *A Soldier's Letters to Charming Nellie.* New York: Neale Publishing Co., 1908.

Reed, Thomas Benton. *A Private in Gray.* Camden, Arkansas: T. B. Reed, 1905.

Richardson, James D. *A Compilation of the Messages and Papers of the Confederacy.* Nashville: United States Publishing Co., 1906.

Ross, John D. Letter. *West Virginia History.* vol. 45. 1984.

Sloan, E. D. Jr., ed., *Memoirs and 1865 Journal of Samuel Wragg Ferguson, 1834-1917, Brigadier General, Confederate States Army.* Greenville, S.C.: Private Printing, 1998.

*Southern Historical Society Papers.* vols. 1-38 (1910), n. s. vols. 1-14 (1959). 1876-1959. Richmond, Va.

Sparks, David S., ed. *Inside Lincoln's Army: The Diary of Marsena Rudolph Patrick, Provost Marshal General, Army of the Potomac.* New York: Thomas Yoseloff, 1964.

Taylor, Richard. *Deconstruction and Reconstruction: Personal Experiences of the Late War.* New York: D. Appleton & Co., 1879.

Thomas, Henry W. *History of the Doles-Cook Brigade.* Atlanta: Franklin Printing & Publishing Co., 1903.

Walker, Francis A. *History of the Second Army Corps in the Army of the Potomac.* New York: Charles Scribner's Sons, 1886.

# Bibliography

Williams, Susan Benson, ed. *Berry Benson's Civil War Book: Memoirs of a Confederate Scout and Sharpshooter.* Athens: University of Georgia Press, 1992.

Wise, George. *History of the Seventeenth Virginia Regiment, C. S. A.* Baltimore: Kelly, Piet & Co., 1870.

Wise, Jennings Cropper. *The Long Arm of Lee: The History of the Artillery of the Army of Northern Virginia.* 2 vols. Lincoln: University of Nebraska Press, 1991.

Woodward, C. Vann, ed. *Mary Chesnut's Civil War.* New Haven: Yale University Press, 1981.

Worsham, John H. *One of Jackson's Foot Cavalry.* James I. Robertson and Bell Irvin Wiley, eds. Wilmington, N. C.: Broadfoot Publishing Co., 1987.

## PUBLISHED SECONDARY SOURCES

Allardice, Bruce S. *More Generals In Gray.* Baton Rouge: Louisiana State University Press, 1995.

Amann, William Frayne. *Personnel of the Civil War.* 2 vols. New York: Thomas Yoseleff, 1961.

Anderson, Cecil W. "P. Tait, Limerick." *North-South Trader.* vol. 10, no. 3, March-April 1983.

Angley, Wilson. *A History of Fort Johnston on the Lower Cape Fear.* Wilmington, N. C.: Broadfoot Publishing Co., 1996.

Atteridge, A. Hilliard. *Famous Modern Battles.* Boston: Small, Maynard and Company Publishers, 1913.

Avery, I. W. *The History of the State of Georgia from 1850 to 1881.* New York: Brown & Derby, Publishers, 1881.

Bailey, James Henry II. *A History of the Diocese of Richmond: The Formative Years.* Richmond: Whittet & Shepperson, 1956.

Bartlett, Thomas and Keith Jeffery, eds. *A Military History of Ireland.* Cambridge: Cambridge University Press, 1996.

Bates, Samuel P. *History of Pennsylvania Volunteers, 1861-5.* 10 vols. Wilmington, N. C.: Broadfoot Publishing Co., 1993.

CLEAR THE CONFEDERATE WAY!

Batson, Mann. *The Upper Part of Greenville County, South Carolina*. Taylors, S.C.: Faith Printing Co., 1993.

Bell, Robert T. *11th Virginia Infantry*. Lynchburg: H. E. Howard, 1985.

Bergeron, Arthur W. Jr. *Guide to Louisiana Confederate Military Units, 1861-1865*. Baton Rouge: Louisiana State University Press, 1989.

Berthoff, Rowland Tappan. *British Immigrants in Industrial America, 1790-1950*. Cambridge: Harvard University Press, 1953.

Bettersworth, John K. *Confederate Mississippi: The People and Policies of A Cotton State in Wartime*. Baton Rouge: Louisiana State University Press, 1943.

Bilby, Joseph G. *Remember Fontenoy! The 69th New York and the Irish Brigade in the Civil War*. Hightstown, N. J.: Longstreet House, 1955.

Black, Robert C. III. *The Railroads of the Confederacy*. Chapel Hill: University of North Carolina Press, 1952.

Booth, Andrew B. *Records of Louisiana Confederate Soldiers and Louisiana Confederate Commands*. Spartanburg, S. C.: Reprint Co., 1984.

Boyle, Frank. *A Party of Mad Fellows: The Story of the Irish Regiments in the Army of the Potomac*. Dayton, Ohio: Morningside Press, 1996.

Brewer, Willis. *Alabama: Her History, Resources, War Record, and Public Men from 1540 to 1872*. Tuscaloosa: Willo Publishing Co., 1964.

Brooks, Thomas Walter and Michael Dan Jones. *Lee's Foreign Legion: A History of the 10th Louisiana Infantry*. Gravehurst, Canada: Watts Printing, 1995.

Brown, Malcolm. *The Politics of Irish Literature: From Thomas Davis to W. B. Yeats*. Seattle: University of Washington Press, 1972.

Burton, William L. *Melting Pot Soldiers: The Union's Ethnic Regiments*. Ames: Iowa State University Press, 1988.

Caravati, Charles M. *Major Dooley*. Richmond: Private Printing, 1978.

Chambers, Lenoir. *Stonewall Jackson*. 2 vols. New York: William Morrow & Co., 1959.

# Bibliography

Christian, W. Asbury. *Richmond: Her Past and Present.* Richmond: L. H. Jenkins, 1912.

Clark, Dennis. "The South's Irish Catholics: A Case of Cultural Confinement." *Catholics in the Old South: Essays on Church Culture.* Randall M. Miller and Jon Wakelyn, eds. Macon, Ga.: Mercer University Press, 1983.

Compton-Hall, Richard. "An Irish Invention." *Submarine Boats: The Beginnings of Underwater Warfare.* New York: Arco Publishing. 1984.

Crook, D. P. *Diplomacy During the American Civil War.* New York: John Wiley & Sons, 1975.

Crute, Joseph H. Jr. *Units of the Confederate States Army.* Midlothian, Va.: Derwent Books, 1987.

Cullop, Charles P. *Confederate Propaganda in Europe, 1861-1865.* Coral Gables, Fla.: University of Miami Press, 1969.

Davis, William C., ed. *The Confederate General.* 6 vols. Harrisburg, Penn.: National Historical Society, 1991.

Dillon, William. *Life of John Mitchel.* London: K. Paul Trench & Co., 1888.

Driver, Robert J., Jr. and Kevin C. Ruffner. *1st Battalion Virginia Infantry, 39th Battalion Virginia Cavalry, 24th Battalion Virginia Partisan Rangers.* Lynchburg: H. E. Howard, 1996.

*Echoes of Glory: Arms and Equipment of The Confederacy.* Alexandria, Va.: Time-Life Books, 1991.

Ellis, John Tracy. *Documents of American Catholic History.* Milwaukee: Bruce Publishing Co., 1956.

Fischer, David Hackett. *Albion's Seed: Four British Folkways in America.* New York: Oxford University Press, 1989.

Folsom, James Madison. *Heroes and Martyrs of Georgia: Georgia's Record in the Revolution of 1861.* Macon, Ga.: Burke, Boykin & Co., 1864.

Fonvielle, Chris E., Jr. *The Wilmington Campaign: Last Rays of Departing Hope.* Campbell, CA.: Savas Publishing Co., 1997.

Foster, Ray F., ed. *The Oxford Illustrated History of Ireland.* Oxford: Oxford University Press, 1989.

CLEAR THE CONFEDERATE WAY!

Fox, William F. *Regimental Losses In the American Civil War, 1861-1865.* Albany, N.Y.: Albany Publishing Co., 1889.

Frassanito, William A. *Antietam: The Photographic Legacy of America's Bloodiest Day.* New York: Simon & Schuster, 1978.

Freeman, Douglas S. *Lee's Lieutenants: A Study in Command.* 3 vols. New York: Charles Scribner's Sons, 1942-1944.

Frey, Jerry. *In the Woods Before Dawn: The Samuel Richey Collection of the Southern Confederacy.* Gettysburg: Thomas Publications, 1994.

Furgurson, Ernest B. *Chancellorsville 1863: The Souls of the Brave.* New York: Alfred A. Knopf, 1992.

Gallagher, Gary W., ed. *The Fredericksburg Campaign: Decision on the Rappahannock.* Chapel Hill: University of North Carolina Press, 1995.

Gannon James P. *Irish Rebels, Confederate Tigers: A History of the 6th Louisiana Volunteers, 1861-1865.* Campbell, Ca. Savas Publishing Co., 1998.

Garland, John Lewis. "Irish Soldiers of the American Confederacy." *Irish Sword.* Dublin: 1949-53.

Griffith, Arthur, ed. *Thomas Davis: The Thinker and Teacher.* Dublin: M. H. Gill & Sons Ltd., 1914.

Hayes-McCoy, Gerard A. *Irish Battles: A Military History of Ireland.* Belfast: Appletree Press, 1969.

Henderson, G. F. R. *Stonewall Jackson and the American Civil War.* New York: Da Capo Press, 1988.

Henderson, Lillian. *Roster of the Confederate Soldiers of Georgia, 1861-1865.* 6 vols. Hapeville, Ga.: Longino & Porter, 1960.

Hennessy, John J. *Return to Bull Run, The Campaign and Battle of Second Manassas.* New York: Simon & Schuster, 1993.

Hernon, Joseph M. *Celts, Catholics and Copperheads: Ireland Views the American Civil War.* Columbus: Ohio State University Press, 1968.

——. "The Irish Nationalists and Southern Secession." *Civil War History.* vol. 12. March 1966.

——. *The Roster of Confederate Soldiers, 1861-1865.* 16 vols. Wilmington, N. C.: Broadfoot Publishing Co., 1996.

# Bibliography

Holden, Walter, ed. "Completely Outgeneralled, the Report of Edward E. Cross at Chancellorsville." *Civil War Times Illustrated.* vol. 34. June-August 1995.

Jensen, Leslie D. "A Survey of Confederate Central Government Quartermaster Issue Jackets, Part II." *Military Collector and Historian.* vol. 41, no. 4. Winter 1989.

Jones, Paul. *The Irish Brigade.* Washington: Robert B. Luce, 1969.

Jones, Terry L. *Lee's Tigers: The Louisiana Infantry in the Army of Northern Virginia.* Baton Rouge: Louisiana State University Press, 1987.

Jordan, Ervin L. Jr. and Herbert A. Thomas Jr. *19th Virginia Infantry.* Lynchburg: H. E. Howard, 1987.

Kee, Robert. *The Green Flag.* 3 vols. New York: Penguin Books, 1989.

Krick, Robert K. "Cedar Mountain." *The Civil War Battlefield Guide.* Boston: Houghton Mifflin Co., 1990.

———. *Lee's Colonels, Lieutenant Colonels and Majors.* Dayton, Ohio: Morningside Press, 1992.

Lankford, Nelson, ed. *An Irishman in Dixie: Thomas Conolly's Diary of the Fall of the Confederacy.* Columbia: University of South Carolina Press, 1988.

Long, E. B. *The Civil War Day by Day.* Garden City, N. Y.: Doubleday & Co., 1971.

Lonn, Ella. *Foreigners in the Confederacy.* Chapel Hill: University of North Carolina Press, 1940.

Luvaas, Jay and Harold W. Nelson. *The U. S. Army War College Guide to the Battles of Chancellorsville and Fredericksburg.* New York: Harper & Row, 1988.

Manarin, Louis H. *15th Virginia Infantry.* Lynchburg: H. E. Howard, 1990.

Manarin, Louis H. and Wallace, Lee A. Jr. *Richmond Volunteers: The Volunteer Companies of the City of Richmond and Henrico County, Virginia, 1861-1865.* Richmond: Westover Press, 1969.

McLeod, Norman C. Jr. "Not Forgetting the Land We Left: The Irish in Antebellum Richmond." *Virginia Cavalcade.* vol. 47, no. 1, winter 1998.

McPherson, James M. *Battle Cry of Freedom: The Civil War Era.* New York: Oxford University Press, 1988.

———. *For Cause and Comrades: Why Men Fought in the Civil War.* New York: Oxford University Press, 1997

Miller, Kerby A. *Emigrants and Exiles: Ireland and the Irish Exodus to North America.* New York: Oxford University Press, 1985.

Miller, Randall M. and Jon L. Wakelyn. *Catholics in the Old South: Essays on Church and Culture.* Macon, Ga.: Mercer University Press, 1983.

Morahan, Larry. "Cleburne's Kin: The Untold Story of the Irish Confederates." *Southern Partisan.* Fourth quarter, 1995.

Nixon, Raymond Blalock. *Henry W. Grady, Spokesman of the New South.* New York: Alfred A. Knopf, 1943.

———. "Private William McCarter and the Irish Brigade at Fredericksburg." *Civil War Regiments: A Journal of the American Civil War.* Vol. 4, 1995.

O'Brien, Michael. *Rethinking the South: Essays in Intellectual History.* Baltimore: Johns Hopkins University Press, 1988.

O'Cathaoir, Brendan. *John Mitchel.* Dublin: Clodhanna Teoranta, 1978.

O'Connor, Frank, ed. *A Book of Ireland.* London: Collins, Sons & Co., 1959.

O'Reilly, Frank A. *Stonewall Jackson at Fredericksburg: The Battle of Prospect Hill, December 13, 1862.* Lynchburg: H. E. Howard, 1993.

Ragan, Mark. K. *Union and Confederate Submarine Warfare in the Civil War.* Mason City, IA.: Savas Publishing Co., 1999.

Raus, Edmund J. Jr. *A Generation on the March: The Union Army at Gettysburg.* Lynchburg: H. E. Howard, 1987.

Reidenbaugh, Lowell. *33rd Virginia Infantry.* Lynchburg: H. E. Howard, 1987.

———. *27th Virginia Infantry.* Lynchburg: H. E. Howard, 1993.

Rietti, J. C. *Military Annals of Mississippi.* Spartanburg, S. C.: Reprint Co., 1976.

Robertson, James I., Jr. *Stonewall Jackson: The Man, the Soldier, the Legend.* New York: Macmillan, 1997.

# Bibliography

————. *The Stonewall Brigade*. Baton Rouge: Louisiana State University Press, 1963.

Salley, A. S., Jr. *South Carolina Troops in Confederate Service*. vol. 1. Columbia, S. C.: R. L. Bryan Co., 1913.

Sears, Stephen W. *Landscape Turned Red: The Battle of Antietam*. New Haven: Ticknor & Fields, 1983.

Shafer, Louis S. "The Trout Boat St. Patrick." *Confederate Underwater Warfare: An Illustrated History*. Jefferson, N. C.: McFarland & Co., 1996.

Shannon, Fred Albert. *The Organization and Administration of the Union Army, 1861-1865*. 2 vols. Cleveland: Arthur H. Clark Co., 1928.

Shokes, Stephen. "The Irish Volunteers of Charleston." *North-South Traders Civil War*, vol. XXIV, no. 3, May-June 1997.

Spiers, E. M. "Army Organizations and Society." *A Military History of Ireland*. Thomas Bartlett and Keith Jeffery, eds. Cambridge: Cambridge University Press, 1996.

Stackpole, Edward J. *The Fredericksburg Campaign: Drama on the Rappahannock*. Harrisburg, Penn.: Military Service Publishing Co., 1957.

Stampp, Kenneth M. *America In 1857: A Nation on the Brink*. New York: Oxford University Press, 1990.

Stegeman, John F. *These Men She Gave: A Civil War Diary of Athens, Georgia*. Athens: University of Georgia Press, 1964.

Tucker, Phillip Thomas. *The Confederacy's Fighting Chaplain: Father John B. Bannon*. Tuscaloosa: University of Alabama Press, 1992.

————. *The History of the Irish Brigade*. Fredericksburg, Va.: Sergeant Kirkland's Museum & Historical Society, 1996.

Van Der Vat, Dan. *Stealth at Sea: The History of the Submarine*. Boston: Houghton Mifflin Co., 1995.

Wakelyn, Jon L. *Biographical Dictionary of the Confederacy*. Westport, Conn: Greenwood Press, 1977.

Wallace, Lee A., Jr. *1st Virginia Infantry*. Lynchburg: H. E. Howard, 1984.

————. *A Guide to Virginia Military Organizations, 1861-1865*. Lynchburg: H. E. Howard, 1986.

———. *17th Virginia Infantry.* Lynchburg: H. E. Howard, 1990.

Walsh, Louis J. *John Mitchel.* Dublin: Talbot Press, 1934.

Warner, Ezra, Jr. *Generals in Gray: Lives of the Confederate Commanders.* Baton Rouge: Louisiana State University Press, 1959.

Whan, Vorin E. *Fiasco at Fredericksburg.* State College: Pennsylvania State University Press, 1961.

White, Gregory C. *This Most Bloody & Cruel Drama: A History of the 31st Georgia Volunteer Infantry.* Baltimore: Butternut and Blue, 1997.

Widener, Ralph W., Jr. *Confederate Monuments: Enduring Symbols of the South and the War Between the States.* Washington: Andromeda Associates, 1982.

Wiley, Bell Irvin. *The Life of Johnny Reb: The Common Soldier of the Confederacy.* Baton Rouge: Louisiana State University Press, 1943.

# Notes

## Introduction: Irish Green and Confederate Gray

1. John Keely, "Civil War Diary Relates Record of Famous Atlanta Company," *The Atlanta Constitution Magazine*, March 15, 1931.

2. John Lewis Garland, "Irish Soldiers of the American Confederacy," *The Irish Sword*, vol.1 (Dublin: 1949-53), 174-80.

## Chapter 1: Irish Green and Confederate Gray: The Irish in the American South

1. Ella Lonn, *Foreigners in the Confederacy* (Chapel Hill: University of North Carolina Press, 1940), 481.

2. Dennis Clark, "The South's Irish Catholics: A Case of Cultural Confinement," in *Catholics in the Old South: Essays on Church Culture*, Randall M. Miller and Jon Wakelyn, eds. (Macon, Ga.: Mercer University Press, 1983), 196-197 and 208.

3. Ibid., 198.

4. David Hackett Fischer, *Albion's Seed: Four British Folkways in America* (New York: Oxford University Press, 1989), 618.

5. Ibid., 620.

6. Rowland Tappan Berthoff, *British Immigrants in Industrial America, 1790-1950* (Cambridge, Mass.: Harvard University Press, 1953), 9.

7. Kerby A. Miller, *Emigrants and Exiles: Ireland and the Irish Exodus to North America* (New York: Oxford University Press, 1985), 347. The famine that caused the Irish hegira was not due to a lack of food in Ireland. Crop yields in 1846 and 1847 were bountiful, but produce of all kinds was reserved for export. John Mitchel believed the Great Famine was the result of a calculated British policy to clear Ireland of its "excess population." Of the famine, Mitchel sarcastically wrote in 1861, "Ireland, perhaps, was the only country in the world which had both surplus produce for export and surplus population for export—too much food for her people, and too many people for her food." Mitchel recalled that Henry A. Wise, later Virginia governor and a Confederate general, was in Brazil during the famine and "was surprised to see unloaded at Rio abundance of the best quality of packed beef from Ireland." (Wise was United States minister to Brazil

from 1844 to 1847.) Perhaps this experience gave Wise, an anti-nativist Democrat, a sympathetic perspective on the plight of immigrant Irish Catholics. See John Mitchel, *The Last Conquest of Ireland (Perhaps)* (Dublin, 1861: reprint, London: Burns, Oates & Washbourne, no date), 82 and 8.

8. Charles M. Caravati, *Major Dooley* (Richmond, Va.: private printing, 1978). The biographical information on the Dooley clan is largely taken from this booklet available through the Maymont Foundation in Richmond.

9. Ibid., xiv.

10. Norman C. McLeod Jr., "Not Forgetting the Land We Left," Virginia Cavalcade, vol. 47, (Richmond, Virginia: Winter 1998), 37.

11. Berthoff, *British Immigrants*, 9.

12. Fischer, *Albion's Seed*, 621.

13. Berthoff, *British Immigrants*, 7.

14. Lonn, *Foreigners*, 481. The 85,000 estimate includes only the eleven "old South" Confederate states. If the Border States of Kentucky, Maryland, and Missouri, all of which contributed soldiers to Confederate armies, are included, the number of Irish natives in the South swells to more than 175,000. See John Lewis Garland, "Irish Soldiers," 174-80.

15. Lonn, *Foreigners*, 30.

16. Caravati, *Dooley*, 6-7.

17. Joseph M. Hernon Jr., *Celts, Catholics and Copperheads: Ireland Views the American Civil War* (Columbus: Ohio State University Press, 1968), 1.

18. Richard Taylor, *Destruction and Reconstruction: Personal Experiences of the Late War* (New York: D. Appleton & Co., 1879), 10.

19. Hernon, *Celts*, 121.

20. Michael O'Brien, *Rethinking the South: Essays on Intellectual History* (Baltimore: Johns Hopkins University Press, 1988), 120. O'Brien alludes to Eric Foner's collection of essays, *Politics and Ideology in the Age of the Civil War* (New York: Oxford University Press, 1980).

21. Kenneth M. Stampp, *America in 1857: A Nation on the Brink* (New York: Oxford University Press, 1990), 37.

22. Ibid., 37.

23. James M. McPherson, *Battle Cry of Freedom: The Civil War Era* (New York: Oxford University Press, 1988), 32.

24. S. C. Hayes to Jefferson Davis, January 6, 1864, War of the Rebellion: *Official Records of the Union and Confederate Armies*, vol. 3, no. 4, 4-6. Hereinafter cited as *OR*.

25. Paul Jones, *The Irish Brigade* (Washington: Robert B. Luce, 1969), 67.

26. Ibid., 14 and 68.

27. Anthony M. Keiley, *In Vinculis or The Prisoner of War* (New York: Blelock & Co., 1866), 166.

28. Randall Miller and Jon Wakelyn, eds., *Catholics in the Old South: Essays on Church Culture* (Macon, Ga.: Mercer University Press, 1983), 7-8.

# Notes

29. Hernon, *Celts*, 65; Lonn, *Foreigners*, 28.

30. Hernon, *Celts*, 65.

31. Ibid., 66.

32. Miller and Wakelyn, *Catholics*, 237.

33. James Henry Bailey II, *A History of the Diocese of Richmond* (Richmond: Whittet & Shepperson, 1956), 148.

34. Stampp, *America in 1857*, 37.

35. I. W. Avery, *The History of the State of Georgia from 1850 to 1881* (New York: Brown & Derby, 1881), 26.

36. Bailey, *Richmond Diocese*, 115.

37. Ibid., 117.

38. Ibid., 118.

39. Lowell Reidenbaugh, *33rd Virginia Infantry* (Lynchburg: Howard, 1987), 2.

40. John Beauchamp Jones, *A Rebel War Clerk's Diary at the Confederate States Capital* (Philadelphia: J. B. Lippincott & Co., 1866), 273.

41. William Porcher Miles to Jefferson Davis, November 19, 1861, General and Staff Officers Compiled Service Records of P. T. Moore, National Archives Microfilm Roll no. 181, Microcopy no. 331.

42. Hernon, *Celts*, 26.

43. Ibid., 17.

44. Michael Cavanagh, *Memoirs of Gen. Thomas Francis Meagher, Comprising the Leading Events of His Career* (Worcester, Mass.: Messenger Press, 1892), 399 n.

45. Ibid., 38.

46. Ibid., 417.

47. Brendan O'Cathaoir, *John Mitchel* (Dublin: Clodhanna Teoranta, 1978), 22.

48. Miller and Wakelyn, *Catholics*, 202.

49. Ibid., 205.

50. Ibid., 359-360.

51. Miller and Wakelyn, *Catholics*, 364.

52. "Banner Presentation to the Irish Volunteers," from the *Charleston Courier*, September 17, 1861, reprinted by the *Charleston News and Courier Presses*, Charleston, South Carolina, 1878, 30-33. The nuns who crafted the Irish Volunteers flag were members of an Irish order. The Sisters of Mercy were founded in Dublin in 1831 by Catherine McAuley, who is commemorated on Ireland's five pound note today. As to the flag's design, some readers may be startled by the seeming incongruity of Confederate or Southern symbols juxtaposed with Irish icons. Actually the synthesis was a quite common one. Before the war, Charleston's Irish militia company, the Irish Volunteers, commanded the respect of the Southern city's native majority and sported fine military regalia. Artifact collector Stephen Shokes recently uncovered Irish militia uniform items in Charleston. The find, presented in a collector's magazine, illuminates this pre-war Irish military presence in the South. "The Irish Volunteers of Charleston" emblazons a plate of this Irish militia company. Fifteen stars adorn the plate, which features the harp,

a liberty cap, and the caption, "Liberty or Death." Uniform buttons display a single centered shamrock surrounded by stars. Irish companies like this switched to Confederate service with the outbreak of the war. See Stephen Shokes, "The Irish Volunteers of Charleston," *North-South Traders Civil War*, vol. XXIV, no. 3, May-June 1997. Oblique references to things Irish in the Confederate army also can be gleaned from various sources. Private Alfred Bellard of the 5th New Jersey found evidence of an Irish Confederate at Yorktown in 1862, although neither he nor his editor realized it. "I sent home by one of the men a pipe bowl make out of laurel root upon which was carved a heart and hand, meaning I suppose that he was heart and hand in the service of his country. It was made by a rebel soldier. . . " Bellard wrote in his memoirs, *Gone for a Soldier*. The heart and hand, the Claddagh symbol, is distinctly Irish, and the pipe, in Irish called a dudeen, could have been left behind by Irish Confederates in Virginia or Alabama regiments at Yorktown. See David Herbert Donald, ed., *Gone for a Soldier: The Civil War Memoirs of Private Alfred Bellard*, (Boston: Little, Brown & Company, 1975), 205.

53. "Banner Presentation," *Charleston Courier*, 30-33.

54. Ibid.

55. Miller and Wakelyn, *Catholics*, 208.

56. Cornelius M. Buckley, trans., *A Frenchman, A Chaplain, A Rebel: The War Letters of Pere Louis-Hippolyte Gache, S. J.* (Chicago: Loyola University Press, 1981), 30. The Daughters of Charity, led by the religious community at Emmitsburg, Maryland, mounted a massive medical service organization during the war. These devout Catholic women operated hospitals on several battlefields, in numerous cities across the continent and in both capitals. The Hippocratic nature of medical service meant that Catholic hospitals served all whom needed aid, regardless of allegiance. However, these hospitals were more often in Confederate cities. Of the forty Daughters of Charity war hospitals, seventeen were operated as Confederate medical centers, while only seven were Union hospitals. The rest were listed as serving soldiers from both armies. The French Daughters of Charity, founded in the seventeenth century, united with a group of American nuns, the Sisters of Charity of Emmitsburg, Maryland, in 1850. The Emmitsburg religious community was founded in 1809 by the United States' first Catholic saint, Mother Elizabeth Ann Seton. The Emmitsburg sisters, no doubt inspired by the order's motto, "The Charity of Christ Crucified Urges Us," selflessly served the soldiers of the war. The Daughters of Charity's Confederate hospitals were found in Mississippi, Alabama, Florida, Georgia, Louisiana, and Virginia. See Betty Ann McNeill, D.C., "Civil War Services of the Daughters of Charity," Military Service, Civil War Accounts, Archives of Saint Joseph's Provincial House, Emmitsburg, Maryland, ASJPH 7-5-1-1.

57. Miller and Wakelyn, *Catholics*, 237.

58. Ibid.

59. Lee A. Wallace Jr., *1st Virginia Infantry* (Lynchburg: H. E. Howard), 15-16; Nancy Hartnagel, "Military Chaplaincy Tied to Legend of St. Martin of Tours,"

# Notes

Arlington Catholic Herald, vol. 23, no. 8 (Arlington, Virginia: February 26, 1998), 11. There were twenty-eight Catholic Confederate chaplains; forty priests served with the Union army.

60. "Chaplain Matthew O'Keefe of Mahone's Brigade," *Southern Historical Society Papers* (Richmond: 1876-1959), vol. 25: 176.

61. Ibid., 182.

62. Ibid., 180.

63. Joseph T. Durkin, ed., *Confederate Chaplain: A War Journal of James B. Sheeran, C. S. R.* (Milwaukee: Bruce Publishing Co., 1960), 5.

64. Ibid., 21.

65. Ibid., 31.

66. Durkin, *Confederate Chaplain*, 128.

67. Ibid., 154.

68. Phillip Thomas Tucker, *The Confederacy's Fighting Chaplain: Father John B. Bannon* (Tuscaloosa: University of Alabama Press, 1992), 167.

69. Ibid., 182.

70. J. F. J. Caldwell, *The History of a Brigade of South Carolinians, First Known as "Gregg's" and Subsequently as "McGowan's Brigade"* (Dayton, Ohio: Morningside Press, 1984), 175 n.

71. John Tracy Ellis, *Documents of American Catholic History* (Milwaukee: Bruce Publishing Co., 1956), 394.

72. Ibid., 399.

73. Buckley, *Gache*, 158.

74. Ibid., 119.

75. Ibid., 158-159.

76. Buckley, *Gache*, 227.

77. James I. Robertson Jr., *Stonewall Jackson: The Man, The Soldier, The Legend* (New York: Macmillan, 1997), 312.

78. Bailey, *Richmond Diocese*, 161.

79. Ibid., 160; Thomas Jefferson McManus, "Sketch of the History of the Catholic Church in Martinsburg, West Virginia," *Papers on the History of the Catholic Church in Virginia,* (Published by the Fifth Annual Convention of the Catholic Benevolent Union of the State of Virginia, June 1875), 38, 13. Generally the state's Catholic churches received donations and other aid from both Union and Confederate soldiers as they marched through Virginia.

80. Bailey, *Richmond Diocese*, 152-153.

81. Ibid., 151.

82. Ibid., 152.

83. Ibid., 156.

84. Robert Kee, *The Most Distressful Country,* vol. 1 of *The Green Flag* (New York: Penguin Books, 1989), 265.

85. O'Cathaoir, *Mitchel*, 5. Mitchel's most enduring nationalist catchphrase: "Ireland for the Irish."

86. Ibid., 6.

87. Kee, *Most Distressful Country*, 261.

88. Ibid., 267. John Mitchel was disgusted with O'Connell's anti-slavery initiatives, believing the issue distracted Irish attention from more pressing problems at home. Mitchel said O'Connell "poured forth his fiery floods of eloquence in denunciation, not of the British Government, but of *American Slavery*, with which he had nothing on earth to do." Mitchel also battled with "The Liberator's" son, John O'Connell, over the slavery issue. In 1845, Mitchel took particular umbrage when the younger O'Connell returned donations for the Repeal Association because they had been raised by the Irish in a Southern state. O'Connell believed the money tainted by the existence of slavery in the state. Mitchel came to the belief that the slavery issue was used by the British government, with the O'Connells as their dupes, to drive a wedge between Irish revolutionaries and their Irish-American supporters, many of whom were Southerners. See Mitchel, *Last Conquest*, 61 and 80-81.

89. John Mitchel, *Jail Journal, or Five Years in British Prisons* (Poole, England: Woodstock Books, reprint, 1996), 150.

90. Ibid., 154-155.

91. Kee, *Most Distressful Country*, 254.

92. Jones, *The Irish Brigade*, 14. Irish nationalist ideology, going back to the political thoughts of Thomas Davis, certainly would have been in concert with the Southern position. Davis, the beloved leader of Irish nationalist thought until his untimely death in 1845, almost certainly would have cleaved to the Confederacy, at least on most political issues. Davis himself could have propounded the Southern stand for states' rights, local control of government and economic self-reliance without interference from a distant central bureaucracy. He wrote, "Centralization [by which he meant the Irish government under the Union with Great Britain] is at least as great a foe to freedom, to spirit, and to prosperity, as aristocracy." Davis called the central government in Ireland "an official despotism." See Arthur Griffith, ed., *Thomas Davis: The Thinker and Teacher*, (Dublin: M. H. Gill & Son Ltd., 1914), 4.

93. Jones, *The Irish Brigade*, 95.

94. Ibid., 13.

95. Mitchel, *Jail Journal*, 1876 edition introduction.

96. O'Cathaoir, *Mitchel*, 7.

97. William Dillon, *Life of John Mitchel* (London: K. Paul Trench & Co., 1888), 100 and 129-130. One of Mitchel's Irish biographers, Louis J. Walsh, gave a retrospective of Mitchel's Southern allegiance in 1934. "The men who might have explained the Southern Cause to the world sleep in 'The Wilderness,' or where Stonewall Jackson fell at Chancellorsville; and the result has been that most people even in Ireland, where the effects of historical propaganda should be apparent to everybody, have accepted the Yankee legend that the North were fighting for virtue and justice all

through the Civil War, and that the South fought only for slavery and the degradation of man. . . As a matter of fact, however, nobody who knows Mitchel would ever have expected him to be on any side in America except that of the Confederates. There was a great deal more involved in the American Civil War than the question of Abolition. . . It was a struggle between two civilisations—the one static, agricultural, content to live on the land of its fathers and refusing to sacrifice its fundamental life, based on the land, for a temporary increase of wealth; the other dynamic, eager for wealth at any price and at any cost, and always seeking expansion. Mitchel saw in the Northern States just another example of that 'Anglo-Saxon civilization' which he hated and which he was convinced would end some day in disaster for those who clung to it." See Louis J. Walsh, *John Mitchel* (Dublin: Talbot Press, 1934), 86-87. In the same vein, Malcolm Brown wrote in 1972: "Mitchel hated the English, as everybody knows, but he hated the Yankees no less." Mitchel once said of England and the Union, "I despise the civilization of the nineteenth century and its two highest expressions and grandest hopes most especially." These were familiar words to Irish nationalists, reminiscent of Thomas Davis's attack on both Englishism and Yankeeism, according to Brown. In defending the South, Mitchel believed he was combating the British military/industrial system, which he had hated in Ireland. The British system was not confined to the British Isles. "Now I meet that evil power here [in America] also; he is everywhere, and nowhere more active and mischievous than in these United States," Mitchel wrote before secession. See Malcolm Brown, *The Politics of Irish Literature: From Thomas Davis to W. B. Yeats* (Seattle: University of Washington Press, 1972), 138, 142.

98. Cavanagh, *Meagher*, 369. The Irish in America were confused by the differing allegiances of Meagher and Mitchel. A South Carolina company of Confederates named themselves the Meagher Guards until it was realized that Meagher was a Yankee. In New York, an Irish company in the "Republican Rifles," later the 37th New York Volunteers, called itself the Mitchel Light Guard. See Cavanagh, 332.

99. Hernon, *Celts*, 93. Northern Irish leaders recruited for the Union army using the argument that the South and England were allies and thus fighting against the South struck a blow against the British. This recruiting propaganda quickly became unquestioned fact in the North. But no true alliance existed between England and the Confederacy. The British government played both sides of the fence in the war. Certainly there were limited, mutually beneficial mercantile contracts between the South and British companies, but the Crown was very careful not commit to any formal alliances with the Confederacy. A stronger case could be made that a fruitful alliance burgeoned between England and the Union during the conflict. There were obvious natural affinities between these two Anglo-Abolitionist-Industrial powers. Social, political and economic threads formed a strong tether binding the two countries together. The issue of Union recruiting in Ireland presents a typical example of how Britain juggled the two American powers, and how Britain's policy and attitude aided the North, not the South. Ostensibly, the Crown's Foreign Enlistment Act forbade recruiting in the United Kingdom for foreign army service. This helped pacify Confederate fears that

## CLEAR THE CONFEDERATE WAY!

Yankee soldiers were flooding in from the United Kingdom. At the same time the government turned a blind eye to Union attempts to pay Irishmen to emigrate as laborers. These "laborers," everyone knew, usually ended up in Union blue. Perhaps Britain pursued this cynical policy because the Queen's government saw emigration/recruiting as a convenient scheme to continue the clearance of the land in Ireland. It is ironic that the myth of an Anglo-Confederate alliance helped Union recruitment in Ireland and at the same time helped British landowners banish Irish peasants from their farms. Today, there is tangible proof of an Anglo-Union connection. It is a statue of Abraham Lincoln standing in Lincoln Square, Manchester, erected after the war. The statue's inscription extols the Union's fight against slavery, and even seems to blame the Confederacy for what was the Union blockade of cotton exports from the South. "This statue commemorates the support that the working people of Manchester gave in the fight for the abolition of slavery during the American Civil War. By supporting the Union under President Lincoln, at a time when there was an economic blockade by the Southern states, the Lancashire cotton workers were denied access to raw cotton, which caused considerable unemployment throughout the cotton industry." In contrast, there are no Confederate monuments in England. But there is a Confederate memorial of sorts in Ireland. A commemorative plaque near Portadown, County Armagh, marks the birthplace of the forbears of one of the Confederacy's greatest heroes, Lieutenant General Thomas J. "Stonewall" Jackson.

100. John Mitchel, "Lincoln and His Proclamation," *Richmond Daily Enquirer*, October 1, 1862.

101. Mitchel, "Recognition Historically Treated," *Richmond Daily Enquirer*, December 11, 1862.

102. Mitchel, editorial in *Richmond Daily Enquirer*, December 16, 1862.

103. Mitchel, editorial in *Richmond Daily Enquirer*, December 20, 1862.

104. Mitchel, editorial in *Richmond Daily Enquirer*, December 27, 1862.

105. Dillon, *Life of Mitchel*, 199.

106. Hernon, *Celts*, 55.

107. Mitchel, editorial in *Richmond Daily Examiner*, January 6, 1864. This idea that the South under the Union would be as Ireland under the British crown may have been widely understood. Private Azariah Bostwick of the 31st Georgia despaired that the failure of the Confederacy would mean abject slavery for all Southerners. Without Southern independence, Bostwick believed, "We will be to the North what Ireland is to England, a slave of the darkest kind." Perhaps Bostwick read Mitchel's editorials on the matter. See Gregory C. White, *This Most Bloody & Cruel Drama: A History of the 31st Georgia Volunteer Infantry* ( Baltimore: Butternut and Blue, 1997), 167.

108. Kee, *Most Distressful Country*, 262.

109. Gerard A. Hayes-McCoy, *Irish Battles: A Military History of Ireland* (Belfast: Appletree Press, 1969), 291.

# Notes

## Chapter 2: Irish Confederates in Battle:
## The War before Fredericksburg

1. Bailey, *Richmond Diocese,* 145. As to the company's uniform and accessories, the militia company was issued gray, cadet-style uniforms in 1859, but 1861 accounts specifically report the wearing of green uniforms on parade that spring. By some accounts the company's ceremonial pikes had been seized as souvenirs from John Brown's raiders in 1859. If it is true that the pikes were taken from the abolitionist insurgents, the weapons, now in the hands of Confederate rebels, held even more symbolism. As an aside, it is interesting to note that when the Confederacy drilled black troops in 1865, they were issued Irish-style pikes, not muskets. For uniform information, see Louis H. Manarin and Lee A. Wallace Jr., *Richmond Volunteers: The Volunteer Companies of the City of Richmond and Henrico County, Virginia, 1861-1865.* (Richmond: Westover Press, 1969), 168-169.

2. Ibid.

3. Ibid., 144.

4. Bailey, *Richmond Diocese,* 146.

5. Joseph T. Durkin, ed., *John Dooley Confederate Soldier: His War Journal* (Ithaca, N. Y.: Georgetown University Press, 1945), xx.

6. E. D. Sloan Jr., ed., *Memoirs and 1865 Journal of Samuel Wragg Ferguson, 1834-1917, Brigadier General, Confederate States Army,* (Greenville, S.C.: Private Printing, 1998), 4-9. Ferguson wrote his memoir of this battle in 1900. He attributed this passage to Lt. Col. Frederick G. Skinner, but evidence points to the distinct probability that Col. Patrick T. Moore uttered this sentence. It is likely that Ferguson, writing thirty-nine years later, confused Skinner's account of the battle with Moore's experience in the charge. In other words, Skinner told Ferguson of Moore's pre-charge speech to the 1st Regiment, and related Moore's wounding, and Ferguson remembered it as Skinner's own experience. It was Moore who was wounded in the head at Bull Run, not Skinner. Likewise, the Irishman Moore would have invoked what was the Gaelic war-cry, which Ferguson spelled "Foy ga ballah." Skinner likely was not familiar with the term. Furthermore, Skinner had no opportunity to give the regiment a talk before the charge, but rode into the fray when Moore fell. It was likely Moore, a naturalized citizen himself, who "told the boys that they were all free born Americans," or as American as a native born Virginia soldier. Skinner was wounded in the head at the Second Battle of Manassas, maybe another reason for the memoir's confusion. Perhaps Skinner and the Old First were still using the Irish phrase in battle in the summer of 1862.

7. Charles T. Loehr, *War History of the Old First Virginia Infantry Regiment, Army of Northern Virginia* (Richmond: Old First Virginia Association, William Ellis Jones, printer, 1884), 9.

8. Francis Potts, "Diary kept by Francis Potts, a private in Company C, 1st Regiment Virginia Volunteers July 14, 1861-September 21, 1861." Virginia State Library Archives. The battle narrative, and quotes of Dooley, Skinner, Seagers and

McRichards, are taken from Potts' unpublished diary. Potts compared the Montgomery Guard to the Connaught Rangers, a famous command of Irish troops in the British army. The Guard wore gray uniforms with prewar regulation formal black hats. At Manassas, Potts tented with James Mitchel, a son of Irish nationalist John Mitchel, and another Irishman, John D. Keiley Jr., later a brigade quartermaster and editor of the *Freeman's Journal*. Potts later became paymaster for Longstreet's corps and penned a poignant scene of Lee at Appomattox. See Chapter 4.

    9. Loehr, *War History*, 18.

    10. William F. Fox, *Regimental Losses in the American Civil War, 1861-1865* (Albany, N. Y.: Albany Publishing Co., 1889), 560. The 33rd Virginia suffered 146 killed and wounded, the fourth largest regimental loss among Confederate units; the 27th Virginia lost 141 men, number five on the list.

    11. Wallace, *1st Virginia Infantry*, 18.

    12. Taylor, *Destruction and Reconstruction*, 52-53.

    13. Ibid., 68.

    14. Ibid.

    15. Ibid.

    16. Reidenbaugh, *33rd Virginia Infantry*, 2.

    17. George R. Bedinger, unpublished letter, Fredericksburg and Spotsylvania National Military Park Manuscript Collection, vol. 30.

    18. James I. Robertson Jr., *The Stonewall Brigade* (Baton Rouge: Louisiana State University Press, 1963), 13.

    19. John O. Casler, *Four Years in the Stonewall Brigade*, James I. Robertson Jr., ed. (Dayton, Ohio: Morningside Press, 1971), 80.

    20. Robert J. Driver Jr. and Kevin C. Ruffner, *1st Battalion Virginia Infantry, 39th Battalion Virginia Cavalry, 24th Battalion Virginia Partisan Rangers* (Lynchburg: H. E. Howard, 1996), 1.

    21. Buckley, *Gache*, 43.

    22. Emma Cassandra Riely Macon and Reuben Conway Macon, *Reminiscences of the Civil War* (private printing, 1911), 153.

    23. Taylor, *Destruction and Reconstruction*, 76.

    24. Henry B. Kelly, in "Stonewall Jackson in the Shenandoah" by John D. Imboden, in *Battles and Leaders of the Civil War*, Robert U. Johnson and Clarence C. Buel, eds., vol. 2, (New York: Century Co., 1884-89), 296 n.

    25. Ibid.

    26. Taylor, *Destruction and Reconstruction*, 76.

    27. Thomas Bartlett and Keith Jeffery, *A Military History of Ireland* (Cambridge: Cambridge University Press, 1996), 2 and 459 n. The authors believe this sweeping statement by perhaps the greatest thinker of the age should have been ignored. They point out that Voltaire had no military experience. Nevertheless, Voltaire's indictment of the Irish soldier has jaundiced the world's attitude toward Irish soldiery ever since. Military historians from Mathew O'Conor to Gerard A. Hayes-McCoy to Grady

# Notes

McWhiney have dealt with Voltaire's stereotypical view of the reckless, but ineffective, unreliable and undisciplined Irish soldier. Taylor simply was reiterating this stereotype. Hayes-McCoy believes Irish soldiers in general historically have been excellent fighters, but in Irish wars lacked the training, technology and leadership of their British opponents. Irish historian Standish O'Grady noted that Sir Richard Bingham, the sixteenth-century British president of Connaught, much preferred Irish soldiers to English ones in 1595. Bingham referred to "the unserviceableness of the English companies" under his command and complained about "the growing weakness of the [British] army owing to the runaways, of whom are many." Writing in the nineteenth century, Standish O'Grady stated, "And the runaways were always English, for the Queen's Irish soldiers, being drawn from a warrior caste, were, while in her service, engaged in the work which they loved, indeed, the only work for which they were fitted." And of the English soldiers, one of Bingham's captains wrote, "Our new [English] soldiers for the most part could not tell how to handle their pieces, so that the captains were drawn to take away their bullets and powder and give them to the Irish." Irishmen, then, have not always been denigrated as poor soldiers. See Standish O'Grady, ed., *Pacata Hibernia or A History of the Wars in Ireland during the reign of Queen Elizabeth*, two vols., (London: Downey & Co. Ltd., 1891), lvi-lvii.

28. Lt. Col. Arthur James Lyon Fremantle, *Three Months in the Southern States* (Lincoln: University of Nebraska Press, 1991), 232.

29. Bell Irvin Wiley, *The Life of Johnny Reb: The Common Soldier of the Confederacy* (Baton Rouge: Louisiana State University Press, 1943), 323. See also Garland, 175.

30. Clement A. Evans, *Confederate Military History: A Library of Confederate States History*, extended edition (Wilmington, N. C.: Broadfoot Publishing Co., 1987-89), vol. 6: 433-434.

31. Edward McCrady, "The Boy Heroes of Cold Harbor," *Southern Historical Society Papers*, vol. 25: 234-239.

32. Ibid.

33. Ibid.

34. Ibid.

35. Willis Brewer, *Alabama: Her History, Resources, War Record, and Public Men from 1540 to 1872* (Tuscaloosa: Willo Publishing Co., 1964), 601.

36. Buckley, *Gache*, 118.

37. Louis H. Manarin, *15th Virginia Infantry* (Lynchburg: H. E. Howard, 1990), 7.

38. Annie Laurie Sharkey, "An Old Confederate's Story of Irish Wit," *Confederate Veteran* (Nashville: Confederate Southern Memorial Association, 1893-1932), vol. 24: 77.

39. Lee A. Wallace Jr., *17th Virginia Infantry* (Lynchburg: H. E. Howard, 1990), 108.

40. Fremantle, *Three Months*, 300.

## CLEAR THE CONFEDERATE WAY!

41. "Thrilling Experiences of Captain N. J. Rawlings," memoir, Fredericksburg and Spotsylvania National Military Park Manuscript Collection, vol. 131: 1-2.

42. Durkin, *Confederate Chaplain*, 4.

43. Wallace, *17th Virginia Infantry*, 73.

44. Elijah Henry Sutton, *Grand Pa's War Stories* (private printing, 1896), 26-27.

45. Janet B. Hewett, *Supplement to the Official Records*, (Wilmington, N. C.: Broadfoot Publishing Co., 1996), vol. 24, pt. 2, no. 36: 83.

46. Driver and Ruffner, *1st Battalion*, 4.

47. James Power Smith, "Stonewall Jackson in Winter Quarters at Moss Neck," address in Winchester, Va., January 19, 1898. Jedediah Hotchkiss Papers, Library of Congress; Robertson, *Stonewall Jackson*, 668 and 907n.

48. "Report of Maj. D. B. Bridgford," *OR*, vol. 21, no. 1: 641.

49. Driver and Ruffner, *1st Battalion*, 3.

50. James Power Smith, "Stonewall Jackson's Last Battle," *Battles and Leaders*, vol. 3: 212.

51. Driver and Ruffner, *1st Battalion*, 3.

52. Ibid.

53. C. G. Chamberlayne, ed., *Ham Chamberlayne, Virginian: Letters and Papers of an Artillery Officer in the War for Southern Independence, 1861-1865* (Richmond: Dietz Printing Co., 1932), 90.

54. Driver and Ruffner, *1st Battalion*, 20.

55. Ibid. 22.

56. Ibid., 22-23.

57. Durkin, *Confederate Chaplain*, 3.

58. Robert K. Krick, "Cedar Mountain," *The Civil War Battlefield Guide* (Boston: Houghton Mifflin Co., 1990), 73.

59. *OR*, vol. 11, pt. 2, no. 1: 571.

60. Catherine Thom Bartlett, *My Dear Brother: A Confederate Chronicle* (Richmond: Dietz Press, 1952), 56.

61. Ibid., 57.

62. Buckley, *Gache*, 193.

63. Durkin, *Confederate Chaplain*, 14-15.

64. W. B. Taliaferro, "Jackson's Raid Around Pope," *Battle and Leaders*, vol. 2: 509 n.

65. Robert Healy in "Jackson's 'Foot-Cavalry' at Second Bull Run," by Allen C. Redwood, 55th Virginia Regiment, *Battles and Leaders*, vol. 2: 536 n.

66. Driver and Ruffner, *1st Battalion*, 27; Taliaferro, *Battles and Leaders*, 508 n.

67. Driver and Ruffner, *1st Battalion*, 27.

68. Hewett, *Supplement to the Official Records*, vol. 24, pt. 2, no. 36: 83.

69. Ibid.

70. Terry L. Jones, *Lee's Tigers: The Louisiana Infantry in the Army of Northern Virginia* (Baton Rouge: Louisiana State University Press, 1987), 130.

71. William A. Frassanito, *Antietam: The Photographic Legacy of America's Bloodiest Day* (New York: Simon & Schuster, 1978), 124.

72. Jones, *Lee's Tigers*, 130.

73. Stephen W. Sears, *Landscape Turned Red: The Battle of Antietam*, (New Haven, Conn.: Ticknor & Fields, 1983), 243.

74. Ibid., 243-44. For endearing insights into Meagher's charisma and charm, as well as a glimpse at what was probably a tragic alcoholic affliction, see Kevin E. O'Brien, ed., *My Life in the Irish Brigade: The Civil War Memoirs of Private William McCarter, 116th Pennsylvania Infantry* (Savas Publishing Co., 1996). By 1864, Meagher's alcoholism was even more acute. Provost Marshal General Marsena Patrick gave tangible evidence of this in his diary entry of Thursday, August 18, 1864. "Genl. Meagher is lying in the tent of the chaplain of the 20th as drunk as a beast, and has been so since Monday, sending out his servant for liquor and keeping his bed *wet and filthy*! I have directed Col. Gates to ship him tomorrow if he does not clear out." David S. Sparks, ed., *Inside Lincoln's Army: The Diary of Marsena Rudolph Patrick, Provost Marshal General, Army of the Potomac*, (New York: Thomas Yoseloff, 1964), 414-415.

## Chapter 3 The Fighting Race At Fredericksburg: Irish Tragedy and Northern Defeat

1. Sutton, *Grand Pa's War Stories*, 24.

2. Keely, "Civil War Diary."

3. Ibid.

4. Frank A. O'Reilly, *Stonewall Jackson at Fredericksburg: The Battle of Prospect Hill, December 13, 1862* (Lynchburg: H. E. Howard, 1993), 89.

5. *OR*, vol. 21, no. 1: 658.

6. O'Reilly, *Prospect Hill*, 89.

7. Ibid., 90.

8. James Madison Folsom, *Heroes and Martyrs of Georgia: Georgia's Record in the Revolution of 1861* (Macon: Burke, Boykin & Co., 1864), 35.

9. Keely, "Civil War Diary." Evidently no admirer of Meagher, whom he referred to as the "one who won so unenviable a distinction in 1848," Keely did give credit to the Irish Brigade and the Irish soldier in general. The brigade, he said, "was composed of gallant men."

10. Samuel P. Bates, *History of Pennsylvania Volunteers, 1861-5*, (Wilmington, N. C.: Broadfoot Publishing Co., 1993), vol. 1: 590-608. Keely's encounter with the Irish in the 2nd Pennsylvania Reserves is a reminder that there were many Irishmen in the Army of the Potomac who were not part of the Irish Brigade.

11. W. H. Johnson, "Correct Report of Casualties in the 19th Ga. Reg't," *Southern Confederacy* (Atlanta) December 30, 1862.

12. *OR*, vol. 21, no. 1: 659.

13. Keely, "Civil War Diary."

14. Ibid.

15. Joseph White Woods, "Reminiscences" from UDC Bound Typescripts no. 144, vol. 6, Georgia Archives; copy in Fredericksburg and Spotsylvania National Military Park Manuscript Collection, vol. 127.

16. "A Gallant Irishman at Fredericksburg," *Charleston (S.C.) Daily Courier,* December 30, 1862. Michael Corcoran was an Irish Union officer who had led the 69th New York at Manassas. He later raised the Corcoran Legion but was killed in a riding accident in December 1863.

17. *Southern Watchman,* (Athens, Ga.) February 25, 1863.

18. "Gallant Irishman," *Charleston Daily Courier.*

19. Sutton, *Grand Pa's War Stories,* 21.

20. Ibid., 20.

21. "Gallant Irishman," *Charleston Daily Courier.*

22. "Report of General Joseph Kershaw," *OR,* vol. 21, no. 1: 589.

23. Ibid.

24. Ibid., 590-91.

25. William Allan, *The Army of Northern Virginia in 1862* (Boston: Houghton Mifflin Co., 1892), 507.

26. "Report of General Lafayette McLaws," *OR,* vol. 21. no. 1: 581.

27. Ibid., 582.

28. "Report of Colonel Robert McMillan," *OR,* vol. 21, no. 1: 608.

29. Hernon, *Celts,* 122.

30. "Return of Casualties of the Union Forces," *OR,* vol. 21, no. 1: 125-145. Looked at by another measure, although the Irish Brigade's casualty ratio was a staggering 38.5 percent, its losses by proportion were by no means the highest in the army. Caldwell's brigade lost 47.9 percent killed, missing and wounded. The four regiments of Allabach's brigade suffered a 42.5 percent casualty ratio.

31. William Corby, *Memoirs of Chaplain Life: Three Years with the Irish Brigade in the Army of the Potomac* (New York: Fordham University Press, 1992), 377; A. Hilliard Atteridge, *Famous Modern Battles* (Boston: Small, Maynard and Co. Publishers, 1913), 12. Atteridge described Russell at the Battle of Alma, September 20, 1854, as "a stout, jolly-looking Irishman," and a pioneer of war correspondents, though with little knowledge of warfare in 1854. It is difficult to say what Russell really knew of Albuera and Fontenoy.

32. Hernon, *Celts,* 41n; Cavanagh, *Meagher,* appendix, 14; David P. Conyngham, *The Irish Brigade and Its Campaigns* (New York: Fordham University Press, reprint, 1994), 222.

33. Paul Jones, *The Irish Brigade,* 124.

34. Frank Boyle, *A Party of Mad Fellows: The Story of the Irish Regiments in the Army of the Potomac* (Dayton, Ohio: Morningside Press, 1996), 166.

# Notes

35. Phillip Thomas Tucker, *The History of the Irish Brigade* (Fredericksburg, Va.: Sergeant Kirkland's Museum & Historical Society, 1995), 5; O'Brien, *My Life in the Irish Brigade*, 40 and 240 n. 3.

36. Hernon, *Celts*, 18n; St. Clair A. Mulholland, *The Story of the 116th Pennsylvania Volunteers in the War of the Rebellion*, Lawrence Frederick Kohl, ed. (New York: Fordham University Press, 1996), 57; *A Book of Ireland*, Frank O'Connor, ed. (London: Collins, Sons & Co., 1959), 65.

37. Kee, *Ourselves Alone*, vol. 3 of *The Green Flag*, 177-178. A more believable Fredericksburg Fenian story was told by Thomas Francis Galwey, an officer in the Hibernian Guard, Company B of the 8th Ohio Infantry. In Galwey's version, a Fenian meeting took place while the armies were in winter camp after the Battle of Fredericksburg. This meeting was convened by a civilian, an Irish newspaperman who represented James Stephens, the founder in 1858 of the Irish Republican Brotherhood. The unnamed emissary rowed across the river from the Confederate side, and carried passes from both governments, signed by Confederate Secretary of State Judah P. Benjamin and Union Secretary of War Edwin Stanton. Fenians from both armies met under guard in a ravine near Falmouth. The delegations were forbidden to discuss the Civil War, and pledged to unite against the British crown one day. Galwey remembered, a "vast Fenian Army, made up of Confederate and Union Fenians, would later strike against England." This never came to pass. See Thomas Francis Galwey, *The Valiant Hours* (Harrisburg, Penn.: The Stackpole Co., 1961), 244-245.

38. Janet B. Hewett, *The Roster of Confederate Soldiers, 1861-1865*, (Wilmington, N. C.: Broadfoot Publishing Co., 1996), vol. 15: 11-12.

39. "Meagher's Report," and "J. B. Kershaw's Report," *OR*, vol. 21, no. 1: 241-242, and 591. Brigadier General Joseph B. Kershaw reported the capture of an "embroidered guide flag of the Sixty-ninth New York Regiment," which was forwarded to division command. This flag was probably a green silk camp color but far from being returned through enemy lines, it hung as a trophy of battle at General McLaws' headquarters.

40. Henry H. Baker, *A Reminiscent Story of the Great Civil War: A Personal Experience*, (New Orleans: Ruskin Press, 1911), 49.

41. Durkin, *John Dooley*, 116-117.

42. J. J. McDaniel, *Diary of Battles, Marches and Incidents of the Seventh South Carolina Regiment*, Fredericksburg and Spotsylvania National Military Park Manuscript Collection, vol. 29, 18-19.

43. "Col. Robt. McMillan," *Southern Watchman*, February 25, 1863.

44. William T. Shumate, "A Story of Slaughter," in Mann Batson, *The Upper Part of Greenville County, South Carolina* (Taylors, S. C.: Faith Printing Company, 1993), 428.

45. George E. Pickett, *The Heart of a Soldier* (New York: Seth Moyle, 1913), 66.

46. "Col. Robt. McMillan," *Southern Watchman*, February 25, 1863.

47. Ibid.

48. "Meagher's Report," *OR*, 242.

49. *OR*, vol. 21, no. 1: 129-145. For the heroic sacrifices of the brigade's regimental commanders, see Kevin E. O'Brien, ed., "Private William McCarter and the Irish Brigade at Fredericksburg," in *Blood on the Rappahannock: The Battle of Fredericksburg (Civil War Regiments: A Journal of the American Civil War)*, 1995, vol. 4, no. 4: 66.

50. "Meagher's Report," *OR*, 242.

51. *Fighting for the Confederacy: The Personal Recollections of General Edward Porter Alexander* (Chapel Hill: University of North Carolina Press, 1989), 177.

52. Thomas Francis Galwey, "Fredericksburg and the Assault on Marye's Heights," *The Catholic World*, December 1889, vol. 1, no. 297, 373.

53. Francis A. Walker, *History of the Second Army Corps in the Army of the Potomac* (New York: Charles Scribner's Sons, 1886), 172.

54. Vorin E. Whan, *Fiasco at Fredericksburg* (State College: Pennsylvania State University Press, 1961), 87.

55. 'Meagher's Report," *OR*, 243.

56. "James Kelly's Report," *OR*, vol. 2, no. 1: 371-372.

57. "Meagher's Report," *OR*, vol. 11, pt. 2, no. 1: 778. Colonel John R. Brooke, commander of the 53rd Pennsylvania, remembered that Meagher and most of the brigade were not engaged at Seven Pines or Fair Oaks, as the North called the battle. Brooke's account strikes at the heart of one of the Irish Brigade's most celebrated battle portraits—the charge of the Irish Brigade, led by Meagher, at Fair Oaks—pictured in *Harper's Weekly*. While Brooke remembered that Colonel Robert Nugent's regiment, the 69th New York, might have fought in the battle, the Pennsylvanian said the charge of the Irish Brigade was a fabrication. "The Irish Brigade was not engaged," Brooke reported in an 1884 letter to Second Corps historian Francis A. Walker. "The main body of the brigade was near what was afterwards used as a supply depot for our corps...After the battle...Meagher moved forward across an open field on his front to the edge of the wood beyond, and in which wood the fighting had been done." This was the "charge" pictured in *Harper's Weekly*, Brooke wrote. The brigade's casualties at Fair Oaks were due to a stray shell that struck them while at the rail depot, he related. Brooke went on to praise the brigade generally, but he saved a potent personal rebuke for its high profile leader. "I had a high regard for the bravery of the Irishmen, but despised Meagher, who never, to my personal knowledge, did any service in battle while commanding that brigade. He is now dead and I have no wish to continue his memory, but as a soldier he was the sorriest charlatan I ever knew." (See John R. Brooke to Francis Walker, May 28, 1884. Mark Edgar Richards Collection, United States Army Military History Institute.)

58. "Rufus King Jr.'s Report," *OR*, vol. 11, pt. 2, no. 1: 59.

59. "Meagher's Report," *OR*, vol. 11, pt. 2, no. 1: 71.

60. Ibid., 74.

61. Walter Holden, ed., "Completely Outgeneralled: The Report of Edward E. Cross at Chancellorsville," *Civil War Times Illustrated*, June-August 1995, vol. 34, no. 3: 83.

# Notes

62. Paul Jones, *The Irish Brigade*, 254; Cavanagh,*Meagher*, 333, 345.

63. Thomas Bartlett and Keith Jeffery, "An Irish Military Tradition?" *A Military History of Ireland* (Cambridge: Cambridge University Press, 1996), 20. The authors recognize that the history and culture of Ireland have been shaped by "martial themes," but caution that "traditions can be, and frequently are, invented." Bartlett and Jeffery, 2.

64. Joseph G. Bilby, *Remember Fontenoy! The 69th New York and the Irish Brigade in the Civil War* (Hightstown, N. J.: Longstreet House, 1995), 15, 17.

65. E. M. Spiers, "Army Organizations and Society," *Military History of Ireland*, 349.

66. Ibid., 352.

67. Ibid.

68. Ibid.

69. Kee, *The Bold Fenian Men*, vol. 2 of *The Green Flag*, 250.

70. Ibid., 229.

71. Larry Morahan, "Cleburne's Kin: The Untold Story of the Irish Confederates," *Southern Partisan*, (fourth quarter, 1995), 17. Also see John Lewis Garland, "Irish Soldiers," 176.

72. Paul Jones, *The Irish Brigade*, 101.

73. G. F. R. Henderson,*Stonewall Jackson and the American Civil War* (New York: De Capo Press, 1988), 559n. John Mitchell, in an 1863 letter to Dublin's *The Nation* newspaper, estimated there were already 40,000 native Irishmen in Southern armies.

74. *OR*, vol. 21, no. 1: 48-61 and 538-545.

75. Lorenzo Thomas, Adjutant General, Army Headquarters, to General Meagher, February 18, 1862, *OR*, vol. 1, no. 3: 895.

76. A. Lincoln to T. Francis Meagher, June 16, 1863, *OR*, vol. 3, no. 3: 372.

77. *Augusta Daily Constitutionalist*, April 22, 1862; Lonn, *Foreigners*, 92. The idea of a distinctly Irish company attracted recruits for the Confederacy. Lonn writes that special ethnic companies "seemed to hold a particular attraction for Irishmen; the green flag seemed to exert a magnetic control over the brawny sons of the Emerald Isle. Their fondness for their own companies is explicable: the Irishman fights better shoulder to shoulder with Irishmen as comrades, and always yearns to reflect honor on 'Ould Ireland.' The strongest inducement in winning Irish recruits was the reputation of the company."

78. William L. Burton, *Melting Pot Soldiers: The Union's Ethnic Regiments* (Ames: Iowa State University Press, 1988), 180.

79. Kee, *Most Distressful Country*, 123.

80. Keiley, *In Vinculis*, 177.

81. W. H. Andrews, *Footprints of a Regiment: A Recollection of the 1st Georgia Regulars, 1861-1865* (Atlanta: Longstreet Press, 1992), 99.

82. Lonn, *Foreigners*, 33.

83. Wallace, *17th Virginia Infantry*, 113.

84. Lonn, *Foreigners*, 33.

85. Braxton Bragg to Jefferson Davis, August 22, 1864, *OR*, vol. 3, no. 4: 6. There is no evidence in the *OR* that this was done.

86. Hernon, *Celts,* 15. Unquestionably, peer and local public pressure persuaded many Irishmen to join the ranks of each army. See James M. McPherson, *For Cause and Comrades: Why Men Fought in the Civil War* (New York : Oxford University Press, 1997), 113-114. Although McPherson chose an example of an Irishman with Union sentiments, it is a telling point that the mother of the Irish Union soldier rued the day he and his brother had joined the army. McPherson could have as easily found an anti-Union Hibernian for illustrative purposes.

87. Henderson, *Stonewall Jackson,* 559.

88. *Southern Watchman,* February 25, 1863.

89. Fred Albert Shannon, *The Organization and Administration of the Union Army, 1861-1865* (Cleveland: Arthur H. Clark Co., 1928), 78. Shannon wrote: "Undoubtedly the large bounties attracted far too many of the worst type."

90. Charles P. Cullop, *Confederate Propaganda in Europe, 1861-1865* (Coral Gables, Fla.: University of Miami Press, 1969), 108 and 113.

91. James D. Richardson, *A Compilation of the Messages and Papers of the Confederacy* (Nashville: U. S. Publishing Co., 1906), 628.

92. Lonn, *Foreigners,* 221-222.

93. Ibid., 222.

94. Hernon, *Celts,* 32.

95. Ibid.

96. Cullop, *Propaganda,* 105.

97. Ibid., 104.

98. Ibid., 113.

99. Ibid.

100. Ibid., 108.

101. Ibid., 104.

102. Hernon, *Celts,* 23.

103. Lonn, *Foreigners,* 31-32; Hernon, *Celts,* 11, 38-39 n; McPherson, *Battle Cry,* 606.

104. About 144,000 Irish natives served in the Union armies. Using the population figures from E. B. Long, *The Civil War Day by Day* (Garden City, N. Y.: Doubleday & Co., 1971), 707-702, the following calculations can be made: Confederate—40,000 divided by 5,449,400 (total white population) = .00734; Union—144,000 divided by 19, 034,400 (total white and free Negro) = .00756.

105. Hernon, *Celts,* 18.

106. Galwey, "Fredericksburg and the Assault on Marye's Heights," *Catholic World,* 373.

107. J. B. Polley, *A Soldier's Letters to Charming Nellie* (New York: Neale Publishing Co., 1908), 90.

108. Miller, *Emigrants and Exiles,* 343.

109. "The Irish Brigade," *Southern Watchman*, February 25, 1863. A reprint of an article in the *Irish American*.

110. Boyle, *Mad Fellows*, 251.

111. Hernon, *Celts*, 19.

112. Ibid., 120.

113. Ibid., 19.

114. Joseph M. Hernon Jr., "The Irish Nationalists and Southern Secession," *Civil War History*, March 1966, vol. 12: 43.

115. Hernon, *Celts*, 6.

116. Roy F. Foster, ed., *The Oxford Illustrated History of Ireland* (Oxford: Oxford University Press, 1989), 204-205. Another mercantile tie between Ireland and the Confederacy was more successful. Peter Tait, the proprietor of the Limerick Clothing Factory, contracted with the Confederate government to supply Southern armies with uniforms. Colonel James A. Weston, acting as a Confederate agent in London, wrote North Carolina Governor Zebulon Vance October 29, 1863, attesting to the quality of Irish-made Confederate uniforms. "I beg to call the particular attention of the Quartermaster Department to the clothing from Mr. Peter Tait of Limerick. In quality, price & style, I think it will be found unequalled by any clothing yet sent to the Confederacy." Tait, a transplanted Scot, manufactured uniforms for the British army from 1851. His Limerick factory featured power-driven machines and mass production methods, and employed thousands in Limerick, even through famine years. Tait's factory made Limerick one of the world's largest clothing manufacturing centers. During the Civil War, the Limerick factory provided the South with British army style eight-button jackets of cadet gray kersey with fine wool broadcloth collars. The ornate brass buttons bore the stamp, "P. Tait, Limerick." An 1866 Limerick newspaper account reported that a Tait blockade runner landed a shipment of 4,400 jackets and pants at Wilmington, North Carolina, on December 29, 1864. Tait uniforms were used mainly by the Army of Northern Virginia later in the war. Peter Tait was mayor of Limerick from 1866 to 1868. See Cecil W. Anderson, *North-South Trader*, vol. 10, no. 3 (March-April, 1983), 17-18; Leslie D. Jensen, "A Survey of Confederate Central Government Quartermaster Issue Jackets," *Military Collector and Historian*, vol. XLI, no. 4 (Winter 1989), 162; *Echoes of Glory: Arms and Equipment of The Confederacy* (Alexandria, Virginia: Time-Life Books, 1991), 119, 139; James A. Weston to Zebulon Vance, October 29, 1863, North Carolina State Archives, GP 170.

117. Paul Jones, *The Irish Brigade*, 209.

118. Hernon, *Celts*, 120.

119. Ibid., 33.

120. McPherson, *Battle Cry*, 609-610.

121. Hernon, *Celts*, 19.

122. Ibid.

123. Ibid.

124. Ibid., 22.

125. Ibid., 23.

126. Ibid., 22.

127. Ibid.

128. Ibid., 23.

129. Durkin, *John Dooley*, 116.

130. S. C. Hayes to Jefferson Davis, January 6, 1864, *OR*, vol. 3, no. 4: 4-6.

131. Braxton Bragg to Jefferson Davis, August 22, 1864, *OR*, vol. 3, no. 4: 6.

## Chapter 4  The Irish Fight Continues: The War After Fredericksburg

1. Edmund J. Raus Jr., *A Generation on the March: The Union Army at Gettysburg* (Lynchburg: H. E. Howard, 1987), 37, 65, 66, 74, 132. After Chancellorsville, the charismatic leader Meagher resigned. At Gettysburg, he was replaced by Col. Patrick Kelly of the 88th New York. The brigade's strength of 701 men and officers really comprised only a handful of companies. About 200 Irish Brigade members were on provost duty during this campaign. The New York regiments were the most depleted. Meagher's own 69th New York was down to seventy-five men. The 63rd New York counted only two companies of 112, and the 88th New York's 126 men made up two thin companies. The 116th Pennsylvania showed 123 men in four small companies. The 28th Massachusetts was the only Irish Brigade unit even close to regimental strength with 265 men. Fighting in the Wheat Field at Gettysburg, the tiny brigade took enormous casualties, but had little effect on the battle. After Gettysburg, the brigade counted only 503 men, suffering 198 casualties of 532 engaged.

2. Keely, "Civil War Diary."

3. Ibid.

4. Ernest B. Furgurson, *Chancellorsville 1863: The Souls of the Brave* (New York: Alfred A. Knopf, 1992), 218.

5. Keely, "Civil War Diary."

6. Ibid.

7. Ibid.

8. Ibid.

9. Ibid.

10. Varina D. Brown, *A Colonel at Gettysburg and Spotsylvania: Col. Joseph Newton Brown* (Columbia: The State Co., 1931), 85.

11. Durkin, *John Dooley*, 105.

12. Ibid., 106-107.

13. Ibid., 107. Lieutenant Keiningham was an officer in the Montgomery Guard's neighboring company, the Old Dominion Rifles, Company D.

14. Brown, *Colonel at Gettysburg*, 85.

15. Durkin, *John Dooley*, 217-218.

16. Dillon, *Life of Mitchel*, 180.

17. Durkin, *John Dooley*, 115.

18. Hewett, *Supplement to the Official Records*, vol. 34, pt. 2, no. 36: 210-211.

19. W. S. Dunlop, *Lee's Sharpshooters, or the Forefront of Battle* (Little Rock: Tunnah & Pittard, Printers, 1899), 368.

20. Ibid., 369.

21. Ibid.

22. J. C. Rietti, *Military Annals of Mississippi* (Spartanburg, S. C.: Reprint Co., 1976), 140-141.

23. Caldwell, *The History of a Brigade of South Carolinians*, 121.

24. Ibid., 141.

25. Report of William N. Pendleton, *OR*, vol. 26, pt. 1, 1046.

26. Jennings Cropper Wise, *Chancellorsville to Appomattox*, vol. 2 of *The Long Arm of Lee: The History of the Artillery of the Army of Northern Virginia* (Lincoln: University of Nebraska Press, 1991), 797.

27. Ibid.

28. Chamberlayne, *Ham Chamberlayne*, 222.

29. Wise, *Long Arm*, 797-798.

30. Ibid., 798.

31. Chamberlayne, *Ham Chamberlayne*, 222.

32. Wise, *Long Arm*, 298.

33. Ibid.

34. Ibid.

35. Thomas S. Doyle, "Memoir," August 12, 1867, Fredericksburg and Spotsylvania National Military Park Manuscript Collection, vol. 67: 13.

36. Ibid., 14.

37. Ibid.

38. H. M. Hamill, "A Boy's First Battle," *Confederate Veteran*, vol. 7: 540.

39. James Cooper Nisbet, *4 Years on the Firing Line*, Bell Irwin Wiley, ed. (Jackson, Tenn.: McGowat-Mercer Press, 1963), 140.

40. William H. Nulty, *Confederate Florida: The Road to Olustee* (Tuscaloosa: University of Alabama Press, 1990), 218.

41. Hamill, "Boy's First Battle"; P. W. Alexander in "Some Florida Heroes," *Confederate Veteran*, vol. 11: 363.

42. "Some Florida Heroes," *Confederate Veteran*, 363-364.

43. Ibid.

44. Ulysses S. Grant, *Personal Memoirs of U. S. Grant*, 2 vols. (New York: Charles L. Webster & Co., 1886), vol. 2: 276.

45. Evans, *Confederate Military History*, vol. 16: 200-202

46. Keiley, *In Vinculis*, 24.

47. Ibid., 19.

48. George S. Bernard, *War Talks of Confederate Veterans* (Petersburg, Va.: Fenn & Owen, 1892), 129 and 122.

49. Keiley, *In Vinculis*, 28. For more on Keiley's battle experience, see George S. Bernard, *War Talks*, 60-65. Though wounded at Malvern Hill in 1862, Keiley took part in the Chancellorsville Campaign, fighting in Mahone's Brigade at Salem Church. In command of the Petersburg Riflemen, he wrote a comprehensive account of the battle in a May 7, 1863, letter to Capt. Daniel Dodson. The letter was published May 13, 1863, in the *Petersburg Express*.

50. Keiley, *In Vinculis*, 183.

51. A. M. Keiley to James A. Seddon, September 28, 1863, *OR*, vol. 6, no. 2: 326-327.

52. Keiley, *In Vinculis*, 142-143.

53. Ibid., 31.

54. Ibid., 51.

55. Sgt. James Reilly to Adjutant General Samuel Cooper, in *A History of Fort Johnston on the Lower Cape Fear*, by Wilson Angley (Wilmington, N. C.: Broadfoot Publishing Co., 1996), 68.

56. Ibid.

57. "Report of Major B. W. Frobel," *OR*, vol. 12, pt. 2, no. 1: 607.

58. Mary Lasswell, ed., *Rags and Hope: The Recollections of Val C. Giles, Four Years with Hood's Brigade, Fourth Texas Infantry, 1861-1865* (New York: Coward-McCann, 1961), 132.

59. William Lamb, "The Defense of Fort Fisher," *Battles and Leaders*, vol. 4: 642.

60. W. H. C. Whiting, *OR*, vol. 42, pt. 1, no. 1: 998.

61. Ibid., 1002.

62. Ibid., 1005.

63. Lamb, "The Defense of Fort Fisher," *Battles and Leaders*, 651.

64. Ibid., 652.

65. Ibid., 653.

66. "Return of Major James Reilly's Sword," *Confederate Veteran*, 1894, vol. 2: 119.

67. Chris E. Fonvielle, Jr., *The Wilmington Campaign: Last Rays of Departing Hope* (Campbell, CA.: Savas Publishing Co., 1997), 293.

68. Lamb, "The Defense of Fort Fisher," *Battles and Leaders*, 653.

69. Lawrence Lee to John A. Reilly, November 21, 1983, Fredericksburg and Spotsylvania National Military Park Manuscript Collection, vol. 104.

70. Francis Potts, *The Death of the Confederacy: The Last Week of the Army of Northern Virginia as Set Forth in a Letter of April 1865* (Richmond: Private printing for A. Potts, 1928), 12.

71. Ibid.

72. Ibid., 15.

73. Nelson Lankford, ed., *An Irishman in Dixie: Thomas Conolly's Diary of the Fall of the Confederacy* (Columbia: University of South Carolina Press, 1988), 3.

74. Potts, *Death*, 8.

75. Ibid., 6.

76. Ibid., 5.

77. Ibid., 11.

78. Ibid., 14.

79. Ibid. Potts' narrative here exemplifies the enormous love and respect Lee's troops had for the vanquished commander. Two examples of Irish affection for Robert E. Lee grace the *Recollections and Letters* of General Lee compiled by his son, Captain Robert E. Lee, in 1904. One Federal soldier, "Irish all over," had served with Lee in the regular army, and brought him food in Richmond after the surrender. "The old Irishman, as soon as he saw him, drew himself up and saluted . . . with tears streaming down his cheeks," reported Captain Lee. "Goodbye, Colonel! [The man knew Lee as a colonel in the regular army.] God bless ye! If I could have got over in time I would have been with ye!" the Irish soldier said upon leaving. In Alexandria in 1869, a "very stout and unprepossessing Irishwoman" delivered an embrace and a kiss to Admiral Smith Lee thinking he was the general. "My boy was with you in the war, honey, and I must kiss you for his sake," she told the admiral. See Captain Robert E. Lee, *Recollections and Letters of General Robert E. Lee*, (Garden City, N. Y.: Garden City Publishing Co., 1904), 159 and 351.

80. Potts, *Death*, 15.

## Chapter 5 Conclusion:
## Irish Confederates After the War

1. Chamberlayne, *Ham Chamberlayne*, 79.

2. C. Vann Woodward, *Mary Chesnut's Civil War* (New Haven: Yale University Press, 1981), 589.

3. Ibid., 820.

4. O'Cathaoir, *Mitchel*, 27; Dillon, *Life of Mitchel*, 221.

5. Ibid., 27.

6. Kee, *Most Distressful Country,* 269.

7. O'Cathaoir, *Mitchel*, 23; Dillon, *Life of Mitchel*, 302, 305-306. Mitchel's often ridiculed claim that the Union was simply another incarnation of British hegemony was proven rather true after the war. It is an overlooked fact of the war's aftermath that Ireland gained no advantage in United States diplomacy with Britain in repayment of the great numbers of Northern Irishmen who fought for the Union. In fact, far from aiding the Irish independence movement, the post-war United States government on at least one occasion went out of its way to stymie it. The Yankee government in fact dispatched American troops to thwart a Fenian attempt to strike a blow against Britain in the spring

of 1866. In April, Maj. Gen. George Gordon Meade, formerly commander of the Army of the Potomac and the Union hero of Gettysburg, moved United States forces with an alacrity seldom shown in the war against Irish troops attempting an invasion of Canada. Meade, commanding Atlantic Division troops, captured Fenian military leaders and their ship, the *Ocean Spray*, at Eastport and Lubec, Maine, as they were attempting to establish a base to occupy nearby Campobello Island off the Maine coast. Six weeks later, May 31 through June 2, 1866, Meade interposed an American force between 7,000 Irish soldiers at Ogdensburg, New York, and another Irish army advancing toward Fort Erie, Ontario. Launching an attack from North Buffalo, New York, Fenian insurgents had routed Toronto volunteer militia at a battle at Limestone Ridge, Ontario. But their invasion depended on their base on the New York side of the border. United States forces posted a warship on the Niagara River and cut off the insurgents from their supplies and reinforcements. Meade again rounded up the Fenian leaders. In this incident, the United States Secretary of War Edwin Stanton seemed to be at the beck and call of the British ambassador. The Union government was not interested in aiding the Irish who purportedly had fought for the North to gain an American ally for the Irish independence movement. Meade, in an operation that efficiently and ruthlessly destroyed the Irish attack on Canada, seemed to have forgotten the Irish Brigade that once fought so bravely in his volunteer army. From that time on, the United States and Britain formed one of the strongest alliances the world has ever known. So much for Irish allegiance to the Union. See Malcolm Brown, *The Politics of Irish Literature: From Thomas Davis to W. B. Yeats*, (Seattle: University of Washington Press, 1972), 199-200.

8. Claudine Rhett, "Sketch of John C. Mitchel, of Ireland, Killed While in Command of Fort Sumter," *Southern Historical Society Papers*, vol. 10: 272. Mitchel's final words perhaps were an embellishment that recalled the last words of Patrick Sarsfield, the hero of Limerick. Sarsfield died at the head of an Irish Brigade in a French victory over British forces at Landen, Belgium, in 1693. As Sarsfield bled to death on that foreign field, his last words were, "Oh! that this were for Ireland." See *The Poems of Thomas Davis*, (New York: D. & J. Sadlier & Co., 1866), 150

9. Durkin, *John Dooley*, xv.

10. "Our Army Correspondence," *Southern Watchman*, May 27, 1863.

11. Benjamin Stiles, letter of April 4, 1862, Mackay-Stiles Collection, Southern Historical Collection, University of North Carolina Library, no. 470.

12. Colonel Robert McMillan, "Memoir," Fredericksburg and Spotsylvania National Military Park Manuscript Collection, vol. 127.

13. Hillary Abner Herbert, "A Short History of the Eighth Alabama Regiment," The Hilary Abner Herbert Papers, Southern Historical Collection, University of North Carolina Library, vol. 2, no. 2.

14. Avery, *History of Georgia*, 456-457.

15. William C. Davis, ed., *The Confederate General*, 6 vols., (Harrisburg, Penn.: National Historical Society, 1991), vol. 1: 134-135.

# Notes

16. Jon L. Wakelyn, *Biographical Dictionary of the Confederacy*, (Westport, Conn.: Greenwood Press, 1977), 306-307.

17. John Beauchamp Jones, *A Rebel War Clerk's Diary*, 43.

18. Dan Van Der Vat, *Stealth at Sea: The History of the Submarine*, (Boston: Houghton Mifflin Co., 1995), 16-19 and 30-32. See also Richard Compton-Hall, "An Irish Invention," in *Submarine Boats: The Beginnings of Underwater Warfare* (New York: Arco Publishing, 1984), 32-44; Louis S. Schafer, "The Trout Boat St. Patrick" in *Confederate Underwater Warfare: An Illustrated History* (Jefferson, N. C.: McFarland & Co., 1996), 155-158. The Irish involvement with the submarine is even older than the Civil War. Robert Fulton, an Irish-American with Irish nationalist sympathies, used French help to design and construct an earlier submarine, the *Nautilus*, 1798-1801. The idea then was that his sub would be used to attack British warships. Fulton is more famous for inventing the first steam-powered surface warship.

A recent book on the subject of Civil War submarines is Mark K. Ragan's *Union and Confederate Submarine Warfare in the Civil War* (Savas Publishing Co., 1999). Ragan has tapped into thousands of previously unused documents, including Confederate Secret Service papers, all of which demonstrate that both sides built and launched a large number of workable, and surprisingly advanced, submarines.

19. Loehr, *War History of the Old First*, 15; Dillon, *Life of John Mitchel*, 173.

20. Durkin, *John Dooley*, xv.

21. Chamberlayne, *Ham Chamberlayne*, 200.

22. Durkin, *John Dooley*, 176.

23. Caravati, *Major Dooley*, 75.

24. P. T. Moore to G. W. Randolph, August 8, 1862, Moore's compiled service record.

25. James Longstreet to Randolph, August 2, 1862, Moore's CSR.

26. E. Lewis Moore to the *Wilmington (N. C.) Weekly Star*, November 3, 1893.

27. James Reilly to E. Lewis Moore, "Return of Major James Reilly's Sword," *Confederate Veteran*, vol. 2: 119.

28. Richard S. Ewell, "Capt. B. T. Walshe, A Gallant Confederate," *Confederate Veteran*, 1898, vol. 6: 576.

29. B. T. Walshe, "Louisianans in the Virginia Army," *Confederate Veteran*, vol. 6: 177.

30. Evans, *Confederate Military History*, vol. 8: 349-350.

31. A. M. Keiley , William T. Joynes, J. M. Venable, John Lyon to Maj. Gen. George L. Hartsuff, April 10, 1865, *OR*, vol. 46, pt. 3, no. 1: 698.

32. Chamberlayne, *Ham Chamberlayne*, ix.

33. Bailey, *Richmond Diocese*, p. 147; William D. Henderson, *12th Virginia Infantry*, (Lynchburg: H. E. Howard, 1984), 135. For more on Keiley's post-war career, see W. Asbury Christian, *Richmond: Her Past and Present* (Richmond, Va.: L. H. Jenkins, 1912) and Armistead Churchill Gordon, *Memories and Memorials of William Gordon McCabe*, 2 vols., (Richmond, Va.: Old Dominion Press, 1925).

34. Susan Benson Williams, ed., *Berry Benson's Civil War Book: Memoirs of a Confederate Scout and Sharpshooter* (Athens: University of Georgia Press, 1992), 201.

35. Raymond Blalock Nixon, *Henry W. Grady, Spokesman of the New South* (New York: Alfred A. Knopf, 1943), 344.

36. Ibid., 25.

37. Ibid., 345.

38. Ibid., 329.

39. Ibid., 340.

40. Keely, "Civil War Diary."

41. Ibid.

42. Ibid.

# Epilogue

1. Cavanagh, *Meagher*, 470.

2. Patrick Cleburne, *OR*, vol. 52, pt. 2, no. 1: 587.

3. Cleburne, *OR*, 590.

4. Ibid., 589.

5. Cleburne, *OR*, vol. 52, pt. 2, no. 1: 592.

6. Ibid., 590.

7. W. H. T. Walker to Jefferson Davis, January 12, 1864, *OR*, vol. 52, pt. 2, no. 1: 595.

8. Patton Anderson to Leonidas Polk, January 14, 1864, *OR*, 598.

9. Jefferson Davis to W. H. T. Walker, January 13, 1864, *OR*, 596.

10. James A. Seddon to Joseph Johnston, January 24, 1864, *OR*, 606-607.

11. J. E. Johnston to Lt. Gen. Hardee, Major-Gens. Cheatham, Hindman, Cleburne, Stewart, Walker; Brig. Gens. Bate and P. Anderson, January 31, 1864, *OR*, 608.

12. Walter P. Lane, *The Adventures and Recollections of General Walter P. Lane,* (Austin: Pemberton Press, 1970), 90-91.

13. Henry Baker, *A Reminiscent Story*, 50.

14. Garland, "Irish Soldiers," 177.

15. Ibid.

16. John Berrien Lindsley, *Military Annals of Tennessee (Confederate)* (Nashville: J. M. Lindsley & Co., 1886), 152.

17. Ibid., 153.

18. J. B. Polley, "The Charming Nellie Papers," *Confederate Veteran*, vol. 4: 345-346.

# INDEX

# Index

343

# Index

# Index